REINHOLD NIEBUHR ON POLITICS

REINHOLD NIEBUHR ON POLITICS

His Political Philosophy and Its Application to Our Age as Expressed in His Writings

EDITED BY

HARRY R. DAVIS

Professor of Government, Beloit College

AND

ROBERT C. GOOD

Assistant Professor of International Relations
The Social Science Foundation
The University of Denver

New York

CHARLES SCRIBNER'S SONS

PRINTED IN THE UNITED STATES OF AMERICA
LIBRARY OF CONGRESS CATALOG CARD NUMBER 60-6326

ACKNOWLEDGMENTS

The Editors acknowledge with thanks permission granted by the following publishers to reprint material written by Reinhold Niebuhr taken from the works cited:

DOUBLEDAY & COMPANY, INC.

RELIGION AND FREEDOM OF THOUGHT by Perry Miller, Robert L. Calhoun, Nathan M. Pusey, Reinhold Niebuhr. Copyright 1954 by The Union Theological Seminary. Reprinted by permission of Doubleday & Company, Inc.

HARCOURT, BRACE & COMPANY, INC.

SCIENCE AND MAN edited by Ruth Nanda Anshen. Copyright 1942 by Harcourt, Brace and Company, Inc.

HARPER & BROTHERS

AN INTERPRETATION OF CHRISTIAN ETHICS by Reinhold Niebuhr
CHRISTIAN FAITH AND THE COMMON LIFE by Reinhold Niebuhr and others
THE NATURE OF RELIGIOUS EXPERIENCE by Reinhold Niebuhr and others
GOALS OF ECONOMIC LIFE edited by A. Dudley Ward. Copyright Harper & Brothers
THE ORGANIZATIONAL REVOLUTION by Kenneth E. Boulding. Copyright Harper & Brothers

CHARLES SCRIBNER'S SONS

by Reinhold Niebuhr

BEYOND TRAGEDY, copyright 1937 by Charles Scribner's Sons; THE CHILDREN OF LIGHT AND THE CHILDREN OF DARKNESS, copyright 1944 by Charles Scribner's Sons; CHRISTIAN REALISM AND POLITICAL PROBLEMS, copyright 1953 by Reinhold Niebuhr; CHRISTIANITY AND POWER POLITICS, copyright 1940 by Charles Scribner's Sons; DISCERNING THE SIGNS OF THE TIMES, copyright 1946 by Charles Scribner's Sons; FAITH AND HISTORY, copyright 1949 by Charles Scribner's Sons; THE IRONY OF AMERICAN HISTORY, copyright 1952 by Charles Scribner's Sons; MORAL MAN AND IMMORAL SOCIETY, copyright 1933 by Charles Scribner's Sons; THE NATURE AND DESTINY OF MAN, copyright 1941 by Charles Scribner's Sons; PIOUS AND SECULAR AMERICA, copyright © 1958 by Reinhold Niebuhr; REFLECTIONS ON THE END OF AN ERA, copyright 1934 by Charles Scribner's Sons; THE SELF AND THE DRAMAS OF HISTORY, copyright 1955 by Reinhold Niebuhr; THE STRUCTURE OF NATIONS AND EMPIRES, copyright © 1959 by Reinhold Niebuhr.

edited by John A. Hutchison

CHRISTIAN FAITH AND SOCIAL ACTION, copyright 1953 by Charles Scribner's Sons.

edited by John Lewis, Karl Polanyi, Donald K. Kitchin

CHRISTIANITY AND THE SOCIAL REVOLUTION.

THE RICHARD R. SMITH COMPANY

THE HERITAGE OF THE REFORMATION edited by Elmer J. F. Arndt.

STUDENT CHRISTIAN MOVEMENT PRESS LIMITED

THE CHURCH AND THE DISORDER OF SOCIETY, Volume III, Amsterdam Assembly Series.

UNIVERSITY OF NOTRE DAME PRESS

From Reinhold Niebuhr's article, "Power and Ideology in National and International Affairs" in THEORETICAL ASPECTS OF INTERNATIONAL RELATIONS, edited by William T. R. Fox, University of Notre Dame Press, 1959.

Some of the material in this volume was first published in the following journals: *The American Scholar; Christian Century; Christianity and Crisis; Christianity and Society; Commentary* ("Will Civilization Survive Technics?" Volume 1, December 1945, copyright by the American Jewish Committee); *The Commonweal; Fortune* (copyright 1942, 1957 *Fortune*); "The Hazen Pamphlets" published by the Edward W. Hazen Foundation; *International Organization; Messenger; The Nation; The New Leader; New Republic; The Progressive; Radical Religion; Religion in Life* (copyright 1932 by the Abingdon Press, Inc.); *The Reporter; Social Action; Theology; The Virginia Quarterly Review; World Politics; World Tomorrow; The Yale Review* (copyright 1951 Yale University Press).

Editors' Introduction

When he proposed that Reinhold Niebuhr be invited to deliver Edinburgh's renowned Gifford Lectures, John Baillie said, "Intellectually, Niebuhr is head and shoulders, he is legs and ankles above any other American."

The honors accorded the prophet in a far country have been lavished upon him at home too. It may surely be said that the towering teacher of Christian ethics from Union Theological Seminary is one of the mighty spirits of our times. For forty years we have been reading his incisive thought in our leading journals. Through eighteen of his volumes we have been jostled by his polemic, instructed by his commentary, and enlightened by the brilliance of his analysis.

Niebuhr's eminence as a prophet and theologian is now being matched by his rapidly growing reputation as a political theorist. Increasingly he is cited, reprinted and critically analyzed by students of international relations and political philosophy.

For Niebuhr, theology and politics are not really separate fields, but two perspectives on a single reality, each helping to illumine the data of the other. His central concerns clearly bridge the two disciplines: the nature and destiny of man, the perplexities of social ethics, the conditions of human community. Out of such concerns Niebuhr naturally emerges, not as a political scientist narrowly defined, but as a political and moral philosopher in the grand manner. His calipers are not calibrated in micromillimeters but in yards and rods, for they are designed to span the height and depth of the human soul rather than to record those minutiae of human behavior susceptible of precise measurement.

Yet Niebuhr, it must be stressed, has disparaged neither reason nor science. His position is that these instruments ought to be understood and used, not worshipped. In his awareness of the ability of the sinful self to appropriate reason to its own ends, Niebuhr is more rational than the rationalists. In his insistence on examining the presuppositions of the scientific method, he is more truly scientific than the devotees of contemporary scientism.

Though Niebuhr is foremost a political and moral philosopher, he has always been vitally engaged with the practical affairs of our troubled times. Equally impressive, he has used experience powerfully as an empirical test of the adequacy of his own presuppositions. Anyone familiar with the development of his thought knows how painful was the process by which he moved from one frame of reference to another as each in turn proved to be an inadequate guide to the complexities of the human situation. He has made perfectly explicit the frame of reference which he finally found sufficient: his understanding of the classical and Biblical version of the Christian faith.

Reinhold Niebuhr's political writings, though extensive, have never been systematic. While we have from him a magnum opus on theology, *The Nature and Destiny of Man,* there is no equivalent work on politics. Further, some of his best writing on political themes appears in his occasional pieces, often published in journals not widely accessible. Thus the reader wishing to study "Reinhold Niebuhr on Politics" has been obliged to consult at least a half dozen books and to search out literally hundreds of articles. Because of this and some alleged difficulties with Niebuhr's dialectical style, many readers have found samples of his work interesting but not fully and immediately comprehensible. These circumstances have set certain limits to his audience.

The editors seek to make available Niebuhr's political thought in convenient, complete and organized form. The intention is to present the structure of his matured philosophy of politics rather than to deal with the evolution of his thought. The editors have tried to include the best of his political writings from whatever source. Accordingly, the present materials have been taken from sixteen of his books and some one hundred and seventy of his many hundreds of articles, besides several selections heretofore unpublished.

The dispersion of Niebuhr's political writings throughout his books, learned articles, and journalistic pieces also gives rise to the elaborate technique used in constructing this compendium. Strands of various lengths and from many sources have been woven into logical chapters and finally a coherent whole. Thus, the editors have tried to avoid some of the hazards of compendia—the danger of incoherence and incompleteness when snippets or large blocks of material are placed in disjointed sequence; or the loss of authenticity and the flavor of the author's style when his work is paraphrased. The editors hope that the present method has combined authenticity with readability and completeness.

One hazard has remained, that of using materials out of context. The editors have guarded against this mortal scholarly sin, not only by using their own best judgment in selecting and combining materials, but through the generous cooperation of Dr. Niebuhr himself. He was consulted at the outset. He advised as the text grew. He reviewed the final version before granting it his approval. Occasional modifications have been made in the original text to effect smooth transitions and to eliminate dated material. These too have been reviewed by Dr. Niebuhr and have received his imprimatur.

The design and purpose of the volume required the violation of some scholarly formalities. Since the purpose was to present all important aspects of Niebuhr's political philosophy in a complete and readable book, it was decided not to clutter the text with dots and brackets indicating those deletions and minor revisions made for the sake of clarity and cohesion. However, the original source of each excerpt has been recorded in notes collected at the end of the volume. The reader wishing to examine a given excerpt in its original context will want to refer to its source.

The editors make no apology for the inevitable overlap of ideas and arguments, though they have attempted to keep these repetitions to a minimum. The volume is an integral whole and the editors hope it will be read as such; yet they know that it will be read selectively too and thus feel it important to make each section reasonably self-contained. Further, Niebuhr's dialectical mode of thought often results in analysis so tightly constructed that it cannot easily be divided and inserted into separate pigeonholes. Any specific argument is likely to reflect some larger argument. Thus basic formulations are often reintroduced to preserve the full strength and integrity of Niebuhr's treatment.

The structure of the compendium deliberately reflects Niebuhr's own approach to the political problem. His professional life has been devoted as much to polemics as to scholarship; he has "inveighed against" as much as he has "stood for." His mature position developed as a reaction against frames of reference he found to be frustratingly inadequate. So the volume begins with Niebuhr's examination of the contemporary crisis and his analysis of the false solutions offered by the liberal creed and by communist doctrine. These views, he maintains, misunderstand the source and depth of evil in the world and thus offer the false hope of overcoming the crisis more or less easily. Because of their errors, they serve at best to conceal, and at worst to deepen, the crisis.

False assumptions about human nature have also confused the problem of man's formal study of himself and his society. Part Two of the compendium begins with Niebuhr's incisive critique of contemporary social science and a brief overview of his own realistic approach to human polity.

The ground thus cleared, Niebuhr erects his system of political thought

—a massive structure, with its footings deep in the Biblical understanding of man and history. From this foundation it rises to encompass the classic subject matter of political philosophy: the sources and manifestations of power, the relationship of individual and community, the uses and abuses of government. Binding the whole together is a theory of Christian political ethics. It runs its trusses and braces the full height and breadth, relating every problem of community and government on the one hand to the necessarily fundamental understanding of human nature, and on the other to the topmost pinnacle where, in the concept of the law of love, the imposing structure brushes against the infinite. For, Niebuhr insists, a responsible approach to the problem of justice must maintain contact with "both the moral imperative of the love commandment and the fact of the persistence of self-love in actual history." Fresh and perspicacious treatments of pacifism, natural law, and democracy are special strengths of the Niebuhrian ethic.

The architecture of Niebuhr's political and ethical thought is anything but simple. It is full of dialectical cantilevers. The whole is suspended in marvellous tension like some Gothic cathedral that rises and is held fast only by the elaboration of opposing forces. Man as creature is counterpoised with man as creator. Necessity is juxtaposed with freedom, possibility with impossibility, love with law, sin with grace, history with eternity. Idealism is set in tension with realism as are their extremes, sentimentalism and cynicism. Order is balanced against justice as are their perversions, tyranny and anarchy. The presuppositions of liberalism and conservatism are laid each against the other, while the policies of socialism and laissez-faire are held in delicate balance. No one of these perspectives may be ignored or minimized without damaging Niebuhr's complex synthesis.

In the light of such intricate dialectics, the student might be excused for failing to label Niebuhr's approach. He identifies with political realism—except when he is flaying the realists for their failure to understand the normative dimension of life. He appreciates idealism—except when he is scoring the idealists for their failure to assess the resistance of all men to the normative dimension of life. If we call him a "Christian realist" it is because he himself has often used the term and because he has emphasized the insights of realism as a corrective to the optimism of contemporary thought. Expressed differently, Niebuhr's philosophy seeks to put "political realism into the service of justice."

By whatever label, it would be very unNiebuhrian to understand Niebuhr's thought as a fixed system. He warns against too confident and closed a science of politics. He inveighs against traditional "natural law" and all forms of legalism. "Niebuhrianism," if such exists, is a constellation of perspectives, Biblically derived and validated by experience—

understandings about human nobility and sin; human anxiety and the quest for security through power; the ambiguous role of reason, morality and religion; the nemesis of pride and power; and the persistent, disturbing intervention of a Divine "oughtness" in human undertakings.

These understandings issue in a commitment concerning the nature of man and his destiny, the nature of God and the meaning of history; and Niebuhr's political science and political ethic are a dynamic response to that commitment. To freeze these understandings into a rigid, completely coherent system would do violence to their spirit. At the center is no system, but the concerned, searching, believing, understanding and acting person. No amount of rational knowledge or meticulous obedience to moral standards can substitute for the self's repeated encounters with God, when all pretensions of pride are shattered, and the self is freed again to work for the loving relationship and the just community.

This surely is to describe Niebuhr's own life. His labors in the field of practical politics, national and international, have been immense. He has courageously and persistently applied in action the central beliefs and insights of his political theory and ethic. Moreover, the experience of grappling with the basic political issues of his generation has influenced profoundly the development and exposition of his theory. For these reasons, as well as for their intrinsic wisdom, Part Three of the compendium is devoted to Niebuhr's writings on selected contemporary political problems.

"In actual life," he has written, ". . . no clear distinction between moral principles and strategy can be made. This is why Christian convictions that deal only with ultimate principle and exclude strategic issues tend to become wholly irrelevant." In his applied writings, all the elements in Niebuhr's complex perspective and elaborate dialectic come brilliantly alive. Here it is also demonstrated that in practice he rarely remains suspended in a state of dialectical balance. His view of historical responsibility requires that he decide, advocate, and act, just as his understanding of justification by faith enables him to act, even while remaining sensitive to the frailty and partiality of all human action.

The materials used in Part Three are drawn largely from Niebuhr's occasional and journalistic writings, as distinct from his more systematic work. They deal with problems of the day. But in no sense were they written in the first instance, nor included in this volume, as detailed policy papers or exhaustive "scholarly" studies. Their value is in illuminating Niebuhr's general approach to the great issues of public affairs. In some instances, events have overtaken Niebuhr's views as recorded in these pages, rendering them somewhat dated. Yet, they remain instructive examples of his ceaseless attempt to relate perennial truths and insights to the swift flow of current events.

In the course of planning and compiling this volume, the editors enjoyed the assistance of a remarkably devoted advisory committee, the members of which reviewed each phase of the project and commented usefully on each of the sections as they emerged from the scissors and paste of the editing process. The editors are pleased to acknowledge with gratitude their debt to Charles Burton Marshall, Hans J. Morgenthau, E. E. Schattschneider, Arthur Schlesinger, Jr., and Arnold Wolfers. Full responsibility for all editorial *faux pas* and for editorial sins of omission or inclusion rests of course with the editors.

Mr. Davis recognizes with gratitude his debt to Professor John H. Hallowell, Director of the Lilly Endowment Research Program in Christianity and Politics, Duke University, for an unusually favorable opportunity to forward work on this project as a member of a summer research conference in 1958; and to Dean Ivan M. Stone and President Miller Upton of Beloit College for their encouragement and support.

Mr. Good expresses his appreciation to Professor C. Dale Fuller, formerly Director of the Social Science Foundation, University of Denver, and to Dr. Arnold Wolfers, Director of the Washington Center of Foreign Policy Research of the Johns Hopkins University, for their generosity in helping to make available the time necessary to assist in producing this volume.

Finally, we speak, we are certain, for literally thousands of Dr. Niebuhr's students, friends and admirers, and particularly for his colleagues in political science and theology, when we say to him a plain but profound "thank you." His wisdom, insight and courage as a scholar and prophet are happily matched by a quality of authentic humility which was revealed to us in his delightful and total lack of prideful self-consciousness about his written work. Our indebtedness has been gratefully incurred; it is utterly impossible of repayment.

HARRY R. DAVIS
ROBERT C. GOOD

Contents

Part II. POLITICAL PHILOSOPHY

The Study of Politics

The Process of Politics

Christian Ethics and Politics

International Politics

REINHOLD NIEBUHR ON POLITICS

PART ONE

The Crisis

CHAPTER I

The Contemporary Crisis

Our civilization has been engulfed in obvious and widespread political and social confusion since the second decade of this century. One world war has followed another; and the second conflagration has left the world in even deeper distress and less assurance for the future than the first. While Western civilization has been the center and source of the world's disorders, the social confusion and political tumult have spread from this center into the whole world.[1]

I. *The Three Crises of Western History*

In our own Western history the crisis in which we stand is in fact the third in a series. The first was the fall of the Roman Empire. The second was the decay of feudalism and the rise of our own bourgeois democratic society. A brief survey of what occurred in these crises may illumine our own situation.

The prestige of Rome had been so great, the Pax Romana had become one of the "eternal verities" to such a degree, that men were threatened with despair when they saw this great system of "law and order" crumbling before their eyes. Furthermore, they felt that Christianity had lost its meaning, because they assumed that Christian truth had validated itself by arresting the decay of Roman civilization and that its final inability to stop the decay had invalidated it.

This sense of despair and confusion prompted Augustine to write one of the most important books of our spiritual history: *The City of God.* In it he affirmed that the Christian religion contained an interpretation of life and history that made it possible to anticipate and to discount the periodic catastrophes of history. Every empire, every "city of this world," he declared, would have to break down ultimately because its "peace was based on strife." Which is to say that such social peace as is achieved in any civilization rests upon a precarious equilibrium of social forces. This equilibrium may degenerate into anarchy if there is no strong organizing center in it. And it may degenerate into tyranny if the organizing center destroys the vitality of the parts.

The new medieval society was, on the whole, built upon Christian presuppositions as defined by St. Augustine. But as medieval civilization finally integrated and organized the vast political and ethnic vitalities of Europe and achieved the social peace and equilibrium of the "golden" thirteenth century, it subtly compounded the complacency of a stable society with the profounder insights of Augustine. Augustine's conception of the tentativity of all historic achievements was lost. Medieval Christianity tended to define the characteristic social relations of a feudal-agrarian society as absolute and final. The invariable mistake of all cultures is that they tend to forget the relative character of such social justice and social peace as are achieved in a given civilization. And the greatest illusion of all historic cultures is that they mistake the precarious stability of their civilization for the final peace.

At the precise moment when medieval society celebrated its arrangements as essentially final, it proved that it was unable to absorb a new factor into its life and law, thus producing the second great crisis in Western history. That new factor was expanding commerce. The vital agent of that new factor was the businessman. The businessman found himself excluded from the political and economic organization of feudal society. By a series of evolutionary and revolutionary processes, including the Cromwellian revolution in England, the revolution in France, and our own American revolution, the businessman finally established a new society, capitalistic in economic form and, broadly speaking, democratic in political form.

Our present civilization is one that has developed largely under the leadership of the bourgeois classes. It has been supplanting feudalism, beginning with the fourteenth century. It rose to its greatest heights in the nineteenth and the early part of the twentieth century. And it finds itself in one of the deepest crises of world history in our own generation.[2]

II. *The Disorders of a Technical Civilization*

The most immediate cause of our distress could be defined as the inability and unwillingness of modern men and nations to re-establish community, or to reconstruct justice, under conditions which a technical civilization has created. We know, of course, that no human society has ever been free of corruption, of injustice and domination.[3] But while there is thus no perfect peace or order in any human community, there are times and seasons when a tolerable justice, hallowed by tradition and supplemented by personal discipline and goodness, gives society a long period of social stability. There are other times when the sins of the fathers are visited upon the children; and new social forces rise up as the "vengeance of the Lord" against traditional injustice. We are living in such a time. This is a period of judgment in which the structures and systems of community which once guaranteed a tolerable justice have themselves become the source of confusion and injustice.

We are witnessing, and participating in, the decline of a European civilization, together with a wide confusion in a world community. And the immediate occasion for the social and political confusion of our day is the progressive development of technics.[4] We have not been able to develop political and social instruments which are adequate for the kind of society which a technical civilization makes possible and necessary. The atomic bomb is in a sense only the most recent and the most dramatic symbol of this deep inner contradiction which cleaves our whole society. The ever increasing introduction of technics into the fields of production and communications constantly enlarges the intensity and extent of social cohesion in modern man's common life; and also tends constantly to centralize effective economic power. The effect of technics upon communications is to create a potential world community, which we have not been able to actualize morally and politically. The effect of technics upon production is to create greater and greater disproportions of economic power and thus to make the achievement of justice difficult. The one represents the international aspect of our crisis and the other the domestic aspect. We might well consider each in turn.[5]

The first impetus of a technical society toward world community was an imperialistic one. The European nations, armed with new technical-economic power, used their power to establish their dominion in Africa and Asia. They then came in conflict with each other over the spoils of their imperial thrusts. More recently the African and Asiatic world has risen in rebellion and opposition to this dominion. Their first resentment was against economic and political injustices, resulting from this new expansion of European power. More recently they have felt, even more keenly than the economic and political injustices, the pretension of ethnic superiority which the white races expressed in establishing their power.

Thus the development of new technical power created a potential, but not an actual, world community. The new power was exercised too egoistically to establish world-wide community. Some of the imperial powers gradually developed a sense of imperial responsibility which mitigated the exploiting tendencies of imperialism. Nevertheless the total effect of the expansion of technical power has been to give international tensions a world-wide scope and to involve the world in two conflicts of global dimensions.[6] The false answer to the problem of this anarchy is the tyrannical unification of the world. The instruments of a technical civilization, having increased the anarchy of our world, made the tyrannical alternative to anarchy more cruel in its methods, and enhanced the possibility of success for its ambitions of world dominion.[7]

Meanwhile, the introduction of technics into the various national economies tended to destroy the more organic and traditional forms of community on the national level. Urban life produced atomic individuals who lacked the social disciplines of the older and more organic societies and industrialism substituted dynamic inequalities and injustices in place of the more static inequalities of an agrarian society.[8]

The modern machine long since has divorced the skill of the worker from his tool. It has to a certain degree divorced the worker from his skill, which is now increasingly in the machine. It has thus made the worker powerless, except insofar as common organized action has given him a degree of social and political power. It has on the other hand constantly increased the power of fewer and fewer centers of economic authority. It may be regarded as an axiom of political justice that disproportions of power increase the hazard to justice; for to be armed with power means that the temptation to do what one wants increases. And what one wants immediately is usually not the common welfare.[9]

Thus modern industrial society was unable to establish a tolerable justice or to give the vast masses involved in modern industry a basic security. Consequently a virtual civil war between the new industrial classes and the more privileged and secure classes and landowners and owners of industrial property tended to destroy the unity of industrial nations. The healthiest modern nations are those who (like America) have been sufficiently privileged to have been able to avoid a desperate struggle between the industrial and middle classes; or those who (like Britain and some of its dominions and some of the smaller nations of northern and western Europe) have been able to mitigate this conflict by religious and moral resources of a special order. Nevertheless the total effect of the rise of a technical civilization and an industrial society has been the destruction of community on the national level and the extension of conflict on the international level.[10]

III. *The Confusions of an Inadequate Culture*

Every great crisis in world history represents a breakdown both in the organization of civilization and in the life of a culture. It is a spiritual as well as a political and economic crisis. The two aspects of life may be distinguished, even though the distinction is slightly arbitrary, by the words "civilization" and "culture." Civilization is the body of a culture. Culture is the spirit of a civilization. Civilization means the political, economic, and social arrangements and mechanisms by which the life of men is ordered. Culture means the philosophical, esthetic, and religious ideas and presuppositions that inform the political organization and that in turn emerge from it.

Ideally an adequate culture would not be involved in the breakdown of a civilization. For an adequate culture would be an interpretation of the meaning of life and history, which would comprehend the periodic breakdowns of civilization as inevitable and would seek to appropriate the lessons to be learned from those breakdowns for the building of a better civilization. Actually this never quite happens for the reason that every culture tends to appropriate certain ideas and conceptions, which are the characteristic products and illusions of its own civilization, into its system of "eternal truths" and to imagine that life would be meaningless without them. It thus brings life fairly close to meaninglessness because the ideas that it regards as eternal are actually being destroyed in the crisis. Furthermore, this spiritual confusion tends to accentuate the political and social crisis; for in every great crisis confusion is worse confounded by the insistence of some that the very illusions that the crisis is challenging and destroying belong to the eternal verities, which cannot be destroyed.

So it is that modern culture has no perspective from which it can view our contemporary crisis and plan a better world; for all our cultural perspectives are themselves colored by the civilization that is involved. If, for instance, the optimistic assumption underlies a whole culture that the extension of technics inevitably makes for the advancement of the good life, such a culture can do little to save men from confusion and despair if the extension of technics actually aggravates domestic and foreign conflict at a particular juncture of history.

Our modern era, which followed the dissolution of medieval culture and feudal civilization, was ushered in by two great movements, the Renaissance and the Reformation. The Reformation regarded the medieval Catholic interpretation of life and history as too optimistic. Human history, according to the Reformation, never achieves such perfection, either individually or collectively, as the medieval era pretended to have achieved. The Reformation did not believe that there could ever be "Christian" societies, or governments, or economic arrangements in the exact ethical definition of the term. A civilization could be Christian only in the sense that it had a faith that would help it to understand, and contritely to admit, the inevitable egoistic and "sinful" corruption by which all human enterprises, including the church and religious institutions, were tainted.

The Renaissance criticized the Catholic ages from the very opposite point of view. It regarded the Christian interpretation of life as too pessimistic. It believed that the human mind had been fettered by religious authority and corrupted by religious superstition. It had great confidence that the "emancipated" mind would disclose the secrets of nature; penetrate into all the ultimate mysteries of life; exploit the buried treasures of the natural world and make them available for man; explore the complexities of human society and eliminate the social maladjustments that ignorance had perpetuated; finally turn its attention to man himself, to free him of the sorrows and pains, the frustrations and lusts by which he made himself and his fellows miserable.

These promises and hopes of the Renaissance, arising in the fourteenth century and achieving new forms and elaborations particularly in the seventeenth and eighteenth centuries, were sufficiently in accord with many actual achievements of history to defeat and overwhelm all the pessimistic scruples of the Reformation. All the basic beliefs of modern man about himself, his society, and his destiny were defined essentially by the Renaissance and by the various cultural movements that followed in its wake.[11]

Thus, for example, the naturalistic assumptions of modern culture prompted the false belief that history was an extension of the evolutionary process of nature, that this evolutionary process guaranteed a higher and higher achievement of the good, however that good might be defined. It was frequently defined in contradictory terms.

But human freedom breaks the limits of nature, upsetting its limited harmonies and giving a demonic dimension to its conflicts. There is therefore progress in human history; but it is a progress of all human potencies, both for good and for evil. A culture which imagined that history was moving naturally to a wider and more inclusive community, toward the "parliament of mankind and the federation of the world," was naturally completely overtaken by the catastrophe of our era. It was not prepared for the tragic character of human history. It did not anticipate that a potential world community would announce itself to history in global wars. After the First World War the natural attitude of modern culture was to regard the war as a capricious interruption of the stream of progress, occasioned by an evil nation. Even the second world catastrophe was sometimes interpreted in such terms.

The historical optimism of our culture was thus derived from a view of man and history that failed to measure the full dimension of the human spirit and of its historic achievements. Man is able by the technical elaboration of his powers to establish a wider and wider community. But the same skills also arm him with a mighty weapon of individual and collective egoism when he desires to set himself against the community.

Because the struggle between the universal and the particular, between egoism and the community, is a more stubborn struggle on every level, the whole of human history is more tragic than modern culture had assumed; and it will continue to be more tragic because the sources of conflict do not lie in the past. They reappear in every historical level.[12]

The errors and illusions of our culture, which have made an estimate of the crisis of our civilization difficult if not impossible, are, almost without exception, various versions of a single error. They are all expressions of too great an optimism about the goodness of human nature; they all therefore underestimate the difficulties of relating life to life, will to will, interest to interest, in a harmonious social life. They regard the achievement of justice and social peace in human society as a comparatively easy task. It is, as a matter of fact, a very difficult task, which can be accomplished with tolerable success only if its difficulties are fully recognized.[13]

IV. *The Decline of Traditional Faith and the Rise of Political Religions*

To attribute the social confusion of our era to the introduction of technics is to give only the negative cause of our discontent. Nor is an adequate explanation forthcoming by analyzing the failures of our culture simply in terms of its intellectual errors. The more positive cause has been the failure of men and nations either to desire or to achieve a tolerable justice within the new conditions created by expanding technical power. This moral failure cannot be attributed merely to ignorance and sloth. Everywhere there are evidences of the positive thrust of the sinful pride and will-to-power of old oligarchies and new social forces, of old cultures and new ideologies. The religious and spiritual, as well as the social and cultural, forces involved in the readjustments of modern society have contributed to the failure. We must seek rigorously to avoid the temptation to interpret our disaster as the primary consequence of the sins of those classes, nations and faiths with which we are not allied.

Amidst the vast social and cultural movements of modern life it is possible to isolate and define three broad forces, each of which must bear a portion of responsibility for our present situation. The first is the old power of the landlord who dominated the agrarian society; the second is the newer commercial and industrial owners; and the third the rising industrial classes. The Catholic faith had historic affinities with the first class. This affinity placed Catholicism in frequent alliance with feudal-agrarian conservatism and in opposition to both the liberal-democratic forces and Marxist-labor forces. The political situation in Spain and some South American countries exemplifies this tendency with particular vividness. Sometimes efforts to reconstruct the older authoritarianism under modern conditions have betrayed Catholicism into active alliance with fascism, as in Italy, Spain and Austria.

In general, churches, both Catholic and Protestant, are inclined to prefer the social forms of an established order and fail to recognize that new conditions may change an old justice into a new injustice. Thus they are heedless of the divine judgment which challenges every historic social order insofar as it incorporates injustices.

The new commercial-industrial society was informed partly by secular-liberal and partly by Protestant religious and moral viewpoints. The modern liberal culture, incorporating the Renaissance assumptions reviewed above, assumed that a free expression of all forces and interests in society would automatically make for justice. In its most consistent form modern liberalism believed in a pre-established harmony in society, akin to the harmony of non-historical nature which would guarantee justice if only governmental controls were reduced to minimal terms. This *laissez faire* theory did not realize that human freedom expresses itself destructively as well as creatively, and that an increase in human freedom and power through the introduction of technics makes the achievement of justice more, rather than less, difficult than in non-technical civilizations. The liberal culture of our era believed, either that the egoism of individuals, classes and nations was limited and harmless, or it hoped that the expression of self-interest was due to ignorance which could be overcome by growing social and political intelligence. This optimism misread the facts of human nature, as they are known from the standpoint of the Chrisitan faith and as they are attested by every page of history.

While some Protestant churches capitulated to the moral sentimentalities of this secular creed of progress and became uncritical allies of the commercial and industrial oligarchy in modern society, others failed to preserve a prophetic independence of modern middle class culture, even where they maintained a more Biblical faith. Both the Catholic and the Protestant forms of the Christian faith were thus involved in the decay of our civilization and were partially responsible for the rise of new secular religions, which promised the establishment of a more integral community and which rose in revolt against both the Christian and the secular forms of the liberal society.

These political religions sought either cynical or utopian methods of achieving community. Traditional Christianity expressed that side of the Christian truth which appreciates the perennially fragmentary character of all historic achievements and realizes that our final fulfilment is possible only through God's forgiveness. But it neglected the possibility and necessity of achieving community under the new conditions which each age sets and which were particularly challenging under the new conditions of a technical age. The new political religions on the other hand had no sense of the divine judgment and the divine fulfilment which stand against and over all human history. They promised the fulfilment of life either in an idolatrous national community or in an international classless society, conceived in utopian terms.[14]

Thus, the spiritual and religious confusion of our age is an even more profound revelation of the depth of the world crisis than the more obvious technical, social and political perplexities of our day. We can summarize the spiritual situation in the Western world rather simply as follows: most of the so-called Christian nations have ceased long since to be profoundly influenced in their thought and action by Christian presuppositions or imperatives. The vacuum left by the decline of the Christian faith has been filled by various forms of three different faiths:

(1) The liberal faith, which believes that society is moving toward a universal community and a frictionless harmony of all social life by forces inherent in history itself.

(2) The Marxist faith, which believes in the same consummation but has a more catastrophic, rather than evolutionary, idea of the method of social realization.

(3) Fascism, which is distinguished from the first two creeds by its nationalism, particularism and cynicism. Its explicit repudiation of the ethical universalism, which underlies the other two political religions, gives it an avowedly "anti-Christian" character, while the other two forms of political faith are heretical forms of the Christian religion. But fascism shares with the democratic and socialist creed the effort to reduce the meaning of human existence to purely social, political and historically realizable terms.[15] We must now turn our attention to a further analysis of these contemporary creeds.

CHAPTER II

The Soft Utopians: Liberalism

It would have been difficult for the generations of the twentieth century to survive the hazards and to face the perplexities of our age in any event, since every problem of human existence had been given a wider scope than known in previous ages. But our perplexities became the more insoluble and the perils to which we were exposed became the more dangerous because the men of this generation had to face the rigors of life in the twentieth century with nothing but the illusions of the previous two centuries to cover their spiritual nakedness. There was nothing in the creeds and dogmas of these centuries which would have enabled modern men either to anticipate or to understand the true nature of the terrors and tumults to which they would be exposed.[1]

I. *Two Forms of Utopianism*

This is why there is a curious pathos in the conflict between the Western and the Russian world. The Western world, though partly Christian, is primarily informed by the secular religion of faith in progress. The Russian world is animated by the secular creed of faith in redemption through revolution. The conflict is of course something more than an ideological one. But insofar as the conflict is ideological, each side is involved in a situation for which its creed offers no source of understanding.

The liberal creed of progress assumes that men are progressing toward higher and higher forms of social life and more and more inclusive loyalties. The Nazi rebellion against a world community was difficult to explain in terms of this faith and as we shall see was usually put down as a mysterious reversion to barbarism, which would not finally impede the onward march of humanity toward world community. Now the liberal world is confronted not by a cynical, but by a utopian foe, who also believes in world community, not by evolution but by revolution.[2]

For Marxism believes that the revolution will usher in an idyllic society of brotherly love, in which each would give according to his ability and take according to his need. If a period of dictatorship intervenes no one will have to worry, since the whole state apparatus will wither away with the victory of its cause and the universal abolition of property.[3]

In other words two secular religions of world redemption are in conflict with one another. One cannot deny that there is a special pathos in a conflict in the world community between two political forces each of which underestimates the complexities of history and both of which fail to understand the tragic character of human history. The communist creed of world redemption is the more dangerous because it is informed by a hard utopianism, while the liberal world is informed by soft utopianism. *Hard utopianism* might be defined as the creed of those who claim to embody the perfect community and who therefore feel themselves morally justified in using every instrument of guile or force against those who oppose their assumed perfection. *Soft utopianism* is the creed of those who do not claim to embody perfection, but expect perfection to emerge out of the ongoing process of history. The liberal soft utopians are obviously not as dangerous and fanatic as the communist hard utopians; but they are at a disadvantage in their conflict with the hard utopians because they do not understand that history makes the problems of man's togetherness more, rather than less, complex.[4]

II. *The Several Varieties of Liberalism*

We have been using the term, liberal, in a special sense. In the broadest sense, liberalism is rightly identified with the rise of a modern technical society availing itself of democratic political forms and of capitalistic economic institutions. This "liberal society" came to birth in Britain, France and America in opposition to the feudal aristocratic culture of the European past. Liberalism in the broadest sense is therefore synonymous with democracy. Its strategy is to free the individual from the traditional restraints of a society, to endow the governed with the power of the franchise, to establish the principle of the "consent of the governed" as the basis of political society, to challenge all hereditary privileges and traditional restraints upon human initiative, particularly in the economic sphere, and to create the mobility and flexibility which are the virtues and achievements of every liberal society as distinguished from feudal ones.

liberalism

But liberalism has more distinct connotations. One of these connotations arises out of the history of technical societies; the other arises out of the peculiar philosophy of the Renaissance and the French Enlightenment. In the first instance, the narrower connotation of liberalism is identified with the peculiar and unique ethos of middle-class life. But since the middle classes soon found the laboring classes to the left of them, liberalism soon ceased to be the exclusive philosophy of democracy. Even without the rise of labor as a political power, modern democracies, as they developed from commercialism to industrialism, found that the freeing of economic initiative from political restraint was only one side of the problem of justice. The other side was the placing of restraints upon initiative in the interest of security and justice.

Thus in every modern industrial nation the word liberalism achieved two contradictory definitions. It was on the one hand the philosophy which insisted that economic life was to be free of any restraint. In this form it was identical with the only conservatism which nations such as our own, who had no feudal past, could understand. It was the philosophy of the more successful middle classes who possessed enough personal skill, property or power to be able to prefer liberty to security. On the other hand the word was also used to describe the political strategy of those classes which preferred security to absolute liberty and which sought to bring economic enterprise under political control for the sake of establishing minimal standards of security and welfare. It has been rather confusing that both of these strategies go by the name of liberalism.

The semantic difficulties arising from this shift in meaning of the word liberal as a technical civilization moves farther and farther from its original contest with an organic and aristocratic society, are, however, simple compared with the confusions of definition which arise from the fact that liberalism is both a political philosophy, identified with the rising technical civilization, and a total philosophy of life which was elaborated in the French Enlightenment.

The French Enlightenment was liberal in its social policy in the sense that it championed all the extensions of political power and freedom from political control of economic enterprise which characterized the whole middle-class movement in its struggle with the feudal past. But it also had a total philosophy of life based on confidence in the perfectibility of man and on the idea of historical progress.[5] *

Though there appeared variations in this philosophy (differentiations for instance between secular and religious liberals) there developed never-

* In the following observation, Niebuhr notes still another problem of definition: "It must be apparent to anyone that it adds to the semantic confusion if those who do not share the illusions of Diderot and Condorcet are termed 'conservatives.' Such persons would be more accurately defined as 'realists,' particularly since a realistic estimate of perennial factors in the historical and social situation may be put into the service of either a conservative or advancing social policy. It would certainly be wrong to define a labor leader as 'conservative' merely because he knew, as every good labor leader must know, that a collective bargaining agreement is not merely a rational or moral encounter, and that its success depends upon the strength and unity of the force at his disposal."[6]

theless a pretty sharply defined credo which holds all liberalism together. Some of the articles in the credo are:

a. That injustice is caused by ignorance and will yield to education and greater intelligence.

b. That civilization is becoming gradually more moral and that it is a sin to challenge either the inevitability or the efficacy of gradualness.

c. That the character of individuals rather than social systems and arrangements is the guarantee of justice in society.

d. That appeals to love, justice, good-will and brotherhood are bound to be efficacious in the end. If they have not been so to date we must have more appeals to love, justice, good-will and brotherhood.

e. That goodness makes for happiness and that the increasing knowledge of this fact will overcome human selfishness and greed.

f. That wars are stupid and can therefore only be caused by people who are more stupid than those who recognize the stupidity of war.[7]

What then is the liberal creed? It is primarily faith in man; faith in his capacity to subdue nature, and faith that the subjection of nature achieves life's final good; faith in man's essential goodness, to be realized either when man ceases to be spiritual and returns to nature (romanticism), or when he ceases to be natural and becomes rational; and finally, faith in human history which is conceived as a movement upward by a force immanent within it. Whether this faith rests upon Darwin or upon Hegel (that is, whether nature is believed to guarantee progress or whether progress is conceived of as man's "gradual spiritualization" and his emancipation from natural impulses, prejudices and parochial attachments) the optimistic conclusion is the same.[8]

Liberalism is in short a kind of blindness to which those are particularly subject who imagine that their intelligence or the ineluctable processes of history have emancipated them from all the stupidities of the past. It is a blindness which does not see the perennial difference between human actions and aspirations, the perennial source of conflict between life and life, the inevitable tragedy of human existence, the irreducible irrationality of human behavior, and the tortuous character of human history.[9] To sum up, liberalism is based upon illusions as to the nature of man and of history. These two illusions were basic to all the political miscalculations of the Enlightenment and were the source of its errors.[10]

III. *Harmless Man*

Almost every version of liberal culture has some futile and fatuous scheme for lifting men from selfish purposes as painlessly as possible. The simplest idea of all is that which underlies the *laissez faire* social philosophies of the eighteenth and nineteenth centuries. According to these philosophies all conflicting interests in human society, and all competing egoistic drives, would result in harmony rather than conflict if they were only left alone. If political society did not interfere with economic process, economic life would achieve a natural harmony. This idea, which obviates the necessity of either moral or political control upon selfish impulses, was a nice device for eating your cake and having it too. It justified unrestrained selfishness without justifying egoism morally; for it gave the assurance that "each man seeking his own would serve the commonweal." The only difficulty with the idea is that it is not true. The one element of truth in it is that there are indeed certain automatic harmonies in the economic process, and it is wise to maintain them. But on the whole, history, unlike nature, has no natural balances of power. Where power is disproportionate, power dominates weakness and injustice results.[11]

There is a curious irony in the fact that this theory, which wrongly equates history with nature and assumes that human powers and impulses are subject to the same limits which operate in nature, should have been propounded at the precise moment in history when a technical civilization would prove how unbounded human power may become, even as all history has proved how unbounded human ambitions may be. Adam Smith, father of the classical liberal theory, was a contemporary of James Watt, the inventor of the steam engine, at the University of Glasgow. That fact points up the irony nicely, for the steam engine typifies the whole industrial development which made nonsense of Adam Smith's theory. A technical civilization accentuated rather than mitigated the disproportions of economic power which existed in an undynamic agrarian society. Thus a bourgeois world, dreaming of achieving "liberty, equality, and fraternity," developed such monstrous disproportions of social and economic power as to threaten not only the security of those who lacked power but the stability of society itself. The creed of classical liberalism created complacency at the precise moment when Western man should have been morally and politically alert. The drives of human society require management just as much as the impulses of the individual. Without such management they lead to anarchy or tyranny or both.[12]

The theory of the harmlessness of natural man, if only he is not controlled and regulated, is usually compounded with another theory, which is a little more profound. It is the theory that ignorant selfishness is dangerous to society, but that a wise and prudent selfishness knows how to relate the interests of the self to the interests of the whole; so that a wise egoist while seeking his own pleasure, will finally serve "the greatest good of the greatest number." The confidence in the essential virtue of the intelligent man takes various forms. Sometimes intelligence supposedly restrains egoism in its narrow form and broadens it to include the interests of others. Sometimes it is assumed that the intelligence preserves a nice balance between egoistic and altruistic impulses. And sometimes reason throws the weight of its authority on the side of altruism as against egoism.[13]

The French Enlightenment assigned reason the primary function of discerning the "laws of nature" and of destroying man's abortive efforts to circumvent these laws. It was assumed that increasing rationality would gradually destroy the irrational (primarily religious) justifications of special privilege. Or that increasing reason would gradually prompt all men to grant their fellow men justice, the power of logic requiring that the interests of each individual be brought into a consistent scheme of value.[14]

Of course, the Enlightenment was not entirely wrong, either in what it opposed or in what it affirmed. It rightly opposed the obscurantism to which an authoritarian religion is inevitably tempted when it seeks to transmute the symbols of its faith into adequate descriptions of detailed historical occurrences. A religion which has discovered the limits of human knowledge does not improve the inadequacies of this knowledge if it seeks to shackle culture by religious dogma. Such dogmatism invariably leads to a religious sanctification of the viewpoints of a particular age and the morality of a particular class. A genuine passion for humanity animated the Enlightenment in its opposition to divisive dogmatisms which had leagued God with a particular cultural viewpoint or social position.[15]

Nor was the Enlightenment entirely wrong in what it affirmed. Reason, inasfar as it is able to survey the whole field of life, analyzes the various forces in their relation to each other and, gauging their consequences in terms of the total welfare, it inevitably places the stamp of its approval upon those impulses which affirm life in its most inclusive terms. Practically every theory, whether utilitarian or intuitional, insists on the goodness of benevolence, justice, kindness and unselfishness. It is fair, therefore, to assume that growing rationality is a precondition of man's growing morality.

For the measure of our rationality determines the degree of vividness with which we appreciate the needs of other life, the extent to which we become conscious of the real character of our own motives and impulses, the ability to harmonize conflicting impulses in our own life and in society, and the capacity to choose adequate means for approved ends. In each instance a development of reason may increase the moral capacity.

The ability to consider, or even prefer, the interests of others to our own, is not dependent only upon the capacity for sympathy. Harmonious social relations depend upon the sense of justice as much as, or even more than, upon the sentiment of benevolence. This sense of justice is a product of the mind and not of the heart. It is the result of reason's insistence upon consistency.[16]

But the Enlightenment was also productive of dangerous errors. For a consistent rationalism makes human reason God. Reason becomes the universal value which is set above all particular values and is made the criterion of all morality. It is by human reason that all history is to be judged. The fatal error of rationalism is its failure to recognize that reason is universal only in purely formal terms. Logic and mathematics may be universal; but no judgment which fills logical forms with material content is universal. A rationalism which does not recognize this fact invariably mistakes its particular judgments for genuinely universal judgments, failing to see how it has insinuated its partial and finite perspectives into its supposedly universal standards.

Rationalism, in other words, forgets the finiteness and creatureliness of man. It does not subject human righteousness to a transcendent righteousness, the righteousness of God. Thus it tempts men to "go about establishing their own righteousness" and finally degenerates into a fanaticism more grievous than that of dogmatic religion. The logic of the decay of modern culture from universalistic humanism to nationalistic anarchy may be expressed as follows: Men seek a universal standard of human good. After painful effort they define it. The painfulness of their effort convinces them that they have discovered a genuinely universal value. To their sorrow, some of their fellow men refuse to accept the standard. Since they know the standard to be universal the recalcitrance of their fellows is a proof, in their minds, of some defect in the humanity of the non-conformists. Thus a rationalistic age creates a new fanaticism. The non-conformists are figuratively expelled from the human community.[17]

Insofar as human reason really frees the human spirit from the necessities and contingencies of nature it creates the possibility of moral action. Insofar as this emancipation is never complete and rationality is never discarnate, it accentuates the disharmonies of nature. Thus the same human reason which, on the one hand, regards differences of race as accidents of nature, as contingencies to be discounted and defied in the name of rational brotherhood, also gives these differences a spiritual significance, which they do not have in nature. Race pride and prejudice are just as much the fruits of rational freedom as is inter-racial brotherhood. In a word, the very reason, which modern culture has regarded as God, as the principle of universality and as the guarantor of goodness, is really a part of man's problem and not his answer to the problem.[18]

The tragic realities of contemporary history have fully revealed the illusory elements in this confidence in human rationality as the guarantor of increasing social peace and justice. The late Professor Einstein came to the despairing conclusion that if he had to live his life again he would want to be a plumber or a peddler and not a scientist. He based his pessimistic thought upon the fact that scientific freedom was in danger through government restrictions upon science, occasioned by the relation of physics to the whole development of nuclear weapons.

But one may suspect that a deeper problem than that of freedom was agitating the conscience of Einstein. It was the problem of the uneasy conscience of a once "pure" scientist, who had become involved in the guilt and moral perplexities of an atomic age.

Einstein once believed that if he could only get two per cent of the population to disavow war he might succeed in abolishing it. How deeply ironic that this very man should have been the one to write the letter of introduction to President Roosevelt for a group of physicists, whose visit to the President initiated the whole process that finally gave us the hydrogen bomb.

This is a case in which the pure rationalism of another age stumbles upon, and becomes involved in, the perennial problem of sin and guilt. The rationalists had dismissed the problem, which meanwhile reached the monstrous proportions of our atomic age. Furthermore, it was not merely the problem of guilt attendant upon a conscious wrong. It was the guilt in which we became involved even when we were trying to do what is right. Here is the moral dilemma of a civilization which once believed in "progress" and now finds all technical advances to be morally ambiguous.[19]

IV. *Redemptive History*

We have defined the error that underlies all the optimistic illusions of our liberal culture as a too-simple confidence in man, particularly in rational man, and as a too-simple hope in the progressive achievement of virtue in history, by reason of the progressive extension of intelligence. This confidence that human history ultimately answers all its unsolved problems and overcomes all its earlier insecurities, that history is itself a kind of process of redemption, has gained such a strong hold upon modern man because it is actually partly true and because all the tremendous advances of science, technology, and intelligence seemed to justify the belief.[20]

The conception of a redemptive history informs the most diverse forms of modern culture. The French physiocrats believed that progress would be assured by the removal of the irrelevancies of historical restraints from the operation of the laws of nature. Comte on the other hand thought it would be achieved by bringing social process under the control of an elite of social scientists. But this contrast between determinism and voluntarism (which is, incidentally, never composed in modern culture) had no influence upon the shared belief in progress. There is only a slight difference in optimism between the deterministic thought of Herbert Spencer and the modern voluntarism of John Dewey.*

Even Karl Marx, who introduced a provisional historical catastrophism to challenge the optimism of bourgeois life, did not shake the modern conception of a redemptive history basically. He saw in the process of historical development certain "dialectical" elements not observed in bourgeois theories. He knew that there is disintegration as well as increasing integration in history; that there is death as well as growth. But he also believed that a new life and a new age would rise out of the death of an old one with dialectical necessity. Catastrophe was the certain prelude of redemption in his scheme of salvation. The ultimate similarity between Marxist and bourgeois optimism, despite the provisional catastrophism of the former, is, in fact, the most telling proof of the unity of modern culture. It is a unity which transcends warring social philosophies, conflict between which contributed to the refutation of a common hope.

The goal toward which history was presumably moving was variously defined. The most unreflective forms of historical optimism in the nineteenth century assumed that increasing physical comfort and well-being were the guarantee of every other form of advance. Sometimes the enlarging human community was believed to be developing inevitably toward a universal community, for "clans and tribes, long narrowly self-regarding, are finally enlarged and compacted into nations; and nations move inevitably, however slowly, into relations with one another, whose ultimate goal is the unification of mankind." [21]

Sometimes, as in H. G. Wells' *Outline of History,* the historical process is assumed to be moving toward the democratization, as well as the universalization, of the human community. The democratic culmination toward which history was presumably moving was frequently defined in contradictory terms. Libertarians thought they saw a movement toward increasing liberty while equalitarians and collectivists thought they could discern a movement toward more intense social cohesion. Though there are minor dissonances the whole chorus of modern culture learned to sing the new song of hope in remarkable harmony. The redemption of mankind, by whatever means, was assured for the future. It was, in fact, assured by the future.

* For an explication of Niebuhr's views on the role of scientism in the social sciences, see Chapter V.

There were experiences in previous centuries which might well have challenged this unqualified optimism. But the expansion of man's power over nature proceeded at such a pace that all doubts were quieted, allowing the nineteenth century to become the "century of hope" and to express the modern mood in its most extravagant terms. History, refusing to move by the calendar, actually permitted the nineteenth century to indulge its illusions into the twentieth. Then came the deluge. Since 1914 one tragic experience has followed another, as if history had been designed to refute the vain delusions of modern man.[22]

There is always progress in history in the sense that it cumulates wisdom, perfects technics, increases the areas of human cooperation, and extends the human control over nature. But this cannot be regarded as moral progress. There are morally ambiguous elements in human history on every new level of achievement. We ought to have known that. A person progresses from childhood to maturity, but it is not easy to compare the virtue of maturity with the innocency of a child, because mature life achieves higher unities and is subject to greater complexities than child life. It is in fact irrelevant to measure mature virtue with childish innocency because they are incommensurate. So it is with the history of mankind.

The advancement of knowledge may mitigate social conflict, but intelligence may also be the servant of imperial ambition. The applied sciences and technics may multiply human power and increase comfort. But dictators may use the power for destructive ends; and the democratic world may be beguiled by the comforts of bourgeois society into a false security. Modern means of communication may increase the breadth and extent of human communities, but they also enlarge areas of human conflict. Reason may serve as an arbitrator between my interest and those of my fellowmen. In that case, reason is a servant of justice. But reason may, as Bergson observed, also break the communities of primitive life by giving the egoistic urge a new instrument.

Whether one analyzes the advances of history in terms of technics or of intelligence, it is quite apparent that history is not so simple as we have believed. The morally ambiguous note remains in it on every level. The securities of its maturity save us from the insecurities of childhood; but they do not save us from the new insecurities of maturity. The wisdom of maturity is a cure for the ignorance of childhood; but it is no cure for the ignorance of maturity. It is because we have trusted history too much that we understand neither life nor history. History cannot be the answer to our problems, for history is itself our problem. History is, in short, an inadequate god. We have failed to gauge every contemporary problem in its true depth because of this false faith in history. Previous civilizations only made the mistake of misjudging their own history and estimating their own security too highly. We went one step beyond them in pride and pretension. We thought no evil could befall us because we trusted not "Roman civilization" nor medieval culture, but history itself. Yet our error was greater than previous errors, precisely because we believed that history's development of all human potencies also guaranteed the elimination of all human insecurities. The very opposite is the truth. A highly dynamic technical society is more destructive in its decay than a simple agrarian society. Destruction dumped from the skies is more awful than the lethal power of a bow and arrow.[23] The possession of a phenomenal form of destructive power in the modern day has proved to be so fruitful of new fears that the perennial ambiguity of man's situation of power and weakness became more vividly exemplified, rather than overcome. Thus a century which was meant to achieve a democratic society of world-scope finds itself at its half-way mark uncertain about the possibility of avoiding a new conflict of such proportions as to leave the survival of mankind, or at least the survival of civilization, in doubt.

The tragic irony of this refutation by contemporary history of modern man's conception of history embodies the spiritual crisis of our age.[24] We thought that life's meaning was guaranteed by the historical process. We believed in progress. Now we find that an atomic bomb stands at the end of the technical development. And at the end of the hoped for rational-moral progress we find little statesmen, representing little nations, drawing pretensions of omniscience from their military omnipotence, and playing with the powder which might blow up the world.[25]

V. *Liberalism and Christianity*

One reason why the whole of modern liberal Christianity has become infected with the illusions of soft utopianism is because the modern idea of progress seemed to reinforce all the hopes for the progressive triumph of pure love which the soft utopians cherished. The spread of the pacifist movement in modern liberal Christianity, particularly in the Anglo-Saxon countries, to the point where it seemed that the perfectionist hopes of the small sectarian churches would be shared by the whole of Protestantism, was undoubtedly due primarily to the substitution of the idea of progress in liberal Christianity for the truth of the Gospel.* In the words of a typical exponent of the American "social gospel," "the new social order will be based not on fighting but on fraternity . . . not simply because the cooperative fraternal life is the highest ideal of human living but because the spirit and method of cooperation is the scientific law of human progress." [26]

Or perhaps our religious modernism believes simply in human good-

* For Niebuhr's critique of pacifism, see Chapter XIII.

ness and in the necessity of exhorting men to be good or of proving to them that the highest good is the love of one's neighbor. It has not heard the cry of despair from the human heart about its impotence to do the good which it knows. The liberal church offers salvation through endless cascades of moral exhortation, moral admonition and moral instruction. Men, on the whole, know that they ought to do good rather than evil; and they have a shrewd suspicion that usually the good may be defined in terms of generosity toward the brother rather than concern for the self. But they are not fully conscious (though they may be darkly conscious) of the fact that they violate moral commandments by their own impulses of pride and lust for power, and that their anxieties about self make it impossible for them to consider the neighbor.

Furthermore the liberal church, preaching in a catastrophic age in which the communal life of man is torn by a thousand hatreds, in which the newly won freedom of India is almost drowned in the blood of fratricidal strife, in which conflicting rights of Jews and Arabs reveal how terribly complex problems of justice are, and in which the vicious circle of mutual fear between two great centers of power in the community of nations threatens to tear the world apart, blandly advises men and nations to love one another if they would escape disaster. There is in this preaching no understanding either of the complex problems of the justice which is required to preserve a tolerable peace among nations, races and groups which do not love each other, nor yet of the agony of rebirth required if the individual would turn from self-love to love.[27]

Liberal Christianity and modern secular liberalism have become united in the errors and sentimentalities of a soft utopianism, which manages to evade the tragic realities of life and to obscure the moral ambiguity in all political positions. These evasions are achieved by hoping for a progressive alteration of the character of human history. This soft utopianism is free of the sin of fanaticism but it is not without its dangers. The recent encounter of the democratic world with tyrannical Nazism might have proved fatal to civilization had not the common sense of "the children of this world" outweighed the illusions of "the children of light." For the soft utopians were prepared to meet malignant evil with non-resistance, hoping that kindness would convert the hearts of tyrants.[28]

VI. *Liberalism and Nazism*

The fact is that the tragic realities in which Western civilization is involved are really striking refutations of our characteristic liberal credos. It is particularly significant that millions of rational and "idealistic" people refused to take seriously the monstrous perils of Nazi totalitarianism. We talked about it as a "reversion to barbarism" which meant that we could imagine evil in history only as a return to a primitive past. We could not imagine that a mature civilization would produce in its decay, not the evils of nature nor of primitive society, but terrible evils that are relevant to, and possible only in, maturity. We did not understand the difference between nature and history. In nature, beasts of prey lie down to go to sleep when their maws are crammed. In human history, no hunger is ever perfectly satisfied and grows by what it feeds on. Just as the desires of man are infinite so also are the possibilities for good and evil in history. But the possibilities for evil keep abreast of the possibilities for good. The delicate balances of a mature mind are more easily subject to disarrangement (insanity) than the simple psychic processes of a child; and a complex technical society can fall into more utter confusion than a simple agrarian economy. The cruelty of the Nazis was no more like "barbarism" than insanity is childishness. The persistent inclination of modern culture to minimize the monstrous evils against which we must contend, and to interpret them as reversions to nature or to a primitive past, reveals a false estimate of human history and a false confidence in its securities. The conflicts and catastrophes of our era have been the more terrible because we had no philosophy by which we could anticipate them, or understand them when they were upon us.[29]

In a sense, Nazi philosophy had in every case taken neglected portions of the total truth about man and history and fashioned them into perverse but potent instruments against a civilization that did not understand the nature and history of man. For the liberal faith in reason, Nazism substituted the romantic faith in vitality and force. For the simple faith that right creates its own might, it substituted the idea that might makes right. For the hope of liberal democracy that history was in the process of eliminating all partial, national and racial loyalties and creating a universal community of mankind, it substituted a primitive loyalty to race and nation as the final end of life. In place of the sentimental idea that men could easily combine devotion to their own interests with loyalty to universal justice, it proclaimed the cynical idea that there is no justice but that which serves "my" or "our" purpose and interest.

It is wrong to worship force and to make power self-justifying. But such an error could not have arisen in a civilization that had not made the opposite mistake and assumed that men were in the process of becoming purely rational. It is perverse to make the interests of our nation the final end of life. But this error could not have achieved such monstrous proportions if our culture had not foolishly dreamed and hoped for the development of "universal" men, who were bereft of all loyalties to family, race, and nation. It is monstrous to glorify war as the final good. But that error could not have brought us so close to disaster if a comfortable civilization had not meanwhile regarded peace as a final good, and had not expected perfect peace to be an attainable goal of history. It is terrible to conduct the diplomacy and military strategy of nations upon the basis of "all or nothing" policies. But the fury expressed in such policies would not have come so close to success if it had not been met by the illusions of comfortable and fat nations in which the love of ease had been compounded with the caution of prudence, and the two together had resulted in an inability to act. If the lies embodied in the Nazi creed did not contain a modicum of truth and if that modicum of truth had not been directed against our weakness and our illusions, we would not have come so close to disaster.[30]

So the tragic events of modern history have negated practically every presupposition upon which modern culture was built. History does not move forward without catastrophe, happiness is not guaranteed by the multiplication of physical comforts, social harmony is not easily created by more intelligence, and human nature is not as good or as harmless as had been supposed. We are thus living in a period in which either the optimism of yesterday has given way to despair, or in which some of the less sophisticated moderns try desperately to avoid the abyss of despair by holding to credos which all of the facts have disproved.[31]

CHAPTER III

The Hard Utopians: Communism

We do not understand communism if we fail to realize that it is a variant of the same utopianism with which the whole liberal world is infected. But communism turns the soft utopianism of modern culture into a hard and truculent utopianism. While the former dreams of achieving an ideal society of uncoerced justice through the historical development of altruistic as against egoistic purposes, the latter claims to embody a social system in which this miracle has actually taken place. A soft utopianism projects its ideal of a perfect accord between men and nations into the future. It is therefore free of the fanaticism and truculence of the hard utopian who claims to possess the ideal society.[1] The hard utopian creates a fighting community which regards itself as the embodiment and champion of an ideal commonwealth of perfect justice or perfect love, for which it is ready to do battle against all enemies.

I. *A Perverted Religion*

The real perils of the "fighting sect" did not develop fully so long as this form of utopianism remained within the general framework of the Christian faith.* The perils became more apparent as the Marxist movement of the nineteenth century presented a secularized version of sectarian perfectionism. In this version the working class, more particularly the class of industrial workers, were constituted into a messianic class whose triumph over their foes would prove, according to their faith, to be not merely a triumph over particular foes but the final triumph over evil in history. The "saving remnant" of this messianic class would be the "vanguard" of "class-conscious" workers, the members of the Communist Party, whose purposes were so identical with the very purposes of history that every weapon became morally permissible to them and every vicissitude of history was expected to contribute to the inevitability of their victory.

* E.g. the Continental Anabaptist movement in the Reformation period, or the fighting sects of seventeenth century, Cromwellian England. See *Faith and History*, p. 208.

The Christian myth of the Fall was reinterpreted so that an original state of innocency was posited as existing before the rise of private property. In this state man had not lost the communal essence of his existence. The rise of private property constituted the Fall, and the socialization of all property was therefore expected to usher in the kingdom of perfect love on earth, in which, when fully developed, everyone "would give according to his ability and take according to his need." The state was regarded as merely an instrument of class domination. It would "wither away" after all the enemies of this new commonwealth were defeated. An anarchistic millennium would crown the final triumph of the proletariat. Meanwhile a "dictatorship of the proletariat" was morally legitimatized both to practice a tyrannical rule over the faithful and to conduct ruthless conflict against all enemies. There is no question about the religious character of this whole program, despite its ostensible scorn for religion and its pretension to a "scientific" interpretation of the "laws of motion" in history. A "dialectical" process becomes surrogate for the absent God. This process guarantees the victory of the cause which the faithful deem to be unqualifiedly just. Everywhere the sense of the ultimate which characterizes religion reveals itself. It is furthermore a religion indirectly related to Biblical faith but perverted at two points. The first perversion is that it has no sense of a conflict between all men and God. It knows only of a conflict between the righteous and the unrighteous. This conflict is existentially interpreted, with considerable justification, as one between the privileged and the poor. Marxism is thus a secularized version of messianism without the knowledge of the prophets that the judgment of God falls with particular severity upon the chosen people.

The other perversion of Christian faith lies in the expectation of the complete realization of the kingdom of perfect righteousness in history. This utopian hope, partly derived from sectarian Christianity and partly from the general utopian temper of the eighteenth and nineteenth centuries, completely obscures the fact that corruptions of the meaning of life are bound to appear on every level of history, so long as human freedom is real freedom and therefore contains the possibility of evil.

The combined impact of these two perversions generates the fanatic fury of orthodox Marxism. Its non-prophetic messianism endows a particular social force in history with unqualified sanctity and its post-Christian utopianism prompts the illusion of the appearance of a kingdom of perfect righteousness (i.e., a classless society and an anarchistic brotherhood) in history. The self-righteous fury, prompted by these two errors, constitutes the real peril of orthodox communism. Most of the conventional objections to Marxist "materialism" and "atheism" are beside the point. Its materialism is, on the whole, a justified reaction to pietistic religions which do not understand the social character of life and to "spiritual" versions of Christianity which do not understand the unity of individual and collective man in the material and spiritual dimensions of his life. Its ostensible atheism is less significant than its idolatry. It worships a god who is the unqualified ally of one group in human society against all others.

The fanaticism of this new religion rent the social and cultural unity of Western society and helped to create the social confusion out of which the even more primitive political religion of Nazism emerged. The fact that this religion gained a foothold in one particular nation has created an almost fantastic religious situation in the Western world. For thousands of intellectuals and millions of workers, particularly in continental Europe, who were desperately seeking for a sense of meaning in life after the utopianism of a bourgeois culture had ended in disillusionment, were willing to invest all their spiritual capital in this new hope, though it was made even more implausible by the fact that the messianic pretensions of a particular nation were compounded with the messianic pretensions of a particular class. There are still numberless people in the Western world who cling to this hope desperately, even though it becomes increasingly difficult to regard the tortuous politics of an anxious dictatorship as the strategy which will usher in a kingdom of perfect righteousness. That so desperate a hope and faith should still be regarded as credible by many is an indication of the desperation of modern man about the meaning of life.[2]

II. *The Sources of Evil in Communism*

1. THE MONOPOLY OF POWER

If we seek to isolate more specifically the various causes of an organized evil which spreads terror and cruelty throughout the world and confronts us everywhere with faceless men who are immune to every form of moral and political suasion, we must inevitably begin with the monopoly of power which communism establishes. Disproportions of power anywhere in the human community are fruitful of injustice, but a system which gives some men absolute power over other men results in evils which are worse than injustice.

Marxism did not indeed plan the highly centralized power structure of communism; but Marx did plan for a "dictatorship of the proletariat"; and the progressive moral deterioration of such a dictatorship was inevitable rather than fortuitous, for two reasons: The first is that when society is divided into the powerful and the powerless there is no way of preventing the gradual centralization of the monopoly of power. The monopoly of a class becomes the monopoly of the party which claims to be the vanguard of the whole class; the monopoly of the party gradually becomes the monopoly of a small oligarchy who speak at first for the class to other classes who have been robbed of power. But their authority inevitably degenerates into a monopoly of power exercised over their own party and class because no one in the whole community has the constitutional means to challenge and check the inevitable extension of power after which the most powerful grasp. The dictatorship of the oligarchy further degenerates into the dictatorship of a single tyrant. It was significant that a fallen oligarch, such as Trotsky, was as powerless as the most powerless peasant to challenge the rule of the tyrant who had defeated him, or to amend the history of the events written by the victor to justify his victory and to discredit his foe.

Another reason for the excessive concentration of power is that the Marxist theory wrongly assumes that economic power inheres solely in the ownership of property and obscures the power of the manager of property. It therefore wrongly concludes that the socialization of property causes economic power to evaporate when in fact it merely gives a single oligarchy a monopoly of both economic and political power. One pathetic consequence of this error is that the workers of a socialized concern, who are in theory the common owners of the property and are therefore prevented from holding any significant power, are rendered powerless against the managerial oligarchs who run the factory. The inevitable result is the accumulation of injustices more grievous than those which originally inspired the Marxist revolt against a free society.

2. UTOPIAN ILLUSIONS

While the relation of absolute power to complete defenselessness is the basic cause of all the evils of communism, it must be recognized, as we have already pointed out, that the communist tyranny is supported and aggravated by the whole series of pretensions derived from the secular religion which creates the ethos of the communist society. The most significant moral pretension is derived from the utopian illusions of Marxism. According to these illusions every policy of Marxist propaganda and class conflict has the object of hastening the day of historical climax when an ideal classless society will emerge.[3] Nothing is more paradoxical in Marxian theory than that it prompts its adherents to a cynically realistic analysis of human motives in the present instance and yet persuades them to look forward to a paradise of brotherhood after the revolution. For the period after the revolution every orthodox Marxian is a liberal. The eighteenth-century faith in the perfectibility of man is expressed with the greater abandon for having been tentatively veiled and qualified.[4]

The utopian illusions presumably make communism more dangerous rather than more evil. They are responsible for the loyalty of a group of intellectuals to the communist cause. The disillusionment of these idealists in Europe does not prevent a new crop of Asian intellectuals from being taken in by these pretensions. Furthermore, the illusions enable communists to pose as the liberators of every class or nation which they intend to enslave; and to exploit every moral and political weakness of the civilized world as if they had the conscience of civilization in their keeping. But the utopianism is the basis of the evil in communism as well as of its greater danger. It provides a moral façade for the most unscrupulous political policy, giving the communist oligarch the moral warrant to suppress and sacrifice immediate values in the historical process for the sake of reaching so ideal a goal.

3. THE CLASS BASIS OF VIRTUE

The fierce self-righteousness derived from these utopian illusions is accentuated by the Marxist distinction between the classes, according to which the classes which hold property are naturally evil while the "proletariat," the industrial workers, are the messianic class endowed with every virtue. A derivative of this distinction differentiates between the capitalist nations which are by nature "imperialistic" and "militaristic" and the innocent "Peoples' Democracies." The tendency to call white black and black white is accentuated and justified by these unreal distinctions.[5] There is of course nothing in the evidence of history to justify the belief that the historic class organization of society is alone responsible for the tendency of men and societies to take advantage of each other. It would be truer to say that the class organization is a consequence of this tendency in the human heart. It may therefore be checked and minimized but not abolished in a society in which power is equalized and held under social control.[6]

The fury of communist self-righteousness is aggravated furthermore by the Marxist error of equating egoism with the economic motive so that the most powerful oligarch, driven and corrupted by the lust for power, will appear innocent to his own conscience and to his deluded community because he makes no profit and owns no property.

4. THE MANIPULATION OF DESTINY

Another pretension of communism is usually obscured by the stock criticism against Marxism. It is rightly accused of being deterministic, that is, of underestimating the freedom of man and of emphasizing the determined character of his culture and of his convictions, which are said to be rooted in his economic interest. This determinism is at least half true and not nearly as dangerous as a supplementary and contradictory dogma according to which history works toward a climax in which the proletarian class must by a "revolutionary act" intervene in the course of history and thereby change not only history but the whole human situation. For after this act man is no longer both creature and creator of history but purely the creator who "not only proposes but also disposes." This idea involves monstrous claims of both omnipotence and omniscience which support the actual monopoly of power and aggravate its evil. Molotov illustrated the pretensions of omniscience when he declared that the communists, guided by "Marxist-Leninist science," know not only the inner meaning of current events but are able to penetrate the curtain of the future and anticipate its events. This tendency of playing God to human history is the cause for a great deal of communist malignancy.

The seemingly opposite tendency to regard men as the product of economic circumstance supports the pretension; for it makes it possible for an elite to pretend to be the manipulators of the destiny of their fellow men. The pretension reveals the similarity between the Nazi evil, based upon the pretension of Nietzsche's "superman," who makes his power self-justifying, and this kind of superman whose power is ostensibly justified by the fate which appoints him as the creator of historical destiny. Some of the communist fury is the consequence of the frustration of the communist oligarchs, when they discover history to be more complex than anticipated in their logic and find that opposing forces, which are marked for defeat in their apocalypse, show a more stubborn strength and resistance than they anticipated.

5. THE DOMINION OF DOGMA OVER FACTS

The Marxist dogmatism, coupled with its pretensions of scientific rationality, is an additional source of evil. The dogmas are the more questionable because the tyrannical organization prevents a re-examination of the dogmas when the facts refute them. Thus communist irrationality and dogmatism consist of a rigorous adhesion to dogma in defiance of the fact. The communists test every historical fact with ostensible precision and coolness, but their so-called science looks at the world through the spectacles of inflexible dogma which alters all the facts and creates a confused world picture. The greatest danger of communist policy comes from the fact that the communists do not know what kind of a world they live in, and what their foes are like. Their own rigorous dogma obscures the facts and their tyrannical system prevents, for motives of fear, the various proconsuls of their imperium from apprising the men in the Kremlin of the truth.

The rigor of the communist dogmatism creates an ideological inflexibility, consonant with the monolithic political structure. The combination of dogmatism and tyranny leads to shocking irrationalities in communist trials, where the victims are made to confess to the most implausible charges. Since the communist dogma allows for no differences of opinion among the elect, every deviation from orthodoxy is not only branded as treason but is attributed to some original sinful social taint.

It is instructive that the actual monopoly of power accentuates the evil in the ideological pretensions of communism while these pretensions give a spiritual dimension to the evils which flow from a monopoly of power. Thus the evil of communism flows from a combination of political and "spiritual" factors, which prove that the combination of power and pride is responsible for turning the illusory dreams of yesterday into the present nightmare, which disturbs the ease of millions of men in our generation.[7]

III. *Communism and Nazism*

It is deeply ironic that our modern culture, which dreams of the gradual elimination of "methods of force" in favor of "methods of mind" and of the progressive triumph of democratic government over all forms of tyranny, should encounter two forms of tyranny in one generation. It is baffling, as well as ironic, that the two forms of tyranny, Nazism and communism, should be so similar in practice and yet so dissimilar in theory. Unless we are perfectly clear how such contradictory theories of man's moral and political problem can issue in practically identical political institutions and moral behavior, we will not fully comprehend the breadth and depth of our contemporary crisis.

Nazism was the fruit of moral cynicism. Communism is the product of moral and political utopianism. Nazism believed (or believes) that a nation has the right to declare that there are no standards of justice beyond its own interest. Communism dreams of a universal society in which all nations will be related to each other in a frictionless harmony, if indeed nations will not disappear entirely in a universal brotherhood. Nazism raises the self-worship, to which all ethnic groups are prone, to explicit proportions in its theory of a "master race." Communism believes that ethnic distinctions are irrelevant in an ideal society.

Nazism regards power as the final justification of any action. According to its theory a nation which has the power to organize an imperial society beyond its own borders, proves its right to do so by its success.

Communism dreams of an ideal society in which the state "will wither away" and in which every form of coercion, force and power will gradually become irrelevant. Nazism believes in an elite class which manages the affairs of the mass of men. Communism is fiercely equalitarian in theory and hopes for the abolition of all class distinctions. The "dictatorship of the proletariat" is, in theory, provisional. For the dictatorship of a small oligarchy, which has in fact established itself in the communist state, there is no place at all in communist theory.

The contrast in theory between the two systems is practically complete. The question is how almost identical political institutions can develop from these contradictory theories. Nazi theory and practice are consistent. The practice follows by logical necessity from the theory. Communism boasts that it has created a new unity of theory and practice. Yet it presents the modern world with the most shocking disparity between the two.

We have seen that the root of communist utopianism lies in the Marxist analysis of the cause of human egoism. If it should be true that a particular economic institution (private property) is the cause of all human egoism, it would follow of course that the elimination of that institution would make men completely social and would abolish all frictions and competitions in human society. A propertyless society would have no use for the coercive functions of the state. It would wither away. If it should be true that this desirable end cannot be achieved without a world-wide revolution of the propertyless classes against the property owners, the idyllic paradise to be attained would seem to justify the ruthless policies pursued in the conflict. It would seem also to justify a provisional dictatorship, which will give cohesion and striking power to the cohorts of redemption. If this provisional dictatorship seems to have inordinate power, the utopian need not worry over-much about the perils of such power, because, according to his theory, all political power will atrophy in the day when a complete victory has been won.

Thus, communism, as we know it, is a political system in which a provisional moral cynicism, which countenances the defiance of the moral experience of the human race, is justified by a moral utopianism which dreams of the achievement of an ideal world in which property, government, nationality and ethnic distinctions will all disappear. Since the communist hope is an illusion, the objective observer must recognize the provisional cynicism as no different than the basic cynicism of the Nazis even as he knows that a supposedly provisional dictatorship follows the same practices as one which claimed permanent tenure.

While it is important to recognize that diametrically opposite conceptions of human nature may thus produce common unscrupulous and ruthless political practices and despotic political institutions, it is nevertheless important to bear the differences in basic theory in mind. One reason for doing this is that the corruption of an ideal may be politically more dangerous than a frankly cynical political program.[8] Most of our polemic against communism sounds like something left over from the propaganda warfare against Nazism. We think we are making the ultimate condemnation of communism if we insist that its totalitarianism is identical with that of Nazism. Thereby we obscure its greater danger, which is derived from the fact that it is a corruption of a utopian dream and does not stem from the pure moral cynicism which the Nazis avowed.[9]

The Nazis were, for instance, frustrated in their senseless self-worship. It is ridiculous to ask a subject people to violate their sense of self-respect by holding the conqueror in religious veneration. The Russian will-to-power is more subtly related to the communist cause. Russia comes to every nation, which it intends to subjugate, as a "liberator" from "fascist" and "imperialist" oppression. Russian nationalism was related to the liberal dream of the eighteenth century. The difference between the nationalism of the Nazis and the nationalism of the Russian communists is the difference between the "honest" moral cynic and the misguided or self-deceived idealist, who fails to recognize to what degree self-interest corrupts even the most ideal motives. A corrupted ideal may be more potent than a frank defiance of all ideal values. The proof of that higher potency is given by the fact that Russia's so-called "fifth columns" in the Western world are composed not of the miserable traitors who constituted the Nazi dominated "Bund," nor yet of mere Communist Party hacks. They contain thousands of misguided idealists. who still think that Russia is the midwife of an ideal society, about to be born.

But there is an even more important reason for noting the difference between the utopian and the cynical bases of these two forms of tyranny. It will not do to fight a despotism, which had its inspiration in utopianism, merely by calling attention to the crass corruption of the original ideal. It is necessary for a democratic civilization to recognize the weakness in its own life which gave power and plausibility to this dream.[10]

IV. *Communism and Liberalism*

The fact is that Marxism, in its pure form, has been the most potent critic of liberal illusions. Who understands the pretensions of "rational objectivity" in social conflict better than a real Marxist? Or for that matter the invalidity of an absolute distinction between the covert and the overt use of force? Yet the provisional realism of the Marxists quickly results in new illusions and confusions.[11] Those of us who once used Marxist collectivism to counter the error of liberal individualism, Marxist catastrophism to counter false liberal optimism, and Marxist determinism to challenge the sentimentality of liberal moralism and idealism, must now admit that the "truths" which we used to challenge "error" turned out to be no more true (though also no less true) than the liberal ones. But they were more dangerous.[12]

For example, our liberal or democratic culture, which maintained a critical attitude toward political power, became increasingly uncritical toward economic power, assuming it to be the source of justice. Thus property rights were made more absolute in an industrial and commercial society than they were in the older agrarian society despite the fact that a technical civilization created new perils of economic power which did not exist in an agrarian civilization. It was this error which invited, in a sense, first the legitimate criticism, but then the counter-error, of Marxism. For a religious veneration of the institution of property led to a new religion which sought the redemption of mankind through the abolition of property. Since Marxism erroneously assumed that economic power inhered altogether in the ownership of property, failing to recognize that the power of the manager of economic process would persist even in a society devoid of private property, its policy of socialization merely resulted in turning both economic and political power over to a single oligarchy, thus increasing the danger of tyranny. This error, added to all of its other miscalculations of human nature and history, accentuated its drift toward despotism.[13]

We are only beginning to appreciate that the real tragedy of our age lies in the fact that the Marxist alternative to the injustices of our society should have generated cruelties and injustices so much worse than those which Marxism challenged, and should nevertheless be able to gain the devotion of millions of desperate people in Europe and particularly in Asia upon the basis of the original dream as if the dream had not turned into a nightmare.[14] But these gross miscalculations of Marxism must not obscure the errors of a liberal society which gave plausibility and credibility to Marxist illusions. Nor should the evils which have been introduced into modern history by this new fanaticism be allowed to obscure the fact that Marxism is the perversion of a profound truth. It understands, as the purely progressive view of history does not, that civilizations and cultures do not merely grow but that they must die and be reborn if they are to have a new life. Its program of the socialization of property may be a proximate answer to the immediate problem of achieving justice in a technical age, though communism falsely made it an absolute answer to the immediate problem and in addition into an ultimate answer to the ultimate problem of human existence itself. The struggle between rich and poor, between the owners and the workers in modern industrial society, is a fact which Marxism illumined, and which both orthodox Christianity and liberalism were inclined to obscure. But Marxism falsely made it into a final fact of history which was supposed to bear within itself the possibility of an ultimate redemption of history. The illusions of Marxism are thus the end-products of a Christian civilization which either failed to realize the highest possibilities of life in history or which claimed the realization of a perfection that can never be achieved in history.[15]

CHAPTER IV

The Perennial Crisis

Our current history is actually a remarkable illustration of the way Nemesis overtakes the pride of man and how divine judgment is visited upon men and nations who exalt themselves above measure.

The liberal part of our culture thought that the Christian idea of the sinfulness of all men was outmoded. In its place it put the idea of a harmless egoism, rendered innocuous either by a prudent self-interest or by a balance of all social forces which would transmute the selfishness of all into a higher social harmony. The vanity of that idea was proved by the ever more dynamic disproportions of power in our society and the ever greater destruction of community in a technical society. Sometimes the liberal part of our culture conceived the idea of redemption through growth and development. Men suffered (so it was argued) not from sin but from impotence. But fortunately the whole historical process was itself redemptive. It translated man from impotence to power, from ignorance to intelligence, from being the victim to becoming the master of historical destiny. This illusion proved as tragic as the first one. Since the sin of man lies in the corruption of his will and not in his weakness, the possibilities of evil grow with the development of the very freedom and power which were supposed to emancipate man.

The obvious illusions of the liberal world prompted a Marxist rebellion against the whole liberal culture. In place of confidence in a simple harmony of all social forces it proclaimed confidence in a new harmony of society through a revolutionary destruction of property, thus making a social institution the root of evil in man and promising redemption through its destruction. In place of the idea of redemption through endless growth and development it promised redemption through the death of an old order and the rise of a new one. But this was not redemption through the perpetual dying to self of the Christian Gospel. It was the promise of a new life for us through the death of our foes. The prophets of this new religion turned into tyrannical priest-kings who, having lost all sense of the contingent character of all human interests and ideas, filled the world with the cruelty of their self-righteousness.[1]

As political theories Marxism and liberalism are antithetical. As moral and religious theories—and they are moral and religious theories—they are very much alike. Both are evasions of the deeper problems which all men face in seeking a tolerable harmony with their fellow men. Both obscure the fact that the root of man's lust for power and of his cruel and self-righteous judgments on his fellows is in himself and not in some social or economic institution.[2]

Is it not significant that a culture which expects "man" to become master of his historical fate, and "man" to decide what direction his historical development should take, arrives at this tragic end? And that the difficulty is created by the fact that the natural scientist, who is the only scientist faintly approximating the universal *mind* which is to become master of historical destiny, discovers atomic power; and that, confronted with the necessity of bringing this new power of creativity and destructiveness under social and moral control, our generation should find *mind* dissolved into various national minds, whose social objectives are as varied as their language? And that they should find the greater difficulty in achieving a tolerable community, across this chasm of mutual fear, because each is armed with a social philosophy which obscures the partial and particular character of its objective?

When all the elements which enter our present world situation are explicated, it becomes apparent that history's pattern of meaning is more complex than either the communist or the liberal conception of historical progress. Men do not, whether by evolutionary or revolutionary means, exchange their position of creatures of historical process to that of history's masters. They remain rather in the continuous ambiguity both of being mastered and mastering the course of history. Whatever mastery they may achieve over historical processes must still operate in a wide realm of meaning in which both natural and historical factors beyond the control of any particular human will frustrate, deflect and negate, as well as fulfill, human desires and ambitions.

The modern version of an historical redemption from the human predicament of finiteness and freedom is, in short, a particularly flagrant expression of the *Hybris* which tempts man to overestimate the degree of his freedom and which Christian thought recognizes as the root of sin.[3]

But the modern world does not believe in sin. Our secular age has rejected that doctrine more whole-heartedly than any other Christian doctrine. Incidentally, there ought to be some evidence that secular individuals with their easy conscience and their natural self-love are on the way of becoming amiable and non-aggressive individuals. Yet our secular age has spawned hatreds and conflicts of vaster proportions than any known in previous ages.[4] Actually, the doctrine of sin makes an important contribution to any adequate social and political theory for it emphasizes a fact which every page of human history attests. Through it one may understand that no matter how wide the perspectives which the human mind may reach, how broad the loyalties which the human imagination may conceive, how universal the community which human statecraft may organize, or how pure the aspirations of the saintliest idealists may be, there is no level of human moral or social achievement in which there is not some corruption of inordinate self-love.

This sober and true view of the human situation was neatly rejected by modern culture.[5] That culture has not taken the Christian faith seriously because it had a simpler answer to the problems of life. It agreed with Christianity in regarding human history as meaningful, but it assigned a simple meaning to history. The Reformation was meanwhile overwhelmed because it was too pessimistic about the possibilities of history.

An adequate faith for our day must again combine these broken fragments of the Christian tradition. Any culture or any religion that is deficient in the "tragic sense of life" is certainly inadequate to give us light and guidance in a day in which the very securities of a technical society have been transmuted into evil. We need a faith that throws light upon the importance of every historical task and responsibility. But it must on the other hand reveal the limits of all historical striving.

Human existence is precarious and will remain so to the end of history. Human achievement contains a tragic element of frustration and corruption and will contain it to the end of history. There is an ultimate answer to these tragic aspects of human existence, but that answer can be known only to those who have stopped looking for some easy escape from tragedy.

The Christian religion regards history as meaningful but as having no fulfillment of its meaning within itself. In that sense Christianity is "other-worldly." For this reason all modern substitutes for the Christian faith, in which history is fulfilled in some kind of utopia, naturally find the Christian faith incredible because they have a simpler answer to the problems of life. The Christian faith becomes credible only when those simpler answers are refuted by history, as indeed they are bound to be.

According to the Christian faith all finite and historical existence points to a ground and an end beyond itself. This divine end and ground are paradoxically defined as having a double relation to history. God judges the world because there are violations of the law of life on every level of human achievement. God "saves" the world because he has resources of mercy beyond his judgment. But mercy cannot express itself without taking justice seriously. Thus God is pictured as being able to be merciful only by taking the consequences of his judgment upon and into himself. These paradoxes of the Christian faith have sometimes been stated in terms of a wooden literalism that has made them offensive to human intelligence. But it is well to remember that they are a "stumbling block" and "foolishness" even when stated profoundly. The reason for this is that all men would like to believe that they have the power within themselves to complete their lives and their history. But this is exactly what all men lack.

A faith that is able to transcend the catastrophes of history must therefore be able to define both the possibilities of human creativity in history and the limits of human possibilities. It must also be able to clarify the fact that the evils of fanaticism, conflict, imperialism, and tyranny have their source in man's ambition to overleap his limitations and to seek unconditioned power, virtue, and security for his existence.

For this reason historical catastrophe seems to be nothing but chaos, which drives men to despair without the profundities of the Christian faith. And Christian faith becomes vapid and sentimental in periods of stability and peace. It recovers its own profoundest insights precisely in those periods of social chaos when all simpler interpretations of life break down and force men to seek for a profounder interpretation of existence.[6]

PART TWO

Political Philosophy

THE STUDY OF POLITICS

CHAPTER V

The Illusion of Scientific Politics: A Critique

The implicit faith of the past two centuries has hardly prepared us for the kind of frustration through which we must live in the next century or two. For we have been given the task of creating community in larger dimensions than any one or two centuries can accomplish. The frustrations of our age become pathetic rather than tragic when we have no means of either anticipating or comprehending the character of our present experiences. The one unifying element in all strands of modern culture was the idea of progress. We had faith in a redemptive history. This faith, which supposedly made all other interpretations of life completely incredible, is now progressively disclosing itself as the most incredible of all interpretations of life. This refutation of the culture of modern man by contemporary history may be regarded as the real spiritual crisis of our day.

The fact that history is endlessly creative but not redemptive might have been more apparent to modern man had it not been for another illusion in modern culture. This other illusion is closely related to the idea of progress and is indeed frequently the basis for it. It is the illusion that the so-called "methods of science" or "impartial scientific inquiry" or "scientific objectivity" are actually the instruments by which mankind rises to higher and higher degrees of perfection. By scientific impartiality man presumably rises from finite to universal perspectives, from interested to disinterested appraisal of problems of justice, from prejudice and passion to god-like serenity and impartiality. Science will not only unlock the mysteries of existence which have remained closed to the poetic and religious imagination and to the speculations of philosophy but will redeem man from the fragmentary and partial character of his life and actions and guarantee actions of universal validity.

A simple fact has been obscured by this cult of redemption through science. Man is a creature whose rational and vital processes are in organic unity, and there is no "scientific method" by which he can escape from the hopes, fears, ambitions, and anxieties of his own individual existence or those of his nation, civilization, or ethnic group.[1] Thus the opinions which men and groups hold of each other and the judgments which they pass upon their common problems are notoriously interested and unobjective. While the ideological taint upon all social judgments is most apparent in the practical conflicts of politics, it is equally discernible, upon close scrutiny, in even the most scientific observations of social scientists.[2]

The question is why the ideological taint should be so much greater in the field of social judgments than in the natural sciences and why the application of the "scientific method" should be so much less efficacious in removing bias. The answer to that question involves a rigorous examination of the differences between the fields of natural and social sciences and also the difference in the status of the observer in each field.[3]

I. *Differences Between Nature and History*

1. THE COMPLEXITY OF CAUSATION IN HISTORY

In his *Plight of the Social Sciences* Robert MacIver emphasizes the many levels of causation which the social sciences must investigate. Every event in history takes place in a half-dozen or more dimensions—geological, geographic, climatic, psychological, social and personal. This complex causation makes it possible to correlate events plausibly in many different ways usually tempting the observer to "make the field of one's special interest the inclusive ground in which the causes of all relevant phenomena are to be sought." The infinite variety of causal sequences to which every act and event in history is related makes almost every correlation of causes sufficiently plausible to be immune to compelling challenge. Any social theory therefore has some kinship with the procedures of a Rorschach test, which is more revealing about the state of the patient's mind who takes it than about the inkspots which his imagination interprets in terms of various configurations. Obviously absurd correlations can be ruled out, and flagrant bias can be discovered. But no one can give a scientifically conclusive account, for instance, of the fall of the Roman Empire, or of the reason for the rise of Nazism in Germany or for the differences between British and French democracy, which would compel the rejection of a competing or contrasting interpretation. The conclusions arrived at are partly determined by the principle of interpretation with which the inquiry is begun.

2. THE ABSENCE OF SIMPLE RECURRENCES IN HISTORY

There are no simple recurrences in history and therefore no analogies between sequences in various periods of history which could compel us to accept a proposition that a given policy in a certain period will have similar effects as the same policy in another period. Of course, it is only partly true that history is a realm of unique events as distinguished from the exact recurrences of the physical world. For there are cycles, recurrences and analogies in history; if there were not, there would be no basis for scientific investigation. But endless contingencies supervene upon the recurrences. In the physical sciences there can be controlled experiments which may be endlessly repeated until the "right" answer is found, but nothing is exactly repeated in history. Therefore a judgment, for instance, that some "New Deal" policy in America of the twentieth century will expose our nation to the fate of the Roman Empire, on the ground that the latter was the victim of an analogous policy, can neither be asserted nor refuted with certainty. Every reliance upon analogy can be refuted by emphasis upon variants in the compared historical scenes. Toynbee's analogy between the medieval situation of Eastern and Western Christendom and the present conflict between Russia and the West sheds some illumination upon the scene; but not much. For there are too many novel factors in the contemporary situation which do not fit into the analogy.[4] Therefore the analyses of historical patterns must lack the scientific precision which characterizes the conclusions of the natural sciences. In short, they must fail in the test of predictability which is the hallmark of any exact science.[5]

3. THE PROBLEM OF HUMAN FREEDOM IN HISTORY

Modern historical and social sciences have sought to gain firm ground under their feet by the strategy of interpreting the emergence of novelty in history as subject to discernible patterns, analogous to evolution in nature. There are undoubtedly patterns of historical development, but the analysis of such patterns is subject to hazardous attributions of particular events as causes of subsequent occurrences. These attributions are hazardous not only because of the complexity of the causal chain but because human agents are themselves causes within the causal nexus.[6]

The freedom of human agents in the temporal process creates novelties of such dimension and at such a tempo as to distinguish historical change radically from the slow mutations of forms known in nature. It also creates a new dimension of causality of endless complexity and depth. To the degree that men are not free, their actions, both individual and collective, may be predicted with something of the assurance with which a natural scientist charts the recurrences of nature. Insofar as they are free, causal sequences in history reach a height and complexity in which the full understanding of the character of an event would require the knowledge of the secret motive of the agent of the action. History is thus comprised of causalities and sequences, coherences and structures which are not easily comprehended as meaningful.[7]

The field of historical events thus differs radically from the field of natural events in the complexity of the causal chain and by the fact that human agents intervene unpredictably in the course of events. These factors prevent any scientific method from leading to absolutely compelling conclusions, because all alternative conclusions can always be plausibly presented.[8]

There are, of course, valid social or historical sciences. They are most legitimate when the scientists know themselves to be historians, rather than natural scientists; and therefore recognize that their generalizations are hazardous and speculative. The real historians have an instinct for the peculiar quality of history and know the hazards of predictions of the future. Economics, which began under physiocratic illusions, has, in these latter years, become more and more conscious of the endless historical contingencies which it must take into account in its predictions. Economists have therefore become increasingly modest, in contrast to some other social sciences, burdened with more physiocratic illusions about so-called "laws of nature."

Historical facts can be dealt with most "scientifically" when the field of inquiry is reduced to some manageable set of uniformities or recurrences in the behavior of individuals, subject to the same set of natural or historical circumstances—to the attitudes of adolescents or convalescents, for instance, or the behavior of industrial or agricultural labor, or to the conditions of urban life or to the effect of boarding-house existence upon family life. In such, and similar cases, statistical evidence may support generalizations; and uniformities of behavior may be distinguished from the historically variable factors. Sometimes, predictions are inaccurate, even in these modest undertakings, perhaps because the unpredictable freedom of man is not taken into account or perhaps because not enough attention has been given to variable conditioning circumstances.

Efforts to predict elections in previous decades failed miserably because sample opinions were taken from people listed in telephone directories, and their ideological bias did not accurately typify the whole political spectrum. Now the samplings are undertaken more scientifically, that is, with due regard for the various groups of a community and their characteristic biases, based on economic and other interests. But no science can determine whether a Polish worker of Hamtramck, Michigan, will vote according to the prevailing opinion in the CIO, or according to his convictions about the adequacy of an administration policy in clearing up the wartime mystery of the murders in the Katyn forests in Poland. If wider generalizations are attempted, as, for instance, covering groups in the same economic class but under differing historical environment, they become more hazardous. What nonsense history made of the Marxist slogan: "Workers of the World Unite!" It mistakenly assumed the equal disinheritance of industrial laborers in every nation, and incidentally the primacy of their economic interest. There are, no doubt, legitimate generalizations about the character of bourgeois communities as contrasted with agrarian ones. But will any such generalizations do justice to the variables in the middle-class life of France and Britain, of Australia and America?

In any event, no scientific investigations of past behavior can become the basis of predictions of future behavior. Even if an historian is able to establish causal sequences after the event, he cannot make any generalizations about the past the basis of predictions of future actions and events. He cannot do so, not only because he has insufficient knowledge of the complex causes of the past, but because he cannot predict which one of the many tendencies and forces which determine actions, may have a dominant place in the life of individuals and nations. Only one historian, Jacob Burckhardt, was able to foretell the rise of twentieth century tyrannies in the nineteenth century. And no one, as late as the beginning of this century, predicted the nightmare which eventuated from the Marxist dreams of heaven on earth. Marx would certainly have been surprised by contemporary realities. These surprising historical events are a refutation of all purely scientific or metaphysical efforts to interpret the drama of history and to reduce its seeming confusion to some kind of simple meaning.[9]

II. *Knowing Nature and Knowing History*

1. THE INEVITABLE BIAS OF THE INTERESTED SELF

The most fundamental difference between the knowledge of nature and the knowledge and estimate of our fellow men is this: in the knowledge of nature the *mind* of man is at the center of the process of knowing; and the *self* with all its fears, hopes and ambitions is on the circumference. In the knowledge of historical events the *self,* with all its emotions and desires, is at the center of the enterprise; and the *mind* is on the circumference, serving merely as an instrument of the anxious self.

The reason for this difference is obvious. When we look at a flower or a star, at a geological formation or at a problem in chemistry, the prestige and the security of the knower is not involved. The things we see are what they are, and no emotion can change the facts or alter the conclusions. If we try to assess the meaning of some facts of nature for the human enterprise, we are already on a different level of knowledge where the whole weight of human pride and insecurity may be felt.

When we behold not a flower or a star, but a friend or foe; when we estimate not natural sequences, but the course of human history; when we weigh not the actions and reactions of the atoms of nature, but the ambitions and purposes of our competitors and comrades, we are never disinterested observers. We are always part of the drama of life which we seek to comprehend and participants in the conflicts and comradeships which we seek to arbitrate or enjoy. Our judgments of others are mixed with emotions prompted by our strength or our weakness in relation to them. Their virtues and advantages may excite our jealousy or prompt our emulation. Their vices may tempt us to hatred. Their weakness may elicit our pity or their strength arouse our fear. We are involved as total personalities in the affairs of history. Our mind is never a pure and abstract intelligence when it functions amidst the complexities of human relations.[10]

The observers of history thus are selves rather than minds because their interest and their will are more immediately engaged than in the observation of nature. The further they are removed in time or in space from an historical encounter the more they can become pure mind, that is, the more they can scientifically analyze without the corruption of passion and interest. Thus the field of historical observation presents us with infinite grades of engagement from the obvious engagement of the practical statesman, through the observations of social scientists who stand upon some contemporary ground of impartiality, to the observations of social and historical scientists of a subsequent age who have gained a perspective in time upon the scene of conflict between various interests and passions.[11] * These various shades of engagement also de-

* In the following passages, however, Niebuhr acknowledges that history provides no escape from partiality. "It is well to remember that there is no vantage point, individual or collective, in human history from which we can judge past events with complete impartiality. It is true of course that some periods of history are, or appear to be, sufficiently dead to seem irrelevant to the contest of interests and values which color our judgments in the present moment. But we can never be sure. Our judgment of Hamilton or Jefferson is still partly determined by contemporary party prejudice; and even an analysis of the causes of the decline of ancient Rome is certain to be mixed with social and political convictions, derived from contemporary situations." [12]

"We recently had a vivid reminder of the relativity of historical knowledge, when two former ambassadors to Spain, both historians, Claude Bowers and Carleton Hayes,

termine the degree to which selves rather than minds must be appealed to. If it is a self rather than a mind, no scientific method can compel a self to cease from engaging in whatever rationalization of interest may seem plausible to it. The field of historical events is too complex and too lacking in exact analogies in its recurrences to coerce the mind to a particular interpretation of the causal sequences. But, even if the mind could be coerced, the historical observer may always turn out in the end to be an agent in history rather than an observer of it, with a sufficient stake in the contests of history to defy conclusions which should compel the mind but will not compel the interested self.[14]

2. THE HIDDEN DOGMAS OF SOCIAL SCIENCE

In the words of Francis Bacon, the father of modern empiricism: "Our method is continually to dwell on things soberly . . . to establish forever a true and legitimate union between the experimental and the rational faculty. . . . Those therefore who are determined, not to conjecture or guess, but to find out and know; not to invent fables and romances of the world, but to look and dissect the nature of the real world must consult only things themselves." This empirical ambition, which is responsible for all the triumphs of the natural sciences, gave modern culture a special animus against "dogma." But unfortunately it was not prepared to deal with the hidden dogmas in the prescriptions of science itself. It was therefore not prepared for the illusions which spread in the name of "empiricism." It is important to consult the evidence of "things themselves." But inquiries cannot be undertaken without presuppositions or what James B. Conant has called "conceptual schemes." These conceptual schemes are the hidden dogmas. They are usually the more potent for being implicit rather than explicit. "Science," declares Conant, "is an interconnected series of concepts and conceptual schemes, which have developed as a result of observation and experimentation, and are fruitful of experimentation and observation."[15]

Conant's regard for the necessity of "conceptual schemes" reveals the impossibility of observing the "things themselves" without a frame of meaning for the inquiry. Among natural scientists these conceptual schemes are assumed to be limited and to be subject to constant re-examination in the light of empirical evidence; for empirical observa-

reported on the civil war in Spain. The one was favorable and the other unfavorable to the Spanish Republican cause. Mr. Bowers regarded the civil war in Spain as a prelude to the World War, and Mr. Hayes thought of it as a prelude to our present cold war with Russia. Both are honest historians and neither falsified the facts; but they chose very different facts and subjected all relevant facts to contrasting interpretations. Mr. Hayes is a liberal Catholic while Mr. Bowers stands in the Jeffersonian tradition."[13]

tion may prove the tentative conceptual scheme to be at variance with the facts. Thus the first empirical science of the modern period, astronomy, invalidated the conceptual schemes underlying Ptolemaic and Aristotelian astronomy by the evidence of facts which pointed to a different astronomical order than had been assumed in the older pre-Copernican astronomy. From that day to this, it has been assumed that it is a fairly simple procedure to change conceptual schemes when the evidence of the "facts" discredits them. But an "empirical" culture was not prepared to deal with the problem of wide, rather than specific, conceptual schemes, that is, with presuppositions of inquiry which referred not to a specific type of being under scrutiny, but with the very character of being itself. Ideally these conceptual schemes were subject to re-examination; but practically they proved themselves powerful enough to determine the evidence by which they were supposed to be tested. Thus Professor John Dewey, the most typical of modern naturalistic philosophers, never tired of insisting that the "experimental method" must be rigorous enough to re-examine its own hypotheses. But it never occurred to him that his insistence that the "methods of science" could be transferred from the field of nature to that of history, and that only the intrusion of irrelevant religious and political authority prevented this consummation, rested upon an erroneous and unexamined presupposition. That was the universally held belief of modern culture that the realm of history was essentially identical with the realm of nature. This belief reduced history to the realm of necessity and obscured the freedom of man and the reality of the drama of history.[16]

Actually, the modern "scientific" examinations of the human scene upon close analysis do, in fact, betray the influence of a variety of religious or ultimate presuppositions which are no less potent for being unconfessed and no more true for being regarded as scientific. The religious presuppositions which form the framework for most modern scientific examinations of the human scene contain two very dubious articles, which must be held responsible for most of the errors and illusions in these examinations: a) the idea of the perfectibility of man and b) the idea of progress. The errors into which the examination is betrayed are reinforced by a characteristic method of the inquiry. That method is to examine man as if he were no more than one of the many objects in nature, which the scientific method will be able to comprehend fully if only its tools are sufficiently precise and the scientist is sufficiently objective.

Any careful observation of any structure of reality, of sequences and causes, even if its frame of reference is inadequate, will yield some truth. It is therefore not surprising that modern social and psychological sciences have been able to teach us a great deal about man and his community. But it is also significant that these disciplines have been fruitful of many errors and illusions on the ultimate level. Indeed, frequently their conclusions do not conform to the obvious facts of human experience. They are held to the more desperately as this contradiction is noted by a stray non-conformist and dissenter. The fact that the presuppositions have determined the conclusions is obscured by the insistence that the conclusions have been arrived at by empirical, or "scientific" observation. The prestige of the "scientific method" plays a part in giving authority to the modern creed, analogous to the service which the priestly incantations had in establishing the creeds of more explicitly religious eras.[17]

3. IDEOLOGY AND THE SCIENTIFIC METHOD

Judgments in the field of history are ultimately value judgments in the sense that they do not intend merely to designate the actions which lead to desired ends but that they seek to give guidance on the desirable. Even the skeptics who try to reduce the concept of desirability to that of "the desired" must admit that human beings have a remarkable penchant for masking what they desire under the idea of the desirable. Indeed it is the very nature of ideology to confuse the two, not because they are identical but because the desirability or "value" of an end is necessary to sanction the fact that it is desired.

The question is in what degree the scientific method can unmask precisely this tendency to pretend a wider value for an act than merely its gratification of the desires of the agent. The scientific method is obviously most potent when we limit the question to specific and narrow ends and ask what is desirable to achieve the end of health, or security, or the national interest, or the preservation of civilization. But every specific end is enmeshed in a vast system of ends and means; and we cannot ascertain the desirability of an immediate end without making value judgments about the total schemes of meaning in which such judgments are made or by which they are informed.

We cannot criticize these total schemes of meaning scientifically for every scientific procedure presupposes them. If metaphysics is, as Collingwood claims, the analysis of the presuppositions of our sciences, we can come to terms with the adequacy of the total structure of meaning by metaphysical analyses. The scientific method may help us in detecting an ideological taint in which some partial and parochial interest is sanctified by the prestige of the whole value scheme. Let us take the ideological conflict in modern technical society as an illustration. Even where the liberal world is not subject to the Marxist challenge, there is an ideological conflict between the more favored and the less favored members of the community. It is to be noted that in the more healthy societies this conflict does not result in a disruption of the community because it takes place against the background of value systems which do rough justice to both the individual and social dimension of human existence. But the degree to which individuality and individual initiative is cherished on the one hand, and social solidarity and security on the other, is clearly ideological. The bourgeois community tends to be libertarian and the industrial workers tend, even when they are not Marxist, to be equalitarian and collectivist. In this situation it is interesting to note what social science can and cannot do. A careful analysis of social sequences and causalities can refute the more extravagant claims of each side. There is, for instance, pretty conclusive evidence that an uncontrolled economy does not automatically make for justice, and that a compounding of political and economic power, according to collectivist programs, will threaten both justice and liberty. Those societies in which there is a relative degree of impartial social observation mitigate the ideological conflict, but they cannot eliminate it. They are powerless to do so because of the existential intimacy between interest and idea. The classes which prefer liberty to security are those which already have a high measure of security through their social and professional skills, and who do not like to have their economic power subjected to political power. The classes on the other hand which prefer security to liberty are on the whole devoid of special skills and therefore lack individual security. They are exposed to the perils of a highly integrated technical society, and therefore fear insecurity more than they fear the loss of liberty. There can be no scientific dissolution of these preferences. It is probably true that the health of a democratic society depends more upon the spirit of forbearance with which each side tolerates the irreducible ideological preferences of the other than upon some supposed scientific resolution of them, because the scientific resolution always involves the peril that one side or the other will state its preferences as if they were scientifically validated value judgments.[18] Insofar as impartiality is possible, it is a moral and religious as much as a scientific achievement. A contrite recognition of the interested character of our views and actions must always lie behind the achievement of relative disinterestedness. The achievement involves the whole of the personality and is therefore not purely intellectual or scientific.[19]

The point of view here expressed does not deny that men must observe and interpret the flow of historical events with as much honesty and wisdom as possible. Historical sciences will continue to be elaborated and scientific schemes invented to reduce conscious and unconscious ideological taints in historical observations. Philosophical disciplines will be judged and scrutinized on the basis of the adequacy of their guard against the temptation of the observer to pretend to more absolute knowledge than a finite creature has the right to claim. All such efforts belong to the legitimate improvement of human culture. But none of them can obviate the necessity of using a scheme of meaning for the correlation of the observed data of history, which is not the consequence but the presupposition of the empirical scrutiny of historical data. The more the whole panorama of history is brought into view, the more obvious it becomes that the meaning which is given to the whole is derived from an act of faith in the sense that the concept of meaning is derived from ultimate presuppositions about the character of time and eternity, which are not the fruit of detailed analyses of historical events.

Whether these ultimate presuppositions of meaning constitute an adequate framework for the correlation of all relevant historical facts is a question which can be approached rationally. It is possible, at least, to reject all concepts of the unity of history which make some vitality, event or value within history itself into a premature and idolatrous center of its meaning. If such idolatries are rejected it will become apparent that the real center of meaning for history must transcend the flux of time. To believe that the story of mankind is one story because the various disparate stories are under one divine sovereignty is therefore not an arbitrary procedure. On the contrary it prevents ages and cultures, civilizations and philosophies, from arbitrarily finding the center of history's meaning within their own life or achievements and from seeking the culmination and fulfillment of that meaning prematurely in the victory of their cause or the completion of their particular project. In summary every larger frame of meaning, which serves the observer of historical events in correlating the events into some kind of pattern, is a structure of faith rather than of science.[20]

III. *Managing Nature and Managing History*

1. VOLUNTARISM AND DETERMINISM

It is obvious that the self's freedom over natural process enables it to be a creator of historical events. Both its memory of past events and its capacity to project goals transcending the necessities of nature enable it to create the new level of reality which we know as human history. But the self is not simply a creator of this new dimension, for it is also a creature of the web of events, in the creation of which it participates.

This double relationship naturally causes great perplexities and gives rise to some rather simple contradictory theories which emphasize either man's role as creator, or his role as creature. The tendency to equate history with nature and to confuse the "laws of nature" with those of history has given rise, since the French Enlightenment, to a determinism which minimizes the creative role of man. The most consistent application of this determinism is the economics of *laissez faire,* drawn from physiocratic theory, and warning men from interference with the "natural" processes and "natural" balances of history.

But the tendency to equate history with nature can also prompt a contradictory voluntaristic theory according to which man is called upon to use scientific technics to manage history, as he has managed nature. Many modern social scientists since Comte have been influenced by this voluntarism, and have naively insisted on the possibility of transferring the "scientific method" learned in the natural sciences to the management of human affairs. Aldous Huxley has satirized the dreams of such voluntarists in his *Brave New World.*

This interesting combination of determinism and voluntarism usually presupposes a vaguely defined elite of scientists who have the omniscience to manage the events in which ordinary mortals are merely creatures, for the sake of directing them to "socially approved" ends.[21] It includes the sociologist who is conducting scientific experiments to determine how the altruistic motives of men can be strengthened and the egoistic impulses weakened. It also includes the anthropologist who proposes scientific breeding in order to eliminate eugenically the present "apeman" who is not capable of managing affairs in a technical age; and the biologist who thinks that the study of social insects will give us some useful clues for managing the next stage in human evolution; or the group of social scientists who propose a world-wide study of human aggressiveness; or the psychologists who want to study the relation between hunger and racial prejudice; or the educator who proposes a tyrannically controlled system of international education in order to insure the absence of national prejudices from the education; or the political scientist who would organize a world government with power to suppress national interests on the ground that "nationalistic parochialism" has become "criminal" at this stage of human development.[22]

The excessive voluntarism which underlies this theory of an elite is encouraged by the excessive determinism, which assumes that most men are creatures with simple determinate ends of life, and that their "antisocial" tendencies are quasi-biological impulses and inheritances which an astute social and psychological science can overcome or "redirect" to what are known as "socially approved" goals.

It would be absurd to claim any degree of unanimity in these disciplines, for frequently a debate rages between excessive determinists and excessive voluntarists. In the field of anthropology which has lately entered the lists in the study and direction of contemporary culture, a strong school of cultural determinists challenges the voluntarists. The determinists rightly recognize that man is the creature of his culture and fail to see that he is also the creator of it. Thus a cultural determinist may rather amusingly challenge the excessive voluntarism of a psychologist. Leslie White in *The Science of Culture* quotes Professor Gordon Allport, who observes: "The United States spent two billion dollars in the invention of the atomic bomb." Professor Allport goes on to ask, "What is there absurd in spending an equivalent sum if necessary on the discovery of the means of control?" Obviously such reasoning assumes that the vast and complex processes of action and interaction between human wills and desires can be brought "under control" if only sufficient money is spent on the enterprise.

Mr. White, who regards this view as "unsound," proceeds to challenge it with an equally unsound view: "Wars are struggles between social organisms, called nations, for survival, struggles for the possession and use of the resources of the earth, for fertile fields, coal, oil, and iron deposits. . . . No amount of understanding will alter or remove the basis of this struggle any more than an understanding of the ocean's tides will diminish or terminate the flow."

There is an absolute contradiction between these two theories insofar as one assumes and the other denies that there can be an elite group with minds pure enough to transcend the "struggle between social organisms" and powerful enough to compose the struggle.

But the theories have much in common; in each case the historical process is regarded as similar in kind with the natural process. In the one view, the wars of history are regarded as perfectly analogous to "the ocean's tides." In the other, what man can do about the peril of an atomic bomb is regarded as equally manageable as the physical forces which produced the bomb.[23]

One may well wonder how the social and psychological sciences, which have proved their value on so many levels of human experience, should generate so many naive miscalculations on the ultimate level of political wisdom. Perhaps the miscalculations are the fruits of two errors which characterize all merely naturalistic approaches to the problems of human behavior. First, it is not understood that the "nature" which is to be mastered and manipulated contains the self, with all of its guile of spirit; and that the mind which is supposed to master nature is also involved in this same self, with all of the capacities of self-deception. Most of the pretentious analogies between the mastery of natural and of historical evil are therefore misleading.[24] Second, it is not understood that man's freedom imparts a stubborn recalcitrance to his actions which makes him finally "unmanageable." It transmutes all of nature's necessities into indeterminate ambitions which will always prevent that simple harmony which is the utopia of both democratic and communist idealists. This unique freedom is the generator of both the destructiveness and the creativity of man. Most of the efforts to manage the historical process would actually destroy the creativity with the destructiveness.[25] *

Perhaps the real difficulty in these dreams of a "rationally ordered" historic process is that the modern man lacks the humility to accept the fact that the whole drama of history is enacted in a frame of meaning too large for human comprehension or management. It is a drama in which fragmentary meanings can be discerned within a penumbra of mystery; and in which specific duties and responsibilities can be undertaken within a vast web of relations which are beyond our powers.

A sane life requires that we have some clues to the mystery so that the realm of meaning is not simply reduced to the comprehensible processes of nature. But these clues are ascertained by faith, which modern man has lost. So he hovers ambivalently between subjection to the "reason" which he can find in nature and the "reason" which he can impose on nature. But neither form of reason is adequate for the comprehension of the illogical and contradictory patterns of the historic drama, and for anticipating the emergence of unpredictable virtues and vices. In either case, man as the spectator and manager of history imagines himself to be freer of the drama he beholds than he really is; and man as the creature of history is too simply reduced to the status of a creature of nature, and all of his contacts to the ultimate are destroyed.[27]

2. EGOISM, AGGRESSIVENESS AND THE SOCIAL SCIENCES

Since the eighteenth century there has been a good deal of speculation on the relation between "egoism" and "altruism," and about the elimination of the one in favor of the other. But the mixture of the self's concern with itself and its creative and responsible interests is infinitely varied. Children in their relation to their parents, soldiers dealing with their officers, workmen and office people seeking tolerable relations with their

* Niebuhr cites a glaring example of this error in the following lines: "In a naive psychologist's view of utopia, B. F. Skinner's *Walden II,* we are presented with the vision of an ideal community of six hundred souls who have been conditioned to a life of perfect harmony, free of all excessive ambition or jealousy. The psychologist who has created this community admits that he has 'managed' the development of the individual components of the harmonious community and that there are, therefore, similarities between him and the notorious dictators of our day. But he feels that there is a great distinction between him and them because he has done what he has done for the good of the community. The community meanwhile lacks the heroic and noble elements in human nature as completely as destructive animosities."[26]

superiors, develop an almost instinctive method of appealing, on the one hand, to the sympathies of those who have greater power than they and, on the other hand, trying to satisfy the vanity or pride, the sense of power or the sense of importance of their superiors. The taint of egoism, both individual and collective, is taken for granted by all men of affairs in government and business. Indeed, the wisdom of common sense takes human egoism for granted in *all* forms of human relations, and reacts with gentle or harsh cynicism to it according to its degree, its vexatiousness and possibly according to the degree of self-deception in the critic. The wisdom of the "man in the street" never fails to comprehend the mixture of creativity and self-concern in the behavior of all his fellows. This is the achievement of a genuine non-academic "empiricism."

In contrast, the academic wisdom deals abstractly with this mixture of motives in human behavior. The wisest understanding of the complexities is characteristic of those disciplines which are most genuinely related to the historical studies and those which pride themselves least on their empiricism, for example, economics and political science.

The errors in modern culture in regard to the mixture of self-regard and creativity in human behavior occur principally in those disciplines of our culture which pride themselves particularly on their methods of empirical observation. These disciplines have an almost universal attitude toward the problem of egoism. It consists in regarding self-interest as ordinate and harmless, provided it is not unduly frustrated by what Holbach defined as "bad rulers." In the modern context this means any political, cultural or religious effort to criticize, suppress or transmute egoism. They also look for specific causes of inordinate forms of egoism, which become in effect the causes of egoism in general so that the progressive elimination or mitigation of the factor of self-regard is assumed in these analyses.

Professor Dewey summarizes a great deal of modern sociological and psychological theory of human nature in his *Human Nature and Conduct*. He asserts: "Moralists are led, perhaps, to think of human nature as evil because of its reluctance to yield to control, its rebelliousness under the yoke. But this explanation only raises another question. Why did morality set up rules so foreign to human nature? . . . We are forced therefore to consider the nature and origin of the control of human nature with which morals has been occupied. . . . Control has been invested in an oligarchy. Indifference to regulations has grown in the gap which separates the rules from the ruled. Parents, priests, chiefs, and social censors have supplied aims which were foreign to those upon whom they were imposed, the young, laymen, ordinary folk. A few have administered and given rules; and the mass have with reluctance and in a passable fashion, obeyed." Professor Dewey, following this diagnosis of the contradictions in which human beings are involved by reason of the fact that "there is a law in their members which wars against the law that is in their minds," proceeds to prescribe a cure. It consists of a more "scientific" projection of rules and aims of human conduct, and would be formulated by more competent "rulers" than parents and priests. It would overcome the contradiction between man's self-regard and his social impulses by a more scientific channeling of all the "drives" in human nature. Dewey naturally promises that the scientific knowledge of human nature will work all the transformations which the knowledge of nature accomplished. It will particularly provide more competent rules to which men will not be so reluctant to conform because they will be constructed in greater accordance with the potentialities of human nature.

The most impressive modern psychological version of the Enlightenment theory of an essentially harmless self-regard, which becomes harmful only when frustrated, is given by the Neo-Freudian Erich Fromm, in his *Man for Himself*. He presents the thesis that men must first seek their own happiness, whereupon they may then love others as a "phenomenon of abundance." "Authoritarian religion" interferes with this simple fact of human nature by confronting the selfish self with the "command" to love the neighbor. Naturally a contradiction is established between the natural desires of the self and the moral command. Fromm sees very clearly that love is not a simple command to be obeyed. It is truly a phenomenon of abundance. The self, which is engrossed with its own security or prestige, is not free to love. But Fromm does not see that the security of the self is furnished not by its own efforts at security, but by the love of others. He also does not realize that the desire for security or for prestige is, like all human desires, indeterminate. There is no point at which the self, seeking its own, can feel itself self-satisfied and free to consider others than itself. The concern for others is as indeterminate as the concern for itself. These concerns are not in the "id" on the one hand and the "super-ego" on the other hand. Fromm has merely elaborated Freud's picture of the "ego" as torn between the demands of the "id" and the "super-ego."

"The demand to love our neighbors as ourselves is the strongest defense against human aggressiveness and is a superlative example of the unpsychological attitude of the cultural super-ego," declares Freud. "The command is impossible to fulfill. The enormous inflation of love can only lower its value and not remedy the evil. Civilization pays no heed to all of this. It merely prates that the harder to obey the more laudable the obedience."

Actually there is no such tension between a pleasure-seeking "id" and a demanding "super-ego," not to speak of a "cultural super-ego." The ego is not an embarrassed broker between the two forces. The fact is that there are indeterminate desires within the self, both for self-aggrandizement and for self-giving. The failure to recognize this fact makes Freudianism, whether in its early or in its later and refined forms, quite irrelevant to political problems. For political life must deal with the bewildering mixture of self-concern and creativity on all levels of community.

There is no "empirical" evidence for Freud's thesis that "aggressiveness" increases with the wider and wider demands upon the self with an ever-widening social organization. The evidence for this thesis is taken from neurotic individuals but is irrelevant to the behavior of "normal" individuals, who are involved in varied mixtures of ambition (not "aggressiveness") and creative concern for family, community, nation and civilization. This miscalculation probably accounts for the difference between the therapeutic success of Freudianism in dealing with deranged persons or neurotic individuals, and its irrelevance to any political problem faced by modern men. It is significant that the professional jealousies which Freud encountered in his early life as he rose to success and the element of jealousy which entered into the friction between him and Jung in later years are not explained in any Freudian theory. Only one of the younger colleagues who were envious of his success was obviously neurotic.[28]

There have, in fact, been many elaborate theories evolved about the roots of human aggressiveness. The anthropologists have a particular penchant for discovering those roots in the early toilet training or in the methods of mothers for swaddling children. The Germans, the Japanese and the Russians have all been analyzed in the hope of discovering the secret of their aggressive behavior in their traditions of child training. Significantly it has not been determined whether collective aggressiveness is merely the cumulation of individual forms of aggressiveness or whether it is the fruit of an undue docility among the individuals of a nation which provides fodder for the aggressiveness of its leaders.

A very noted psychologist, Dr. Brock Chisholm, former head of the World Health Organization, thinks that human aggressiveness is derived from the fact that "we are civilized too early" which is to say that we are prompted to regard our "natural human urges as bad." Thus we "distrust and hate ourselves" and from this self-hatred arises "aggressive feelings against others." This aggressiveness could be cured very easily if mothers' clinics were established which would teach mothers that "babies need, not just want but need, uncritical love, love whose manifestations are quite independent of the babies' behavior." Such love will create the feeling of "belonging" which in a "successful development process should spread gradually to include family, friends and fellow citizens and in the little world this has become, it can no longer safely stop at national boundaries." We must now have "large numbers of people who have grown emotionally beyond national boundaries" and we, therefore, need a greater emphasis on "uncritical love" and "freedom from the 'conviction of sin.' "

It is not explained how both liberal and Marxist civilizations which have long since disavowed doctrines which Dr. Chisholm abhors should have generated so much "aggressiveness." [29]

Thus modern social and psychological scientists are forever seeking to isolate some natural impulse such as "egoism" or "aggressiveness" and to manage it; with equal vanity they are trying to find a surrogate for Plato's and Aristotle's disinterested "reason" in a so-called "scientific method." Their inability to discover the corruption of self-interest in reason or in man's rational pursuits and to measure the spiritual dimension of man's inhumanity and cruelty gives an air of sentimentality to the learning of our whole liberal culture. Thus we have no guidance amid the intricacies of modern power politics except as the older disciplines, less enamored of the "methods of natural science," and the common sense of the man in the street supply the necessary insights.[30]

For the common sense of ordinary men is seldom under the illusion that the jealousies and envies which infect even the most intimate human relations are merely the defects of an undisciplined mind. They are known to be temptations for saint as well as sinner; for the wise man and fool. Practical statesmen do not regard the will-to-power of a strong man as the vestigial remnant of barbarism. All common-sense political wisdom seeks to harness and to restrain, to make use of, and to guard against, the power impulse. A common-sense regulation of economic life does not treat the economic motive as a force which is about to be eliminated from human society. It knows that motive to be one facet of the power of self-interest which must be harnessed, deflected, beguiled and transmuted in the interest of the commonweal but which can never be completely suppressed.

The common-sense wisdom of mankind is even more aware of the recalcitrant power of egoistic interest in collective action. Nations and groups do not possess an integral consciousness as does the individual. But they do have an inchoate will; and that will is capable of only vagrant affirmations of ideals and values beyond its own interest. No one is particularly shocked by George Washington's dictum that a nation is not to be trusted beyond its own interest. That bit of cynicism is common currency in the affairs of mankind; and statesmen would be impeached if their policies ventured too far beyond its warning.[31]

IV. *The Validity and Limits of the Scientific Method*

The foregoing analysis does not invalidate the social sciences or prove that they ought to be reduced to statistical proportions in order to become purer sciences. Both the logical and the analytical powers of reason remain instruments by which partial and particular points of view are corrected, and the whole stuff of historical reality is brought under examination. We must continue to seek to understand what things are and how they came to be what they are in history as well as in nature.[32] And to this end an *inductive* social science is useful. Such a science will not speak vaguely about general concepts such as, for example, property or planning. It will ask what the institution of property is in an agrarian as against an industrial situation. It will recognize that a peasant's relation to the soil is of a different order from the relation of either an owner or a worker to a factory. It will study the effects of socialization of property and will probably conclude that there were important economic as well as social reasons for Britain's socialization of coal which do not necessarily justify the plan for socializing steel. It will recognize the necessity of guaranteeing human welfare in areas in which a market economy does not satisfy human wants as, for instance, in housing and medical services. But it will not assume that human desires are naturally ordinate and that they can be satisfied by government agencies without the necessity of some restraint upon inordinate, or at least disproportionate, demands.[33] It will understand that there is no magic in either logic or the scientific method which will coerce men or nations to subordinate the particular to the universal interest or to correct the partial by a more universal insight. Reason in history remains permanently ambiguous, being both the servant and the master of all of history's vitalities.[34] *

There is, thus, no "scientific method" which could guarantee that statesmen who must deal, let us say, with the social and political consequences of atomic energy could arrive at the kind of "universal mind" which operated in the discovery of atomic energy. Statesmen who deal with this problem will betray "British," "American," or "Russian" bias,

* Niebuhr points out that the term "scientific" has two connotations. "It means 'empirical' or an atttitude of 'humility before the fact,' or the inductive rather than the deductive method. It also, somewhat strangely, means 'rational' which could imply that empirical methods must avail themselves of strictly logical tools to avoid caprice; but it may also imply that rational coherence is regarded as the test of truth. In the latter case the two connotations of scientific, 'empirical' and 'rational,' would stand in contradiction; because the test of rational coherence might prompt men to deny obvious facts because they violated, or appeared to violate, the test of rational coherence. It is particularly important to note this in the study of man, who is both a creature and creator and who does not fit easily into any system of rational or natural coherence." [35]

not because they are less intelligent than the scientists but because they are forced to approach the issue in terms of their responsibility to their respective nations. Their formulation of a solution is intimately and organically related to the hopes, fears, and ambitions of nations. They must deal with history as a vital and not a rational process. As a vital process it is always something less and something more than reason. It is less than rational insofar as the power impulses of nations express themselves as inexorably as the force of a stampeding herd of cattle. It is something more than rational insofar as human beings have aspirations and loyalties transcending both impulse and prudence. Man is a heaven-storming creature whose highest ideals are curiously compounded with his immediate and mundane interests. The Marxist dream of a universal classless society, mixed with the power impulses of a Russian state and the anxieties of a precarious dictatorship, is a nice symbol of what historical reality is like. Our so-called democratic world is a little more rational; but the mixture of democratic idealism and the quest for profits of a vast American economic machine must be almost as bewildering to the outside observer as the Russian mixture.

The collective mixtures of ideals and interests are more vivid than individual expressions of human spirituality, but every individual life is governed less by prudence and rationality and more by what lies below the level of reason and rises above the level of rational calculation than a scientific culture understands.[36]

This persistent misunderstanding of human nature by modern psychologists and social scientists belongs to the deepest pathos of our age. Either the full dimension of man's spirit is not recognized and he is reduced to the level of nature's forms of life; or his spirit is obscured; or the spiritual dimension of human existence is falsely regarded as virtuous and it is not recognized that the worst forms of human wrong-doing are spiritual; or the spiritual character of evil is recognized and falsely identified with "religion" and salvation is promised through the decay of religion.

These wise men insist upon investigating human nature with scientific objectivity, which means that they will not look at themselves with introspective humility. They therefore do not know themselves. They know nothing about the treason in the human heart because they have evaded the fact that there is treason in their own.

Historically we live in a world in which evil and good are embattled in such a way as to illumine the terrible depths and the awful heights of the human enterprise.[37] Because man in his grandeur and in his misery, in his high aspirations and in their egoistic corruption, is and always will be a more complex creature than modern culture has understood, his history is more tragic and his redemption from self-seeking, whether individual or collective, more difficult and always less final than we have assumed.[38] The dimension of this whole scene is so great that only the judgment and the grace of God can give it a frame of meaning.

But the wise men of our day insist that human nature is flat. They run about with little measurements which can measure whatever is irrelevant but do not touch the heights and depths which are relevant. If we should ever fall into the deep abyss of an atomic conflict, we may be quite certain that on the night before the conflict begins some psychological association will bestow a medal upon an outstanding scientist for having found the key to the problem of eliminating aggressiveness from human life.[39]

CHAPTER VI

The Relevance of Christian Realism: An Orientation *

I. *Idealism and Realism*

The terms "idealism" and "realism" are not analogous in political and in metaphysical theory; and they are certainly not as precise in political, as in metaphysical, theory. In political and moral theory "realism" denotes the disposition to take into account all factors in a social and political sitation which offer resistance to established norms, particularly the factors of self-interest and power. In the words of a notorious "realist," Machiavelli, the purpose of the realist is "to follow the truth of the matter rather than the imagination of it; for many have pictures of republics and principalities which have never been seen." This definition of realism implies that idealists are subject to illusions about social realities, which indeed they are.

"Idealism" is, in the esteem of its proponents, characterized by loyalty to moral norms and ideals, rather than to self-interest, whether individual or collective.[1] The idealists believe that self-interest should be brought under the discipline of a higher law, which is correct, for evil is always the assertion of some self-interest without regard to the whole, whether the whole be conceived as the immediate community, or the total community of mankind, or the total order of the world. The good is, on the other hand, always the harmony of the whole on various levels. Devotion to a subordinate and premature "whole" such as the nation, may of course become evil, viewed from the perspective of a larger whole, such as the community of mankind. The idealist may thus be defined as the person who seeks to bring self-interest under the discipline of a more universal law and in harmony with a more universal good.[2]

In the opinion of its critics, however, idealism is characterized by a disposition to ignore or be indifferent to the forces in human life which

* The several themes identified in this brief orientation are developed at length in the chapters which follow.

offer resistance to universally valid ideals and norms. This disposition, to which Machiavelli refers, is general whenever men are inclined to take the moral pretensions of themselves or their fellow men at face value; for the disposition to hide self-interest behind the façade of pretended devotion to values transcending self-interest is well-nigh universal. Man is a curious creature with so strong a sense of obligation to his fellows that he cannot pursue his own interests without pretending to serve his fellow men. The definitions of "realists" and "idealists" emphasize disposition, rather than doctrines; and they are therefore bound to be inexact. It must remain a matter of opinion whether or not a man takes adequate account of all the various factors and forces in a social situation.[3]

At the level of political policy, realistic and idealistic approaches may be identified in analogous, but somewhat different, terms. For the realist, all plans for the future are dominated by the question: Where do we go from *here?* The broken process of history is emphasized and it is believed that new ventures in political organization, however broad their field and bold their purpose, remain under certain conditions and limitations which human history never transcends. For the idealist, the primary concern is not with perennial conditions but with new possibilities, and not with the starting point but with the goal.

The realists understand that certain perennial problems of political organization emerge in new forms, but are of the same essence on each level of the political integration of human society. The idealists are more conscious of novel and radical elements in a new situation and are inclined to believe and hope that old problems and vexations will disappear in the new level of political achievement.

These differences of temper and viewpoint are finally focussed upon a crucial issue: the problem of power. The realists know that history is not a simple rational process but a vital one. All human societies are organizations of diverse vitalities and interests. Some balance of power is the basis of whatever justice is achieved in human relations. Where the disproportion of power is too great and where an equilibrium of social forces is lacking, no mere rational or moral demands can achieve justice.

The idealists are inclined to view history from the standpoint of the moral and social imperatives which a rational analysis of a situation generates. Thus, for example, they look at the world and decide that its social and economic problems demand and require a "federation of the world." They think of such a federation not primarily in terms of the complex economic and social interest and vitalities, which must be brought into and held in a tolerable equilibrium. Least of all do they think of the necessity of some dominant force or power as the organizing center of the equilibrium. They are on the whole content to state the ideal requirements of the situation in as rigorous terms as possible.[4]

II. *Self-Love: the* Civitas Terrena

Augustine was, by general consent, the first great "realist" in Western history. He deserves this distinction because his picture of social reality in his *Civitas Dei* gives an adequate account of the social factions, tensions, and competitions which we know to be well-nigh universal on every level of community; while the classical age conceived the order and justice of its *polis* to be a comparatively simple achievement, which would be accomplished when reason had brought all subrational forces under its dominion.

This difference in the viewpoint of Augustine and the classical philosophers lies in Augustine's Biblical, rather than rationalistic or idealistic conception of human selfhood with the ancillary conception of the seat of evil being in the self. According to Augustine the self is an integral unity of mind and body. It is something more than mind and is able to use mind for its purposes. The self has, in fact, a mysterious identity and integrity transcending its functions of mind, memory, and will. It must be observed that the transcendent freedom of this self, including its capacity to defy any rational or natural system into which someone may seek to coordinate it (its capacity for evil) makes it difficult for any philosophy, whether ancient or modern, to comprehend its true dimension. This conception of selfhood is drawn from the Bible, rather than from philosophy, because the transcendent self which is present in, though it transcends, all of the functions and effects, is comprehensible only in the dramatic-historical mode of apprehension which characterizes Biblical faith.

Augustine's conception of the evil which threatens the human community on every level is a corollary of his doctrine of selfhood. "Self-love" is the source of evil rather than some residual natural impulse which mind has not yet completely mastered. This excessive love of self, sometimes also defined as pride or *superbia,* is explained as the consequence of the self's abandonment of God as its true end and of making itself "a kind of end." It is this powerful self-love or, in a modern term, "egocentricity," this tendency of the self to make itself its own end, or even to make itself the false center of whatever community it inhabits, which sows confusion in every human community.

Augustine's description of the social effects of human egocentricity or self-love is contained in his definition of the life of the "city of this world," the *civitas terrena,* which he sees as commingled with the *civitas dei.* The "city of this world" is dominated by self-love to the point of contempt of God; and is distinguished from the *civitas dei* which is actuated by the "love of God" to the point of contempt of self. This "city" is not some little city-state, as it is conceived in classical thought.

It is the whole human community on its three levels of the family, the commonwealth, and the world.

The *civitas terrena* is described as constantly subject to an uneasy armistice between contending forces, with the danger that factional disputes may result in "bloody insurrection" at any time. Augustine's realism prompts him to challenge Cicero's conception of a commonwealth as rooted in a "compact of justice." Not so, declares Augustine. Commonwealths are bound together by a common love, or collective interest, rather than by a sense of justice; and they could not maintain themselves without the imposition of power. "Without injustice the republic would neither increase nor subsist. The imperial city to which the republic belongs could not rule over provinces without recourse to injustice. For it is unjust for some men to rule over others."

This realism has the merit of describing the power realities which underlie all large-scale social integrations whether in Egypt or Babylon or Rome, where a dominant city-state furnished the organizing power for the Empire. It also describes the power realities of national states, even democratic ones, in which a group, holding the dominant form of social power, achieves oligarchic rule, no matter how much modern democracy may bring such power under social control. This realism in regard to the facts which underlie the organizing or governing power refutes the charge of modern liberals that a realistic analysis of social forces makes for state absolutism, so that a mild illusion in regard to human virtue is necessary to validate democracy. Realistic pessimism did indeed prompt both Hobbes and Luther to an unqualified endorsement of state power; but that is only because they were not realistic enough. They saw the dangers of anarchy in the egoism of the citizens but failed to perceive the dangers of tyranny in the selfishness of the ruler. Therefore they obscured the consequent necessity of placing checks upon the ruler's self-will.[5]

III. *Love: the* Civitas Dei

If Augustine's realism is contained in his analysis of the *civitas terrena,* his refutation of the idea that realism must lead to cynicism or relativism is contained in his definition of the *civitas dei,* which he declares to be "commingled" with the "city of this world" and which has the "love of God" rather than the "love of self" as its guiding principle. The tension between the two cities is occasioned by the fact that, while egoism is "natural" in the sense that it is universal, it is not natural in the sense that it does not conform to man's nature who transcends himself indeterminately and can only have God rather than self for his end. A realism becomes morally cynical or nihilistic when it assumes that the universal characteristic in human behavior must also be regarded as normative. The Biblical account of human behavior, upon which Augustine bases his thought, can escape both the illusions of a too consistent idealism and the cynicism of a too consistent realism because it recognizes that the corruption of human freedom may make a behavior pattern universal without making it normative. Good and evil are not determined by some fixed structure of human existence. Man, according to the Biblical view, may use his freedom to make himself falsely the center of existence; but this does not change the fact that love rather than self-love is the law of his existence in the sense that man can only be healthy and his communities at peace if man is drawn out of himself and saved from the self-defeating consequences of self-love.[6]

At the same time any Christian political thought which exploits the law of love without considering the power of the law of self-love is betrayed into sentimentality. As David Hume observed: "Politics must assume the selfishness of men, however we may speculate on the degree of their unselfishness and however much we may seek to increase that degree above the level of our political arrangements." [7] Indeed, Augustine's doctrine of love as the final norm must be distinguished from modern sentimental versions of Christianity which regard love as a simple possibility and which think it significant to assert the obvious proposition that all conflicts in the community would be avoided if only people and nations would love one another. Augustine's approach differs from modern forms of sentimental perfectionism in the fact that he takes account of the power and persistence of egoism, both individual and collective, and seeks to establish the most tolerable form of peace and justice under conditions set by human sin.[8]

It must be equally emphasized that the Augustinian formula for the leavening influence of a higher upon a lower loyalty or love, is effective in preventing the lower loyalty from involving itself in self-defeat. It corrects the "realism" of those who are myopically realistic, who see only their own interests and fail thereby to do justice to their interests where they are involved with the interests of others. There are modern realists, for instance, who, in their reaction to abstract and vague forms of international idealism, counsel the nation to consult only its own interests. In a sense collective self-interest is so consistent that it is superfluous to advise it. But a consistent self-interest on the part of a nation will work against its interests because it will fail to do justice to the broader and longer interests, which are involved with the interests of other nations. A narrow national loyalty on our part, for instance, will obscure our long range interests where they are involved with those of a whole alliance of free nations. Thus the loyalty of a leavening portion of a nation's citizens to a value transcending national interest will save a realistic nation from defining its interests in such narrow and short range terms as to defeat the real interests of the nation.[9]

Whatever the defects of Augustine's approach may be,* we must acknowledge his immense superiority both over those who preceded him and who came after him. As has already been pointed out, a part of that superiority was due to his reliance upon Biblical rather than idealistic or naturalistic conceptions of selfhood. But that could not have been the only cause, else Christian systems before and after him would not have been so inferior. Or were they inferior either because they subordinated the Biblical-dramatic conception of human selfhood too much to the rationalistic scheme, as was the case with medieval Christianity culminating in the thought of Thomas Aquinas? or because they did not understand that the corruption of human freedom could not destroy the original dignity of man, as was the case with the Reformation with its doctrines of sin, bordering on total depravity and resulting in Luther's too pessimistic approach to political problems? As for secular thought, it has difficulty in approaching Augustine's realism without falling into cynicism or in avoiding nihilism without falling into sentimentality. Hobbes' realism was based on an insight which he shared with Augustine, namely, that in all historical encounters the mind is the servant and not the master of the self. But he failed to recognize that the self which thus made the mind its instrument was a corrupted and not a "normal" self. Modern realists know the power of collective self-interest as Augustine did; but they do not understand its blindness. Modern pragmatists understand the irrelevance of fixed and detailed norms; but they do not understand that love as the final norm must take the place of these inadequate norms. Modern liberal Christians know that love is the final norm for man; but they fall into sentimentality because they fail to measure the power and persistence of self-love. A generation which finds its communities imperiled and in decay from the smallest and most primordial community, the family, to the largest and most recent, the potential world community, might well take counsel of Augustine in solving its perplexities.[10]

* For Niebuhr's critique of Augustine, see *Christian Realism and Political Problems*, pp. 137–145.

THE PROCESS OF POLITICS

CHAPTER VII

Human Nature and the Will-to-Power

I. *Human Nature and Politics*

The following pages are devoted to the task of analyzing the moral resources and limitations of human nature, of tracing their consequences and cumulative effect in the life of human groups, and of weighing political strategies in the light of the ascertained facts. The ultimate purpose of this task is to find political methods which will offer the most promise of achieving ethical social goals for society. Such methods must always be judged by two criteria: first, do they do justice to the moral resources and possibilities in human nature and provide for the exploitation of every latent moral capacity in man? Second, do they take account of the limitations of human nature, particularly those which manifest themselves in man's collective behavior? [1]

Modern optimists would argue that the second question, with its implied pessimistic reservations upon their utopian dreams, is predicated upon the assumption that human nature does not change, while it is their own belief that human nature is surprisingly malleable and is to a large degree the product of its environment. The question is whether they have not confused human nature with human behavior. Human behavior is constantly changing under the influence of various stimuli. The differences in the behavior of a Chinese Buddhist monk, a British aristocrat, a Prussian general, an American go-getter, an expatriated artist, and a Russian worker are very considerable. But a certain common human nature underlies all this varied behavior. Its common characteristics have been obscured by the rationalistic illusions which began in the eighteenth century, and which lost sight of common human traits in their emphasis upon the variable factors of education and environment.[2]

Recently a considerable number of political scientists have become aware of the relevance of Christian conceptions of human nature for the assessment of man's collective capacities and incapacities for justice and civic virtue. In secular political theory the tendency is to elaborate cynical and undemocratic social theories upon the basis of pessimistic interpretations of human nature; or to expound sentimental political theories upon the basis of a too optimistic interpretation of human nature. This contradiction between cynicism and sentimentality in political theory is partly derived from the separation of two elements in the Christian doctrine of man, the cynics emphasizing the sinful egoism of man and the sentimentalists emphasizing his dignity and greatness.[3]

II. *Humanist and Christian Views of Man*

Western civilization rests upon two sources—Greek classical thought and Biblical, Hebraic-Christian faith. These two sources are in agreement in their common appreciation of and emphasis upon the dignity and uniqueness of man. The alliance between them is, however, always uneasy, because they disagree on the character of man's unique gifts. For classical, as for modern secular, humanism, the emphasis lies heavily upon man's rational endowments, his logical and analytical faculties—in short, his "reason"—as the mark of his uniqueness. The Biblical view regards man's reason as only a part of his unique endowment, which it defines as the "image of God" and which it describes as a radical form of freedom in the human person. It is the total person, in the unity of will, memory, and understanding, which bears the "image of God."

According to the classical and modern secular view every extension and development of the human mind represents a clear gain. This is why, in the modern period, man's rational conquest of nature increased the prestige of rational humanism so significantly, and why this humanism had such an optimistic view of the moral consequences of man's conquest of nature, and of the development of technical civilization.

According to the Christian view the dignity of man and the "misery" of man are inextricably interwoven in his freedom. Every extension of freedom therefore involves the possibility of both good and evil; for evil is never merely the inertia of "nature" against the operation of "mind." Evil is in the person and not in nature. It is man's inclination to "self-love," his undue concern for himself. This defect is not overcome by any extension of mind; for if the center of personality is not changed, the mind still remains the servant of the self.

One reason why the Christian view has achieved a new relevance today is because modern developments have proved that there is a more intimate relation between what Madison called man's reason and self-love than the rationalists have assumed. The force of sin is stronger than humanism understands; and therefore the necessity of "grace" is greater. By "grace" we must understand every force in life and history which persuades and beguiles self-centered man to forget himself and to realize himself by letting go of himself and seeking the good of his fellows.

Modern, like classical, humanism removes every mystery from human selfhood. Christianity, on the other hand, declares that man stands so far above and beyond all relations of nature and reason that he can understand himself only in his relation to God. Modern humanism tends to equate the "dignity" of man with his virtue. Christianity, on the other hand, recognizes that the "dignity" of man consists precisely of that freedom which makes it possible for man to sin.[4]

III. *Man as Creature and Free Spirit*

As the classical view of man is determined by Greek metaphysical presuppositions, so the Christian view is determined by the ultimate presuppositions of the Christian faith. The Christian faith in God as Creator of the world transcends the canons and antinomies of rationality, particularly the antinomy between mind and matter, between consciousness and extension. God is not merely mind who forms a previously given formless stuff. God is both vitality and form and the source of all existence. He creates the world. This world is not God; but it is not necessarily evil simply because it is not God. Indeed, being God's creation, it is good.

The consequence of this conception of the world upon the view of human nature in Christian thought is to allow an appreciation of the unity of body and soul in human personality which idealists and naturalists have sought in vain. Furthermore it prevents the idealistic error of regarding the mind as essentially good or essentially eternal and the body as essentially evil. But it also obviates the romantic error of seeking for the good in man-as-nature and for evil in man-as-spirit or as reason. Man is, according to the Biblical view, a created and finite existence in both body and spirit.[5]

Thus, the Chritian faith teaches that the world is not evil because it is temporal, that the body is not the source of sin in man, that individuality as separate and particular existence is not evil by reason of being distinguished from undifferentiated totality, and that death is no evil though it is an occasion for evil, namely the fear of death. The Biblical view is that the finiteness, dependence and the insufficiency of man's mortal life are facts which belong to God's plan of creation and must be accepted with reverence and humility.[6]

Another characteristic of the Christian view of man is that he is understood primarily from the standpoint of God, rather than from the uniqueness of his rational faculties or his relation to nature. He is made in the "image of God." It has been the mistake of many Christian rationalists to assume that this term is no more than a religious-pictorial expression of what philosophy intends when it defines man as a rational animal. Whereas in fact the human spirit has the special capacity of standing continually outside itself in terms of indefinite regression. Consciousness is a capacity for surveying the world and determining action from a governing center. Self-consciousness represents a further degree of transcendence in which the self makes itself its own object in such a way that the ego is finally always subject and not object. The rational capacity of surveying the world, of forming general concepts and analyzing the order of the world, is thus but one aspect of what Christianity knows as "spirit." The self knows the world, insofar as it knows the world, because it stands outside both itself and the world, which means that it cannot understand itself except as it is understood from beyond itself and the world.

The essential homelessness of the human spirit is the ground of all religion; for the self which stands outside itself and the world cannot find the meaning of life in itself or the world. It cannot identify meaning with causality in nature; for its freedom is obviously something different from the necessary causal links of nature. Nor can it identify the principle of meaning with rationality, since it transcends its own rational processes, so that it may, for instance, ask the question whether there is a relevance between its rational forms and the recurrences and forms of nature. It is this capacity of freedom which finally prompts great cultures and philosophies to transcend rationalism and to seek for the meaning of life in an unconditioned ground of existence.[7]

While these paradoxes of human self-knowledge are not easily reduced to simpler formulae, they all point to two facts about man. The obvious fact is that man is a child of nature, subject to its vicissitudes, compelled by its necessities, driven by its impulses, and confined within the brevity of the years which nature permits its varied organic forms, allowing them some, but not too much, latitude. The other less obvious fact is that man is a spirit who stands outside of nature, life, himself, his reason and the world.[8]

The behavior of collective man naturally has its source in this anatomy of human nature. If we examine the constants and variables in that behavior, the most apparent constant factors are obviously derived from those aspects of human nature which constitute man a creature of nature, namely his natural hungers and needs, and the natural forces of cohesion in his communities, such as the sense of kinship. But natural necessity is not the only source of the constant factors. Some are derived from the unvarying way in which man's unique freedom manifests itself, such as his yearning for an ultimate good and his inevitable abuse of his freedom. However, freedom is, of course, also the source of the unique and variable factors in social behavior and therefore of the unpredictable character of historical events.[9]

In the Christian view, then, for man to understand himself truly means to begin with a faith that he is understood from beyond himself, that he is known and loved of God and must find himself in terms of obedience to the divine will. This relation of the divine to the human will makes it possible for man to relate himself to God without pretending to be God; and to accept his distance from God as a created thing, without believing that the evil of his nature is caused by this finiteness. Man's finite existence in the body and in history can be essentially affirmed, as naturalism wants to affirm it. Yet the uniqueness of man's spirit can be appreciated even more than idealism appreciates it, though always preserving a proper distinction between the human and the divine. Also the unity of spirit and body can be emphasized in terms of its relation to a Creator and Redeemer who created both mind and body. These are the ultra-rational foundations and presuppositions of Christian wisdom about man.

IV. *Man as Sinner*

This conception of man's stature is not, however, the complete Christian picture of man. The high estimate of the human stature implied in the concept of "image of God" stands in paradoxical juxtaposition to the low estimate of human virtue in Christian thought. Man is a sinner.[10]

Indeed, it is man's radical and boundless freedom which is the basis of the self's destructive as well as creative powers; and there is no simple possibility of making nice distinctions between human destructiveness and creativity. In the words of Pascal, the "dignity of man and his misery" have the same source. Man stands perpetually outside and beyond every social, natural, communal, and rational cohesion. He is not bound by any of them, which makes for his creativity. He is tempted to make use of all of them for his own ends; that is the basis of his destructiveness. One may go further and declare that the limitless character of man's ideals of perfection and the inordinancy of human lusts and ambitions have their common root in the capacity of man to stand out of, and survey, any historical or natural situation which surrounds him.[11]

While the Bible consistently maintains that sin cannot be excused by, or inevitably derived from, any other element in the human situation than man himself, it does admit that man was tempted. In the myth of the Fall the temptation arises from the serpent's analysis of the human situation. The serpent depicts God as jealously guarding his prerogatives against the possibilty that man might have his eyes opened and become "as God, knowing good and evil." Man is tempted, in other words, to break and transcend the limits which God has set for him. The temptation thus lies in his situation of finiteness and freedom.

That is, the occasion for man's temptation lies in the two facts taken together: his greatness and his weakness, his unlimited and his limited knowledge. Man is both strong and weak, both free and bound, both blind and far-seeing. He stands at the juncture of nature and spirit; and is involved in both freedom and necessity. His sin is never the mere ignorance of his ignorance. It is always partly an effort to obscure his blindness by overestimating the degree of his sight and to obscure his insecurity by stretching his power beyond its limits.

In short, man is anxious. Anxiety is the inevitable concomitant of the paradox of freedom and finiteness in which man is involved. Anxiety is the internal precondition of sin, the internal description of the state of temptation.

It is not possible to make a simple separation between the creative and destructive elements in anxiety; and for that reason it is not possible to purge moral achievement of sin as easily as moralists imagine. The same action may reveal a creative effort to transcend natural limitations, and a sinful effort to give an unconditioned value to contingent and limited factors in human existence. Man may, in the same moment, be anxious because he has not become what he ought to be, and also anxious lest he cease to be at all.

The parent is anxious about his child and this anxiety reaches beyond the grave. Is the effort of the parent to provide for the future of the child creative or destructive? Obviously it is both.

The statesman is anxious about the order and security of the nation. But he cannot express this anxiety without an admixture of anxiety about his prestige as a ruler and without assuming unduly that only the kind of order and security which he establishes is adequate for the nation's health.

The philosopher is anxious to arrive at the truth; but he is also anxious to prove that his particular truth is the truth. He is never as completely in possession of the truth as he imagines. That may be the error of being ignorant of one's ignorance. But it is never simply that. The pretensions of final truth are always partly an effort to obscure a darkly felt consciousness of the limits of human knowledge. Man is afraid to face the problem of his limited knowledge, lest he fall into the abyss of meaninglessness. Thus fanaticism is always a partly conscious, partly unconscious attempt to hide the fact of ignorance and to obscure the problem of skepticism.

Anxiety, of course, must not be identified with sin because there is always the ideal possibility that faith will purge anxiety of the tendency toward sinful self-assertion. The ideal possibility is that faith in the ultimate security of God's love will overcome all immediate insecurities of nature and history. That is why Christian orthodoxy has consistently defined unbelief as the root of sin, or as the sin which precedes pride. It is significant that Jesus justifies his injunction, "Be not anxious" with the observation, "For your heavenly Father knoweth that ye have need of these things." The freedom from anxiety which he enjoins is a possibility only if perfect trust in divine security has been achieved.[12]

Thus man's sin is defined as rebellion against God. The Christian estimate of human evil is so serious precisely because it places evil at the very center of human personality: in the will. This evil cannot be regarded complacently as the inevitable consequence of his finiteness or the fruit of his involvement in the contingencies and necessities of nature. Sin is occasioned precisely by the fact that man refuses to admit his "creatureliness" and to acknowledge himself as merely a member of a total unity of life. He pretends to be more than he is. Nor can he, as in both rationalistic and mystic dualism, dismiss his sins as residing in that part of himself which is not his true self, that is, that part of himself which is involved in physical necessity. In Christianity it is not the eternal man who judges the finite man; but the eternal and holy God who judges sinful man. Nor is redemption in the power of the eternal man who gradually sloughs off finite man. Man is not divided against himself so that the essential man can be extricated from the non-essential. Man contradicts himself within the terms of his true essence. His essence is free self-determination. His sin is the wrong use of his freedom and its consequent destruction.

Man is an individual but he is not self-sufficing. The law of his nature is love, a harmonious relation of life to life in obedience to the divine center and source of his life. This law is violated when man seeks to make himself the center and source of his own life. His sin is therefore spiritual and not carnal, though the infection of rebellion spreads from the spirit to the body and disturbs its harmonies also. Man, in other words, is a sinner not because he is one limited individual within a whole but rather because he is betrayed by his very ability to survey the whole to imagine himself the whole.[13]

V. *Pride and the Will-to-Power*

The Bible defines sin in moral as well as religious terms. The religious dimension of sin is man's rebellion against God, his effort to usurp the place of God. The moral and social dimension of sin is injustice. The ego which falsely makes itself the center of existence in its pride and will-to-power inevitably subordinates other life to its will and thus does injustice to other life. Man is insecure and involved in natural contingency; he seeks to overcome his insecurity by a will-to-power which overreaches the limits of human creatureliness. Man is ignorant and involved in the limitations of a finite mind; but he pretends that he is not limited. He assumes that he can gradually transcend finite limitations until his mind becomes identical with universal mind. All of his intellectual and cultural pursuits, therefore, become infected with the sin of pride. Man's pride and will-to-power disturb the harmony of creation.[14] We must now examine more carefully the ways in which sin expresses itself as both pride and the lust for power, and the consequences of these evils for social relations.

The most significant distinction between the human and the animal world is that the impulses of the latter are "spiritualized" in the human world. Human capacities for evil as well as for good are derived from this spiritualization. There is of course always a natural survival impulse at the core of all human ambition. But this survival impulse cannot be neatly disentangled from two forms of its spiritualization.

The one form is the desire to fulfill the potentialities of life and not merely to maintain its existence. Man is the kind of animal who cannot merely live. If he lives at all he is bound to seek the realization of his true nature; and to his true nature belongs his fulfillment in the lives of others.

The will-to-live is thus transmuted into the will to self-realization; and self-realization involves self-giving in relations to others. When this desire for self-realization is fully explored it becomes apparent that it is subject to the paradox that the highest form of self-realization is the consequence of self-giving, but that it cannot be the intended consequence without being prematurely limited. Thus the will-to-live is finally transmuted into its opposite in the sense that only in self-giving can the self be fulfilled, for: "He that findeth his life shall lose it; and he that loseth his life for my sake shall find it."

On the other hand the will-to-live is also spiritually transmuted into the will-to-power or into the desire for "power and glory." Man, being more than a natural creature, is not interested merely in physical survival but in prestige and social approval. Having the intelligence to anticipate the perils in which he stands in nature and history, he invariably seeks to gain security against these perils by enhancing his power, individually and collectively. Possessing a darkly unconscious sense of his insignificance in the total scheme of things, he seeks to compensate for his insignificance by pretensions of pride.

The conflicts between men are thus never simple conflicts between competing survival impulses. They are conflicts in which each man or group seeks to guard its power and prestige against the peril of competing expressions of power and pride. Since the very possession of power and prestige always involves some encroachment upon the prestige and power of others, this conflict is by its very nature a more stubborn and difficult one than the mere competition between various survival impulses in nature.

Since the survival impulse in nature is transmuted into two different and contradictory spiritualized forms, which we may briefly designate as the will-to-live-truly and the will-to-power, man is at variance with himself. The power of the second impulse places him more fundamentally in conflict with his fellow man than liberalism realizes. The fact that he cannot realize himself, except in organic relation with his fellows, makes the community more important than bourgeois individualism understands. The fact that the two impulses, though standing in contradiction to each other, are also mixed and compounded with each other on every level of human life, makes the simple distinctions between good and evil, between selfishness and altruism, with which liberal idealism has tried to estimate moral and political facts, invalid. The fact that the will-to-power inevitably justifies itself in terms of the morally more acceptable will to realize man's true nature means that the egoistic corruption of universal ideals is a much more persistent fact in human conduct than any moralistic creed is inclined to admit.

If we survey any period of history, and not merely the present tragic era of world catastrophe, it becomes quite apparent that human ambitions, lusts and desires are more inevitably inordinate, that both human creativity and human evil reach greater heights, and that conflicts in the community between varying conceptions of the good and between competing expressions of vitality are of more tragic proportions than was anticipated in the basic philosophy which underlies liberal civilization.[15]

In one form of the pride of power, the human ego assumes its self-sufficiency and self-mastery and imagines itself secure against all vicissitudes. It does not recognize the contingent and dependent character of its life and believes itself to be the author of its own existence, the judge of its own values and the master of its own destiny. This proud pretension is present in an inchoate form in all human life but it rises to greater heights among those individuals and classes who have a more than ordinary degree of social power.

Closely related to the pride which seems to rest upon the possession of either the ordinary or some extraordinary measure of human freedom and self-mastery, is the lust for power which has pride as its end. The ego does not feel secure and therefore grasps for more power in order to make itself secure. It does not regard itself as sufficiently significant or respected or feared and therefore seeks to enhance its position in nature and in society.

In the one case the ego seems unconscious of the finite and determinate character of its existence. In the other case the lust for power is prompted by a darkly conscious realization of its insecurity. The first form of the pride of power is particularly characteristic of individuals and groups whose position in society is, or seems to be, secure. In Biblical prophecy this security is declared to be bogus and those who rest in it are warned against an impending doom. Thus the second Isaiah describes the pride of Babylon in the words: "Thou saidst, I shall be a lady forever; so that thou dost not lay these things to thy heart." The impending doom is defined as a revelation of the weakness and insecurity of Babylon: "Thy nakedness shall be uncovered; yea, thy shame shall be seen." In the same way the first Isaiah warns the rulers of Israel who are described as "the crown of pride" that their "glorious beauty is a fading flower." He declares that in the day of judgment the "Lord of hosts" will be vindicated and will be "for a crown of glory and for a diadem of beauty." In other words history invariably shatters the illusions of those who overestimate the power of human life and in the day of judgment God is revealed as the true source and end of life as the "crown of glory."

The second form of the pride of power is more obviously prompted by the sense of insecurity. It is the sin of those who, knowing themselves to be insecure, seek sufficient power to guarantee their security, inevitably of course at the expense of other life. It is particularly the sin of the advancing forces of human society in distinction to the established forces. Among those who are less obviously secure, either in terms of social recognition, or economic stability, or even physical health, the temptation arises to overcome or to obscure insecurity by arrogating a greater degree of power to the self.

In international life between the World Wars, Great Britain with its too strong a sense of security, which prevented it from taking proper measures of defense in time, and Germany with its maniacal will-to-power, were perfect symbols of the different forms which pride takes among the established and the advancing social forces. The inner stability and external security of Great Britain was of such long duration that she may be said to have committed the sin of Babylon and declared, "I shall be no widow and I shall never know sorrow." Germany on the other hand suffered from an accentuated form of inferiority long before her defeat in World War I. Her boundless self-assertion which literally transgressed all bounds previously known in religion, culture and law was a very accentuated form of power impulse which betrayed a marked inner insecurity.

Sometimes the lust for power expresses itself in terms of man's conquest of nature, in which the legitimate freedom and mastery of man in the world of nature is corrupted into a mere exploitation of nature. Man's sense of dependence upon nature and his reverent gratitude toward the miracle of nature's perennial abundance is destroyed by his arrogant sense of independence and his greedy effort to overcome the insecurity of nature's rhythms and seasons by garnering her stores with excessive zeal and beyond natural requirements. Greed is in short the expression of man's inordinate ambition to hide his insecurity in nature.

However, since man's insecurity arises not merely from the vicissitudes of nature but from the uncertainties of society and history, it is natural that the ego should seek to overcome social as well as natural insecurity and should express the impulse of "power over men" as well as "power over matter." The peril of a competing human will is overcome by subordinating that will to the ego and by using the power of many subordinated wills to ward off the enmity which such subordination creates. The will-to-power is thus inevitably involved in the vicious circle of accentuating the insecurity which it intends to eliminate. "Woe to thee," declares the prophet Isaiah, "that spoilest, and thou was not spoiled; and dealest treacherously, and they dealt not treacherously with thee! when thou shalt cease to spoil, thou shalt be spoiled." The will-to-power in short involves the ego in injustice. It seeks a security beyond the limits of human finiteness and this inordinate ambition arouses fears and enmities which the world of pure nature, with its competing impulses of survival, does not know.

The school of modern psychology which regards the will-to-power as the most dominant of human motives has not yet recognized how basically it is related to insecurity. Adler attributes it to specific forms of the sense of inferiority and therefore believes that a correct therapy can eliminate it. Karen Horney relates the will-to-power to a broader anxiety than the specific cases of the sense of inferiority which Adler enumerates. But she thinks that the will-to-power springs from the general insecurities of a competitive civilization and therefore holds out hope for its elimination in a cooperative society. This is still far short of the real truth. The truth is that man is tempted by the basic insecurity of human existence to make himself doubly secure and by the insignificance of his place in the total scheme of life to prove his significance. The will-to-power is in short both a direct form and an indirect instrument of the pride which Christianity regards as sin in its quintessential form.

We have provisionally distinguished between the pride which does not recognize human weakness and the pride which seeks power in order to overcome or obscure a recognized weakness. This distinction is justified only if regarded as strictly provisional. The fact is that the proudest monarch and the most secure oligarch is driven to assert himself beyond measure partly by a sense of insecurity. This is partly due to the fact that the greater his power and glory, the more the common mortality of humankind appears to him in the guise of an incongruous fate. Thus the greatest monarchs of the ancient world, the Pharaohs of Egypt, exhausted the resources of their realm to build pyramids, which were intended to establish or to prove their immortality. A common mortal's fear of death is thus one prompting motive of the pretensions and ambitions of the greatest lords.

But furthermore, the more man establishes himself in power and glory, the greater is the fear of tumbling from his eminence, or losing his treasure, or being discovered in his pretension. Poverty is a peril to the wealthy but not to the poor. Obscurity is feared, not by those who are habituated to its twilight but by those who have become accustomed to public acclaim. Nor is this sense of insecurity of the powerful and the great to be wholly discounted as being concerned with mere vanities. Life's basic securities are involved in the secondary securities of power and glory. The tyrant fears not only the loss of his power but the possible loss of his life. The powerful nation, secure against its individual foes, must fear the possibility that its power may challenge its various foes to make common cause against it. The person accustomed to luxury and ease actually meets a greater danger to life and mere existence in the hardships of poverty than those who have been hardened by its rigors.

The will-to-power is thus an expression of insecurity even when it has achieved ends which, from the perspective of an ordinary mortal, would seem to guarantee complete security. The fact that human ambitions know no limits must therefore be attributed not merely to the infinite capacities of the human imagination but to an uneasy recognition of man's finiteness, weakness and dependence, which become the more apparent the more we seek to obscure them, and which generate ultimate perils, the more immediate insecurities are eliminated. Thus man seeks to make himself God because he is betrayed by both his greatness and his weakness; and there is no level of greatness and power in which the lash of fear is not at least one strand in the whip of ambition.[16]

VI. *Intellectual, Moral and Spiritual Pride*

The Biblical and distinctively Christian conception of sin as pride and self-love finds various expressions in the observable behavior of men. Besides pride of power, two other types may be distinguished: pride of knowledge and pride of virtue. The third type, the pride of self-righteousness, rises to a form of spiritual pride, which is at once a fourth type and yet not a specific form of pride at all but pride and self-glorification in its inclusive and quintessential form.[17] *

The intellectual pride of man is of course a more spiritual sublimation of his pride of power. Sometimes it is so deeply involved in the more brutal and obvious pride of power that the two cannot be distinguished.

* For Niebuhr's treatment of the validity as well as the corruption of intellectual, moral and religious norms in political relations, see Chapter XI.

Every ruling oligarchy of history has found ideological pretensions as important a bulwark of authority as its police power. But intellectual pride is confined neither to the political oligarchs nor to the savants of society. All human knowledge is tainted with an "ideological" taint. It pretends to be more true than it is. It is finite knowledge, gained from a particular perspective; but it pretends to be final and ultimate knowledge. Exactly analogous to the cruder pride of power, the pride of intellect is derived on the one hand from ignorance of the finiteness of the human mind and on the other hand from an attempt to obscure the known conditioned character of human knowledge and the taint of self-interest in human truth.

Moral pride is revealed in all "self-righteous" judgments in which the other is condemned because he fails to conform to the highly arbitrary standards of the self. Since the self judges itself by its own standards it finds itself good. It judges others by its own standards and finds them evil, when their standards fail to conform to its own. This is the secret of the relationship between cruelty and self-righteousness. When the self mistakes its standards for God's standards it is naturally inclined to attribute the very essence of evil to non-conformists.

One might add that the sin of self-righteousness is not only the final sin in the subjective sense but also in the objective sense. It involves us in the greatest guilt. It is responsible for our most serious cruelties, injustices and defamations against our fellow men. The whole history of racial, national, religious and other social struggles is a commentary on the objective wickedness and social miseries which result from self-righteousness.

The sin of moral pride, when it has conceived, brings forth spiritual pride. The ultimate sin is the religious sin of making the self-deification implied in moral pride explicit. This is done when our partial standards and relative attainments are explicitly related to the unconditioned good, and claim divine sanction. For this reason religion is not simply, as is generally supposed, an inherently virtuous human quest for God. It is merely a final battleground between God and man's self-esteem. In that battle even the most pious practices may be instruments of human pride. The same man may in one moment regard Christ as his judge and in the next moment seek to prove that the figure, the standards and the righteousness of Christ bear a greater similarity to his own righteousness than to that of his enemy. The worst form of class domination is religious class domination in which, as for instance in the Indian caste system, a dominant priestly class not only subjects subordinate classes to social disabilities but finally excludes them from participation in any universe of meaning. The worst form of intolerance is religious intolerance, in which the particular interests of the contestants hide behind religious absolutes. The worst form of self-assertion is religious self-assertion in which under the guise of contrition before God, He is claimed as the exclusive ally of our contingent self.

Christianity rightly regards itself as a religion, not so much of man's search for God, in the process of which he may make himself God; but as a religion of revelation in which a holy and loving God is revealed to man as the source and end of all finite existence against whom the self-will of man is shattered and his pride abased. But as soon as the Christian assumes that he is, by virtue of possessing this revelation, more righteous, because more contrite, than other men, he increases the sin of self-righteousness and makes the forms of a religion of contrition the tool of his pride.

Indeed the final mystery of human sin cannot be understood if it is not recognized that the greatest teachers of this Reformation doctrine of the sinfulness of all men used it on occasion as the instrument of an arrogant will-to-power against theological opponents. There is no final guarantee against the spiritual pride of man. Even the recognition in the sight of God that he is a sinner can be used as a vehicle of that very sin. If that final mystery of the sin of pride is not recognized the meaning of the Christian gospel cannot be understood.

It must be added that it is not necessary to be explicitly religious in order to raise moral pride to explicit religious proportions. Stalin can be as explicit in making unconditioned claims as the pope; and a French revolutionist of the eighteenth century can be as cruel in his religious fervor as the "God-ordained" feudal system which he seeks to destroy. The hope of modern culture that the elimination of religion might result in the elimination of religious intolerance is fallacious. Religion, by whatever name, is the inevitable fruit of the spiritual stature of man; and religious intolerance and pride is the final expression of his sinfulness. A religion of revelation is grounded in the faith that God speaks to man from beyond the highest pinnacle of the human spirit; and that this voice of God will discover man's highest not only to be short of the highest but involved in the dishonesty of claiming that it is the highest.[18]

CHAPTER VIII

Groups in the Struggle for Power

I. *"Moral Man and Immoral Society"*

A sharp distinction must be drawn between the moral and social behavior of individuals and of social groups, national, racial, and economic; and this distinction justifies and necessitates political policies which a purely individualistic ethic must always find embarrassing. When we speak of "moral man and immoral society" we state the intended distinction too unqualifiedly, but it is nevertheless a fair indication of the argument to which the following pages are devoted.

Individual men may be moral in the sense that they are able to consider interests other than their own in determining problems of conduct, and are capable, on occasion, of preferring the advantages of others to their own. They are endowed by nature with a measure of sympathy and consideration for their kind, the breadth of which may be extended by an astute social pedagogy. Their rational faculty prompts them to a sense of justice which educational discipline may refine and purge of egoistic elements until they are able to view a social situation in which their own interests are involved with a fair measure of objectivity.

But all these achievements are more difficult, if not impossible, for human societies and social groups. In every human group there is less reason to guide and check impulse, less capacity for self-transcendence, less ability to comprehend the needs of others and therefore more unrestrained egoism than the individuals who compose the group reveal in their personal relationships.

The inferiority of the morality of groups to that of individuals is due in part to the difficulty of establishing a rational social force which is powerful enough to cope with the natural impulses by which society achieves its cohesion; but in part it is merely the revelation of a collective egoism, compounded of the egoistic impulses of individuals, which achieve a more vivid expression and a more cumulative effect when they are united in a common impulse than when they express themselves separately and discretely.[1]

Even when the individual is prompted to give himself in devotion to a cause or community, this egoism may still be evidenced. In the family for instance, it may express itself in part within the family circle and in part through the family. Devotion to the family does not exclude the possibility of an autocratic relationship toward it. The tyranny of the husband and father in the family has yielded only very slowly to the principle of mutuality.

But even if perfect mutuality should be attained within the family circle, the family may still remain a means of self-aggrandizement. The solicitous father wants his wife and children to have all possible advantages. His greater solicitude for them than for others grows naturally out of the sympathy which intimate relations prompt. But it is also a projection of his own ego. Families may, in fact, be used to advertise a husband's and father's success and prosperity. The truth is that every immediate loyalty is a potential danger to higher and more inclusive loyalties, and an opportunity for the expression of a sublimated egoism.

The larger social groups above the family, communities, classes, races and nations, all present men with the same twofold opportunity for self-denial and self-aggrandizement; and both possibilities are usually exploited. Patriotism is a high form of altruism, when compared with lesser and more parochial loyalties; but from an absolute perspective it is simply another form of selfishness. The larger the group the more certainly will it express itself selfishly in the total human community. It will be more powerful and therefore more able to defy any social restraints which might be devised. It will also be less subject to internal moral restraints. The larger the group the more difficult it is to achieve a common mind and purpose and the more inevitably will it be unified by momentary impulses and immediate and unreflective purposes. The increasing size of the group increases the difficulties of achieving a group self-consciousness, except as it comes in conflict with other groups and is unified by perils and passions of war. It is a rather pathetic aspect of human social life that conflict is a seemingly unavoidable prerequisite of group solidarity.

Furthermore the greater the strength and the wider the dominion of a community, the more will it seem to represent universal values from the perspective of the individual. There is something to be said for Treitschke's logic, which made the nation the ultimate community of significant loyalty, on the ground that smaller units were too small to deserve, and larger units too vague and ephemeral to be able to exact, man's supreme loyalty. Treitschke was wrong only in glorying in this moral difficulty.

Thus, try as he will, man seems incapable of forming an international community with power and prestige great enough to bring social restraint upon collective egoism. He has not even succeeded in disciplining anti-social group egoism within the nation. The very existence of human sympathies has therefore resulted in the creation of larger units of conflict without abolishing conflict. So civilization has become a device for delegating the vices of individuals to larger and larger communities.[2]

Unquestionably there is this alloy of projected self-interest in patriotic altruism. The man in the street, with his lust for power and prestige thwarted by his own limitations and the necessities of social life, projects his ego upon his nation and indulges his anarchic lusts vicariously. So the nation is at one and the same time a check upon, and a final vent for, the expression of individual egoism.

The combination of unselfishness and vicarious selfishness in the individual thus gives a tremendous force to group egoism, which neither religious nor rational idealism can ever completely check.[3]

Our contemporary culture fails to realize the power, extent and persistence of group egoism in human relations. It may be possible, though it is never easy, to establish just relations between individuals within a group purely by moral and rational suasion and accommodation. In inter-group relations this is practically an impossibility. The relations between groups must therefore always be predominantly political rather than ethical; that is, they will be determined by the proportion of power which each group possesses at least as much as by any rational and moral appraisal of the comparative needs and claims of each group.[4]

II. *The Pride of Groups and Nations*

Strictly speaking, only individuals are moral agents, and group pride is therefore merely an aspect of the pride and arrogance of individuals. It is the fruit of the undue claims which they make for their various social groups. Nevertheless, as we have seen, some distinctions must be made between the collective behavior of men and their individual attitudes. This is necessary in part because group pride, though having its source in individual attitudes, actually achieves a certain authority over the individual and results in unconditioned demands by the group upon the individual. Whenever the group develops organs of will, as in the apparatus of the state, it seems to the individual to have become an independent center of moral life. He will be inclined to bow to its pretensions and to acquiesce in its claims of authority, even when these do not coincide with his moral scruples or inclinations.

A distinction between group pride and the egoism of individuals is necessary, furthermore, because the pretensions and claims of a collective or social self exceed those of the individual ego. The group is more arrogant, hypocritical, self-centered and more ruthless in the pursuit of its ends than the individual.

The egoism of racial, national and socio-economic groups is most consistently expressed by the national state.[5] The modern nation is the human group of strongest social cohesion, of most undisputed central authority and of most clearly defined membership. The church may have challenged its pre-eminence in the Middle Ages, and the economic class may compete with it for the loyalty of men in our own day; yet it remains, as it has been since the seventeenth century, the most absolute of all human associations.

What is the basis and reason for the cohesive power and selfishness of nations? If we begin with what is least important or least distinctive of national attitudes, it must be noted that nations do not have the direct contact with other national communities which is prerequisite to the recognition of common interest. They know the problems of other peoples only indirectly and at second hand. Since both sympathy and justice depend to a large degree upon the perception of need, which makes sympathy flow, and upon the understanding of competing interests which must be resolved, it is obvious that human communities have greater difficulty than individuals in achieving ethical relationships.[6]

More importantly, loyalty to the nation state is strengthened by the fact that the state gives the nationalist sentiments and collective impulses of the nation such instruments of power and presents the imagination of individuals with such obvious symbols of its discrete collective identity that the national state is most able to make absolute claims for itself, to enforce those claims by power, and to give them plausibility and credibility by the majesty and panoply of its apparatus. In the life of every political group, whether nation or empire, which articulates itself through the instrument of a state, obedience is prompted by the fear of power on the one hand and by reverence for majesty on the other. The temptation to idolatry is implicit in the state's majesty. Rationalists, with their simple ideas of government resting purely upon the consent of the governed, have never appreciated to what degree religious reverence for majesty is implicit in this consent.[7]

In other words the nation is a corporate unity, held together much more by force and emotion than by mind. Since there can be no ethical action without self-criticism, and no self-criticism without the rational capacity of self-transcendence, it is natural that national attitudes can hardly approximate the ethical. Even those tendencies toward self-criticism in a nation which do express themselves are usually thwarted by the governing classes and by a certain instinct for unity in society itself. For self-criticism is a kind of inner disunity, which the feeble mind of a nation finds difficulty in distinguishing from dangerous forms of inner conflict. So nations crucify their moral rebels with their criminals upon the same Golgotha, not being able to distinguish between the moral idealism which surpasses, and the anti-social conduct which falls below that moral mediocrity on the level of which every society unifies its life. While critical loyalty toward a community is not impossible, it is not easily achieved.[8]

Perhaps the most significant moral characteristic of the nation is its hypocrisy. Self-deception and hypocrisy is an unvarying element in the moral life of all human beings. It is the tribute which immorality pays to morality; or rather the device by which the lesser self gains the consent of the larger self to indulge in impulses and ventures which the rational self can approve only when they are disguised. One can never be quite certain whether the disguise is meant only for the eye of the external observer or whether, as may usually be the case, it deceives the self. Naturally this defect in individuals becomes more apparent in the less moral life of nations. Yet it might be supposed that nations, of whom so much less is expected, would not be under the necessity of making moral pretensions for their actions. There was probably a time when they were under no such necessity. Their hypocrisy is both a tribute to the growing rationality of man and a proof of the ease with which rational demands may be circumvented. The dishonesty of nations is a necessity of political policy if the nation is to gain the full benefit of its double claim upon the loyalty and devotion of the individual, as his own special and unique community and as a community which embodies universal values and ideals.[9]

Sinful pride and idolatrous pretensions are thus an inevitable concomitant of the cohesion of large political groups. This is why it is impossible to regard the lower morality of groups, in comparison with that of individuals, as the consequence of the inertia of "nature" against the higher demands of individual reason. It is true of course that the group possesses only an inchoate "mind" and that its organs of self-transcendence and self-criticism are very unstable and ephemeral compared to its organs of will. A shifting and unstable "prophetic minority" is the instrument of this self-transcendence, while the state is the organ of the group's will.

Still, the egoism of nations must be understood as a characteristic of the spiritual life, and not merely an expression of the natural impulse of survival. The most conclusive proof of this proposition is the fact that its most typical expressions are the lust-for-power; pride (comprising considerations of prestige and "honor"); contempt toward the other; hypocrisy (the inevitable pretension of conforming to a higher norm than self-interest); and finally the claim of moral autonomy by which the self-deification of the social group is made explicit by its presentation of itself as the source and end of existence.

It cannot be denied that the instinct of survival is involved in all these spiritual manifestations of egoism; but that is equally true of individual life. Every human self-assertion, whether individual or collective, is therefore involved in the inconsistency of claiming, on the one hand, that it is justified by the primary right of survival and, on the other hand, that it is the bearer of interests and values larger than its own and that these more inclusive values are the justification of its conflict with competing social wills. No modern nation can ever quite make up its mind whether to insist that its struggle is a fight for survival or a selfless effort to maintain transcendent and universal values.

The nation to which the individual belongs transcends the individual life to such a degree in power, majesty, and pseudo-immortality that the claim of unconditioned value can be made for it with a degree of plausibility. The significance of this claim is that through it human pride and self-assertion reach their ultimate form and seek to break all bounds of finiteness. The nation pretends to be God. A certain ambiguity which envelops this claim has already been noted. Collective egoism does indeed offer the individual an opportunity to lose himself in a larger whole; but it also offers him possibilities of self-aggrandizement beside which mere individual pretensions are implausible and incredible. Individuals "join to set up a god whom each of them then severally and tacitly identifies with himself, to swell the chorus of praise which each then severally and tacitly arrogates to himself." [10] [11]

Since nations constitute an extreme case of the sinful pride of groups, perhaps the best that can be expected of them is that they should justify their hypocrisies by a slight measure of real international achievement, and learn how to do justice to wider interests than their own, while they pursue their own.[12]

The special "immorality of groups" helps, incidentally, to explain the recalcitrance and stubbornness of the man of power. This recalcitrance is not simply due to personal defects or self-deceptions. The real cause lies in the representative character of the oligarch. He expresses not only his own impulses but those of a social group, a class or a nation. He is the incarnation of a *raison d'état*.[13]

It may be that group pride represents a particular temptation to individuals who suffer from specific forms of the sense of inferiority. The relation of modern fascist nationalism to the insecurity and sense of inferiority of the lower middle classes is therefore significant. But it hardly can be denied that extravagant forms of modern nationalism only accentuate a general characteristic of group life and collective egoism; and that specific forms of inferiority feeling, for which this pride compensates, only accentuate the general sense of inferiority from which all men suffer.

Collective pride is thus man's last, and in some respects most pathetic, effort to deny the determinate and contingent character of his existence. The very essence of human sin is in it. It can hardly be surprising that this form of human sin is also most fruitful of human guilt, that is of objective social and historical evil. In its whole range from pride of family to pride of nation, collective egoism and group pride are a more pregnant source of injustice and conflict than purely individual pride.

The pride of nations is, of course, not wholly spurious. Their claim to embody values which transcend their mere existence has foundations in fact. It is the very character of human life, whether individual or collective, that it incarnates values which transcend its immediate interests. A particular nation or group of nations may actually be the bearers of a "democratic civilization" or of a communist one. Men are not animals and never fight merely for existence, because they do not have a mere animal existence.

But the real pride of nations consists in the tendency to make unconditioned claims for their conditioned values. The unconditioned character of these claims has two aspects. The nation claims a more absolute devotion to values which transcend its life than the facts warrant; and it regards the values to which it is loyal as more absolute than they really are.

The fact that human pride insinuates itself into the struggle of the Christian religion against the pride and self-will of nations merely proves how easily the pride of men can avail itself of the very instruments intended to mitigate it. The church, as well as the state, can become the vehicle of collective egoism. Every truth can be made the servant of sinful arrogance, including the prophetic truth that all men fall short of the truth. This particular truth can come to mean that, since all men fall short of the truth and since the church is a repository of a revelation which transcends the finiteness and sinfulness of men, it therefore has the absolute truth which other men lack.[14]

Human vitalities, then, express themselves from collective as well as individual centers, and both may be endlessly elaborated. Any premature definition of what the limits of these elaborations ought to be inevitably destroys and suppresses legitimate forms of life and culture. But this capacity for human creativity also involves the destructive capacity of human vitality. Vitalities may be developed inordinately. Various forms of vitality may come in conflict with one another, or one form may illegitimately suppress another. The tension among the various forms may threaten or destroy the harmony and peace of the community.[15]

The limitations of the human imagination, the easy subservience of reason to prejudice and passion, and the consequent persistence of irrational egoism, particularly in group behavior, make social conflict an inevitability in human history to its very end.[16]

III. *The Perennial Struggle for Power*

All communal life represents a field of vitality, elaborated in many forms which are related to each other in terms of both mutual support and of potential conflict.[17] Yet communal life is most accurately analyzed, not as Aristotle and Stoic rationalists analyze it—as merely an order of vitalities which is prevented from falling into chaos by its conformity to particular structures which reason may ascertain. It should be recognized rather as a vast series of encounters among human selves and their interests. The encounters are indeed regularized into patterns and stabilities, and the habit of conformity to these stabilities mitigates the encounters. But these social patterns are not "eternal laws" and they cannot hide the essential character of social life as an encounter between myself and another, whether individually or collectively, and whether the encounter is creative or destructive, cooperative or competitive. Political life, that is, has to deal primarily with human selves and not with either mind, on the one hand, or sub-rational vitalities, on the other.[18]

The perennial importance of power in social organization is based upon two characteristics of these selves. The one is the unity of vitality and reason, of body and soul. The other is the force of human sin, the persistent tendency to regard ourselves as more important than anyone else and to view a common problem from the standpoint of our own interest. The second characteristic is so stubborn that mere moral or rational suasion does not suffice to restrain one person from taking advantage of another. Legal authority may be more sufficing; but there is no legal authority which does not imply sanctions or the threat of coercive action against recalcitrance. The first characteristic, the unity of vitality and reason in human nature, guarantees that egoistic purposes will be pursued with all vital resources which an individual or collective will may control.[19]

Consequently the perfect accord between life and life is constantly spoiled by the inordinate concern of each life for its own weal, especially as expressed in the corporate egoism of contending groups. Human society is full of the friction of cross purposes.[20] Indeed it is in a perpetual state of war.[21]

Disputes may of course be composed and conflicts arbitrated. The conflict of interest and passion among races, classes, nations, and individuals can be arbitrated into a tolerable harmony by wise statesmanship and astute methods of adjudication.[22] Conscience may appeal to conscience and reason to reason. There are in fact no conflicts in which these appeals are not made, even when the conflict has become physical. But in every conflict of interest the possibility of marshalling every possible resource on either side is implied. Most human conflicts are composed, or subdued, by a superior authority and power, without an overt appeal to force or without the actual use of force, either violent or nonviolent. But the calculation of available resources on either side is as determinative in settling the outcome of the struggle as more purely rational or moral considerations.[23]

The contest of power, then, is the heart of political life.[24] To understand politics is to recognize the elements of power which underlie all social structures—the play of power which may be obscured or submerged, but which cannot be eliminated.[25] The peace of the world is always, as St. Augustine observed, something of an armistice between opposing factions. There is no perfect harmony in history, no peace within the limits of understanding.[26]

IV. *Types of Power and Their Relationship*

The spiritual and physical faculties of man are able, in their unity and interrelation, to create an endless variety of types and combinations of power, from that of pure reason to that of pure physical force. It is hardly necessary at this point to prove that reason may be the instrument of the ego in advancing its claims against another. When it is so used it is a "power" which supports the claims of one life against another. The shrewd do take advantage of the simple. A rational solution of a conflict may be a very unjust one, if the more robust has "overpowered" the weaker intellect.

But there are other spiritual faculties which may serve the same purpose. One man may keep another enslaved purely by "soul" force. Such soul force may consist of spiritual vitalities of various kinds, mental and emotional energy, the possession or the pretension of virtue, the prestige of an heroic life, or of a gentle birth. It follows that Gandhi's identification of "soul force" with nonegoistic motives and "body force" with egoistic ones, is almost completely mistaken. The type of power used by the will to effect its purposes does not determine the quality of the purpose or motive.

Pure physical force is always a last resort in individual relations. It is determinative in these relations only on primitive levels. All civilized relations are governed more by spiritual than by physical facets of power. It is significant that they are not, for that reason, naturally more just.

The forms of power which are developed collectively display an even wider variety of types. On the whole, social power rests upon differentiations of social function. The soldier is the bearer of physical force in advanced societies, not because he is physically strong, but because he has the instruments, and masters the techniques, of physical conflict. The priest has social power (especially potent in the organization of early empires) because he mediates the authority of some ultimate majesty and endows the political authority of a given oligarchy with this sanctity. The ownership and the control of property and economic process represents partly physical and partly spiritual power. It is physical in so far as the wealth created by the economic process is physical. It is spiritual in so far as the right to use and control this physical force is derived from law, custom, the prestige of function and other similar considerations.

The modern belief that economic power is the most basic form, and that all other forms are derived from it, is erroneous. The first landlords were soldiers and priests who used military and religious forms of social power to possess and to acquire land. Economic power, before the modern period, was derivative rather than primary. It was used to enhance the comforts of the oligarchs of society and to insure the perpetuation of their social eminence from generation to generation. But it did not give them their initial eminence. In modern Germany, Nazi political oligarchs transmuted political power into economic power. In the bourgeois period economic power did tend to become more fundamental and to bend other forms to its purposes. In democratic societies it was, however, always under some restraint from the more widely diffused political power of the common man, inhering in the universal right of suffrage.

It has been an error in both liberal and Marxist social interpretations to identify ownership with economic power. The control and manipulation of economic process is also a form of economic power. It gives workers minimal power resources to set against the power of ownership; and the managers of economic process are acquiring an even larger share of power. James Burnham's *The Managerial Revolution* is a one-sided correction of the error of identifying ownership with economic power too simply. The error contributes to the political miscalculations of Marxism. For when it abolishes economic ownership it may merely merge both economic and political power in the hands of an oligarchy which controls both political and economic processes.

Political power deserves to be placed in a special category, because it rests upon the ability to use and manipulate other forms of social power for the particular purpose of organizing and dominating the community.[27] The political power in any society is held by the group which commands the most significant type of non-political power, whether it be military prowess, priestly prestige, economic ownership or the ability to manipulate the technical processes of the community.[28] The political oligarchy usually possesses at least two forms of significant social power. In all early empires these two forms were the priestly and the military power, which were either merged in one class, or combined through intimate collaboration between the military and the priestly classes.

Modern democracies tend toward a more equal justice partly because they have divorced political power from special social functions. They endowed all men with a measure of it by giving them the right to review the policies of their leaders. This democratic principle does not obviate the formation of oligarchies in society; but it places a check upon their formation, and upon the exercise of their power. It must be observed, however, that the tyrannical oligarchy of fascism arrived at its eminence by the primary use of political power (the demagogic manipulation of the masses) and then gradually acquired the other forms of power: the control of economic process, the pretension of religious sanctity, and the control of, or collaboration with, military power.

The shifting interrelations of various types of power in human society are determined by a wide variety of historical developments from the technical to the religious level of social existence. Thus the development of modern commerce gave the middle classes new economic power. They used it to challenge the priestly-military oligarchy of feudal society. They undermined the power of land-ownership with the more dynamic economic power of the ownership of bank stock. The development of modern technical industry had a twofold effect. It both enhanced the economic power and wealth of the owners and manipulators of economic process, and it gave industrial workers a form of power (exercised for instance by their refusal to cooperate in an interrelated economic process) which the common men of agrarian societies did not have.

Sometimes a shift in power relations has a much more spiritual origin. Who can deny that the development of prophetic religion, which challenges rather than supports political majesty in the name of the majesty of God, helps to destroy priestly-military oligarchies and to create democratic societies? In this way the prophetic elements in Christianity have contributed to the rise of modern democratic societies, just as conservative elements in the Christian tradition have strengthened the pretensions of oligarchies by their uncritical identification of political power with the divine authority.

The complexity of the technical, rational and prophetic-religious factors which contributed to the rise of modern democracies illustrates the complex and intimate involvement of all these factors in the whole historical process. The interweaving of these various strands in the total fabric of historical development refutes both vitalists and rationalists.

No form of individual or social power exists without a modicum of physical force, or without a narrow pinnacle of "spirit" which transcends the conflict and tension of vital forces. But the tension and balance of such forces in any given social situation include vitalities and powers which manifest the complex unity of spirit and nature, of reason and force, in the whole of human existence.[29]

CHAPTER IX

The Necessity and Basis of Community

I. *The Individual and the Community*

The self's physical and spiritual need of others is naturally satisfied not only in casual and transient but in permanent relationship. Man is a "social," or as Aristotle has it, a "political" animal. Human communities rise from nature to every type of historical artifact. The simplest, most primordial and most persistent community is the family, which is rooted in nature, that is, in hetero-sexuality. The family lies naturally at the basis of the larger community, which is no more in primitive life than an enlarged family, with kinship feeling as the force of cohesion. Civilization gradually welds these larger families together into more powerful communities. The guile of priests and skill of warriors are operative in this enterprise, signifying the place of organized physical force and of the ideological factor in the forces of social cohesion.

The relation of the individual to the community is a complex one which could be defined as consisting of vertical and horizontal dimensions. In the vertical dimension the individual is related to the community in two sharply contradictory forms. He looks up at the community as the fulfillment of his life and the sustainer of his existence. By its organization his physical and moral needs are met. Morally the community is, in the words of Hegel, the individual's "concrete universality." [1]

The highest reaches of individual consciousness and awareness, then, are rooted in social experience and find their ultimate meaning in relation to the community. The individual is the product of the whole sociohistorical process, though he may reach a height of uniqueness which seems to transcend his social history completely. His individual decisions and achievements grow into, as well as out of, the community and find their final meaning in the community. Even the highest forms of art avail themselves of tools and forms, of characteristic insights and styles which betray the time and place of the artist; and if they rise to very great heights of individual insight they will also achieve a corresponding height of universal validity. They will illustrate, or penetrate into, some universal, rather than some particular and dated experience, and thereby will illumine the life of a more timeless and wider community.[2]

But this suggests another direction in which the individual may look in the vertical dimension, about which Hegel knew little because he, in common with most rationalists, could not comprehend the heights of human selfhood above the dimension of reason. The individual looks down upon the community because he is, as it were, higher than it. It is bound to nature more inexorably than he. It knows nothing of a dimension of the eternal beyond its own existence. It therefore clings to its life desperately and may sacrifice every dignity to preserve its mere existence. The highest moral ideal to which it can aspire is a wise self-interest, which includes others in its ambition for security. Looking down at the community from his individual height the individual is embarrassed by the difference between the moral standards of the community and his own.

Much of the world's progress has arisen from this embarrassment, for it has tended to lift the standards of the community. Whenever communities throttle the individual's uneasiness and insist that the collective sense of the good is absolute, they sink, as does modern totalitarianism, into a consistent brutality. On the other hand, the idea that the individual's uneasy conscience about collective morality can be easily transposed into collective action leads to sentimentality. This has been particularly apparent in the bourgeois ethos which erroneously imagined that communities were only provisional entities, to be dispensed with as soon as the individual had become fully emancipated. Looked at from above, the community is the frustration of the individual, even as it is his fulfillment when looked at from below. No historical progress can change the twofold relation of the individual to the community in the vertical dimension. The community will always remain both the fulfillment and the frustration of the individual.

The individual experiences his relation to the community horizontally, rather than vertically, whenever his community is in conflict with other communities. As we have seen, in moments of competition or conflict between communities, the individual tends to become identified with his community so that its pride and prestige become his own. Indeed its majesty is frequently a compensation for his own real or seeming insignificance. This fact makes the pride of national and racial communities particularly attractive to individuals who suffer from various forms of individual frustration.[3]

As a consequence of the paradoxical relationship of the individual and the community, both freedom and communal order are requirements of human life. Man requires freedom in his social organization because he is "essentially" free, which is to say that he has the capacity for indeterminate transcendence over the processes and limitations of nature. This freedom enables him to make history and to elaborate communal organizations in boundless variety and in endless breadth and extent. But he also requires community because he is by nature social. He cannot fulfill his life within himself, but only in responsible and mutual relations with his fellows.

Liberal democrats are inclined to believe that freedom is primarily a necessity for the individual, and that community and social order are necessary only because there are many individuals in a small world, so that minimal restrictions are required to prevent confusion. Actually the community requires freedom as much as the individual; and the individual requires order as much as does the community.

Both the individual and the community require freedom so that neither communal nor historical restraints may prematurely arrest the potencies which inhere in man's essential freedom and which express themselves collectively as well as individually. It is true that individuals are usually the initiators of new insights and the proponents of novel methods. Yet there are collective forces at work in society which are not the conscious contrivance of individuals. In any event society is as much the beneficiary of freedom as the individual. In a free society new forces may enter into competition with the old and gradually establish themselves. In a traditional or tyrannical form of social organization new forces are either suppressed, or they establish themselves at the price of social convulsion and upheaval.

The order of the community is, on the other hand, a boon to the individual as well as to the community. The individual cannot be a true self in isolation. Nor can he live within the confines of the community which "nature" establishes in the minimal cohesion of family and herd. His freedom transcends these limits of nature, and therefore makes larger and larger social units both possible and necessary. It is precisely because of the essential freedom of man that he requires a contrived order in his community.[4]

Thus the obligation to limit the struggle for power, to build and to perfect communal life, is not merely forced upon us by the necessity of coming to terms with the rather numerous hosts whom it has pleased an Almighty Creator to place on this little earth beside us. Community is an individual as well as social necessity; for the individual can realize himself only in intimate and organic relation with his fellowmen. Love is therefore the primary law of his nature; and brotherhood the fundamental requirement of his social existence.[5]

II. *The Organic Foundations of Community*

In building and preserving any kind of community, we must give due weight to the following factors:

1. The inclination of the individual to consider other than his own needs. Without this capacity for justice, the harmony and order of communities would depend purely upon coercion. In social philosophies such as that of Thomas Hobbes, the presupposition that men are consistently egoistic naturally leads to political conclusions in which freedom is sacrificed to the supposed necessities of order and no guarantees of justice are given.

2. Despite the capacity of men to consider the needs and interests of others, they also have an inclination to follow their own interests with little regard for the larger interests. This inclination must be defined not merely as "self-interest" but as "particular" interest in contrast to a more universal system of interests. The particular interest may be that of the family or of an economic group, in contrast to that of the national community; or the interest of the national community in contrast to that of the community of nations.

3. Traditional, historical, organic, and natural forces of communal cohesion such as common language, ethnic kinship, geographic factors, common experiences, and common perils. All of these factors operate below the level of conscious decision and bind men together in ways which are not explicitly coercive on the one hand but are on the other hand not the contractual relations of the business community. They create large areas of habitual rather than voluntary association, but their cohesive force is implicit rather than explicit and covert rather than overt.

4. The conscious contrivances of statecraft which seek to prevent partial and parochial interests from clashing in chaotic competition or conflict, which provide channels for the maximum degree of cooperation, which suppress undue recalcitrance against minimal standards of justice and order, which equalize fortuitous inequalities in the interest of justice, and which create a larger community than is possible upon the basis of the "natural" limits of human sympathy and concern for the neighbor.[6]

1. COMMUNITY AS ORGANISM AND ARTIFACT

The considerations listed above suggest the two cohesive elements in all communities: the organic ties of nature and history, and the conscious contrivances of men in positions of authority. These two elements are necessary because man is both creature and creator, a unity of vitality and reason. Thus, the social coherence of life can never be purely contrived and rational. It must include an interpenetration of all powers and potencies, emotional and volitional as well as rational.[7]

Every human community, then, is both organism and artifact. It is an organism insofar as it is integrated by loyalties, forms of cohesion and hierarchies of authority which have grown unconsciously with a minimum of conscious contrivance. The concept of "organism" is of course only roughly applicable to anything in history because historical developments, even in primitive communities, are never purely unconscious.

The community and its authorities are artifacts insofar as the form of cohesion and the integration of the community have been consciously contrived. The early empires were artifacts rather than organisms insofar as the imperial cohesion, above the level of the city-states which were the components of empire, was contrived by the military and priestly statesmen.

All early civilizations, including our European one until the disintegration of the traditional society of the Middle Ages, were more nearly organisms than artifacts. Kings and their ministers did, of course, consciously manipulate the loyalties which furnished the bonds of community; but no one thought of the possibility of forming a community or even a government purely by an act of the will. The "social contract" theory had not yet been conceived. The principle of legitimacy in dynastic rule was, for example, one symbol of the organic quality of traditional communities. It expressed the significance of continuity as a source of authority.[8]

Communities are in fact created less by political mechanism than by attitudes of mutual respect and trust. Society is older than human history and exists wherever individuals establish these relations of mutual reverence and trust. The family is usually the beginning of society because here nature aids the imagination and consanguinity creates an atmosphere of mutual trust. The family is enlarged by the fortunes and the needs of war; the resulting clans may amalgamate into larger units through intermarriage of leaders or through other exigencies; and the emerging national or racial group is formed by similar forces.[9] *

The communities of the world, imperial and national, which have achieved a high degree of integration, all have had some core of ethnic homogeneity, though various and heterogeneous elements may be on the periphery. They have also been bound together by particular and unique cultural forces such as a common language; common religious, legal and moral concepts; economic mutuality; and common traditions

* See *The Structure of Nations and Empires,* pp. 150–81, for a comprehensive survey of modern nations and the variety of factors out of which the national communities grew.

and experiences. The authority of the government in such communities is not infrequently derived from the same history from which the community derived its unity. The prestige of the House of Orange in Holland, for instance, is intimately related to the history of the Dutch emancipation from Spain. Not infrequently the source of unity in a national community, the root of its collective self-consciousness, is provided by the experience of facing a common foe. This experience of arriving at communal self-consciousness through encounter with an enemy is a particularly significant symbol of the role which particularity plays in establishing national communities.

Geographic limitation, ethnic and cultural uniqueness distinguishing this from other communities, and a common history, usually embodying comradeship in meeting a common foe, all contribute to the cohesion of communities. Governments develop to express and to perfect the unity thus achieved, but they do not create what they must presuppose.[10]

One must also include under the "organic" aspect of community the force of mutually and historically acknowledged rights and responsibilities, in comparison with the "inalienable" rights which are worthless if no community acknowledges them. One must further include standards of justice which have developed by slow and unconscious growth rather than by conscious political intervention. Finally, to the organic aspects one must reckon the hierarchies of authority which develop in every political and economic realm, and which contribute to the organization of the community and often symbolize its unity and continuity.[11]

To illustrate, the institution of monarchy—more precisely the hereditary principle by which sovereignty is transmitted from generation to generation—is symbolic of the fact that the authority by which a community orders its life is not merely a conscious contrivance, as the "social contract" theory of government wrongly supposed. It is, further, something more than the particular governments which are made and unmade by popular will. It represents the slow accretion of authority and prestige at one particular center which is transmitted and perfected by the organic processes of history. Conscious intent, which is symbolized by parliamentary government, is an important element in the establishment of justice; but the adjustment of interest to interest, and the mutual acknowledgment of rights which proceeds "providentially" and not by conscious contrivance, is symbolized by the continuities of the monarchy.

The rich symbolism of the British coronation ceremony is itself a product of history. The anointment and enthronement, the scepter, rod and crown, are acts and symbols which historic experience has elaborated, beginning with Zadok's anointment of King Solomon. Poetic symbols such as these are so important in our communal life because they represent many processes of justice and slow developments of authority which are too complex and inexact to be scientifically apprehended. They must be grasped imaginatively. Of course the monarchy symbolizes not only the historic continuities of a healthy organic society, but the unity of a people beyond party division, and the majesty of the state beyond the authority of particular governments, made and unmade at the people's will. How can a nation or any community arrive at a consciousness of its total unity without such poetic symbols? [12]

Even a tyrant may serve, in perverse fashion, as the symbol of community. The pathos of Stalinism is instructive because it clearly reveals that the same power which corrupts is also able to secure uncritical compliance with, and acceptance of, its pretensions. It does this partly because it is able to suppress all critical estimates of its character, but also because there is a disposition in the human heart to attribute moral character to the symbol of the community. For if that symbol is acknowledged to be as tainted as it actually is, the very meaning of man's social existence is called into question.

The long history of absolute monarchy is instructive on the same point. All absolute monarchs were invested in the imagination of the subjects with virtues which they did not possess, particularly in the days of their youth. The resultant disillusionment was never politically potent as long as it operated within the framework of the system of monarchy. But ultimately the disillusionments and resentments did generate the democratic rebellions against absolute monarchs. It may be worth recording that in the present day, when monarchs have been shorn of their power and the obvious moral ambiguities of power have been removed, there is no limit to the adulation which a constitutional monarch receives from his or her "subjects." The individual's imagination insists on as pure a symbol of the community and its majesty as possible.

We even see this imagination at work in democracies, particularly in the case of a President like Eisenhower, who seems to stand partly above the party conflicts. It is interesting to observe that even the most sophisticated are inclined to adopt the attitude of the naive Russian peasants, who were wont to say: "The nobles are bad, but the Tsar is good." The ultimate symbol must be kept inviolate as long as possible, even in defiance of the facts.[13]

2. THE ERROR OF THE SOCIAL CONTRACT THEORY

Government presupposes community and cannot create it for the simple reason that the authority of government is not primarily the authority of law nor the authority of force, but the authority of the community itself. Laws are obeyed because the community accepts them as corresponding, on the whole, to its conception of justice. This is particularly true of democratically organized communities. But it is well to observe that even in traditional, non-democratic communities of the past there was a discernible difference between tyranny and legitimate government. It consisted precisely in the fact that a legitimate government relied primarily upon the implicit consent of the community.

Even in a national constitutional system, such as our own, we have seen how limited is the power of law whenever a portion of the community adheres to moral standards which differ from those of the total community. We have had this experience both with the prohibition movement and with the question of civil rights for Negroes in southern states. The police power of a government cannot be a pure political artifact. It is an arm of the community's body. If the body is in pieces, the arm cannot integrate it.

It should be noted, of course, that the priority of the community to its laws and its use of force does not mean that both law and force may not have limited efficacy in perfecting the organization and preserving the integrity of the community. Good constitutions provide for the rational arbitrament of many conflicting and competing forces which might otherwise tear the community apart. Preponderant force in one part of the community may also so shape the social forces of the total community that its use need not be perpetual. Thus the preponderant force of the northern states decided the issue whether our nation was a nation or merely a federation of states. But force is no longer necessary to guarantee the loyalty of the southern states to our union.[14]

The symbol of modern man's belief that both community and government are merely artifacts, that is, the creations of the human will and reason, is the social contract theory, which was propounded by such divergent theorists as the liberal democrat John Locke, the proponent of royal absolutism Thomas Hobbes, and the totalitarian democrat Rousseau. The theory assumed a mythical "state of nature" before the rise of civil society, to which the various theorists attributed contradictory virtues and vices. For Thomas Hobbes the state of nature meant the "war of all against all"; for John Locke it was a state of imperfect order and harmony, suffering from the "inconvenience" of allowing every man to be "a judge in his own case." For Rousseau it was a state of unabridged freedom.

None of these presuppositions, of course, remotely resembled the character of primitive society. Indeed the reality of primitive society, of organic communities which developed into more advanced civilizations, proves the invalidity of the assumptions underlying the social contract theory. For the community is as primordial as the individual. The social contract theory was primarily the expression of the individualism and voluntarism of the rising business community. It was beguiled by its possession of mobile and flexible instruments of power and by the disintegration of traditional society to assume that all men had the power not only to determine their own destinies but the destiny of their communities.

This excessive voluntarism was of course accompanied by a confident rationalism. It was thought that men would only have to exercise their reason to conceive of more just social and political integrations. Both faith and tradition (for religion was obviously a support of tradition) were discredited. Were they not simply the "superstitions" which a more astute intelligence would dissolve?

These uncritical approaches to the past flowered in the French Enlightenment, but they characterized the social viewpoints of modernity from the seventeenth to the nineteenth century. They were motivated by a strong desire for justice within the context of the emerging commercial and industrial community. But they were blind to the contributions which the traditional organs of community made to communal integration, failing to recognize that, even if the price in justice which they exacted was too high, they did serve as organs of integration.[15]

One reason why the social contract conception of government has a particular plausibility with us is because the United States came closer to a birth by "contract" than any other nation. But the preamble of our constitution declares that its purpose is to establish a "more perfect union." That is a very telling phrase which presupposes a previous union. This previous union was in fact established on the battlefield in a common struggle against a common foe; it needed only to be made "more perfect." It may be observed in passing that, though the thirteen colonies had never enjoyed sovereignty, they did not find it too easy to submit what had only been potential, and not actual, sovereignty to the authority of the federal union. We fought a civil war before it was proved that they had in fact done this without reservations.[16]

Thus we must conclude that even the wisest statecraft cannot create social tissue. It can cut, sew and redesign social fabric to a limited degree. But the social fabric upon which it works must be "given." [17] *

* In Chapter XXI Niebuhr applies his thesis on the relation of community and government to the problem of establishing world government.

CHAPTER X

Structures of Power

I. *The Structures of Power and Their Corruptions*

All social cooperation on a larger scale than the most intimate social group requires a measure of coercion.[1] The limitations of the human mind and imagination, the inability of human beings to transcend their own interests sufficiently to envisage the interests of their fellowmen as clearly as they do their own makes force an inevitable part of the process of social cohesion.[2]

It is true, as we have seen, that the internal order and peace of a community and its security and stability in the total community of nations is not maintained by power alone. Internal peace and justice are maintained only on the basis of organic cohesions and by a decent organization of the mutually dependent and partially conflicting vitalities of national life. External peace depends upon the same principles of organization.

Yet the internal justice of a community is never so perfect and the accommodation of interests so complete that any society could dispense with the alloy of coercion in the amalgam of its social peace. Nor is it possible to secure the external peace of a community in the partial, and sometimes total, anarchy of nations, without balancing power against power in times of peace and without setting power against power in times of war.[3]

All communities, then, are more or less stable or precarious harmonies of human vital capacities. They are governed by power. The power which determines the quality of the order and harmony is not merely the coercive and organizing power of government. That is only one of the two aspects of social power. The other is the balance of vitalities and forces in any given social situation. These two elements of communal life—the central organizing power, and the equilibrium of power—are essential and perennial aspects of community organization; and no moral or social advance can redeem society from its dependence upon these two principles.

Since there are various possibilities of so managing and equilibrating the balance of social forces in a given community that the highest possible justice may be achieved, and since the organizing principle and power in the community is also subject to indeterminate refinement, communal order and justice can approximate a more perfect brotherhood in varying degree. But each principle of communal organization—the organization of power and the balance of power—contains possibilities of contradicting the law of brotherhood. The organizing principle and power may easily degenerate into domination and tyranny. It may create a coerced unity of society in which the freedom and vitality of all individual members are impaired. Such a tyrannical unification of life is a travesty on brotherhood. Again, the principle of the balance of power is always pregnant with the possibility of anarchy. These twin evils, tyranny and anarchy, represent the Scylla and Charybdis between which the frail bark of social justice must sail. It is almost certain to founder upon one rock if it makes the mistake of regarding the other as the only peril.[4]

Consequently political community must be brought into being by considering first how the creation of a power and authority at its center may check the tendency toward distintegration. The second consideration is how a proper equilibrium among the various units may check the tendency toward domination from the center. This is the correct approach toward the difficult problem of government in general.[5]

And since human history defies, rather than observes, the limits in which nature confines both mutual dependence and conflict, it becomes a task of conscious political contrivance in human history to mitigate conflict and to invent instruments for the enlarging mutualities of social existence.[6] While no society can maintain its health if the individuals who compose it do not have some sense of responsibility for their fellow men, it is also true that no society could live if it did not harness, equilibrate and deflect, as well as sublimate and suppress, self-interest. Human society is partly an artful contrivance which enables men to serve one another indirectly, even though their primary motives may be to serve themselves.[7]

The statesman, as the artful contriver, avoids tyranny by balancing the vitalities, powers, interests of life into a tolerable equilibrium. But such an equilibrium has the peril of anarchy in it if it is not organized and directed. This organization means that we must give some one, some class, some government, some nation, or some group of nations, more authority than others. There is no way of completely obliterating the distinction between the rulers and the ruled, however much we may give the ruled the chance to check the rulers. But where there are rulers, there may also be tyrants.[8]

It is important both to recognize the higher possibilities of justice in every historic situation, and to know that the twin perils of tyranny and anarchy can never be completely overcome in any political achievement. These perils are expressions of the sinful elements of conflict and dominion, standing in contradiction to the ideal of brotherhood on every level of communal organization. There is no possibility of making history completely safe against either occasional conflicts of vital interests (war) or against the misuse of the power which is intended to prevent such conflict of interests (tyranny).[9]

II. *The Balance of Power and the Peril of Anarchy*

All political community and justice are achieved by coercing the anarchy of collective self-interest into some kind of decent order by the most attainable balance of power. Such a balance, once achieved, can be stabilized, embellished, and even, on occasion, perfected by more purely moral considerations. But there has never been a scheme of justice in history which did not have a balance of power at its foundation.[10] That is, the domination of one life by another is avoided most successfully by an equilibrium of powers and vitalities, so that weakness does not invite enslavement by the strong. Without a tolerable equilibrium no moral or social restraints ever succeed completely in preventing injustice and enslavement. In this sense an equilibrium of vitality is an approximation of brotherhood within the limits of conditions imposed by human selfishness.

But an equilibrium of power is not brotherhood. The restraint of the will-to-power of one member of the community by the counter-pressure of power by another member results in a condition of tension.[11] Such a balance of power does not exclude love. In fact, without love the frictions and tensions of a balance of power would become intolerable. But without the balance of power even the most loving relations may degenerate into unjust relations, and love may become the screen which hides the injustice.

Family relations are instructive at this point. Women did not gain justice from men, despite the intimacy of family relations, until they secured sufficient economic power to challenge male autocracy. There are Christian "idealists" today who speak sentimentally of love as the only way to justice, whose family life might benefit from a more delicate "balance of power."

Naturally the tensions of such a balance may become overt; and overt tensions may degenerate into conflict.[12] The principle of the equilibrium of power is thus a principle of justice insofar as it prevents domination and enslavement; but it is a principle of anarchy and conflict insofar as its tensions, if unresolved, result in overt conflict.[13]

It is sometimes possible to shift the balance without overt violence, though probably not without some risk of violence. Sometimes the balance can only be shifted by violence. Whether one prefers an established social peace or the dangers and actualities of violence concomitant with the shifting of social equilibria, depends upon the degree of justice realized in the peace. Any state of social injustice which reduces a part of the population to such penury and oppression as to make the risk of its violent overthrow a preferable alternative is bound to issue in revolution.[14] *

III. *The Organization of Power and the Peril of Tyranny*

Social life, when not consciously managed and manipulated, does not develop perfect equilibria of power. Its capricious disproportions of power generate various forms of domination and enslavement. Human society therefore requires a conscious control and manipulation of the various equilibria which exist in it.[15]

A balance of power is in fact a kind of managed anarchy. But even so it is a system in which anarchy invariably overcomes the management in the end. An equilibrium of power without the organizing and equilibrating force of government is potential anarchy which becomes actual anarchy in the long run.[16]

Thus society requires more positive organs of communal integration, which are chiefly three: government, social hierarchy and property. Of these three, the social hierarchy, which provides for integration below the level of obvious government, is not so much an "institution" as a general social phenomenon.[17] If we define phenomena of social hierarchy and stratification as "below the level of government," we can do this only tentatively. For all subordination of life to leadership in the various activities of the community is in a sense "government," though pluralistic and democratic communities have understood how to create independent centers of authority without relating them to state authority. The establishment of grades of authority inevitably leads to social stratification because grades of privilege invariably are related to grades of authority and power.

Property is related to this stratification because it is the primary instrument for transmitting authority and privilege from generation to generation. It is this function of property which makes the institution morally

* The principles of modern democracy are essentially extensions and elaborations of the strategy of balance of power (Chapter XVI). Other contemporary applications of the strategy include the efforts of democratic states to prevent undue concentrations of economic power within their domestic orders (Chapter XVIII), and attempts by the Western alliance to stabilize the relations among nations (Chapter XXV).

so ambiguous. For property as the consequence of mixing our labor with nature (John Locke) and property as the right of inheriting power and privilege are certainly in different categories of moral legitimacy.[18]

There are some very obtrusive evidences of the perennial nature of these social hierarchies in our daily life. Begininng with the family, we know of integrations of the community in which power and competence are the levers of authority to subordinate some men to others. Conservatives have generally derived explicit analogies from the authority of the father in order to justify monarchy. Locke spent most of his polemic fire upon this analogy in his *Two Essays on Civil Government*. But the conservatives were certainly in closer accord with history than the social contract theorists who posited a wholly mythical "state of nature." The family is indeed the embryo of all social integration.

Above the level of the family we meet the pattern of integration and coordination of life through subordination on every hand: schools with more than one teacher have a "principal"; and school sytems with more than one school have a "superintendent"; churches are supervised by a bishop. The extreme congregational polity of sectarian churches, which is the counterpart in the religious community of the libertarianism and equalitarianism of the modern age, was modified by experience; and the modification was obscured by giving the effective bishops the title of "superintendent." The industrial life of the nation is integrated from factory foreman to superintendent, to manager, to owner. In every sphere of life this integration of the community through social hierarchy has proved necessary and inevitable.[19]

1. THE FUNCTIONS OF GOVERNMENT

Turning specifically to the organ of government, it is clear that there must be an organizing center within a given field of social vitalities [20]—a center of authority and power to act as an organ of the will of the community both in establishing its unity and in giving it cohesion in competition with other communities.[21] This center must arbitrate conflicts from a more impartial perspective than is available to any party of a given conflict; it must manage and manipulate the processes of mutual support so that the tensions inherent in them will not erupt into conflict; it must coerce submission to the social process by superior power whenever the instruments of arbitrating and composing conflict do not suffice; and finally it must seek to redress the disproportions of power by conscious shifts of the balances whenever they make for injustice.

It is obvious that the principle of government, or the organization of the whole realm of social vitalities, stands upon a higher plane of moral sanction and social necessity than the principle of the balance of power.

The latter without the former degenerates into anarchy. The principle of government is, moreover, a more conscious effort to arrive at justice than the principle of balance of power. It belongs to the order of the historical while the power balance belongs, on the whole, to the order of the natural.

Rousseau's and Hobbes' social contract theories of government have such contradictory estimates of the "state of nature" because both fail to understand the ambiguous character of social equilibrium without the interference of government. Rousseau sees only the elements of harmony within it, and Hobbes only the elements of conflict and anarchy. Rousseau on the other hand sees only the principle of domination in government and Hobbes only the principle of order.[22]

Actually, not only the abuse of human freedom but also its responsible exercise require that human society have a cement of cohesion transcending the natural sociality of animal existence. All structures of justice do indeed presuppose the sinfulness of man, and are all partly systems of restraint which prevent the conflict of wills and interests from resulting in a consistent anarchy. But they are also all mechanisms by which men fulfill their obligations to their fellow men, beyond the possibilities offered in direct voluntary and personal relationships.[23]

A conscription law in a democracy, for instance, may represent, not so much the unjust claims of a national community upon the individual, as the recognition by many individuals that it is fairer for an impartial judge to determine what order of preference family duties and specific skills ought to have in relation to the duty to defend the nation and the skill of the potential soldier. Taxation schedules are another case in point. Any system of taxation is coercive as it impinges upon the individual taxpayer. But the same taxpayer who feels the coercion when he pays the tax may vote for it as the most equitable way of distributing the common burdens of a community, and also as a method of supporting his own long-range sense of duty toward the community as against a short-range disinclination to do so.[24]

Thus, though it is true that government must have the power to subdue recalcitrance, it also has a more positive function. It must guide, direct, deflect and rechannel conflicting and competing forces in a community in the interest of a higher order. It must provide instruments for the expression of the individual's sense of obligation to the community as well as weapons against the individual's anti-social lusts and ambitions.[25] Indeed, a healthy society forces practically all people to be just beyond their natural inclinations by establishing standards of justice which gain the moral assent of the majority of the population but yet operate against the immediate inclinations even of some of the good people who helped to establish the standards.[26]

2. THE SOURCES OF GOVERNMENTAL AUTHORITY

The question of the sources of governmental power or authority has been consistently raised in history. A simple cynical answer to this question is given by many. It is that authority stems from force and that the government or nation has authority which has the capacity to compel obedience to its decisions. But this answer rests upon a too simple identification of physical force and authority. It neglects the factor of prestige as a source of authority.

It is true that no government can either exercise internal authority or marshal the community's strength for conflict with other communities without a minimal degree of physical force as one of the ingredients of its power.[27] Indeed force alone may be a tentative source of power, at the beginning of a reign or after a revolution. Coercion enforces obedience until the authority of government has been established, when it may win uncoerced consent by its prestige.[28] But authority dependent purely upon force is rightly regarded as insufferable in the long run because force connotes unwilling obedience against the inclinations of the members of the community. In short, authority must rest upon either implicit or explicit consent rather than merely upon the force to compel conformity to its will.

This is to say that the attempt of a government to exercise internal authority without at least implicit consent destroys community. It generates resentments which require more and more force to suppress. Hence despotisms are short-lived even if they combine fraud with force to generate a spurious consent. In conflict situations *among* communities it is taken for granted that military force is the *ultima ratio*. But it is equally true, though not equally obvious, that force alone is subject to a law of diminishing returns even in the external relations of communities.[29]

We have suggested that the "consent" ingredient of authority may be either implicit or explicit. The prestige of political authority in traditional communities seems so absurd to the modern mind that a great chasm would seem to exist between democratic governments deriving the authority of the "ruler" from "the consent of the governed" and the traditional rulers who derive their prestige from such claims as that of incorporating the cosmic order. But while the chasm is great it is not as great as the modern imagination assumes.[30] Traditional government is more legitimate than pure democrats are inclined to believe because it has enough implicit consent to dispense with fraud and to rely on only a minimum of force. And while democratic government relies upon explicit consent for the authority of a particular government, it must also rely on implicit consent for the authority of the system of government which permits the alternation of particular governments by popular will.[31]

Indeed, the democratic principle which derives the authority of government from the "consent of the governed" and exalts the "sovereign people" as the source of all authority does not describe so simple a process as Locke and other rationalist democratic theorists assumed. The explicit consent which is given or withheld from particular parliamentary governments, expressing the will of a people at a given moment, may be more or less rational. But the authority and majesty of a governmental system which allows this alternation of particular governments is not so simply rational. As other theorists such as Hume, Burke and Montesquieu have shown, this authority rests upon habits of loyalty and confidence in its stability; in short, upon an implicit consent derived not so much from rational calculations as from emotions, habits and traditions, growing out of organic and historical experiences, and analogous to the sources of loyalty in traditional communities.[32]

In any case, if we define majesty or prestige as the principal source of the community's consent, and thus of the government's authority, it is necessary to identify the component elements of prestige. These differ somewhat as between traditional and modern democratic polities.

Before the rise of democracy, legitimate governments drew their authority from various ideological systems which were identical in their emphasis upon justifying the authority of government chiefly by its ability to maintain peace and order, providing the order was not bought at too great a price of justice. Justice is always a secondary, but not a primary, source of authority and prestige. The primary source is the capacity to maintain order, because order is tantamount to existence in a community and chaos means non-existence.

The ability to maintain order in traditional governments since the rise of the first empires in Egypt and Babylon rested on the authority derived on the one hand from the prestige of continued rule and on the other hand from the prestige gained through the claim that the political order was an extension and an application of the cosmic order. In the one case the "legitimacy" of dynastic inheritance guaranteed the transmission of authority from generation to generation. In the other case idolatrous claims were made for the priest-kings and God-kings of Egypt and Babylon in order that both legitimacy in the narrow sense and in the sense of the ultimacy of the order would guarantee the "majesty" necessary to prevent chaos. In both cases, reverence for an order which a given generation could not create but from which it could benefit was involved. This is the valid religious element in the majesty of government. The priests did not create this reverence for Providence but they could manipulate it. They were, therefore, the chief agents of the "organization of consent" in the ancient empires.[33]

The substance of the prestige of the national kings rests on the legitimacy of their rule, and that legitimacy is established by dynastic succession. Kings of the Christian nations were never thought to be divine, yet they still claimed to rule by "divine right." The right was inherited from their fathers. The principle of dynastic legitimacy is so absurd a principle of selection of men fit to rule that its persistence throughout all history, despite the weight of injustice which absolute monarchy created, must have some fairly obvious cause. That cause is the prevention of anarchy, the avoidance of competing claims to the throne upon the death of the monarch. Dynastic legitimacy from the Egyptian Pharaohs to the kings of contemporary nations was a fairly simple way of insuring implicit consent and thus dispensing with the necessity of a clash of force to determine the right to rule.[34]

Further, in all traditional societies religious and philosophical claims are obviously used to increase the prestige of the ruler. It is significant that priests and soldiers were partners in both primitive and civilized traditional societies. The soldiers were the obvious wielders of force, but the priests or priest-kings were more potent in the partnership because they organized and manipulated the ideological system which gives the soldier the right to use force in the interest and in behalf of the community. It must be understood that the term "priest" is used symbolically. It includes the political oligarchs of an atheist communist state, who have recently given abundant proof that they can maintain ascendancy over the soldier.

The religious prestige of the ancient dynasty, then, both obscured the force which established it and made force less necessary in preserving its authority. But it is wrong to assume that religion is the only ideological source of prestige for the authority of government. Aristotle manages to veil both the factor of force and the interested nature of dominion in his study of politics. For him, the relation between the political order and the cosmic order is established by a rational law which imitates the reason of the cosmos. This metaphysical method of obscuring the factors of interest and power in the dominion of the community differs from the religious approach. Yet from Plato to Hegel the philosophical identification of some contingent establishment of political order with the cosmic order is not as different from the religious sanctification of dominion as it may at first appear. It is surely significant, for instance, that both Plato and Aristotle took the Athenian city-state for granted as the final form of political community, thus betraying that the purest reason must begin with some historical presuppositions.

In any case traditional communities, whether city-states or empire, were as interested in proving that the ruler used his power disinterestedly because he had contact with or embodied the cosmic, divine order as modern liberalism is concerned to prove that dominion is responsive to the public interest, empirically determined.[35] Study of the sanctificationist tendencies of Christianity, Islam, communism and even Buddhism will illumine the ability of the impulse to dominion on every level to use the most varied and contradictory religious impulses and philosophies as instruments of its purposes.[36] *

In short, the ideological support for political power in traditional communities, whether of Pharaoh, Emperor, Pope or King, whether in pagan or in Christian cultures, was contained in the twin emphases upon Providence: the stability of a dynastic house, transmitting authority through the generations; and its relation to cosmic or divine order and intention. Through all these millennia it was order, and not justice or freedom, which was the primary concern of the architects of political community.

But the authority of traditional community produced injustice as well as order. And so the modern democratic society slowly came into being, in which the prestige of justice was added to that of order as a source of authority, and freedom and equality were adopted as standards of justice. A free society must have a proper reverence for the principle of government as a source of order, but also a proper insistence that the power of government be brought under control of the people and that the majesty of government be partly derived from its capacity for justice. This ideological shift resulted from a variety of factors; so that the culture and climate which supports democratic authority in the Western world is thus drawn partly from the peculiar flexibilities and necessities of a technical society, partly from the Christian tradition which values the individual as transcending any social process and political community, and partly from modern secularism and empiricism which generated the temper of criticism and punctured the religious pretensions which were the source of so much political authority in the past.[37]

Obviously, the achievement of justice, or the reputation or hope for its achievement, is the chief source of prestige with which we have to deal in estimating the authority of a modern government in both its internal and external relations. We can affirm that any authority without this element of prestige is defective. But we cannot say exactly how much or how little of prestige and force can be compounded in authority. We can only define authority resting solely on force as detrimental to the justice of the community and to its effectiveness in competition or conflict with other communities.[38]

* For elaboration of this thesis, see Chapters VI and VII of *The Structure of Nations and Empires*.

3. DOMINATION AND TYRANNY

Ideally the coercive power of government is established by the whole society and is held responsible to it. The most obvious rational check which can be placed upon the use of coercion is to submit it to the control of an impartial tribunal which will not be tempted to use it for selfish ends. Thus society claims the right to use coercion but denies the same right to individuals. The police power of nations is a universally approved function of government. The supposition is that the government is impartial with reference to any disputes arising between citizens, and will therefore be able to use its power for moral ends.[39]

Actually the ideal is never completely attained even in the most democratic societies. The oligarchy which helps to organize a community gains its position either by the military prowess by which it subjugated the community or by some priestly prestige which gave its will and law an authority beyond its own power, or (as in modern states) by some special measure of power or skill with which it organized the vital forces of the community. Government is thus at once the source of order and the root of injustice in a community. Thus the external peace between communities is marred by competitive strife and the internal peace by class domination. Both forms of sin are related to the insecurity of the community. It must make itself powerful to ward off the peril of the external foe; and it must allow an oligarchy to arise within it to ward off the peril of anarchy.

The indictment of the nations by the prophets of the Old Testament was concerned with these two facets of collective sin. Israel was indicted for seeking its own ends, rather than the will of God. The prophets sought to make nations as well as individuals conform to the absolute and final possibilities of human existence. The other facet of the prophetic indictment concerned the "elders," the "princes" and the "judges" of Israel. They were accused of exploiting their eminence in the community for their own advantage. This second indictment calls attention to the inevitable corruption of government because the coercive power required to maintain order and unity in a community is never a pure and disinterested power. It is exercised from a particular center and by a particular group in society.

In the modern period the liberal society assumed that it had destroyed every specific center of power in the community by the democratic checks which were placed upon the organs of government. But this proved to be an illusion. The proletarian revolt against bourgeois society was prompted by resentment against the injustices which arose from the inordinate power of the commercial and industrial oligarchy of modern society. The new communist society made the same mistake in turn. It assumed that the destruction of an oligarchy whose power rested in ownership would create an idyllic society without oligarchic power. But this new society came under the tyrannical power of a new oligarchy of political overlords, who combined economic and political power in a single organ. These modern errors prove the persistence of the tendency of the organs of order in a community to become instruments of injustice. The same power required to establish the unity of a society also becomes the basis of injustice in it because it seeks its own ends, rather than the common weal.[40]

Aside from the sinful proclivities of the rulers themselves, there is in every community as such an instinctive avoidance of social conflict, and a superficiality in dealing with the roots of social disaffection, which increase the possibility of the unjust use of the police power of the state against individuals and groups who break its peace, no matter how justified their grievance. A community may be impartial in using coercion against two disputants whose dispute offers no peril to the life and prestige of the community. But wherever such a dispute affects the order or the prestige of the community, its impartiality evaporates. The prejudice and passion with which a staid, genteel and highly cultured New England community conducted itself in the Sacco-Vanzetti case is a vivid example. For these reasons it is impossible to draw too sharp a moral distinction between the use of force and coercion under the control of impartial tribunals and its use by individuals and groups who make it a frank instrument of their own interests.[41]

The ruler's abuse of power may take one of two forms. It may actually be the dominion which one portion of the community exercises over the whole of the community. Most governments until a very recent period were in fact just that; they were the consequence of conquest by a foreign oligarchy. But even if government does not express the imperial impulse of one class or group within the community, it will, if its pretensions are not checked, generate imperial impulses of its own towards the community. It will be tempted to destroy the vitality and freedom of component elements in the community in the name of "order." It will identify its particular form of order with the principle of order itself, and thus place all rebels against its authority under the moral disadvantage of revolting against order *per se*. This is the sin of idolatry and pretension in which all government is potentially involved.[42]

Failure to perceive the moral ambiguity of government reveals the moral naivete of every form of absolutistic political theory. It identifies the national community with the universal and fails to recognize that the nation is also an egocentric force in history, tempted on the one hand to claim a too unconditioned position in relation to the individuals and to the subordinate institutions in the national community; and on the other hand to became a source of anarchy in the larger community of nations. Furthermore it identifies the interests of the ruler or the ruling oligarchy of a community too simply with the interests of the community. Therefore it fails to provide checks against the inordinate impulses to power to which all rulers are tempted. Hobbes identifies the interests of the ruler with those of the community in the following implausible words: "In monarchy the private interest is the same with the public interest because no prince can be rich and glorious nor secure, whose subjects are poor or weak or contemptible." [43]

This latter error may be made by some optimists as well as pessimists. The political theory of Rousseau contains the conception of a "general will" which is supposedly the final harmony of conflicting individual wills. This conception obscures the fact that there is a conflict of wills in every living community, and that the victorious will is at least partly fashioned and crystallized by the ruling oligarchy which has the instruments to express it. In a democratic society there is presumably some concurrence between the will of the rulers and that of the majority; but the Rousseauistic conception leads to constitutional forms which offer inadequate safeguards to the minority.

Marxist social theory betrays striking similarities to Rousseau's conceptions. It fails to anticipate the rise of a ruling group in a socialist society. When the group does arise, the theories are forced to obscure the initiative of the rulers, and to pretend that the policies at which the leaders arrive represent merely the expression of what the multitude has conceived.[44]

Contrary to the illusions of the absolutists, governmental tyranny is not only real; it is in fact worse than war. In the first place tyranny is itself a "cold war" which destroys life, liberty, and culture. But further, it must inevitably lead to war—it includes overt conflict as an inevitable fruit of its type of rule. In the long run it drives subject peoples to rebellion. It becomes more and more obvious that irresponsible power, whether economic or political, cannot be trusted. To allow tyranny to grow means to have war in the end. The only alternative is wider and wider submission to the ever growing ambition of tyrants. Even if nations and peoples were abject enough to submit to the will of the tyrant for a decade, they would rise against him in the end, after bitter experience had taught them that death may be preferable to a life bereft of all liberty and self-respect.[45]

Further, the same factors which make for an uneasy peace within a social group tend to aggravate intergroup conflict. Power sacrifices justice to peace within the community and destroys peace between communities. It is not true that only governments cause war. Nevertheless the whole history of mankind bears testimony to the fact that the power which prevents anarchy in intra-group relations encourages anarchy in inter-group relations. Every social group tends to develop imperial ambitions which are aggravated by the lusts of its leaders and privileged groups.[46]

The proclivity of unrestrained rulers to behave tyrannically is well illustrated by the relations of victors to vanquished after World War II. This does not mean that our cause against either Germany or Japan was not "just." We were indeed the executors of God's judgment yesterday. But we might have remembered the prophetic warnings to the nations of old, that nations which become proud because they were divine instruments must in turn stand under the divine judgment and be destroyed. The virtues of men have only a short-range efficacy. We may be virtuous in this context; and just in that relationship; and the instruments of divine judgment in performing such and such a peculiar responsibility. But this does not guarantee our virtue tomorrow. The same power which encompasses the defeat of tyranny may become the foundation of a new injustice.[47]

Our behavior during the early years of the occupation of Germany should remind us that there is something very ugly in the contrast between absolute power and absolute weakness, between luxury and poverty. Nothing was spared to make the American soldier, and more particularly an officer, comfortable. And little was done to make the almost intolerable lot of overcrowded Germans a little easier. One wonders whether men are incapable of self-restraint, when the social restraints of power no longer operate. The contrast of power and weakness is as fruitful of arrogance as the contrast of poverty and wealth is of self-indulgence. Even the best men, who know that no man deserves the absolute power he holds in such a situation, find difficulty in avoiding a certain note of arrogance in their relation to an occupied population. Among the best it assumes an air of patronizing kindness and among the worst, of brutality. An army of occupation is a vivid reminder of the necessity of striving for both equality and liberty as the basis of justice. Where these are lacking, life is brutalized.[48]

Not only government, but the two institutions of property and social stratification are in the same position of moral ambiguity. Both are necessary instruments of justice and social order, and yet both are fruitful of injustice. Both have, no less than government, grown up organically in traditional civilizations in the sense that they were unconscious adaptations to the needs of justice and order. Both were, even as government, productive of injustice. The injustice was inevitable because the economic and other privileges attendant upon special function tended to be in excess of the necessities of the function performed.[49]

Thus every civilized community tends to create and to suffer from an oligarchy which once performed a creative task in organizing the community. It tends to become increasingly burdensome in the period of decay when it exacts more wealth from the community than its services deserve or require, and when it reveals instincts of survival as a special class which come in direct conflict with the defensive needs of the community as a whole.[50]

It is a fact that those who hold great economic and political power are more guilty of pride against God and of injustice against the weak than those who lack power and prestige. Wherever the fortunes of nature, the accidents of history or even the virtues of the possessors of power, endow an individual or a group with power, social prestige, intellectual eminence or moral approval above their fellows, there an ego is allowed to expand. It expands both vertically and horizontally. Its vertical expansion, its pride, involves it in sin against God. Its horizontal expansion involves it in an unjust effort to gain security and prestige at the expense of its fellows.[51] The mighty men are like tall trees whose branches rob neighboring trees of the sunshine they require for their life. In other words, the social sin of the mighty is that they demand too high a price from society for the services they render. They not only demand it but get it. They get it because they control the organs by which society comes to self-consciousness and thinks and acts.

So whether the mighty men are priestly rulers, military chieftains, or economic overlords they always become involved in the same self-destructive process. At first they create social peace and a modicum of justice by their power. Then they disturb social peace and destroy justice by the exactions of their power. They involve society in internal strife by demanding exorbitant rewards for the service they render; also they involve it in external strife by using their control of their fellow men for the satisfaction of their imperial ambitions beyond the borders of their own social system. Thus injustice is the social consequence of pride; and the inevitable fruit of injustice is self-destruction.[52]

It is the business of politics so to organize the vitalities of human existence that a "commonwealth" will be created out of the conflicting forces and interests of human life, a task which has never been achieved in history without setting force, as the instrument of order, against force as the instrument of anarchy. The basic problem of politics is how to prevent the force which is an instrument of order on one level of social organization from becoming the instrument of either anarchy or tyranny on the next level of social integration. *Quis custodiet custodes ipsos?* [53]

CHAPTER XI

Rational, Moral and Religious Norms

I. *Norms and Their Corruptions* *

It is significant that most genuine community is established below and above the level of conscious moral idealism. Below that level we find operative the strong forces of nature and nature-history, sex and kinship, common language and geographically determined togetherness. Above the level of idealism the most effective force of community is religious humility. This includes the charitable realization that the vanities of the other group or person from which we suffer are not different in kind, though possibly in degree, from similar vanities in our own life. It also includes a religious sense of the mystery and greatness of the other life, which we violate if we seek to comprehend it too simply from our own standpoint.

Genuine community, then, whether between men or nations, is not established merely through the rational realization that we need one another, though indeed we do. Genuine community is established only when the knowledge that we need one another is supplemented by the recognition that "the other," that other form of life, or that other unique community, is the limit beyond which our ambitions must not run and the boundary beyond which our life must not expand.[1] Not logic, but love lies at the foundation of a human community.[2]

Insofar as modern men have solved their social problems and achieved communities in which the individual has a tolerable freedom and the community preserves a tolerable stability, and classes are related to each other in a tolerable justice, it will be found that both components of our culture, the Hebraic and the Hellenic, the Biblical and the classical,

* Any analysis of the factors which limit the conflicts of power and make for community must take full account of both the realities and limitations of man's capacity for justice—of the disciplining effect of rational and moral norms and inner religious checks, and of the corruption of those norms into ideology, self-righteousness, and fanaticism. Both the validity and the distortion of such norms are grounded in the nature of the human self; "intellectual, moral and spiritual pride" especially account for the distortions here considered (see Chapter VII).

the religious and the rational have made, if not equal, yet equally necessary contributions to this result.

At its best the Biblical faith guarded the "facts" of freedom and responsibility and acknowledged the self-concern of the self, which a more pretentious empiricism denied. It also introduced a sense of the dramatic quality of history and the uniqueness of its various occasions which underlies the empiricism of an Edmund Burke as contrasted with the alleged empiricism of the French Revolution. At its best, the Renaissance faith introduced the disciplines of rational discrimination which religious dogmas effaced or obscured.

At their worst, the two forces of piety and rationalism introduced similar errors into the social situation in the very debate in which they polemicised against their respective errors. There is an ironic quality in the debate between the pious and the rationalistic exponents of freedom and justice. Each accuses the other of introducing false absolutes into the contingencies of history. For the pious, the absolute is the will of God; and for the rationalists, it is the dictate of reason. Yet each side is guilty in its own way of the error of which it accuses the other.

The pious conceive the worship of God to be a guarantee against the worship of idols, that is, against undue reverence for or loyalty to contingent and finite values. Ideally the worship of the true God does emancipate the soul from the worship of self, either individually or collectively. Actually the history of religious fanaticism proves that it is fairly easy to claim identity between the absolute and the contingent value, and thus to claim divine validity for a "Christian" civilization despite all of its moral ambiguities, and to use the Christian faith as a weapon against the foe in all kinds of historic encounters.

Reason, according to the faith of a rationalistic culture, will dissolve all these irrationalities and force men to claim for themselves only those privileges which will fit into a total scheme of coherence. Reason, argued Condorcet, would force the privileged to yield their privileges, and education would arm the simple with new weapons against the shrewd. But were not most injustices due as much to the shrewd taking advantage of the simple as of the strong taking advantage of the weak? And after all, it was Aristotle who gave the most plausible and rational justification of slavery when he declared the institution to be the natural consequence of the difference in the endowments of men, of whom the intelligent were by nature destined to command while the unintelligent were by nature "tools."

The simple fact is that neither the classical, the medieval nor the modern rationalists recognized that it is as easy to identify the interest of the self with a universally acknowledged right or value as to identify it with the will of God. That is why we have had such an ironic conflict between the pious and the rationalists, each of them aware of the hypocrisy of the other but neither of them aware of the dishonesty in themselves. Ideally a Christian faith makes for humility and charity because it subjects both the claims and the pretensions of the self to an ultimate judgment. Actually religion makes for fanatic claims as frequently or more frequently than it generates charity, for reasons already analyzed.

Ideally the cultivation of reason makes for "reasonableness." It moderates claims by weighing each claim against competing claims and by challenging traditionally established privileges with the question whether they are justified by social function or any consideration of the commonweal. Actually the logical process does no more than work out conclusions on the basis of the premises upon which the process is based.[3]

The similar corruptions of fanaticism in both piety and rationalism are particularly instructive. They both point to the tendency of finite and creaturely man to think more highly of himself than he ought to think. The problem of community is confused more by these absolutistic pretensions than by the hunger for bread and by the competition for the resources of the earth. The pious try to moderate the pretension by subjecting human pride to divine judgment. The rationalists seek to bring it under critical social scrutiny. Both methods of restraint are necessary; but both methods are also defective. One might claim that it is possible to realize why they are defective from the standpoint of the Christian faith but not from the Hellenic modern standpoint. But this understanding must not be regarded as eliminating the defect.[4]

II. *Reason and Ideology*

The rationalists from the Stoics to Kant have correctly assessed the role of reason in morality, but have not been able to relate it to the dynamic aspects of life. It is true that reason discloses the "moral law." It reveals, or at least suggests, the total field of life in which obligation moves. The rational man is thus able to recognize the mutual relationships between, let us say, life in Africa and life in America, which the ignorant man does not see and for which he therefore recognizes no obligation. Furthermore, reason discloses how uncontrolled impulses create anarchy both within the self and within the social whole. Against this anarchy it sets the ideal of order. Reason tries to establish a system of coherence and consistency in conduct as well as in the realm of truth. It conceives of its harmonies of life with life not only in ever wider and more inclusive terms, but also works for equal justice within each area of harmony by the simple fact that the special privileges of injustice are brought under rational condemnation for their inconsistency.[5]

Thus reason may extend social impulses beyond the immediate objectives which nature prompts; it may insist upon harmony in the whole field of vital impulses; and it may reveal all the motives which prompt human action and all the consequences which flow from it so that honest error and dishonest pretensions are reduced. The development of community and justice does depend to some degree upon the extension of rationality.[6]

Yet there is no evidence that reason is becoming progressively disembodied. It always remains organically related to a particular center of vitality, individual or collective; and it is therefore always a weapon of defense and attack for this vitality against competing vitalities, as well as a transcendent force which arbitrates between conflicting vitalities. A high perspective of reason may as easily enlarge the realm of dominion of an imperial self as mitigate expansive desires in the interest of the harmony of the whole.[7] For in the field of history it is no pure mind which observes the facts, but an anxious reason, organically related to an anxious ego, reacting with pity or scorn, with fear or pride, to the greatness or the weakness, to the promised support or the threatened peril, of this or that competitive expression of human vitality.[8]

The relation of interest to historical knowledge is so obvious and inevitable that it is somewhat surprising that it came fully into view so late in the history of culture, and that Marxism, a polemic creed, should have been the primary agent of its discovery. The Marxist sponsorship of the theory of ideology was unfortunate, for Marxism discredited itself so quickly by becoming the prisoner of its own ideological presuppositions, that it has seemed unnecessary to deal seriously with the Marxist theory. Yet Marxism stumbled upon an important, and in some respects an insoluble, problem in the realm of historical knowledge.[9] Marxist theory has become a source of moral and political confusion because it attributes ideology to economic class interest alone, when as a matter of fact the ideological taint is a permanent factor of human culture on every level of advance.[10]

The subservience of reason to interest in political life may be illustrated many times over. For example, one of the pre-election polls in 1944 announced that college graduates were in favor of Dewey two to one, while the faculties of various institutions were for Roosevelt a little better than two to one. Usually these graduates stood well to the left of the professors in their college days. But they voted two to one for Dewey after they became established as more or less privileged members of a privileged class of owners and managers in our industrial process.

It does not take much intelligence to recognize how serious our problems were and some of the necessities of our situation at that time. But the more educated members of our community were not intelligent enough to understand these facts. The reason they were not intelligent enough is because their reason was a servant of their interest. They talked nonsense about free enterprise because they had a privileged position in the free enterprise system which they did not want to yield. Economic determinists may be wrong if they insist that interest determines all of our moral and political attitudes. There is, fortunately, some power and inclination in men to rise above their interests. But rationalists are equally wrong if they imagine that intelligence alone will solve our moral and political problems. For intelligence is corrupted by interest.

When one contemplates these facts one thanks God for democracy which gives the ignorant man just as much power of suffrage as the educated man, despite the apprehensions of the elite of all the ages that the masses are too ignorant to understand the complexities of government. One may also thank God for the wisdom which resides in a hungry belly rather than a sophisticated mind. The hungry belly announces at least that there is something wrong in a society which allows insecurity and hunger; and the sophisticated mind does not always know this, so long as the belly which feeds it is filled. The ignorant man may be too ignorant to make a pair of shoes; but not so ignorant that he does not know if a pair of shoes pinches him. Democracy must depend upon the wisdom of the pinched toe and the empty belly.

This does not mean that we ought not to continue to strive for political and moral perspective in our education. We will always need as much moral transcendence over interest and rational perspective upon conflicting passions as it is possible to secure. But to the end of time the college graduates will vote for the Deweys of their day. They will have known better in their youth but will have forgotten in the complacency of their middle age. They will organize "hate Roosevelt" clubs as they previously organized against Cleveland and Jackson. Therefore "blessed are the poor" not only in the kingdom of heaven, where their humility merits a special reward; but also in the kingdom of earthly justice, where the partial wisdom of their unsatisfied needs is a resource of justice. Without it the nation would be victim of the illusions of the intelligent who are also powerful and privileged, whose eyes are too fat to see clearly and whose minds are too engaged by self-interest to think honestly.[11]

In modern experience, a secular and rationalist age has imagined that it could exorcise fanaticism by disavowing religion. But an age which prides itself upon its scientific objectivity has actually sunk to new levels of cruelty; for the man who knows himself to be absolutely right through the benefit of reason and science is as cruel as those who achieved this fanaticism by religious revelation.[12] An uncritical cult of reason, which manages to derive cruelty and tyranny from its scientific pretensions, thus proves how unreasonable a pretentious reason can be. We have in modern history two lessons in the limits and the corruptions of man's reason, one in the French Revolution and one in modern communism.[13]

Because reason is something more than a weapon of self-interest it can be an instrument of justice; but since reason is never dissociated from the vitalities of life, individual and collective, it cannot be a pure instrument of justice.[14]

III. *Morality and Self-Righteousness*

The problem of the validity and the ideological corruptions of moral concepts in politics can be briefly stated. A moral judgment obviously asserts something about a policy or action which refers, not to the preference or desires of the agent, but to its rightness in a fairly consistent scheme of values, transcending the desires of the agent. The ideological distortion arises from the fact that the agent is bound to view this scheme from the standpoint of his particular interests, individual or collective.

It is a significant fact, which probably refutes all simple hedonistic interpretations of the moral problem, that even the most consistently self-seeking man cannot pursue his own interests without pretending to himself and to others that his good is a part of a consistent total scheme of value. This fact reveals something about the very structure of human nature. It proves that a mature intelligence is always conscious of the system of value greater than his own interest, and he cannot gain the consent of his conscience for his own interests without pretending, at first to himself and then to others (mostly for the purpose of supporting his own self-deception), that his own interest can be fitted into, or may even dominate, the whole system of value. Napoleon was a fairly consistent egoist, but he never tired of assuring himself that his ambitions were in the service of the Revolution or of the honor of France.[15]

The "content" of conscience is obviously very relative to time and place. Yet the minimal terms of our obligations to our neighbors, incorporated for instance in the prohibition of murder, theft and adultery, are fairly universal. Hume rightly observed that the "preference for benevolence over self regard" was universal, certainly more nearly universal than actual benevolence.

Perhaps it would be correct to surmise that the universalities of the "moral law" are derived from intuitions of the self about the essential nature of its selfhood. The self would therefore feel obligated to conform to the "law" written into its nature, including the law of love or the law which is derived from the mutual dependence of persons.

Yet the content of conscience is much more relative than the proponents of the idea of "moral intuitions" realize. These relativities point to the social derivation of the moral law. Man is both an historical and social creature. He does not make his moral judgments in a vacuum. The community in which he lives sets the standards by which he judges himself. There is at least that modicum of truth in the moral relativism propounded by modern anthropologists.

That this is not the whole truth of the matter is proved by the frequency with which "conscience" expresses itself in defiance of the community. The modern martyrs who have given their lives to defy communities which sought to make total claims upon the individual have vividly refuted all theories, whether psychological, sociological or anthropological, which sought to reduce the sense of moral obligation to a purely sociological phenomenon. More particularly they refuted the Freudian theory of the "super-ego" which was no more than the pressure of the community upon the "ego."

It is worth noting however that consistently "liberal" or "bourgeois" notions of conscience as purely individual do not do justice to the fact that the individual is best able to defy a community when his conscience is informed and reinforced by another community, whether religious or political. Perhaps the final paradox of the social and individual dimension of the moral sense is revealed by the fact that the individual may defy a community which directly impinges upon his life and threatens his liberty by its coercion; but his defiance is usually undertaken in the name of another, more inclusive or more worthy, community even though that community makes no overt claims upon him and may exist only in his imagination.[16]

Rightly directed the tension between the individual conscience and the realities in actual communities can be a constant source of power for purifying and broadening the justice and brotherhood of the community.[17] It must be admitted that pure conscience seldom defeats an unjust social system; those who speak against its injustice are primarily its victims. Yet slavery would have persisted if only the slaves had recognized its oppression. A moral element thus enters into every successful challenge of Caesar's authority.[18]

But even though the development of rational and moral resources may indeed qualify the social and ethical outlook, it cannot destroy the selfishness of men and groups. Moral idealism must express itself within the limits of the imagination by which men recognize the true character of their own motives and the validity of interests which compete with their own. The imagination of very few men is acute enough to accomplish this so thoroughly that the selfish motive is adequately discounted and the interests of others are fully understood.[19]

Therefore we must understand to what degree every civilization, as a system of power, idealizes and rationalizes its equilibrium of power and how these rationalizations invariably include standards of morals which serve the moral and spiritual pride of the ruling oligarchy.[20] Thus every national organism seeks to defend itself, and possibly to extend its power and prestige, in competition with other nations; but every nation claims that in doing this it is fighting not only for its own existence but for certain values which transcend its existence. This claim need not be wholly spurious. It cannot be wholly spurious, in fact, if it is to achieve any degree of plausibility. But the claim is always more unqualified than the facts warrant. No nation is ever true to the cause which transcends its national life if there is not some coincidence between the defensive necessities of that cause and the defensive requirements of the national organism. Every nation pretends, on the other hand, that its primary loyalty is to a universal value. This is the element of deceit which is involved in all national life, and in all human existence for that matter; for individuals, as well as nations, sanctify partial and particular interests by identifying them unduly with universal values.[21]

Similarly, all principles of justice which are applied as public policy through the rules and laws governing social relations are on the one hand instruments of mutuality and community; and they contain on the other hand mere approximations of, and positive contradictions to, the ideal of brotherhood. Usually the norms of law are compromises between the rational-moral ideals of what ought to be, and the possibilities of the situation as determined by given equilibria of vital forces. The specific legal enactments are, on the one hand, the instruments of the conscience of the community, seeking to subdue the potential anarchy of forces and interests into a tolerable harmony. They are, on the other hand, merely explicit formulations of given tensions and equilibria of life and power, as worked out by the unconscious interactions of social life. The more positive contradiction to brotherhood in all schemes of justice is introduced by the contingent and finite character of rational estimates of rights and interests and by the taint of passion and self-interest upon calculations of the rights of others. Even the comparatively impartial view of the whole of a society, as expressed particularly in the carefully guarded objectivity of its juridical institutions, participates in the contingent character of all human viewpoints.

The positive relation of principles of justice to the ideal of community and brotherhood makes an indeterminate approximation of love in the realm of justice possible. The negative relation means that all historic conceptions of justice will embody some elements which contradict the law of love. The interests of a class, the viewpoint of a nation, the prejudices of an age and the illusions of a culture are consciously and unconsciously insinuated into the norms by which men regulate their common life. They are intended to give one group an advantage over another. Or if that is not their intention, it is at least the unvarying consequence.[22]

IV. *Religion and Fanaticism*

Ideally religion is the force which brings all individual actions and vitalities into a total harmony by subjecting them all to the realm of meaning. Ideally religion is the principle of harmony which must be substituted for the harmony of nature, once man's freedom has broken the latter and made the equanimity and order of nature unavailable for him. Yet religion is frequently (and some believe always) the force of disharmony in life. It accentuates conflict, generates fanaticism and aggravates the pride and arrogance of individuals and groups.[23]

Every genuine passion for community and social justice will always contain a religious element within it. Religion will always leaven the idea of justice with the ideal of love. It will prevent the idea of justice, which is a politico-ethical ideal, from becoming a purely political one, with the ethical element washed out. The ethical ideal which threatens to become too purely religious must save the ethical ideal which is in peril of becoming too political.[24] Further, the religious sense of the absolute qualifies the will-to-live and the will-to-power by bringing them under subjection to an absolute will, and by imparting transcendent value to other human beings, whose life and needs thus achieve a higher claim upon the self.[25]

Even religious reverence for the "majesty" of the state is legitimate insofar as it embodies and expresses both the authority and power of the total community over all its members, and the principle of order and justice as such against the peril of anarchy. The legitimate majesty of government is acknowledged and affirmed in the Christian doctrine of government as a divine ordinance.[26]

Yet it must be regarded as inevitable that religion, and especially a religion which apprehends the truth about man and God by faith alone, should be used as the instrument of human arrogance. This is done whenever the truth which is held by faith, because it is beyond all human attainment, comes to be regarded as a secure possession. In this form it is no longer a threat to man. It does not mediate judgment upon the false and imperial completions of human life. It becomes, rather, the vehicle of the pretension that the finiteness and sin of life have been overcome.[27]

The most primitive religion is magic; and magic is a kind of crude science which seeks to bend natural and cosmic forces to the human will. Yet there is in even the most primitive religion a suggestion of a higher purpose. This purpose is to bend the human will to the divine will, to discover the ultimate truth about life to which men ought to submit, whatever their inclinations. These two contrasting motives in religion are always at war and never achieve a stable equilibrium. The lowest religion is never purely an effort to bend the world to human wishes; and the highest religion, in actual practice, mixes motives of self-glorification into the honest purpose of subjecting the individual will to the purposes of God.[28]

The most potent form of pretension arises at the very point in culture where the claim is made that all partial perspectives have been transcended, and where it is assumed that a political force in conflict with other forces is in fact a transcendental force, moving above the welter of interest and passion. Modern culture confronts in modern communism exactly the same problem which the Reformation and the Renaissance faced in Catholicism at the dawn of the modern age. The Catholic Church claimed to be, not a particular religious, political, and cultural force imbedded in the feudal order and sanctifying particular political interests, but an absolute and transcendental force. It is because the claim of ultimate and absolute validity is always involved in religion that Marx rightly declared, "The beginning of all criticism is the criticism of religion." That truth must now be applied to Marxism itself insofar as it is not merely a political movement dealing with particular abuses but a religious movement claiming to have a solution for the ultimate problems of human existence.[29]

Fanaticism is, of course, no more simply the fruit of religion than of irreligion. The similarity between the fanaticism of the sects of the Cromwellian revolution and the fanaticism of the various rationalist sectaries of the French Revolution refutes the theories both of traditional religion and of secularism, that utopianism is the result either of faith or want of faith. Religious faith or any system of philosophy may create a universe of meaning which transcends, or seems to transcend, all particular historic norms and concepts. Wherever this transcendent meaning is taken seriously a tolerant attitude is developed toward means, ends, and purposes other than our own. But all systems of meaning, whether founded in religion, philosophy, or science, more frequently tempt men to identify their norms and ends with the final meaning, thus generating fanaticism.[30]

The real problem of human community begins when men who are absolutely certain that they are unselfish and equally certain that they know God's will, come in conflict with other men who have the same certainty but whose political, social and economic convictions have nothing in common with their own. It is at that point that we face the issue of the relativity of all human perspectives; the sinful tendency of finite men to deny this relativity and to claim absolute validity for opinions which God supposedly gave them; the necessity of living by God's will insofar as we can apprehend it for us; and finally the need of forgiving the foe in the knowledge that our own perspectives, ideals and goals are tainted by sin as certainly as his.

All theories which set up too simple wires of guidance between God and man lead to intolerance and strife in the end. The man who thinks it is a rather simple matter to know God's will always ends up by defining that will rather simply and excluding from the Kingdom of God everyone who does not agree with him. A study of the history of religious intolerance and tolerance is a very good antidote for this religious optimism. It is well to remember that the Christian church, which prays daily "forgive us our debts, as we forgive our debtors," has a pretty terrible record of fanaticism. The fanatics were the good people, whether Catholic, Protestant or sectaries, who did not really believe that they were sinners who had to be forgiven.[31]

V. *The Ultimate Validity of Norms*

The ideological taint, the dishonest pretension of universality which accompanies every partial perspective in history, does not mean that significant choices between rival political movements cannot be made; we are still capable of making them, though we are ourselves involved in rationalization and have no absolute and impartial perspective. If there were not some degree of freedom from interest in the human mind, there could be no culture at all, and all life would be no more than a conflict of interests. But our choices will be less confused if we know how to discount the latest ideology, which always presents itself in the guise of a final freedom from rationalization.[32]

From this analysis we may draw insights which are instructive for dealing with this whole problem of the ultimate validity and the ideological corruptions of moral concepts in politics. These insights include: 1) the recognition of the validity of a viewpoint despite the ideological distortion furnished by the interests of its chief proponents; 2) the recognition of the possibility of winnowing truth from error in various ideological positions; and 3) the admission that it is not possible finally to eliminate certain ideological preferences of classes and nations. They must be accepted as the inevitable fruit of the finiteness of man's intelligence and the intimate association between reason and interest in human affairs.[33]

When truth is made the slave of power, one can only hold up one's hands. Truth is always partly corrupted by power and interest. But it is in the margin of purity where truth transcends interest partially that civilization is built and men maintain a sane world, where there is some hope of adjusting interest to interest, life to life, and value to value.[34]

CHRISTIAN ETHICS AND POLITICS

CHAPTER XII

The Problem of the Love Ethic in Politics

I. *The Christian Law of Love*

Moral life is possible at all only in a meaningful existence. Obligation can be felt only to some system of coherence and some ordering will. Thus moral obligation is always an obligation to promote harmony and to overcome chaos. But every conceivable order in the historical world contains an element of anarchy. Its world rests upon contingency and caprice. The obligation to support and enhance it can therefore arise and maintain itself only upon the basis of a faith that it is the partial fruit of a deeper unity and the promise of a more perfect harmony than is revealed in any immediate situation. If a lesser faith than this prompts moral action, it results in precisely those types of moral fanaticism which impart unqualified worth to qualified values and thereby destroy even their qualified worth.

The prophetic faith in a God who is both the ground and the ultimate fulfillment of existence, who is both the creator and the judge of the world, is thus involved in every moral situation. Without it the world is seen either as being meaningless or as revealing unqualifiedly good and simple meanings. In either case the nerve of moral action is ultimately destroyed.[1]

But more than this, Christianity enters the world with the stupendous claim that in the life, death and resurrection of Christ, the expected disclosure of God's sovereignty over history, and the expected establishment of that sovereignty have taken place. In this disclosure of the power and will which governs history, both life and history have found their previously partly hidden and partly revealed meaning.[2]

The Christian faith affirms, further, that the same Christ who discloses the sovereignty of God over history is also the perfect norm of human nature. This perfection is not so much a sum total of various virtues or an absence of transgression of various laws; it is the perfection of sacrificial love.[3]

Every moral standard, rigorously analyzed, proves to be no permanently valid standard at all short of perfect and infinite love. The only adequate norm of human conduct is love of God and of man, through which all men are perfectly related to each other, because they are all related in terms of perfect obedience and love to the center and source of their existence. Christ, who expresses both the infinite possibilities of love in human life and the infinite possibilities beyond human life, is thus a true revelation of the total situation in which human life stands.[4]

The specific content of this love contains three terms: (a) the perfect relation of the soul to God in which obedience is transcended by love, trust and confidence ("Thou shalt love the Lord thy God"); (b) the perfect internal harmony of the soul with itself in all of its desires and impulses ("With all thy heart and all thy soul and all thy mind"); and (c) the perfect harmony of life with life ("Thou shalt love thy neighbor as thyself"). This love of the neighbor, the perfect accord of life with life and will with will, is a derivative of perfect faith and trust in God. Without such trust man is involved in the vicious circle of anxiety and self-sufficiency which inhibits him from genuine concern for the needs of the neighbor. Love between man and man is thus but one facet of the total *justitia originalis*. It is also the final form of that righteousness. Love is the final requirement of human relations, if the freedom of the persons who are involved in mutual relations be considered.[5]

The ethic of Jesus which is founded upon this love is an absolute and uncompromising ethic. It is, in the phrase of Ernst Troeltsch, an ethic of "love universalism and love perfectionism." The injunctions "resist not evil," "love your enemies," "if ye love them that love you what thanks have you?" "be not anxious for your life," and "be ye therefore perfect even as your father in heaven is perfect," all are of one piece, and they are all uncompromising and absolute.[6]

This love absolutism expresses itself in terms of a universalism set against all narrower forms of human sympathy, as well as in terms of a perfectionism which maintains a critical vigor against the most inevitable and subtle forms of self-assertion. The universalistic element appears in the injunctions which require that the life of the neighbor be affirmed beyond the bounds set by natural human sympathy. Love within the bounds of consanguinity and intimate community is regarded as devoid of special merit. An all-embracing love is enjoined because God's love is like that.[7]

The absolutism and perfectionism of Jesus' love ethic sets itself uncompromisingly not only against the natural self-regarding impulses, but against the necessary prudent defenses of the self, required because of the egoism of others. It does not establish a connection with the horizontal points of a political or social ethic, or with the diagonals which a prudential individual ethic draws between the moral ideal and the facts of a given situation. It has only a vertical dimension between the loving will of God and the will of man.[8]

Thus in terms of individual life Jesus' ethical ideal was one of complete disinterestedness, religiously motivated. No one was to seek his own. The man who asked him to persuade his brother to divide an inheritance with him was rudely rebuked. Evil was not to be resisted, the borrower was to be given more than he asked for without hope of return. A special premium was placed upon actions which could not be rewarded. In other words, the prudential motive was treated with utmost severity.[9]

The justification for these demands is put in purely religious and not in socio-moral terms. We are to forgive because God forgives; we are to love our enemies because God is impartial in his love. The points of reference are vertical and not horizontal. Neither natural impulses nor social consequences are taken into consideration. It is always possible, of course, that absolute ethical attitudes have desirable social consequences. To do good to an enemy may prompt him to overcome his enmity; and forgiveness of evil may be a method of redemption which commends itself to the most prudent. It must be observed, however, that no appeal to social consequences could ever fully justify these demands of Jesus. Nonresistance may shame an aggressor into goodness, but it may also prompt him to further aggression. Furthermore, if the action is motivated by regard for social consequences it will hardly be pure enough to secure the consequences which are supposed to justify it. Upon that paradox all purely prudential morality is shattered.[10]

Though Jesus was as indifferent to the social consequences of pure disinterestedness as he was critical of concern for the personal consequences, it is not difficult to draw conclusions in regard to the social ideal implied by such disinterestedness. In practical terms it means a combination of anarchism and communism dominated by the spirit of love. Such perfect love as He demands would obviate the necessity of coercion on the one hand because men would refrain from transgressing upon their neighbor's rights, and on the other hand because such transgression would be accepted and forgiven if it did occur. That is anarchism, in other words. It would mean communism because the privileges of each would be potentially the privileges of all. Where love is perfect the distinctions between mine and thine disappear. The social ideal of Jesus is as perfect and as impossible of attainment as is his personal ideal.[11]

II. *A Law That Is Not a Law*

The law of love is a law and yet not a law. It is a law in the sense that it states the basic requirement of the aggregate existence of humankind. Ideally, a healthy social life is one in which every part, individual and collective, finds its rightful place in the harmony of the whole and serves the commonweal without coercion. Indeed, every social harmony which falls short of perfect love has the seeds of anarchy and death in it. The commandment to love our neighbor as ourself is, therefore, not a mere counsel of perfection in the sense that it merely extends the logic inherent in the possibilities of human action until an ideal is projected which transcends all possibilities. The law of love is really the law of life. It is a basic requirement of human existence which men transgress at their peril. Every transgression disturbs and imperils the social harmony of human existence.

Yet the law of love is not a law. It is a norm but not an obligation. At least it is not an obligation which can be enforced. Every effort to enforce it negates it; for an enforced submission of the will to something other than itself, whether of the individual by society or of the sensible by the intelligible self (to use Kant's distinction), presupposes a conflict between the self and society, or between the self and its higher self, which real love would overcome. For it is of the very character of love that it desires the good freely and without compulsion. The law of love therefore presupposes a human personality which is not at war with itself, that is, a sinless soul. Since, however, sin is a fact of all human existence, the law of love can only be stated in terms of an obligation. Thus the paradox in the simple commandment, "Thou shalt love" (i.e., the paradox of stating a possibility as an obligation when the obligatory feature destroys it is a possibility) is a faithful expression of the basic paradox in all human morality.

With this perspective in mind, the problem of the Christian faith and the common life is easily stated, but not readily solved. The problem is to relate the moral ultimate of Christian faith, the law of love, to the facts and necessities of daily existence. This is a difficult problem precisely because the law of love is not a law at all; and the common life of man in all its relationships requires the restraints of law. Love is an ideal which transcends all law; but the sinfulness of the human heart threatens the common life of man with anarchy if it is not restrained; if natural impulses are not brought under the discipline of accepted standards; if standards are not enforced by some kind of social will, stronger than the potentially recalcitrant will of the individual; and if methods of arbitration are not found for the inevitable conflicts of social will and interest between various members of the human community.[12]

We are very foolish if we try to reduce the love ethic so that it will cover and justify our prudential and relative standards and strategies. To do this is to reduce the ethic to a new legalism; whereas we have seen that the significance of the law of love is precisely that it is not just another law, but a law which transcends all law. Every law and standard which falls short of the law of love embodies contingent factors and makes concessions to the fact that sinful man must achieve tentative harmonies of life with life which are less than the best. It is dangerous and confusing to give these tentative and relative standards final and absolute religious sanction.[13]

III. *The Final Impossibility of Love*

The teachings of Christ have a rigor which points beyond simple historical possibilities. The ethical demands made by Jesus are incapable of fulfillment in the present existence of man. They proceed from a transcendent and divine unity of essential reality, and their final fulfillment is possible only when God transmutes the present chaos of this world into its final unity.[14]

The Christian faith in its profoundest versions has never believed that the Cross would so change the very nature of historical existence that a more and more universal achievement of sacrificial love would finally transmute sacrificial love into successful mutual love, perfectly validated by historical social consequences. In thus conceiving history after Christ as an interim between the disclosure of its true meaning and the fulfillment of that meaning, between the revelation of divine sovereignty and the full establishment of that sovereignty, a continued element of inner contradiction in history is accepted as its perennial characteristic. Sin is overcome in principle but not in fact. Love must continue to be suffering love rather than triumphant love.[15]

So there is indeed a very rigorous ethical ideal in the gospel of Jesus, but there is in it no social ethic in the ordinary sense of the word precisely because the ethical ideal is too rigorous and perfect. The ethic of Jesus was, to begin with, a personal ethic. It was not individual in the sense that He believed in individual perfection abstracted from a social situation. He saw that wealth tempted to covetousness and that poverty prompted the virtue of humility. He spoke of the Kingdom and not of salvation, and the Kingdom meant an ideal social relationship, even though He might emphasize that it proceeded from internal spiritual forces. His ethic was an ethic of love, and it therefore implied social relationships. But it was an individual ethic in the sense that His chief interest was in the quality of life of an individual.

His lack of concern for social and political issues is, however, not as important from the perspective of this problem as the kind of ethical ideal which He actually developed.[16] The law of love is so absolute that its fulfillment is no simple possibility. Love is the law of freedom; but man is not completely free; and such freedom as he has is corrupted by sin. The ideal is an impossibility because both the contingencies of nature and the sin in the human heart prevent men from ever living in that perfect freedom and equality which the whole logic of the moral life demands. The ideal of equality will be relativized, for example, not only by the fortuitous circumstances of nature and history, but by the necessities of social cohesion and organic social life, which will give some men privileges and powers which other men lack; and finally by human sin, for it is inevitable that men should take advantage of privileges with which nature or necessity has endowed them and should enhance them beyond the limits of the one and the requirements of the other.[17]

The same limiting factors prevent man from fully achieving true community. The human imagination is too limited to see and understand the interests of the other as vividly as those of the self. Furthermore the realization of any such system of harmony would require more than individual action. It would require the organization of vast economic and political structures in defiance of, and transcendence over, the contingencies of geography, the fortuitous differences of natural resources, etc. There is, therefore, no historic structure of justice which can fulfill the law of love. The fact of sin introduces an even more stubborn force of corruption into the inertia of nature and finiteness. The man who is limited by time and place does not merely fail to sense the needs of others who live beyond the limits of his time and place. He resists the claim of their necessities upon his conscience and makes demands of his own which are incompatible with their interests.[18]

In classical Christianity it is understood not only that love can be fully realized only at the expense of life itself (the simple moral meaning of the Cross) but also that all historic forms of life, individual and collective, embody a positive contradiction to it. The contradiction to it is not the animal survival impulse of man, but the spiritualized survival impulse, the will-to-power and the pride by which men seek to overcome their finiteness and actually aggravate the competition between life and life. This contradiction is recognized as a permanent element in man's historic situation. Thus it is impossible to construct a social ethic out of the ideal of love in its pure form, because the ideal presupposes the resolution of the conflict of life with life.[19]

The same Cross, then, which symbolizes the love of God and reveals the divine perfection to be not incompatible with a suffering involvement in historical tragedy, also indicates that the perfection of man is not attainable in history. Sacrificial love transcends history. From the standpoint of history mutual love is the highest good. Only in mutual love, in which the concern of one person for the interests of another prompts and elicits a reciprocal affection, are the social demands of historical existence satisfied. The highest good of history must conform to standards of coherence and consistency in the whole realm of historical vitality. All claims within the general field of interests must be proportionately satisfied and related to each other harmoniously. The sacrifice of the self for others is therefore a violation of natural standards of morals, as limited by historical existence.[20]

This is why in political life we must measure realities in terms of possible historical alternatives, and not by comparison with purely ideal possibilities, for political values are highly relative. We never have the chance to choose between pure tyranny and pure freedom; we can only choose between tyranny and relative democracy. We do not have the choice between war and perfect peace, but only between war and the uneasy peace of some fairly decent and stable equilibrium of social forces. We cannot choose between violence and non-violence, but only between violence and a statesmanship which seeks to adjust social forces without violence but cannot guarantee immunity from clashes. We have never had the opportunity—and probably never shall have—to choose between injustice and perfect equality, but only between injustice and a justice which moves toward equality and incorporates some of its values.[21]

The social validity of a moral ideal which transcends social considerations in its purest heights is progressively weakened as it is applied to more and more intricate, indirect and collective human relations. It is not only unthinkable that a group should be able to attain a sufficiently consistent unselfish attitude toward other groups to give it a very potent redemptive power, but it is improbable that any competing group would have the imagination to appreciate the moral calibre of the achievement. Furthermore a high type of unselfishness, even if it brings ultimate rewards, demands immediate sacrifices. An individual may sacrifice his own interests, either without hope of reward or in the hope of an ultimate compensation. But how is an individual who is responsible for the interests of his group to justify the sacrifice of interests other than his own? The moral obtuseness of human collectives makes a morality of pure disinterestedness impossible.[22]

So it is that the *Agape* of Christ, which the New Testament regards as the final norm of human life, would seem to have an even more problematic relevance to the structure of human society than to the structure of individual existence. Can the idea of sacrificial love be anything but an embarrassment when the community's need of social harmony, justice, and peace are considered? The justice of a community requires a careful and discriminate judgment about competing rights and interests. The admonition to be heedless of the interests of the self introduces confusion into such discriminate judgments. In the collective relationships of mankind ruthless aggression must be countered by resolute defense; and the impulse of dominion must be resisted, if slavery is to be avoided. A sacrificial submission to a ruthless antagonist may mean a noble martyrdom if the interests of the self alone are considered. But if interests other than those of the self are sacrificed, this nobility becomes ignoble "appeasement." [23]

It is therefore idle to assume that human society could ever be completely knit together by the perfection of love in which each carries the burdens of all, and the anxieties of each are quieted by the solicitude of all. That is the vision of the Kingdom of God, of the Kingdom of perfect love, which hovers as a possibility and yet impossibility over all human life. Actually the perfect accord between each man and his neighbor is constantly violated by the inordinate concern of each for his own welfare.[24]

CHAPTER XIII

The Case Against Pacifism

The "liberal culture" of modern bourgeois civilization has simply and sentimentally transmuted the supra-historical ideals of perfection of the Gospel into simple historical possibilities. In consequence it defines the good man and the good nation as the man and nation which avoid conflict. Sometimes it merely insists that violent conflict must be avoided. But this finally comes to the same thing because the foe may always threaten us with violent reaction to our non-violent forms of pressure, in which case we must desist from pressing our cause or cease to be "good."

It is the thesis of this analysis that modern liberal perfectionism actually distills moral perversity out of its moral absolutes. It is unable to make significant distinctions between tyranny and freedom because it can find no democracy pure enough to deserve its devotions, and in any case it can find none which is not involved in conflict in its effort to defend itself against tyranny. It is unable to distinguish between the peace of capitulation to tyranny and the peace of the Kingdom of God. It does not realize that its effort to make the peace of the Kingdom of God into a simple historical possibility must inevitably result in placing a premium upon surrender to evil, because the alternative course involves men and nations in conflict, or runs the risk, at least, of involving them in conflict.

On the religious level, modern Christian and secular perfectionism is a very sentimentalized version of the Christian faith and is at variance with the profoundest insights of the Christian religion.[1] The modern liberal Protestant church has tried to eliminate the compromises of the orthodox church by accepting and diluting the ethic of sectarian Christianity. The optimism and rationalism which it inherited from the Enlightenment gave it confidence that the Gospel of love needed only to be adequately preached to be universally accepted. It therefore envisaged a new society, achieved by gradual evolutionary process, and practically identical with the Kingdom of God of the Gospel.[2]

The fact is that this whole pitiless perfectionism, which has informed a large part of liberal Protestantism in America, is wrong not only about war and international politics. It is wrong about the whole nature of historical reality. It worries about some of us "crucifying the Lord afresh" by accepting involvement in war when necessary, and does not recognize that the selfishness of the best of us is constantly involved in the sin of crucifying the Lord afresh. It thinks there is some simple method of extricating ourselves from conflict, when as a matter of fact all justice that the world has ever known has been established through tension between various vitalities, forces, and interests in society. All such tension is covert conflict and all covert conflict may on occasion, and must on occasion, become overt.[3]

I. *Non-Resistance and Non-Violent Resistance*

Probably the most prominent and revealing expression of moralistic perfectionism in modern Christianity and culture has been the phenomenon of pacifism. Curiously enough, the pacifists are just as guilty as their less absolutist brethren of diluting the ethic of Jesus for the purpose of justifying their position. They are forced to recognize that an ethic of pure non-resistance can have no immediate relevance to any political situation; for in every political situation it is necessary to achieve justice by resisting pride and power. They therefore declare that the ethic of Jesus is not an ethic of non-resistance, but one of non-violent resistance; that it allows one to resist evil provided the resistance does not involve the destruction of life or property.

There is not the slightest support in Scripture for this doctrine of non-violence. Nothing could be plainer than that the ethic uncompromisingly enjoins non-resistance and not non-violent resistance. Furthermore, it is obvious that the distinction between violent and non-violent resistance is not an absolute distinction. If it is made absolute, we arrive at the morally absurd position of giving moral preference to the non-violent power which Doctor Goebbels wielded over the type of power wielded by a general. This absurdity is really derived from the modern (and yet probably very ancient and very Platonic) heresy of regarding the "physical" as evil and the "spiritual" as good.[4]

Gandhi, the greatest modern exponent of non-violence, himself contributed to the confusion between non-resistance and non-violent resistance. He frequently spoke of his method as the use of "soul-force" or "truth-force." He regarded it as spiritual in distinction to the physical character of violence. Very early in his development of the technique of non-violence in South Africa he declared: "Passive resistance is a misnomer. The idea is more completely expressed by the term 'soul-force.' Active resistance is better expressed by the term 'body-force.' " A negative form of resistance does not achieve spirituality simply because it is negative. As long as it enters the field of social and physical relations and places physical restraints upon the desires and activities of others, it is a form of physical coercion. In spite of his use of various forms of negative physical resistance, civil disobedience, boycotts and strikes, he seemed to persist in giving them a connotation which really belongs to pure non-resistance. "Jesus Christ, Daniel and Socrates represent the purest form of passive resistance or soul-force," he declares in a passage in which he explains the meaning of what is most undeniably non-violent resistance rather than non-resistance. All this is a pardonable confusion in the soul of a man who was trying to harmonize the insights of a saint with the necessities of statecraft, a very difficult achievement. But it is nevertheless a confusion.[5]

The religious radical is wrong in believing that there is an intrinsic difference between violence and non-violence. The differences are pragmatic rather than intrinsic. The social consequences of the two methods are different, but the differences are in degree rather than in kind. Both place restraint upon liberty and both may destroy life and property. Once the principle of coercion and resistance has been accepted as necessary to the social struggle and to social cohesion, and pure pacifism has thus been abandoned, the differences between violence and non-violence lose their absolute significance, though they remain important.[6]

One may well concede that a wise and decent statesmanship will seek not only to avoid conflict, but to avoid violence in conflict. Its function consists in mitigating the struggle between contending forces, by insinuating the greatest possible degree of social imagination and intelligence into it and by providing the best possible means of arbitration so that violent conflict may be avoided. For social violence is a great evil and ought to be avoided if at all possible. It frequently defeats its own ends. A technical civilization has measurably increased its perils to the whole fabric of civilization and has furthermore increased the hazards of its success as a weapon in the hands of the victims of injustice. When resort is taken to armed conflict, the possessors may have more deadly instruments than the dispossessed. For these and other reasons the avoidance of violence is important in any society, and particularly in the complex society of modern times.[7]

But this pragmatic distinction between violent and non-violent means has nothing to do with the more basic distinction between the ethic of the "Kingdom of God," in which no concession is made to human sin, and all relative political strategies which, assuming human sinfulness, seek to secure the highest measure of peace and justice among selfish and sinful men.[8]

It follows that a Christian's concern over his violation of the ethic of Jesus ought to begin long before the question of violence is reached. It ought to begin by recognizing that he has violated the law, "Thou shalt love thy neighbor as thyself." Out of the violation of that commandment arises the conflict of life with life and nation with nation. It is highly desirable to restrict this conflict to non-violent assertions and counter-assertions; but it is not always possible.[9]

II. *Coercion and Social Justice*

1. LOVE, JUSTICE AND POWER

The tendency toward social irresponsibility in the pacifist position derives not only from the confusion of making an absolute of non-violent resistance, but also from the attempt to apply the personal ethic of sacrificial love to the social problems of war. Pacifists say that Christians must accept suffering instead of inflicting it. This is quite true, so far as personal relations are concerned. But the moral issues of war seldom present themselves in such simple terms. The issue often is whether or not to accept (and thus to inflict) suffering by others, as the victims of aggression or injustice. This issue cannot be resolved by a formula of non-violence which may be quite applicable to individual relations. A social ethic is required.

Whose duty is it to protect the lives and liberties of others? Apparently pacifists who stop short of philosophical anarchism would say the state is responsible, for its primary task is to be the guarantor of order. Non-pacifist Christians today would largely agree as to the delegated, relative, and provisional nature of the authority exercised by the state, and that it applies to unredeemed society under the dispensation of providence as compared with the dispensation of redemption. The issue here is the relation of the Christian to the state.

The very limited concept of Christian citizenship held by pacifist Christians is one of the weaknesses of their position. The responsibility of the Christian to and for the state is recognized up to a point. But when the state has to exercise its admitted central function as guarantor of order, then the state is abandoned on the ground that the Christian has a higher loyalty and code of conduct. The Christian is thus "in the world" until coercion or violence enter the scene, when he becomes "not of the world."

This is a wrong concept of the tension in which the Christian stands, for the demands of the gospel challenge him at every point, and not merely when the state resorts to force. And he is obliged to act responsibly in society at all times, and not merely when the state is at peace. Being in the world, but not of the world, applies to the whole of life.[10]

In general, the pacifist attitude toward political questions puts not only governmental but other forms of "power" in contradiction to "love." This contradiction leaves out the whole problem of the attainment of justice. Justice may be the servant of love, and power may be the servant of justice. Every historic form of justice has been attained by some equilibrium of power. Force in the narrow sense may be an element in the arsenal of power, but power is wider than force. It includes all the vitalities of life by which men seek to accomplish their ends.

Power is not evil. It may be put in the service of good ends. When the ends of men or nations conflict, the conflict may, of course, issue in violence. All sensible people will seek to avoid these violent conflicts whether on the national or international level. But only if one adopts the principle that it is better to suffer injustice than to resort to force can one wholly disavow the use of force. It is possible, though not always advisable, for individuals to suffer injustice rather than let the dispute come to an ultimate issue. But statesmen, responsible for values beyond their own lives, do not have this option. They must seek for justice by an accommodation of interests and they must protect precious values by force if necessary. Even the terrors of a possible atomic conflict cannot disengage them from such responsibilities, though it must naturally make them very hesitant to use a form of force that might spell mutual annihilation.[11]

So great are the perils of complete social disintegration, once violence is resorted to, that it is particularly necessary to oppose romantic appeals to violence on the part of the forces of radicalism. But this cannot be done successfully if absolutistic motifs are erroneously mixed with a pragmatic analysis of the political problem. The very essence of politics is the achievement of justice through equilibria of power. A balance of power is not conflict; but a tension between opposing forces underlies it. Where there is tension there is potential conflict, and where there is conflict there is potential violence. A responsible relationship to the political order, therefore, makes an unqualified disavowal of violence impossible.[12] We know that the best systems of justice which the world has ever known have been filled with positive evil as well as incomplete good. But we also know that in a sinful world systems of justice and civilization are both more precious and more precarious than those imagine who think it easy to substitute some perfect scheme of brotherhood for them.[13]

2. TYRANNY AND THE REQUIREMENT OF JUSTICE

The refusal to recognize that sin introduces an element of conflict into the world invariably means that a morally perverse preference is given to tyranny over anarchy (war). If we are told that tyranny would destroy itself, if only we would not challenge it, the obvious answer is that tyranny continues to grow if it is not resisted. If it is to be resisted, the risk of overt conflict must be taken. The thesis of the 1930s that German tyranny ought not to be challenged by other nations because Germany would throw off this yoke in due time merely meant that an unjustified moral preference was given to civil war over international war, for internal resistance runs the risk of conflict as much as external resistance. Furthermore, no consideration is given to the fact that a tyrannical state may grow too powerful to be successfully resisted by purely internal pressure, and that the injustices which it does to other than its own nationals may rightfully lay the problem of the tyranny upon other nations.

It is not unfair to assert that most pacifists who seek to present their religious absolutism as a political alternative to the claims and counter-claims, the pressures and counter-pressures of the political order, invariably betray themselves into this preference for tyranny. Tyranny is not war. It is peace, but it is a peace which has nothing to do with the peace of the Kingdom of God. It is a peace which results from one will establishing a complete dominion over other wills and reducing them to acquiescence.[14]

Actually the struggle for justice and the struggle for peace have the same sanction in the commandment of love. Both present a moral imperative. But justice normally has the prior claim, for while order may be conducive to justice, there can be no lasting peace without justice. The Biblical concept is expressed by Isaiah: "And the effect of righteousness will be peace" (Isaiah 32:17). The just war position gains strength from the consideration that the triumph of an unjust cause would defeat both the ends of justice and the future hope of peace.[15]

One pacifist critic of our position wrote during World War II: "Most of us would give our right arm to find some sanction for a position in the matter of war which would let us go along with the Government unhaunted by the feeling that Christ has anything to say about our decisions." We would have been truly unChristian if we had held to our non-pacifist convictions during World War II without an uneasy conscience about the evils in our own lives which forced the tragic alternatives of that hour upon us. But we realized, as our pacifist-isolationist Christians did not always seem to realize, that alternative decisions would have left us with an equally uneasy conscience. Might we not counter the assertion of our critic with a parallel assertion running something like this: "Most of us would have given our right arm to be able to go along with William Randolph Hearst, Mr. Wheeler and Mr. Hoover in a policy which avoided American participation in war, unhaunted by the feeling that Christ has anything to do with our decisions." We might give the figure of the accusing Christ a greater relevance if we translated the final part of the phrase to read: "unhaunted by the sense that millions of Jews, Czechs, Poles, Danes, Norwegians, Serbs, Greeks and French, living in the misery of slavery, were accusing us of consigning them to living death by our irresponsibility." The only difficulty with this parallel is that it commits us to one glaring insincerity. We would *not* have "given our right arm" to be able to make such a decision. We find it morally too intolerable to entertain.[16]

Yet the Christian utopians think they can dispense with all structures and rules of justice simply by fulfilling the law of love. They do not realize that the law of love stands on the edge of history and not in history, that it represents an ultimate and not an immediate possibility. They think they might usher in the Kingdom of God if only they could persuade men not to resist tyranny and thus avoid conflict. They do not recognize to what degree justice in a sinful world is actually maintained by a tension of competitive forces, which is always in danger of degenerating into overt conflict, but without which there would be only the despotic peace of the subordination of the will of the weak to the will of the strong.[17]

3. JUST WAR IN THE ATOMIC AGE

In our own day we encounter the problem of war in a new setting. The rapid development of weapons of mass destruction has enormously increased the destructive power in Soviet and Western hands. This has created a new dimension of catastrophe for any future global war. And because of the ramifications of the power blocs, and the tensions between them, there is grave danger that limited wars will become a global war. Obviously, the probability of tremendous, perhaps incalculable, destruction on both sides in a future war needs to be reckoned with when making calculations on the justifiability of any possible war.

However, the notion that the excessive violence of atomic warfare has ended the possibility of a just war does not stand up. The moral problem has been altered, but not eliminated.

The threat of atomic destruction has heightened the criminal irresponsibility of aggression, the employment of war as an instrument of national or bloc policy. Correspondingly, the moral obligation to discourage such a crime or, if it occurs, to deny it victory, has been underscored. The consequences of a successful defense are fearful to contemplate, but the consequences of a successful aggression, with tyrannical monopoly of the weapons of mass destruction, are calculated to be worse. While the avoidance of excessive and indiscriminate violence, and of such destruction as would undermine the basis for future peace remain moral imperatives in a just war, it does not seem possible to draw a line in advance, beyond which it would be better to yield than to resist.

Resistance to aggression, designed to deny it victory and tyrannical control, is not to be equated with victory by those who resist the aggressor. In view of war's new dimension of annihilation, the justification for a defensive war of limited objectives, to prevent conquest and to force an end to hostilities, does not apply equally to the objectives of bringing an aggressor to unconditional surrender and punishment. Because the ultimate consequences of atomic warfare cannot be measured, only the most imperative demands of justice have a clear sanction.

For this reason, the occasions to which the concept of the just war can be rightly applied have become highly restricted. A war to defend the victims of wanton aggression, where the demands of justice join the demands of order, is today the clearest case of a just war. But where the immediate claims of order and justice conflict, as in a war initiated to secure freedom for the oppressed, the case is now much less clear. The claims of justice are no less. But because contemporary war places so many moral values in incalculable jeopardy, the immediate claims of order have become much greater. Although oppression was never more abhorrent to the Christian conscience or more dangerous to the longer-range prospects of peace than today, the concept of a just war does not provide moral justification for initiating a war of incalculable consequences to end such oppression.

While this position gives the claims of order a certain immediate priority over the claims of justice, the fact remains that no lasting peace is possible except on foundations of justice. Nor can the shorter-range prospects be improved unless remedial measures are taken in regard to social injustices likely to erupt as civil and hence international war. Consequently, the restraints imposed by the new dimension of war underline the importance of a vigorous development of methods of peaceful change. For God wills both justice and peace.[18]

For these harsh predicaments of the nuclear age, the pacifists have a simple answer. Let us simply renounce the use of atomic weapons, together with our enemies if possible, but alone if necessary. This answer assumes that it is possible to summon the human will to defy historical development with a resounding "No." But where is this "human will" which could rise to such omnipotence? Unfortunately we do not have moral access to the Russian will. We have to limit ourselves to the will of America and the Western world. Could we possibly, as a nation, risk annihilation or subjugation for the sake of saying "no" to this new development of destruction? Could we risk letting the Russians have the bombs while we are without them? The answer is that no responsible statesman will risk putting his nation in that position of defenselessness. Individuals may, but nations do not thus risk their very existence. Would a gesture of defenselessness possibly soften the Russian heart? That is the other possibility implied in the pacifist solution. The answer is that we have no such assurance. Granted the Russian hope and belief that it has the possibility of bringing its peculiar redemption to the whole world, it is not likely to be impressed by any "moral" gesture from what it believes to be a decadent world. In other words, our will is neither powerful enough nor good enough to accomplish the miracle expected of us in the pacifist position. Yet even a nation can reach the point where it can purchase its life too dearly. If we actually had to use this kind of destruction in order to save our lives, would we find life worth living? [19]

There are, in short, still no easy solutions for these dilemmas of history. There is nothing in the Christian faith which would enable Christians to evade a tragic dilemma which other men face. The development of atomic weapons has heightened the moral dilemmas which periodically generate the pacifist revolt against responsibilities which embody moral ambiguities. But it has not solved them.[20]

III. *Pacifism as Christian Heresy*

If we cannot accept the simple hopes of the pacifists, it is not because we have eliminated Christ from our convictions or decisions. It is because we interpret life, man, history, and even God and Christ in different terms than some of our brethren. We believe that the evil in man is more stubborn, that life and history are more tragic, and that the God who is revealed in Christ is more terrible in His judgments than is envisaged in sentimentalized versions of the Christian faith.[21]

The pacifists do not know human nature well enough to be concerned about the contradictions between the law of love and the sin of man, until sin has conceived and brought forth death. They do not see that sin introduces an element of conflict into the world and that even the most loving relations are not free of it. They are, consequently, unable to appreciate the complexity of the problem of justice. They merely assert that if only men loved one another, all the complex, and sometimes horrible, realities of the political order could be dispensed with. They do not see that their "if" begs the most basic problem of human history.

It is because men are sinners that justice can be achieved only by a certain degree of coercion on the one hand, and by resistance to coercion and tyranny on the other hand.[22]

In this view, most modern forms of Christian pacifism are heretical. Presumably inspired by the Christian Gospel, they have really absorbed the Renaissance faith in the goodness of man, have rejected the Christian doctrine of original sin as an outmoded bit of pessimism, have reinterpreted the Cross so that it is made to stand for the absurd idea that perfect love is guaranteed a simple victory over the world, and have rejected all other profound elements of the Christian gospel as "Pauline" accretions which must be stripped from the "simple gospel of Jesus." It is rather remarkable that so many modern Christians should believe that Christianity is primarily a "challenge" to man to obey the law of Christ; whereas it is, as a matter of fact, a religion which deals realistically with the problem presented by the violation of this law. Far from believing that the ills of the world could be set right "if only" men obeyed the law of Christ, it has always regarded the problem of achieving justice in a sinful world as a very difficult task. In the profounder versions of the Christian faith the very utopian illusions which are currently equated with Christianity have been rigorously disavowed.[23]

Modern pacifism, then, is merely a final fruit of this Renaissance spirit which has pervaded the whole of modern Protestantism. We have interpreted world history as a gradual ascent to the Kingdom of God which waits for final triumph only upon the willingness of Christians to "take Christ seriously." There is nothing in Christ's own teachings, except dubious interpretations of the parable of the leaven and the mustard seed, to justify this interpretation of world history. In the whole of the New Testament, Gospels and Epistles alike, there is only one interpretation of world history. That pictures history as moving toward a climax in which both Christ and anti-Christ are revealed.

The New Testament, in other words, does not envisage a simple triumph of good over evil in history. It sees human history involved in the contradictions of sin to the end. That is why it sees no simple resolution of the problem of history. It believes that the Kingdom of God will finally resolve the contradictions of history; but for it the Kingdom of God is no simple historical possibility. The grace of God for man and the Kingdom of God for history are both divine realities and not human possibilities.

The Christian faith believes that the Atonement reveals God's mercy as an ultimate resource by which God alone overcomes the judgment which sin deserves. If this final truth of the Christian religion has no meaning to modern men, including modern Christians, that is because even the tragic character of contemporary history has not yet persuaded them to take the fact of human sinfulness seriously.[24]

It cannot be denied that these emphases are full of pitfalls for the faithful. There is always the possibility that we will not take Christ as our norm seriously enough, and that we will rest prematurely in the divine mercy.[25] The danger is that we make sin normative when we declare it to be inevitable. We must see the sinfulness of war. But we must also see the sin of egoism in which all life is involved and of which war is the final expression. Furthermore, we must be able to see the difference between the relative virtue of a decent scheme of justice and the real peril of tyranny. A civilization that fights tyrannical barbarism must know at what points its sins approach the barbarism of its foes. But it must also know at what points it is the custodian of values that transcend the sins of its "imperialism." Otherwise its uneasy conscience will betray it into the hands of those who have no moral scruples at all.[26]

IV. *Pacifism as Symbol of the Kingdom*

Nevertheless, it is not possible to regard pacifism simply as a heresy. In one of its aspects modern Christian pacifism is simply a version of Christian perfectionism. It expresses a genuine impulse in the heart of Christianity, the impulse to take the law of Christ seriously and not to allow the political strategies, which the sinful character of man makes necessary, to become final norms.

In medieval ascetic perfectionism and in Protestant sectarian perfectionism the effort to achieve a standard of perfect love in individual life was not presented as a political alternative. On the contrary, the political problem and task were specifically disavowed. This perfectionism did not give itself to the illusion that it had discovered a method for eliminating the element of conflict from political strategies. On the contrary, it regarded the mystery of evil as beyond its power of solution. It was content to set up the most perfect and unselfish individual life as a symbol of the Kingdom of God. It knew that this could only be done by disavowing the political task and by freeing the individual of all responsibility for social justice.

It is this kind of pacifism which is not a heresy. It is rather a valuable asset for the Christian faith. It is a reminder to the Christian community that the relative norms of social justice, which justify both coercion and resistance to coercion, are not final norms, and that Christians are in constant peril of forgetting their relative and tentative character and of making them too completely normative.[27]

Asceticism seeks to achieve a higher degree of individual purity—particularly emancipation from egoism—by mystic discipline of the individual soul, and by withdrawal from the ordinary social relations. The ascetic withdrawal from family, property, and political relations is a proof of its realism. It understands the perennial paradox of man's social life. The most unselfish individual is drawn by his very loyalty to a social group, whether family, race, or nation, into an expression of collective egoism. Individuals may run the risk of annihilation always involved in the practice of complete non-resistance; but it is questionable whether they can justify the same risks when they are dealing with the interests of a group. Perhaps it is even more important that the impulses of both survival and the will-to-power are too strong in the social group to bring a policy of complete non-resistance into the realm of possibilities in collective relationships, even if it could be morally justified. The effort to realize the perfectionist ideals of Christianity can be carried through literally and absolutely only upon an ascetic basis. Thus only can the individual separate himself sufficiently from both the entanglements and natural obligations of broader social life to seek individual purity without being betrayed into either compromise or perversity.[28]

There is, then, a place in Christian thought and life for the kind of goodness that knows martyrdom to be its end and that declares that rather than be involved in the claims and counterclaims of politics, in the struggle for justice with its ambiguous means and its dubious and speculative ends (there is always a risk that the struggle for justice will result not in justice but in anarchy), it would prefer to be defrauded and to die. There is a place for such perfectionism as a symbol of the Kingdom of God, lest we accept the tragic sin in which the struggle for justice involves us as ultimately normative.[29] If any Christian wishes to say that it is incompatible with Christianity to fool with the terrible and sinful relativities of the political world, I for one will accord him my genuine respect and admiration if he leaves the world of politics alone entirely and seeks simply to live by the love commandment in terms which demand an irresponsible attitude toward the problem of collective justice in international and economic terms. Let him, in other words, be a pure pacifist and remind the rest of us, who fool with politics, that we are playing a dangerous game.[30]

Religious pacifism, as a part of a general ascetic and symbolic portrayal of love absolutism in a sinful world, has its own value and justification. A church which does not generate it is the poorer for its lack. But it ought to be clear about its own presuppositions and understand the conflict between the ideal of love and the necessities of natural life.[31]

Religious pacifism ought to recognize, further, that the desire for perfection must invariably express itself parasitically. The celibate disavows the sexual function of procreation in the interest of perfection. The monastics build ideal communities of presumably perfect individuals who have freed themselves of the taint and contamination of the ambiguous institutions of property and government. Both these institutions are necessities of community in a sinful world. They are subject to corruption because they both make use of power for the sake of order or of justice but both can be used for self-aggrandizement. The perfect individuals who flee from these ambiguities are necessarily parasitic on the justice and the order provisionally established by these institutions.[32] The acknowledgment of parasitism will prevent pacifism from being corrupted by pharisaism. It can therefore testify against us without tempting us to resist sinful pharisaism with sinful arrogance.[33]

To sum up: we may admit that the pacifists are right in their conviction that our civilization stands under the judgment of God; no one can have an easy conscience about the social and political anarchy out of which the horrible tyrannies of our age have arisen. But they are wrong in assuming that we have no right or duty to defend a civilization, despite its imperfections, against worse alternatives. They are right in insisting that love is the ultimate law of life. But they have failed to realize to what degree the sinfulness of all men, even the best, makes justice between competing interests and conflicting wills a perennial necessity of history.

The pacifists rightly recognize that it may be very noble for an individual to sacrifice his life or interests rather than participate in the claims and counterclaims of the struggle for justice (of which war may always be the *ultima ratio*). They are wrong in making no distinction between an individual act of self-abnegation and a political policy of submission to injustice, whereby lives and interests other than our own are defrauded or destroyed. They seek erroneously to build a political platform upon individual perfection.[34]

CHAPTER XIV

The Relevance of the Love Ethic to Politics

I. *The Relevance of an Impossible Ideal*

Christianity is a religion with an ethic so pure that it has difficulty in coming to terms with political realities; for in politics moral ideas are inevitably compounded with the practical necessities of conflict and coercion. With its religio-moral ideal of perfect love, it is not quite certain how to approach and what to do with the stubborn realities of the political order; whether it should compromise with them, flee them or be indifferent to them.[1]

Yet Christians must find ways of bringing the love ethic to bear on their political decisions. If the Christian humility which has no illusions about our ideals and structures or about any of the realities of the community is the negative precondition of a Christian social ethic, the positive form of it is the application of the law of love to man's collective relations.

The problem of the application of the law of love to the collective relationships of mankind contains within itself the whole question of the possibility of a Christian social ethic. When Catholic thought embodies the law of love into counsels of perfection and relegates these to the realm of ultimate possibilities of the "supernatural" life in the individual, and when it seeks to regulate the collective relations of mankind by the standards of "justice" which are given in the natural law, it is seeking to come to terms with the realities of the social order which seem to make the law of love inapplicable. This is also behind the logic of the thought of Protestant theologians who, following Luther, relegate love and forgiveness to the heavenly kingdom, as distinguished from the "earthly" one, where "the sword and the law," that is power and coercion, prevail. On the other hand, we have long since learned to recognize the sentimentality of Christian liberalism and other forms of liberalism which regard the establishment of "motives of service" in contrast to the "profit motive" as a simple possibility.

The question is therefore how, if love is not a simple possibility, it may yet be relevant to our political decisions. This question really involves the relevance of our final Christian insights as individuals to our actions as members of the group. As individuals we know the law of love to be final, if we view life through the revelation of Christ. The real problem of a Christian social ethic, then, is to derive from the Gospel a clear view of the realities with which we must deal in our common or social life, and also to preserve a sense of responsibility for achieving the highest measure of order, freedom and justice despite the hazards of man's collective life.[2] We must establish tentative harmonies and provisional equities in a world from which sin cannot be eliminated, and yet hold these provisional and tentative moral achievements under the perspective of the Kingdom of God.[3]

Of course, when the Church proclaims the love commandment to the world as the law of God it must guard against the superficial moralism of telling the world that it can save itself if men will only stop being selfish and learn to be loving. We dare not forget that in us, as well as in those who do not acknowledge the Christian gospel, there is a law in our members that wars against the law that is in our mind. The law of love is not kept simply by being preached. Yet it is the law of life and must be both preached and practiced. It is a terrible heresy to suggest that, because the world is sinful, we have a right to construct a Machiavellian politics or a Darwinian sociology as normative for Christians.

What is significant about the Christian ethic is precisely this: that it does not regard the historic as normative. Man may be, as Thomas Hobbes observed, a wolf to his fellowman. But this is not his essential nature. Let realistic Christians beware that they do not accept the habits of a sinful world as the norms of a Christian collective life. For the Christian only the law of love is normative. He would do well to remember that he is a sinner who has never perfectly kept the law of God. But neither must he forget that he is a child of God who stands under that law.

Frequently, believing Christians are tempted by their recognition of the sinfulness of human existence to disavow their own responsibility for a tolerable justice in the world's affairs. A Christian pessimism which becomes a temptation to irresponsibility toward all those social tasks which constantly confront the life of men and nations—tasks of ordering the productive labor of men, of adjudicating their conflicts, of arbitrating their divergent desires, of raising the level of their social imagination and increasing the range of their social sympathies—such a pessimism cannot speak redemptively to a world constantly threatened by anarchy and suffering from injustice. The Christian gospel which transcends all particular and contemporary social situations can be preached with power only by a Church which bears its share of the burdens of immediate situations in which men are involved, burdens of establishing peace, of achieving justice, and of perfecting justice in the spirit of love. Thus is the Kingdom of God which is not of this world made relevant to every problem of the world.[4]

II. *The Relevancies of Love to Political Life*

1. LOVE AS INDETERMINATE POSSIBILITY AND OBLIGATION

Life in history must be recognized as filled with indeterminate possibilities of love. There is no individual or interior spiritual situation, no cultural or scientific task, and no social or political problem in which men do not face new possibilities of the good and the obligation to realize them.[5]

The love commandment is thus a guide for the approximations of justice and love which make up the woof and warp of everyday existence. It is a challenge, because there is no human situation in which love does not present possibilities of action higher than the conventional and traditional customs and habits of men. While the limitations of nature and the sin of egoism make it impossible for me to love the neighbor as the self, I can never use that final impossibility as an excuse for complacence toward the neighbor's life and interest. There are no exact limits to the degree of imagination with which I may enter into the needs and consider the interests of the neighbor. The love commandment is therefore always a challenge which stands vertically over every moral act and achievement. It defines the dimension, ending in a transcendent Kingdom of God, in which all moral actions take place.

But moral actions are subject not only to this "vertical" challenge, but also to "horizontal" ones. Human life is under obligation not only to perfect every moral attitude in the direction of perfect love, but to extend it in the direction of universal love. A Christian feels a tension not only to make his family life, in a measure, into a symbol of the Kingdom of God, but also to extend the loving relations which prevail in the family to life which is not bound to him by natural consanguinity. He lives under the challenge: "If ye love them that love you, what thanks have ye?"[6]

So there are no limits to be set in history for the achievement of more universal brotherhood, for the development of more perfect and more inclusive mutual relations. All the characteristic hopes and aspirations of Renaissance and Enlightenment, of both secular and Christian liberalism, are right in at least this, that they understand that side of the Christian doctrine which regards the *Agape* of the Kingdom of God as a resource for infinite developments toward a more perfect brotherhood in history. The uneasy conscience of man over various forms of social injustice, over slavery and war, is an expression of the Christian feeling that history must move from the innocency of Adam to the perfection of Christ, from the harmony of life with life in unfree nature to the perfect love of the Kingdom of God. For the freedom of man makes it impossible to set any limits of race, sex, or social condition upon the brotherhood which may be achieved in history.

Even the purest form of *Agape,* the love of the enemy and forgiveness toward the evil-doer, do not stand in contradiction to historical possibilities.[7] While social consequences are not considered in such a moral strategy, it would be shortsighted to deny that it may result in redemptive social consequences, at least within the area of individual and personal relationships. Forgiveness may not always prompt the wrong-doer to repentance; but yet it may. Loving the enemy may not soften the enemy's heart; but there are possibilities that it will.[8] The Christian doctrine of Creation does not set the eternal and divine into absolute contradiction to the temporal and the historical. There are, therefore, validations of *Agape* in actual history, insofar as concern for the other actually elicits a reciprocal response.[9]

To state the point on another level: the most direct relationship of love to the problems of community would seem to be the purifying effect of sacrificial love upon mutual love. Mutual love and loyalty are, in a sense, the highest possibilities of social life, rising above the rational calculations and the power-balances of its rough justice. The grace of sacrificial love prevents mutual love from degenerating into a mere calculation of mutual advantages. If mutual love is not constantly replenished by impulses of grace in which there are no calculations of mutual advantages, mutual relations degenerate first to the cool calculation of such advantages and finally to resentment over the inevitable lack of complete reciprocity in all actual relations. Justice degenerates into mere order without justice if the pull of love is not upon it.[10]

The law of love is, therefore, not a norm of history in the sense that historical experience justifies it. Historical experience justifies more complex social strategies in which the self, individual and collective, seeks both to preserve its life and to relate it harmoniously to other lives. But such strategies of mutual love and of systems of justice cannot maintain themselves without inspiration from a deeper dimension of history.[11]

2. LOVE AS INDISCRIMINATE CRITICISM AND JUDGMENT

The perpetual relevance of the norm of *Agape* to the structure of human existence lies in the fact that it is not only the fulfillment of the self's freedom but also the contradiction of every actual self-realization insofar as every actual self-realization is partly an egoistic and therefore a premature closing of the self within itself. *Agape* is thus, as the final norm of the self as free spirit, a perpetual source of judgment upon every other norm which may be used tentatively to describe the self's duties and obligations.[12] Perfect love is the very ideal which discloses the imperfections of every concrete moral achievement by revealing the alloy of egoism which expresses itself in every act of history, particularly in every collective act.[13]

As a principle of indiscriminate criticism upon all forms of justice, the law of love reminds us that the injustice and tyranny against which we contend in the foe are partially the consequence of our own injustice, that the pathology of Nazi Germany, for example, was partially a consequence of the vindictiveness of the peace of Versailles, and that the ambition of a tyrannical imperialism is different only in degree and not in kind from the imperial impulse which characterizes all of human life.

The Christian faith ought to persuade us that political controversies are always conflicts between sinners and not between righteous men and sinners. It ought to mitigate the self-righteousness which is an inevitable concomitant of all human conflict. The spirit of contrition is an important ingredient in the sense of justice. If it is powerful enough it may be able to restrain the impulse of vengeance sufficiently to allow a decent justice to emerge. The recognition of the law of love as an indiscriminate principle of criticism over all attempts at social and international justice is actually a resource of justice, for it prevents the pride, self-righteousness and vindictiveness of men from corrupting their efforts at justice.[14]

Thus the Christian conception of the relation of historical justice to the love of the Kingdom of God is a dialectical one. Love is both the fulfillment and the negation of all achievements of justice in history. Or expressed from the opposite standpoint, the achievements of justice in history may rise in indeterminate degrees to find their fulfillment in a more perfect love and brotherhood; but each new level of fulfillment also contains elements which stand in contradiction to perfect love. There are therefore obligations to realize justice in indeterminate degrees; but none of the realizations can assure the serenity of perfect fulfillment. If we analyze the realities of history in terms of this formula it will throw light on aspects of history which would otherwise remain obscure and perplexing; and will obviate mistakes which are inevitably made under alternative interpretations. Higher realizations of historic justice would be possible if it were more fully understood that all such realizations contain contradictions to, as well as approximations of, the ideal of love. Sanctification in the realm of social relations demands recognition of the impossibility of perfect sanctification.[15]

3. LOVE AS THE STANDARD FOR DISCRIMINATE DECISIONS

We have seen that the love universalism of Jesus establishes a viewpoint from which human ends may be recognized as proximate and not ultimate, and our loyalties as parochial rather than universal. But it must be emphasized that this love universalism is not inimical to a discriminating social ethic. It maintains relevance to a social ethic by Jesus' insistence that the love of God and the love of neighbor are not competitive; that they are two sides of the same shield.[16] Love is thus a principle of discriminate criticism among various forms of community and various attempts at justice.[17]

The serious and difficult problem is that of the relationship of the heedlessness of perfect love to the discriminate judgments which are required to weigh competing values and interests in the field of social relations. Perfect love is sacrificial love, making no careful calculations between the interests of the self and the other. Perfect justice is discriminate and calculating, carefully measuring the limits of interests and the relation between the interests of the self and the other. The spirit of justice is particularly well served if reason finds the points of coincidence between the interests of the self and those of the other, or if not, if it makes careful and discriminate judgments between them. What can this heedlessness of *Agape* have to do with discrimination?

We cannot doubt that Christians must make their decisions about political and economic alternatives with a sense of responsibility to the divine will as revealed in Christ. But the question is whether there are any criteria whereby we can judge among alternative movements. The love which is the final criterion is obviously a principle of criticism upon all political and economic realities, since it reveals the sinful element of self-seeking and of coercive restraint in all forms of human community. But does it help us to arrive at discriminate choices among alternative systems and policies, since all of them have morally ambiguous elements in them? [18]

To look at human communities from the perspective of the Kingdom of God is to know that there is a sinful element in all the expedients which the political order uses to establish justice. But it must also be recognized that it is not possible to eliminate the sinful element in the political expedients. They are, in the words of St. Augustine, both the consequence of, and the remedy for, sin. If they are the remedy for sin, the ideal of love is not merely a principle of indiscriminate criticism upon all approximations of justice. It is also a principle of discriminate criticism among forms of justice.[19]

The Christian faith does throw light upon the immediate historical issues which man faces. Christianity is not a flight into eternity from the tasks and decisions of history. It is rather the power and the wisdom of God which makes decisions in history possible and which points to proximate goals in history which are usually obscured either by optimistic illusions or by the despair which follows upon the dissipation of these illusions.[20] *

4. LOVE AS CONTRITION AND FORGIVENESS

The heedlessness of love, which sacrifices the interests of the self, enters into calculations of justice principally by becoming the spirit of contrition which issues from the self's encounter with God. In that encounter it is made aware of the contingent character of all human claims and the tainted character of all human pretensions and ideals. This contrition is the socially relevant counterpart of love. It breaks the pride of the implacable contestants and competitors in all human encounters and persuades them to be "kindly affectioned one with another, forgiving one another, even also as God in Christ has forgiven you" (Ephesians 4:32). This spirit lies at the foundation of what we define as democracy. For democracy cannot exist if there is no recognition of the fragmentary character of all systems of thought and value which are allowed to exist together within the democratic frame. Thus the *Agape* of forgiveness as well as the *Agape* of sacrificial love become a leaven in the lump of the spirit of justice. Or rather it would be better to use the other Gospel symbol and define them as the "salt" which arrests the decay in the spirit of justice.[21]

For Christianity is not simply a new law, namely, the law of love. The finality of Christianity cannot be proved by analyses which seek to reveal that the law of love is stated more unambiguously and perfectly in the life and teachings of Christ than anywhere else. Christianity is a religion which measures the total dimension of human existence not only in terms of the final norm of human conduct, which is expressed in the law of love, but also in terms of the fact of sin. It recognizes that the same man who can become his true self only by striving infinitely for self-realization beyond himself is also inevitably involved in the sin of infinitely making his partial and narrow self the true end of existence. It believes, in other words, that though Christ is the true norm (the "second Adam") for every man, every man is also in some sense a crucifier of Christ.

The good news of the Gospel, therefore, is not the law that we ought to love one another. The good news of the Gospel is that there is a resource of divine mercy which is able to overcome a contradiction within our own souls which we cannot ourselves overcome. The grace of God

* Niebuhr's further treatment of love as the standard of discriminate decisions will be found, not only in the remainder of Part II, but also in the applications of Part III.

which is revealed in Christ is regarded by Christian faith as, on the one hand, an actual "power of righteousness" which heals the contradiction within our hearts. In that sense Christ defines the actual possibilities of human existence. On the other hand, this grace is conceived as "justification," as pardon rather than power, as the forgiveness of God, which is vouchsafed to man despite the fact that he never achieves the full measure of Christ. In that sense Christ is the "impossible possibility." Loyalty to him means realization in intention, but does not actually mean the full realization of the measure of Christ. In this doctrine of forgiveness and justification, Christianity measures the full seriousness of sin as a permanent factor in human history.[22]

Thus Biblical faith ends by seeing human history perpetually, and on every level of its achievements, in contradiction to the divine. It sees the possibilities of new beginnings in history only upon the basis of the contrite recognition of this contradiction. Significantly the same suffering love, the same *Agape* of Christ which reveals the divine mercy is also the norm of a new life. Men may have this new life if they discern what they are and what God is in this focal point of God's self-disclosure. Such a point in human history can be regarded both as the beginning of a new age for all mankind and as a new beginning for every individual man who is "called" by it, because both the individual and the collective realities of human existence are fully disclosed in it. If apprehended at all they are so apprehended that the old self, which makes itself its own end, is destroyed and a new self is born. That is why a true revelation of the divine is never merely wisdom but also power.[23]

In its profoundest insights, then, the Christian faith sees the whole of human history as involved in guilt, and finds no release from guilt except in the grace of God. The Christian is freed by that grace to act in history; to give his devotion to the highest values he knows; to defend those citadels of civilization of which necessity and historic destiny have made him the defender; and he is persuaded by that grace to remember the ambiguity of even his best actions. If the providence of God does not enter the affairs of men to bring good out of evil, the evil in our good may easily destroy our most ambitious efforts and frustrate our highest hopes.[24]

III. *Love and the Life of Groups*

Is the love ethic relevant to the life of groups in the same ways that it bears upon the life of individual persons? Though on the whole nations and other collectives are not expected to conform to a moral standard higher than that of a prudent self-interest, yet it is possible to observe the moral debate in the "spiritual life" of nations as well as in individuals, and common-sense moral judgments do cast blame upon nations for a too consistent devotion to their own interests, involving indifference to a wider good. This moral blame is justified; for though no nation will venture beyond its own interest into a system of mutual security, yet the power of even enlightened self-interest is not sufficient alone to prompt such a venture. It must be supported by a concern for a wider good, beyond its own interests.[25] If the conscience of individuals within the community does not operate to concern life within it with the welfare of life outside of it, the collective self-concern of the nation will express itself in narrower and more self-defeating terms. That is why love cannot be declared irrelevant even for the life of the community (chiefly the modern nation) and why the individual conscience must be concerned with the conduct of the community even if its dictates in their purest form are not directly relevant.[26]

Nations are thus subject, as are individuals, to an internal tension between the claims of the self and the larger claim of love. Whether the second claim is tolerably met represents a spiritual issue beyond the mere calculations of prudence. Here is the responsible self in the collective life of mankind. Insofar as nations, even more than individuals, never adequately meet the wider claim, the responsible self is also the guilty self.[27]

Ruling groups within a nation and hegemonic nations in a community of nations face the alternative of dying because they try too desperately to live, or of achieving a new life by dying to self. This alternative is offered when their power, prestige and pride are challenged by the emergence of new social forces in history. The emergence of these new forces is the historic execution of the absolute judgment which constantly hangs over them by reason of their "sin." In history God always chooses "the things which are not, to put to nought things that are" (I Corinthians 1:28). A traditional equilibrium of power, an established structure of justice, a hallowed system of social norms, come under historic judgment when the emergence of new classes or nations, or the acquisition of new technics or powers in the hands of previously subject groups, challenges the established hierarchical structure of power. Such new elements and forces are constantly arising in history.

It is precisely at the point of challenge by new forces that the old structures, powers and forms of life either atrophy and are destroyed, or submit to judgment and are renewed. They atrophy and are destroyed if and when the challenge of new competing forces in history tempts them to make even more extravagant claims for the absolute validity of their power and justice than they have previously made, and to regard the competitor and foe not merely as an interloper but as a foe of all order and justice.

But there is fortunately another possibility in history. The powers and majesties, the institutions and structures of human contrivance do not always meet the challenge of competitive forces by increased rigidity and idolatry. Sometimes the competitive challenge serves to moderate the idolatrous claims. Judgment leads to repentance. There is not as clearly defined an experience of repentance in the life of communities and social institutions as in that of individuals. Yet there is a possibility that old forms and structures of life may be renewed, rather than destroyed by the vicissitudes of history. These experiences establish the validity of the Christian doctrine of life through death for the collective, as well as for the individual, organism.

There are, in fact, indeterminate possibilities of such renewal of the life of groups so that no culture or civilization need die by a fateful necessity of its sin. But the judgments of God are not so clear to nations or cultures that they could escape a final *Nemesis,* when some final triumph or some extraordinary period of stability, or some phenomenal success tempts them to a final form of *Hybris.*

The significance of the contest of the prophets of Israel with the pride of their nation lies precisely in the fact that in the contest it became more and more apparent that only a "saving remnant" within the nation could finally understand the ultimate issue. The prophets warned the nation, but their warnings were heeded only relatively. In the absolute sense Israel, like every other nation, defied them. This is why the messianic hopes for the renewal of the nation became more and more a hope for the redemption of the whole of history. Ideally the Christian community is the "saving remnant" which calls nations to repentance and renewal without the false belief that any nation or culture could finally fulfill the meaning of life or complete the purpose of history.[28] *

IV. *Love Beyond Politics*

Naturally, the justice and harmony which is achieved collectively, through various social strategies, is not the harmony of the Kingdom of God, nor yet identical with the highest possible harmony between individuals in their personal relations. For this reason, there must always be a final distinction between what the Gospel demands of us in the institutions and structures of society and what is demanded in our individual and spontaneous relations. It is equally idle to expect spontaneous and gracious personal relations to take the place of law, or to expect any system of law or any codified relationship to exhaust the possibilities of grace and freedom which can be expressed by individuals above and beyond the law. For, on the one hand, Christians must always reconsider

* The problem of relating the requirements of love and justice to the "national interest" is treated in Chapter XXVI.

the organizations and arrangements through which the toil of men is organized so that impediments to life's more ultimate purposes may be removed. But on the other hand, they must seek to serve God, that is, consider the ultimate purpose of their toil, no matter how inadequate may be the structure of justice in which they are forced to toil.[29]

Which is to say that, finally, beyond and above every human relation as ordered by a fixed structure of justice, by custom, tradition, and legal enactment, there remain indeterminate possibilities of love in the individual and personal encounters of those who are in the structure. Whether men meet their fellow men with generosity or with envy, with imagination or with ambitions of dominion, is a question which cannot be fully solved by the structure of justice which binds them to their fellow men. Human actions can, to a degree, corrupt even the highest structure and they can also partially redeem the worst structure. The fact that slavery was essentially wrong proves the invalidity of regarding structures of justice as irrelevant to love. Yet it did make a difference to a slave whether he was subject to a kind or to a cruel master. The institution was wrong because the disproportions of power in the institution of slavery were such that they could predispose even decent men to unconscious cruelties. But the most adequate institution is still only a bare base upon which the higher experiences of love must be built.

The commandment to love the neighbor as the self must finally culminate in the individual experience in which one self seeks to penetrate deeply into the mystery of the other self and yet stand in reverence before a mystery which he has no right to penetrate. This kind of love is a matter of law in the sense that the essential nature of man, with his indeterminate freedom, requires that human relations should finally achieve such an intimacy. But it is also a matter of grace because no sense of obligation can provide the imagination and forebearance by which this is accomplished. Such intimacy is of course closely related to sacrificial love, for the intermingling of life with life predisposes to sacrificial abandonment of the claims of the self for the needs of the other.[30]

In summary, we must recognize how dialectically the Kingdom of God is related to the sinful world in every moment of existence, offering both judgment and a more excellent way in consideration of every problem of justice. The gospel command of love is surely in the realm of the Kingdom of God. But the Kingdom of God is not simply trans-historical. It is involved in every moment of history. It is a clue to the fact that every moment of history is a moment of judgment. For it reveals the law of life which life defies and for the defiance of which life is destroyed. But it is also a revelation of mercy and grace in human history. It reveals the infinite possibilities under which all human actions take place. The love commandment is, in short, immediately relevant to every moral action.[31]

CHAPTER XV

Love, Justice and the Question of Natural Law

I. *Love and the Necessity of Justice*

In the Christian faith the final law in which all other law is fulfilled is the law of love. But this law does not abrogate the laws of justice, except as love rises above justice to exceed its demands. The ordinary affairs of the community, the structures of politics and economics, must be governed by the spirit of justice and by specific and detailed definitions of rights and duties.[1]

The orthodox Christian church, both Catholic and Protestant, has taken the position that the law of love is not fully applicable to the world of politics, since politics is concerned with the establishment of justice in a "world of sin." The church has admitted, in other words, that, however much egoism must be chastised as sin, it must be taken for granted in man's collective behavior. If the elimination of egoism was not to be hoped for, the church was bound to draw the conclusion that justice in politics must be established by conflict and coercion. Conflict is necessary because relative justice depends upon setting interest against interest in the hope of achieving a degree of equality and stability between conflicting interests. Coercion is necessary in order that organized society may prevent the expression of inordinate egoism on the part of individuals and groups. The lesser, but more relevant, ideal of justice was substituted for the purer ideal of love.

This political realism in the viewpoint of orthodox Christianity stands in wholesome contrast to the romanticism of liberal Christianity, which imagines that it has, in the law of love, a moral ideal which will painlessly transmute the realities of politics.[2] American Christianity, particularly, tends to be irrelevant to the problems of justice because it persists in presenting the law of love as a simple solution for every communal problem.

The effort to substitute the law of love for the spirit of justice instead of recognizing love as the fulfillment and highest form of the spirit of justice, is thus derived from the failure to measure the power and persistence of self-interest. It is because self-interest is not easily overcome in even the life of the "redeemed" that most of the harmonies of life are not the perfect harmonies of fully co-ordinated wills but the tolerable harmonies of balanced interests and mutually recognized claims.[3]

Moreover, justice requires calculated and discriminate judgments between conflicting claims. A Christian justice will be particularly critical of the claims of the self as against the claims of the other, but it will not dismiss them out of hand. Without this criticism all justice becomes corrupted into a refined form of self-seeking. But if the claims of the self (whether individual or collective) are not entertained, there is no justice at all. There is an ecstatic form of *Agape* which defines the ultimate heroic possibilities of human existence (involving of course martyrdom), but not the common possibilities of tolerable harmony of life with life.

But if justice requires that the interests of the self be entertained, it also requires that they be resisted. Every realistic system of justice must assume the continued power of self-interest, particularly of collective self-interest. It must furthermore assume that this power will express itself illegitimately as well as legitimately. It must therefore be prepared to resist illegitimate self-interest, even among the best men and the most just nations. A simple Christian moralism counsels men to be unselfish. A profounder Christian faith must encourage men to create systems of justice which will save society and themselves from their own selfishness.[4]

The closest approximation to a love in which life supports life in voluntary community is a justice in which life is prevented from destroying life and the interests of the one are guarded against unjust claims by the other. Such justice is achieved when impartial tribunals of society prevent men "from being judges in their own cases," in the words of John Locke.[5]

Yet, love remains both the fulfillment and the abyss of the rational ideal of justice. Justice is the highest rational moral ideal because reason must seek to deal with human relations and moral conduct in terms of the ascertainable causes and consequences of action. A good act must be rewarded and an evil one punished. The interest of my neighbor must be guarded; but my own interests deserve protection as well. Yet all rational justice constantly sinks to something less than justice.

Remedial justice fails to "do justice" to the causes which prompted an evil act because it is ignorant of the operations of mind and conscience in that secret place where actions are compounded. If reason should grow imaginative ("Love is justice grown imaginative," declares Santayana), and make shrewd guesses about the source of evil actions, it will result in a fairer justice. But if it should become so sensitive as to recognize that the evil in the other has its sources in the self or the self's society, it will destroy every form of remedial justice. "Let him who is without sin cast the first stone." Thus love is both the fulfillment and the denial of remedial or punitive justice.

Love is related to distributive justice in the same manner. It is "right" that I protect my own interests as well as those of my neighbor. But an imaginative regard for the interests of my neighbor will be concerned for his needs even if they are in competition with mine. Such an imaginative concern for the neighbor's interests transcends all ordinary conceptions of equity and enjoins actions of generosity which no society can ever enjoin or regularize. But this same tendency toward the fulfillment of justice in love leads to the negation of justice by love. The neighbor's interests are avowed rather than my own and no effort is made to protect myself against the neighbor ("resist not evil"). Thus morality is fed by a realm of transcendent possibilities in which the canons of the good established in ordinary experience are both fulfilled and negated. That is why Jesus could symbolize the mercy of God through the impartiality of nature in which the sun shines on the evil and the good and rain falls upon the just and the unjust. The impartiality of nature is something less than human justice—and a symbol of something more, the mercy of God.[6]

To sum up: in so far as justice admits the claims of the self, it is something less than love. Yet it cannot exist without love and remain justice. For without the "grace" of love, justice always degenerates into something less than justice.[7] Thus laws and systems of justice have a negative as well as a positive relation to mutual love and brotherhood. They contain both approximations of and contradictions to the spirit of love.[8] There is therefore no justice, even in a sinful world, which can be regarded as finally normative. The higher possibilities of love, which is at once the fulfillment and the negation of justice, always hover over every system of justice.[9]

II. *The Natural Law Position*

The relation of justice to love contains complexities which may be clarified by considering them in two dimensions. The first is the dimension of rules and laws of justice. The second is the dimension of structures of justice, of social and political organizations in their relation to brotherhood. The difference between the first and second dimension obviously lies in the fact that laws and principles of justice are more abstractly conceived, while structures and organizations embody more the vitalities of history. The contradiction between actual social institutions and arrangements and the ideal of love is obviously greater than between love and the rules and laws of justice.[10]

One might define a more precise descending scale of relativity. The moral principle may be more valid than the political principles which are derived from it. The political principles may have greater validity than the specific applications by which they are made relevant to a particular situation. And the specific applications may have a greater validity than the impulses and ambitions of the social hegemony of a given period which applies or pretends to apply them. There was a greater degree of validity in the ethical content of medieval natural law than in the social and political hegemony of priests and landed aristocrats in the feudal society. And there is more truth in the natural law as Jefferson conceived it than there was justice in the social hegemony of monopolistic capitalism which maintained its prestige by appeals to Jefferson's principles.[11]*

It is in this context, on the level of laws and principles of justice, that the classical problem of the "natural law" may best be treated. The natural law is, according to both Stoic teachers and the Christian fathers, the law of reason. It supposedly establishes universal standards of right conduct and action which are not identical with the standards of love but have equal validity as laws of God. The theory of the natural law is thus the instrument by which the orthodox church adjusted itself to the world after the hope of the *parousia* waned. This was natural enough since the love perfectionism of the Gospels, with its implied anarchism and universalism, was obviously not applicable to the arbitration of conflicting interests and the choice of relative values required in an imperfect world.[12]

Following St. Paul, Christian thought has consistently maintained that the law must be regarded, not simply as something which is given man either by revelation or by the authority of society, but as written in the heart. This can only mean that the requirements of action, dictated by man's essential nature, are a part of his real self. They stand outside of the self in action; that is why they are "law," and appear in the guise of something imposed from without and are only the "form of knowledge and of truth" (Romans 2:20).

The particular content of the voice of conscience is of course conditioned by all the relativities of history. Men may be mistaken in their interpretation of what life is essentially; and conscience may be, in its very content, a vehicle of sin. Yet even in its content the universalities of conscience are at least as significant as its varieties and relativities. One must conclude that the real structure of life, for instance the dependence of man upon his fellowmen which requires both organic and loving rela-

* In various other passages, Niebuhr has drawn still finer distinctions in the scale of moral relativity. A complete catalog would appear to include, in descending order: the love ideal, absolute natural law, relative natural law, "political principles," positive or civil law, basic social structures and institutions, and finally the level of naked power conflicts. See especially *Human Destiny*, pp. 244–57.

tions between them, asserts itself, in spite of all errors, and against the confusion which human egoism and pride introduce into the relations of men.

In theological terms, the original righteousness or perfection is present with sinful man as law, and we may tentatively define this law as derived from man's essential nature and distinguish between organic structure and freedom in man's essential nature. What is usually known as "natural law" in both Christian and Stoic thought is roughly synonymous with the requirements of man as creature, and the virtues defined in Catholic thought as "theological virtues," that is the virtues faith, hope and love, are the requirements of his freedom and represent the *justitia originalis*. This righteousness is not completely lost in the Fall but remains with sinful man as the knowledge of what he ought to be, as the law of his freedom.[13]

Consequently, even if we do not accept the Catholic theory of a highly specific "natural law," we all do accept the reality of principles of justice which transcend the positive enactments of historic states and which are less specific and not so sharply defined as positive law, and yet more specific than the law of love. These are generated in the customs and mores of communities; and they may rise to universal norms which seem to have their source not in particular communities but in the common experience of mankind.[14]

III. *A Critique of Natural Law*

But there are serious difficulties preventing full acceptance of the classical versions of the natural law concept. The primary mistake of Catholic theory is precisely the sharp and absolute distinction which it makes between the natural law which states the requirements of man as creature and the *justitia originalis* which states the requirements of man's freedom. It speaks of an original righteousness which was lost in the Fall and a natural justice which remains essentially uncorrupted by the Fall. This distinction obscures the complex relation of human freedom to all of man's natural functions, and the consequent involvement of all "natural" or "rational" standards and norms in sin. There is therefore no uncorrupted natural law, just as there is no completely lost original justice. The freedom of man sets every standard of justice under higher possibilities, and the sin of man perennially insinuates contingent and relative elements into the supposedly absolute standards of human reason.

Undue confidence in human reason, as the seat and source of natural law, makes this very concept of law into a vehicle of human sin. It gives the sanctity of universality to the peculiar conditions and unique circumstances in which reason operates in a particular historical moment. The confidence of medieval Catholicism in the ability of an unspoiled reason to arrive at definitive standards of natural justice thus became the very vehicle of the sinful pretensions of the age. The social ethics of Thomas Aquinas embody the peculiarities and the contingent factors of a feudal-agrarian economy into a system of fixed socio-ethical principles.

The relativizing effect of both freedom and sin upon all historical norms may be illustrated by a few specific examples. In Catholic natural law all social relations, including family relations, are precisely defined. *Inter alia* it is maintained that the natural law prohibits birth control and also that it enjoins the supremacy of the husband over the wife. The prohibition of birth control assumes that the sexual function in human life must be limited to its function in nature, that of procreation. But it is the very character of human life that all animal functions are touched by freedom and released into more complex relationships. This freedom is the basis of both creativity and sin. Freedom in relation to sex may occasion license and it may also provide for a creative relation between the sexual impulse and other more complex and refined spiritual impulses. It is not possible to escape the natural fact that the primary purpose of bisexuality in nature is that of procreation. But it is not easy to establish a universally valid "law of reason" which will eternally set the bounds for the function of sex in the historic development of human personality.

As for the supremacy of the male over the female, a rationalistic feminism is undoubtedly inclined to transgress inexorable bounds set by nature. On the other hand any premature fixation of certain historical standards in regard to the family will inevitably tend to reinforce male arrogance and to retard justified efforts on the part of the female to achieve such freedom as is not incompatible with the primary function of motherhood. The freedom which is the unique capacity of humankind makes it difficult to set precise standards for all time for any kind of relationship, including the relation between the sexes. The sinfulness of man, on the other hand, makes it inevitable that a dominant class, group, and sex should seek to define as permanently normative a relationship which guarantees its dominance.

The limitations of Catholic natural law theories are revealed with equal clarity when applied to the field of international relations. The Catholic theory of a "just war" is a case in point. The Catholic theory is infinitely superior to the Lutheran relativism and moral skepticism which finally leaves the Christian without any standards by which he might judge the relative justice of his nation's cause. Nevertheless, it assumes that obvious distinctions between "justice" and "injustice," between "defense" and "aggression," are possible. Contemporary history reinforces the clear lessons of the whole of history upon this point. Not all wars are equally just and not all contestants are equally right. Distinctions must be made. But the judgments with which we make them are influenced by passions and interests, so that even the most obvious case of aggression can be made to appear a necessity of defense; and even a war which is judged by neutral opinion to be wholly defensive cannot be waged with completely good conscience because the situations out of which wars arise are charged with memories of previous acts of aggression on the part of those now in defense. Men do have to make important decisions in history upon the basis of certain norms. But they must recognize that all historic norms are touched with both finiteness and sin; and that their sinfulness consists precisely in the bogus claim of finality which is made for them.[15]

In both Stoic and Catholic theory special consideration was given to the situation created by the fact of sin by distinguishing between an absolute and a relative natural law. The former represents the demands of conscience without compromise with the fact of sin. The latter stated the legal and moral necessities of a sinful world. Thus the absolute natural law demanded complete liberty and equality. The relative natural law, on the other hand, defined the necessary coercion of government, the inequalities of property and class, including slavery, and the necessities of conflict. The absolute natural law outlawed war while the relative natural law recognized it as a necessary method of achieving justice in a sinful world.

These distinctions correspond to actual realities in the moral experience which modern secular and Christian utopianism disregards. Nevertheless, just as Catholic rationalism makes too complete a distinction between natural law and the *justitia originalis,* it also tends to differentiate too completely between a relative and absolute natural law. The distinctions are too absolute because it is never possible to define the limits of the force of sin or of the ideal possibilities which transcend sin. One cannot, by definition, determine where and when an inequality of nature or history must be accepted as ineluctable fate and where it must be defied. Nor can one determine in advance where and when tyranny and injustice must be resisted even if such resistance results in overt conflict. If the distinction between relative and absolute natural law is made too sharp, as it is in medieval theory, the inequality and conflict which the relative law allows is accepted too complacently.

There are no precise distinctions between relative and absolute natural law, as there are none between natural law and the law of love, for the simple reason that the freedom of the spirit is so enmeshed in the necessities of nature, and the health and sickness of that freedom are so involved in each other, that it is not possible to make rules isolating certain aspects of nature and sin without having them disturbed by the claims of the law of love as the requirement of freedom.[16]

Thus it was the weakness of both classical and medieval theories that they assumed an order in history conforming to the uniformities of nature. Aristotle was aware of deviations in history, greater than those in nature; but he believed that there was nevertheless one form "which was marked by nature as the best." There is, in other words, no place in this theory of natural law for the endlessly unique social configurations which human beings, in their freedom over natural necessity, construct. The proponents of "natural law" therefore invariably introduce some historically contingent norm or social structure into what they regard as God's inflexible norm. That was the weakness of both classical and medieval social theory; and for that matter of the natural law theories of the bourgeois parties of the eighteenth century, who had found what they regarded as a more empirically perceived "natural law." But the modern empirical intelligence was no more capable than the deductive rational processes of classical and medieval times to construct a social norm not colored by the interests of the constructor, thus introducing the taint of ideology into the supposed sanctities of law.

So the various versions of natural law tend to assume a determinate human freedom and falsely equate the fixed structures of nature and the less fixed structures of human nature. The supposedly fixed structures of human nature are the basis of a law which states those things to be done and not to be done "which follow in an inevitable manner from the fact that man is man" (Maritain). But the indeterminate character of human freedom and the variety and uniqueness of historic occasions produce fewer things about which one may be sure that they must be done or not done than is supposed in Catholic natural law theory.[17]

The errors of natural law theory find expression in an unwarranted confidence in human reason. The perennial mistake of rationalists, whether Stoic, Catholic or modern, is to exempt reason from either finiteness or sin or both, and to derive universal rational norms from this confidence in reason. This mistake may be remedied by a more dialectical analysis of the function of reason. Reason is in fact in an equivocal position between the self-as-subject and the self-as-agent of action, between the self as transcending itself and the anxious self in action. It is the servant of both. Its universal judgments, its effort to relate all things to each other in a system of coherence, can be alternately the instrument by which the self-as-subject condemns the partial and prejudiced actions of the sinful self, and the vehicle of the sinful self by which it seeks to give the sanctity of a false universality to its particular needs and partial insights.[18] Natural law theories which derive absolutely valid principles of morals and politics from reason invariably introduce contingent practical applications into the definition of the principles. This is particularly true when the natural law defines not merely moral but also political principles.[19]

Thus Thomistic definitions of justice are filled with specific details which are drawn from the given realities of a feudal social order and may be regarded as "rationalizations" of a feudal aristocracy's dominant position in society. Bourgeois idealists of the eighteenth century invented new natural law theories and invested them with bourgeois rather than feudal-aristocratic content. The natural law of the eighteenth century was supposed to be descriptive rather than prescriptive. It was, more exactly, a "law of nature" rather than a "law of reason." But its real significance lay in its specific content. The content of this law justified the bourgeois classes in their ideals, just as the older law justified the feudal aristocrats. In short, it is not possible to state a universally valid concept of justice from any particular sociological locus in history.

Nor is it possible to avoid either making the effort or making pretenses of universality which human finiteness does not justify. This inevitable pretense is the revelation of "original sin" in history. Human history is consequently more tragic than Catholic theology assumes. It is not an incomplete world yearning for completion, and finding it in the incarnation. It is a tragic world, troubled not by finiteness so much as by "false eternals" and false absolutes, and expressing the pride of these false absolutes even in the highest reaches of its spirituality. It is not the incarnation as such that is the good news of the gospel, but rather the revelation of a just God who is also merciful.[20]

By equating meaning too simply with rationality, the Christian rationalists inevitably obscure some of the profoundest incongruities, tragic antinomies, and depth of meaning on the edge of the mysteries in human life and history. In Thomism the suprarational truths of faith are not identified with the truths of reason. They illumine a realm of mystery above the limits of the world which is rationally understood and morally ordered. The existence of God is known by reason, though His character as triune God is apprehended by faith.

This means that the finiteness of man's reason and its involvement in the flux of the temporal world is not appreciated. In the realm of morality the rational man feels secure in the virtue which he may achieve by his reason and the justice which he can define by it. This means that the problematic character of all human virtues and the ideological taint in all reasoning about human affairs are not understood. Therefore, grace becomes merely an addition to natural virtue and in no way stands in contradiction to it. Significantly man is essentially defined as a rational creature, just as Aristotle would define him. The true dimension of selfhood, with its indeterminate relations to itself, to God, and to its fellow men, is regarded as an addition, a *donum superadditum*.

Wherever one touches the Thomistic scheme, one finds a perfectly coherent world, a perfectly understood self, a perfectly possible virtue and justice. This coherent world has superimposed upon it an aura of mystery and meaning in which the limitless possibilities of man's and God's freedom find expression. It is a two-story world with a classical base and a Christian second story.[21]

Actually, the ultimate requirements of the Christian ethic are not counsels of perfection or theological virtues of the sort which merely completes an otherwise incomplete natural goodness or virtue. Nor can they be subtracted from man without making his freedom a source of sinful infection. They are indeed counsels of perfection in the sense that sinful man lacks them and is incapable of achieving them. But they are basic and not supplementary requirements of his freedom.[22] The law of love is thus not something extra to be added to whatever morality we establish in our social relations. It is the guiding principle of them.[23]

To summarize the critique: the authority of rational "natural" law is less valid than Catholicism supposes. The whole concept of natural law rests upon a Stoic-Aristotelian rationalism which assumes a human reason untainted by ideology, and which further assumes fixed historical structures and norms that do not in fact exist.[24] That is, Catholic thought does not fully recognize the degree to which historical freedom reaches down into the structural aspects of life. Consequently, the Biblical idea of love as the final norm of life is merely added as an extra "theological virtue" upon the classical ethical system; and the content of "natural law" is made much too specific, rigid, and neat to give adequate moral guidance to men in the unique occasions of history.[25]

IV. *A Limited Natural Law*

While it is important to reject the errors of the natural law theorists, it is just as important to disavow the opposite error of the moral relativists, who deny every validity of general norms. In secular theory this relativism is the fruit of an extreme naturalistic empiricism. In the history of religious thought Lutheran orthodoxy tends to regard reason as so completely involved in the corruption of sin that it has no confidence in any natural law norms.[26]

The fact is that there are some general principles of justice which define the right order of life in a community. There are no living communities which do not have some notions of justice beyond their historic laws, by which they seek to gauge the justice of their legislative enactments. Such are the general principles which have been known as "natural law" in both Catholic and earlier liberal thought. Even when, as in the present stage of liberal democratic thought, moral theory has become too relativistic to make appeal to natural law as plausible as in other centuries, every human society does have something like a natural law concept; for it assumes that there are more immutable and purer principles of justice than those actually embodied in its obviously relative laws.[27]

Thus there is a tenable distinction between ideals of justice and their embodiment in historical or "civil" law. The latter is the consequence of pressures and counterpressures in a living community. It is therefore subject to a greater degree of historical relativity than natural law. Insofar as thought is purer than action natural law is purer than civil law. Furthermore it is important to recognize the validity of principles of justice, rationally conceived, as sources of criticism for the historical achievements of justice in living communities. If the medieval and modern secular theories of natural law claim too much for these rational principles of justice, both secular and Reformation relativists frequently dismiss them as irrelevant or dangerous. Karl Barth's belief that the moral life of man would possess no valid principles of guidance if the Ten Commandments had not introduced such principles by revelation is as absurd as it is unscriptural.

The practical universality of the prohibition of murder for instance in the moral codes of mankind is just as significant as the endless relativities which manifest themselves in the practical application of the general prohibition. There are essentially universal "principles" of justice, by which the formulation of specific rules and systems of justice is oriented.[28]

The principles of natural law by which justice is defined are, however, not so much fixed standards of reason as they are rational efforts to apply the moral obligation implied in the love commandment to the complexities of life and the fact of sin; that is, to the situation created by the inclination of men to take advantage of each other. Any definition of moral rules beyond those which mark the minimal obligation of the self to the neighbor are discovered, upon close analysis, to be rational formulations of various implications of the love commandment, rather than fixed and precise principles of justice. All principles of justice are designed to arbitrate and adjudicate competing claims and conflicting rights. In this adjudication the Aristotelian principle that everyone is to have his due defines the spirit of justice, but the formula contains no indication of what each man's due is. It is equally impossible to derive any specific criteria from the general Thomistic proposition that we ought to do good and avoid evil.

Rules of justice do not follow in a "necessary manner" from some basic proposition of justice. They are the fruit of a rational survey of the whole field of human interests, of the structure of human life and the causal sequences in human relations. They embody too many contingent elements and are subject to such inevitable distortion by interest and passion that they cannot possibly be placed in the same category with the logical propositions of mathematics or the analytic propositions of science. They are the product of social wisdom and unwisdom. Reason itself is not the source of law, since it is not possible to prove the self's obligation to the neighbor by any rational analysis which does not assume the proposition it intends to prove. Yet reason works helpfully to define the obligation of love in the complexities of various types of human relations.[29]

V. *Principles of Justice: Liberty and Equality*

There do exist, then, certain principles of justice, basic conditions set by God to which human life must conform. Though God's order can never be identified with some specific form of social organization, it is very important to arrive at concepts of justice which draw upon the common experience of mankind and set a restraint upon human self-interest.[30]

Obviously the basic social peace of an ordered community is a necessary condition for the very existence of communal life, and is therefore a prerequisite to the achievement of justice. Man requires community as much as liberty. And since both liberty and community are basic requirements, libertarian social theories which are founded on the assumption that liberty is the only basic requirement of man's nature are just as erroneous and just as dangerous as the opposite theories which maintain that liberty must be completely subordinated to the requirements of order and social cohesion.[31]

Consequently if the central problem of politics is the problem of justice, the prior question is how to coerce the anarchy of conflicting human interests into some kind of order, offering human beings the greatest possible opportunity for mutual support.[32] The problem of justice is finally more important than the problem of order; but not immediately so. The instruments of justice can function only within a framework of order.[33]

Beyond the prerequisite of communal order, both "liberty" and "equality" are recognized in Stoic, medieval and modern theories of natural law as transcendent principles of justice.[34] That is, the ideal possibility for men involved in any social situation may always be defined in terms of these two regulative principles. Men's highest good consists in freedom to develop the essential potentialities of their nature without hindrance.[35]

At the same time, a higher justice always means a more equal justice. Since all human morality rests upon the presupposition of the value of all human life and since there are no *a priori* principles by which the value of one life may be preferred to that of another, the problem of dividing the privileges of common human enterprises can only be solved by implicit or explicit standards of equality. That is why equality is also an ideal principle in both Stoic and Christian conceptions of the natural law.[36]

A free society is justified by the fact that the indeterminate possibilities of human vitality may be creative. Every definition of the restraints which must be placed upon these vitalities must be tentative. This is so because all such definitions, which are themselves the products of specific historical insights, may prematurely arrest or suppress a legitimate vitality if they are made absolute and fixed. The community must constantly re-examine the presuppositions upon which it orders its life, because no age can fully anticipate or predict the legitimate and creative vitalities which may arise in subsequent ages.[37]

But the most frequent general principle of justice in the thought of modern as well as Stoic and Catholic proponents of natural law is the principle of equality. The dominant position of the principle of equality in all natural law concepts is significant. Equality stands in a medial position between love and justice. If the obligation to love the neighbor as the self is to be reduced to rational calculation, the only guarantee of the fulfillment of the obligation is a grant to the neighbor which equals what the self claims for itself. Thus equality is love in terms of logic. But it is no longer love in the ecstatic dimension. For the principle of equality allows and requires that the self insist upon its own rights and interests in competition with the rights and interests of the other. Therefore equal justice is on the one hand something less than the law of love and on the other hand the law of love in rational form.[38] In other words, equality is the approximation of the principle of love in the realm of law. It is such an approximation because the principle of the equal affirmation of all life is closest to the ideal of sacrificial love, in which each life is subjected to the necessities of life as such.[39]

This does not mean that any society will ever achieve perfect equality. Equality, being a rational, political version of the law of love, shares with it the quality of transcendence. It ought to be, but it never will be fully realized. Besides the contingencies of nature which arbitrarily benefit some men more than others, social prudence will qualify the ideal. The most equalitarian society will probably not be able to dispense with special rewards as inducements to diligence. Some differentials in privilege will be necessary to make the performance of certain social functions possible. While a rigorous equalitarian society can prevent such privileges from being perpetuated from one generation to another without regard to social function, it cannot eliminate privileges completely.

Nor is there any political technique which would be a perfect guarantee against abuses of socially sanctioned privileges. Significant social functions are endowed by their very nature with a certain degree of social power. Those who possess power, however socially restrained, always have the opportunity of deciding that the function which they perform is entitled to more privilege than any ideal scheme of justice would allow.

The ideal of equality is thus qualified in any possible society by the necessities of social cohesion and corrupted by the sinfulness of men. It remains, nevertheless, a valid principle of natural law, a standard of criticism under which every scheme of justice stands, and a symbol of the principle of love involved in all moral judgments.[40]

The validity of the principle of equality on the one hand and the impossibility of realizing it fully on the other, illustrates the relation of all absolute norms of justice to the relativities of history. The fact that one social class will tend to emphasize the absolute validity of the norm unduly, while another class will be inclined to emphasize the impossibility of achieving it fully illustrates the inevitable "ideological taint" in the application of a generally valid principle, even if the principle itself achieves a high measure of transcendence over partial interest. Equality, like liberty, is a regulative and guiding, but not an absolute, standard.[41]

Indeed, the basic principles of justice logically conflict with each other, and thus are themselves mutually limiting. The Stoics and the medievalists were wiser than the eighteenth century at least in this, that they regarded liberty and equality as requirements of the absolute, but not of the relative, natural law. This is to say they believed liberty and equality to be ultimate but not immediate social norms. Neither one can be fully realized in the complexities of actual history, if for no other reason than that they come into conflict with each other. A society can destroy liberty in its search for equality; it can annul the spirit of equal justice by a too consistent devotion to liberty.[42]

Further, the principle of equality is a relevant criterion of criticism for the social hierarchy, and the principle of liberty serves the same purpose for the community's unity. Yet neither principle could be wholly nor absolutely applied without destroying the community.[43] But since the community may as easily become inordinate in its passion for order as may the various forces in the community in their passions for freedom or equality, it is necessary to preserve a proper balance between order and justice, and to be ready to champion either one against the other.[44]

The experience of Abraham Lincoln might well instruct us on the relative importance of order and justice. Facing civil conflict within the nation Lincoln declared: "My primary purpose is to save the union." It was significant, however, that though Lincoln was prepared to save the union "half slave and half free" it soon became apparent that this could not be done. The union could be saved only by abolishing slavery. This is a nice symbol of the fact that order precedes justice in the strategy of government; but that only an order which implicates justice can achieve a stable peace. An unjust order quickly invites the resentment and rebellion which lead to its undoing.[45]

The real fact is that we need many strategies of social harmony and justice if we are to approximate the law of love in any society. But every strategy of social peace and every system of justice should be regarded as tentative and fragmentary: as embodying some, but not all, of our responsibilities to our fellow men; as adequate for a given historical occasion but not necessarily adequate for all occasions.[46]

Historical contingencies must, therefore, determine whether order must be given preference over justice; and whether equality or liberty must be given preference in the norms of justice, and whether force or prestige should have larger emphasis in authority. Among these contingencies are, for example, the degree of danger to which a community may be exposed, requiring a more than ordinary abridgement of liberty; and the hierarchical necessities of communal integration requiring the qualification of equality.

It is possible, however, to affirm that the absolute want of any of these moral values is an evil. A situation without order means chaos and is therefore bad. An order without justice means that it will become intolerable in the long run. Justice without both liberty and equality is intolerable, though we cannot determine abstractly how much liberty or equality must be sacrificed for the integration of the community. Nor is it possible to determine how large a component of force may have to be tolerated in the authority by which the community integrates its life and effects its external desires and ambitions. There are fixed principles and norms in the political realm, but there is no fixed principle for relating the norms to each other.[47]

VI. *Love Beyond Law*

According to the Christian faith there is only one law, which reads: "Thou shalt love the lord thy God—and thy neighbor as thyself." In this law all other law is both fulfilled and ended.[48] Traditional natural law theory fails to do justice to the relation of love to justice implied by this great commandment. In its conception, natural justice is good as far as it goes, but it must be completed by the supernatural virtue of love. The true situation is that anything short of love cannot be perfect justice. In fact, every definition of justice actually presupposes sin as a given reality. It is only because life is in conflict with life, because of sinful self-interest, that we are required carefully to define schemes of justice which prevent one life from taking advantage of another. Yet no scheme of justice can do full justice to all the variable factors which the freedom of man introduces into human history.

The real situation is that man transcends his own reason, which is to say that he is not bound in his actions by reason's coherences and systems. His freedom consists in a capacity for self-transcendence in infinite regression. There is therefore no limit in reason for either his creativity or his sin. There is no possibility of giving a rational definition of a just relation between man and man or nation and nation short of a complete love in which each life affirms the interests of the other. Every effort to give a definition of justice short of this perfect love invariably introduces contingent factors, conditions of time and place, into the definition.

Love is the only final structure of freedom. Human personality as a system of infinite potentialities makes it impossible to define absolutely what I owe to my fellow man, since nothing that he now is exhausts what he might be. Human personality as the capacity for infinite self-transcendence makes it impossible from my own standpoint to rest content in any ordered relation with my fellow men. There is no such relation that I cannot transcend to imagine a better one in terms of the ideal of love. Provisional definitions of justice short of this perfect love are, of course, necessary. But they are much more provisional than any natural law theory, whether medieval or modern, realizes. The freedom of man is too great to make it possible to define any scheme of justice absolutely in terms of "necessary" standards.[49]

It is specially important to reaffirm the New Testament spirit of freedom over law in our own day, because the task of preserving justice in the rapidly shifting circumstances of a technical society and of preserving personal integrity under conditions of growing human power require that the spirit of love be freed of subservience to traditional codes. It is not wise to alter social customs and traditional restraints upon human expansiveness lightly. The more the historical root of social restraints is known, the greater must be the inclination to deal conservatively with any viable structure of the human community. But no historic structure or traditional restraint deserves the sanctity which is usually ascribed to it. A truly religious morality must appreciate the virtue of historic and traditional forms of justice against attack by abstract forms of rationalism; but it must at the same time subject to constant scrutiny every structure of justice, whether historically, rationally, or Scripturally validated.[50]

If rules and *principles* of justice have an equivocal relation to the ideal of brotherhood, this equivocal character is even more obvious and apparent in the *structures* and systems, the organizations and mechanisms, of society in which these principles and rules are imperfectly embodied and made historically concrete. We have noted the distinction between natural law, as a rational statement of principles of justice, and positive law, which designates the historic enactments of living communities. But an analysis of the equivocal character of the structures of justice must include more than a mere consideration of civil or positive law. It must look beyond legal enactments to the whole structure and organization of historical communities.

This structure is never merely the order of a legal system. The harmony of communities is not simply attained by the authority of law. *Nomos* does not coerce the vitalities of life into order. The social harmony of living communities is achieved by an interaction between the normative conceptions of morality and law and the existing and developing forces and vitalities of the community. Therefore, even more than the principles of justice, the structures of justice and the various forms of communal organization invariably contain contradictions as well as approximations to the ideal of love.[51]

We must conclude that there are *many* norms of conduct, validated by experience, between the conditions of man's creatureliness and the law of love which is the final norm of man's freedom. But they must be held with some degree of tentativity and be finally subordinated to the law of love.[52] Human nature is, in short, a realm of infinite possibilities of good and evil because of the character of human freedom. The love that is the law of its nature is a boundless self-giving. The sin that corrupts its life is a boundless assertion of the self. Between these two forces all kinds of *ad hoc* restraints may be elaborated and defined. We may call this natural law. But we had better realize how very tentative it is. Otherwise we shall merely sanction some traditional relation between myself and my fellow man as a "just" relation, and quiet the voice of conscience which speaks to me of higher possibilities. What is more, we may stabilize sin and make it institutional.[53]

Thus a Christian morality, inspired by the spirit of the New Testament, must be as ready to challenge legalism as relativism. Against relativists it must insist that no man or nation, no age or culture can arbitrarily define its own law. Against legalists it must insist that there is no virtue in law as such (Romans 7:7–25). It does not have the power within itself to compel obedience. All genuine obedience to law is derived from the grace of love, which is more than law. Neither does law have the virtue to define the interests of the self and the neighbor with precision, since there is no completely disinterested intelligence in history. If the faulty criteria of law are not corrected by love, law is always in danger of becoming the instrument of sin.[54]

CHAPTER XVI

Government and the Strategy of Democracy

I. *The Moral Ambiguity of Government* *

To establish justice in a sinful world is the whole sad duty of the political order. There has never been justice without law; and all laws are the stabilization of certain social equilibria, brought about by pressures and counterpressures in society, and expressed in the structures of government.[1]

The basic pattern of man's collective life thus corresponds to Augustine's description of the *civitas terrena,* the concord of which is alternately or simultaneously corrupted by conflict and domination. The conflict is the inevitable consequence of the tendency of partial and particular communities to make themselves their own end. The domination and injustice in the internal structure of particular communities is the consequence of the idolatrous self-worship of the oligarchies which have the responsibility for the order and unity of the community. Thus man's collective, like his individual, life is involved in death through the very strategies by which life is maintained, against both external and internal peril.

But there is life as well as death, virtue as well as sin in these social and political configurations. St. Augustine's Christian realism errs in its too consistent emphasis upon the sinful corruptions of the world's peace. Civilizations and cultures do rise and prosper; and they have periods of creativity and stability before the destructive elements in them overcome the creative ones. Augustine may, in fact, have made the mistake of taking his analogies for the *civitas terrena* from the Roman Empire in the period of its decay, thus failing to do justice to the creative achievement of the *Pax Romana* at its best.[2]

The Bible contains two approaches which, taken together and held in balance, do justice to these moral ambiguities of government. According to the one, government is an ordinance of God and its authority reflects

* The ambiguity in the functioning of government is treated descriptively in Chapter X.

the Divine Majesty. According to the other, the "rulers" and "judges" of the nations are particularly subject to divine judgment and wrath because they oppress the poor and defy the Divine Majesty.

These two approaches do justice to the two aspects of government. It is a principle of order and its power prevents anarchy. But its power is not identical with divine power; it is wielded from a partial and particular locus and it cannot achieve the perfect union of goodness and power which characterizes divine power. The pretension that its power is perfectly virtuous represents its false claim of majesty. This claim elicits alternate moods of reverent obedience and resentful rebellion in history.

The double approach of prophetic criticism and of priestly sanctification of royal or state authority has armed both conservative and radical schools of Christian thought with plausible proof-texts for their respective positions. Only occasionally is the truth in each position properly appreciated. The Dutch, French and Scottish Calvinists of the seventeenth century, along with the Anglican Richard Hooker, probably came closest to a full comprehension of all the complexities of political justice. They distinguished between government as an ordinance of God's providence and the particular form of government which might obtain at a given moment. Thus they freed the religious conscience from undue reverence for any particular government and established a critical attitude toward it, while yet preserving religious reverence for the principle of government. They understood, as the proponents of the secular social contract theory of government did not, that it is not within the power of conscious human will to create government. But unlike Calvin himself the later Calvinists did understand the importance of human action in the formation of particular governments and the responsibility of men for the achievement of justice.[3] *

This dual approach to power means that, from the Christian standpoint, we cannot regard as evil the structures, systems, laws, and conventions by which partly selfish and partly unselfish men are held together in large-scale cooperation. The order and justice which they achieve must be regarded as an approximation of loving community under the conditions of sin.

The interests of justice require, on the other hand, that no perils in these structures and applications of coercive power be obscured. For tyrannical power destroys the very human potential which a human community is intended to serve. That is why power must be "weighed

* For Niebuhr's interpretation of the main historical outlines of Christian thought on government, see *Human Destiny,* pp. 269–84. For some elaboration of the Calvinist position, see *The Self and the Dramas of History,* pp. 171–76. See *An Interpretation of Christian Ethics,* Chapters V and VI for a systematic, though somewhat dated, critique of the positions of Christian orthodoxy and Christian liberalism.

out ounce by ounce," in the words of Sam Rutherford, a seventeenth-century Calvinist. Christianity knows that a healthy society must seek to achieve the greatest possible equilibrium of power, the greatest possible number of centers of power, the greatest possible social check upon the administration of power, and the greatest possible inner moral check on human ambition, as well as the most effective use of forms of power in which consent and coercion are compounded.[4]

Because men are sinners, justice can be achieved only by a certain degree of coercion on the one hand, and by resistance to coercion and tyranny on the other. The political life of man must constantly steer between the Scylla of anarchy and the Charybdis of tyranny.

Human egoism makes large-scale cooperation upon a purely voluntary basis impossible. Governments must coerce. Yet there is an element of evil in this coercion. It is always in danger of serving the purposes of the coercing power rather than the general weal. We cannot fully trust the motives of any ruling class or power. That is why it is important to maintain democratic checks upon the centers of power. It may also be necessary to resist a ruling class, nation or race, if it violates the standards of relative justice which have been set up for it.[5]

II. *The Strategy of Democracy*

The whole development of democratic justice in human society has depended upon some comprehension of these moral ambiguities which inhere in both government and the principle of the equilibrium of power. It is the highest achievement of democratic societies that they embody the principle of resistance to government within the principle of government itself. The citizen is thus armed with "constitutional" power to resist the unjust exactions of government. He can do this without creating anarchy within the community if government has been so conceived that criticism of the ruler becomes an instrument of better government and not a threat to government itself.

The achievements of democracy have been tortuously worked out in human history partly because various schools of religious and political thought had great difficulty in fully comprehending the perils of justice in either one or the other instrument of justice—the organization of power and the balance of power. Usually the school of thought which comprehended the moral ambiguities of government did not understand the perils of anarchy inhering in uncontrolled social life; while those who feared this anarchy were uncritical of the claims and pretensions of government. History had to stumble by tortuous process upon the proper techniques for avoiding both anarchy and tyranny, against the illusions of idealists and of realists who understood only one or the other side of the problem.[6]

Ideally democracy is a permanently valid form of social and political organization in which freedom and order are made to support, and not to contradict, each other. It does justice to two dimensions of human existence: to man's spiritual stature and his social character; to the uniqueness and variety of life, as well as to the common necessities of all men. An ideal democratic order seeks unity within the conditions of freedom; and maintains freedom within the framework of order.[7]

Thus the democratic strategy is two-fold. First, it contributes to the establishment of order and community through the non-violent arbitration and accommodation of social conflict. Second, it seeks to maintain freedom by making power responsible, checking the authority of government, and providing a form of social control over the leaders of society.[8]

1. THE OPEN SOCIETY

Contrary to the belief and expectations of eighteenth-century democrats, a national community is both integrated and divided by many ethnic, cultural, religious and economic groups. Early democratic idealists were too individualistic to appreciate the creative character of these groups or to anticipate the perennial peril of disunity which might arise from them. The founding fathers of America regarded "faction" as an unmitigated evil. The American Constitution was designed to prevent the emergence of the very political parties without which it has become impossible to maintain our democratic processes. Of our early constitutionalists, Madison was realistic enough to recognize the inevitability of factions. But even he tried in every way to circumscribe their development.[9]

Methods of arbitrating these conflicting social interests must be found because various social groups cannot be expected to have perfect, rational conformity of interests. A non-violent expression of the claims and counterclaims of politics is important precisely because political arguments are never merely rational arguments. The threat of force is always implied.[10]

The best political answer to the problem of accommodating and balancing the interests of competing groups is democracy, which in one sense is a permanently valid method of holding all cultural viewpoints under criticism and of achieving an uncoerced harmony among the various social and cultural vitalities.[11] But more than this, a healthy democracy provides for checks and balances upon both the pretensions of men and their lust for power. It never gives all the power to the proponents of any one dogma; it holds all claims to truth under critical review; it balances all social forces, not in an automatic, but in a contrived harmony of power. In this way it distills a modicum of truth from a conflict of error.[12]

An open society manages through this strategy to draw upon the virtues, and to correct the vices, of various components of the community by countervailing influences of other components. The mind of each religious and culture group is freed by these democratic pressures in exactly the same way as interest groups of various kinds are purged of the virulence of their bias, by the challenge which they must meet from other groups.

In this situation the democratic consensus, without which a community cannot survive, must be tentative and precarious; and the required majority, necessary for common action, may be composed from time to time by the most various alliances of groups. But history has proved the consequences in justice to be much higher in this freedom than is possible to attain when the "truth" about justice, as defined by any one religious group or, for that matter, any interest group, remains unchallenged. This is true because the mind by which we define justice is bound, not only by ultimate commitments, but by immediate interests. There is no better way of freeing these various minds than the way which has been found in free society. They would have, if left unchallenged, attempted to dominate the community and provide it with the only ultimate definition of "truth" and "justice."[13]

A free society thus derives general profit from the interested desires of particular groups, each group leaving a deposit of virtue in the community beyond its intentions and interests. The health and justice of the community is preserved, not so much by the discriminate judgment of the whole community, as by the effect of free criticism in moderating the pretensions of every group and by the weight of competing power in balancing power which might become inordinate and oppressive. Democracy in short is not a method which is effective only among virtuous men. It is a method which prevents interested men from following their interests to the detriment of the community—though there must of course be a minimal inclination for justice to furnish a base of community.[14]

2. THE ACCOUNTABLE GOVERNMENT

More obviously and specifically, democracy as government by popular consent is the application of checks and controls against even the groups who hold governmental power. Democracy as a political institution is rooted in the principle of universal suffrage, which arms every citizen with political power and the chance to hold accountable the actions of his rulers, thereby checking the tendency of the community to achieve order at the price of liberty. This procedure implements the thesis that governments derive their authority from the consent of the governed.[15]

Elections are therefore the pride of democracy. It is a great achievement to keep all political power under the scrutiny of the citizens and give the men who organize political life only a short lease of power, which must be periodically renewed. This achievement separates democracy from all forms of authoritarianism, which falsely trust some elite group to wield power over society without subjection to control.[16]

Modern democracies tend toward a more equal justice partly because they have divorced political power from special social functions. They endow all men with a measure of it by giving them the right to review the policies of their leaders. This democratic principle does not obviate the formation of oligarchies in society; but it places a check upon their formation, and upon the exercise of their power.[17]

In sum, a democratic or open society is not a perfect society; on the contrary it allows its imperfections to be published abroad. It is a society which permits and even encourages criticism of itself in the light of universal standards. Such a society has at hand the means of peaceful self-correction. Such a society keeps alive the concern for objective truth and it can never be deceived into substituting the fiat of the state for objective truth. Such a society enables persons to keep their integrity as persons without constant fear of the secret police. Such a society permits minorities to organize for the purpose of changing its policies and even its structure. Such a society is uncorrupted by officially planned terror against its most independent minds and its bravest spirits. Such a society provides a framework in which the Church can preach the Gospel and keep civilization under Christian judgment.[18] Yet we are committed even to the proposition that there are no human institutions, including religious ones, which can safely be made immune to democratic criticism and which can be allowed to dictate the terms and the limits of the unity of the culture. We are committed to democracy as a method of holding all sources of power under restraint and all sources of authority under criticism.[19] The reason this final democratic freedom is right is that there is no historical reality, whether it be church or government, whether it be the reason of wise men or specialists, which is not involved in the flux and relativity of human existence; which is not subject to error and sin, and which is not tempted to exaggerate its errors and sins when they are made immune to criticism.[20]

III. *The Justification and Sources of Democracy*

Democracy has a more compelling justification and requires a more realistic vindication than is given it by the liberal culture with which it has been associated in modern history. The excessively optimistic estimates of human nature and of human history with which the democratic credo has been historically associated are a source of peril to democratic society for contemporary experience is refuting this optimism and there is danger that it will seem to refute the democratic ideal as well.

Democracy, like every other historic ideal and institution, contains ephemeral as well as more permanently valid elements. Democracy is in one sense the characteristic fruit of a bourgeois civilization. Democracy is a "bourgeois ideology" insofar as it expresses the typical viewpoints of the middle classes which have risen to power in European civilization in the past three or four centuries. And the fundamental error in the social philosophy of this democratic civilization is the confidence of idealists in the possibility of achieving an easy resolution of the tension and conflict between self-interest and the general interest.

A free society does indeed require some confidence in the ability of men to reach tentative and tolerable adjustments among their competing interests and to arrive at some common notions of justice which transcend all partial interests. A consistent pessimism in regard to man's rational capacity for justice invariably leads to absolutistic political theories; for they prompt the conviction that only preponderant power can coerce the various vitalities of a community into a working harmony. But a too consistent optimism in regard to man's ability and inclination to grant justice to his fellows obscures the perils of chaos which perennially confront every society, including a free society. In one sense a democratic society is particularly exposed to the dangers of confusion. If these perils are not appreciated they may overtake a free society and invite the alternative evil of tyranny.

Thus modern democracy requires a more realistic philosophical and religious basis, not only in order to anticipate and understand the perils to which it is exposed; but also to give it a more persuasive justification. Man's capacity for justice makes democracy possible; but man's inclination to injustice makes democracy necessary. In all non-democratic political theories the state or the ruler is invested with uncontrolled power for the sake of achieving order and unity in the community. But the pessimism which prompts and justifies this policy is not consistent; for it is not applied, as it should be, to the ruler. If men are inclined to deal unjustly with their fellows, the possession of power aggravates this inclination. That is why irresponsible and uncontrolled power is the greatest source of injustice.

The consistent optimism of our liberal culture has prevented modern democratic societies both from gauging the perils of freedom accurately and from appreciating democracy fully as the only alternative to injustice and oppression. When this optimism is not qualified to accord with the real and complex facts of human nature and history, there is always danger that sentimentality will give way to despair and that a too consistent optimism will alternate with a too consistent pessimism.[21]

The facts about human nature which make a monopoly of power dangerous and a balance of power desirable are best understood from the standpoint of the Christian faith. The democratic wisdom which learns how to avoid and negate conflicting ideologies, based upon interest, may be of course the result of experience rather than of special Christian insights. But it cannot be denied that Biblical faith is unique in offering three insights into the human situation which are indispensable to democracy.

The first is that it assumes a source of authority from the standpoint of which the individual may defy the authorities of this world. ("We must obey God rather than man.") The second is an appreciation of the unique worth of the individual which makes it wrong to fit him into any political program as a mere instrument. A scientific humanism frequently offends the dignity of man, which it ostensibly extols, by regarding human beings as subject to manipulation and as mere instruments of some "socially approved" ends. It is this tendency of a scientific age which establishes its affinity with totalitarianism, and justifies the charge that a scientific humanism is harmless only because there is not a political program to give the elite, which its theories invariably presuppose, a monopoly of power.

The third insight is the Biblical insistence that the same radical freedom which makes man creative also makes him potentially destructive and dangerous, that the dignity of man and the misery of man therefore have the same root. This insight is the basis of all political realism in which secular theory, whether liberal or Marxist, is defective; it justifies the institutions of democracy more surely than any sentimentality about man, whether liberal or radical.[22]

But Christianity cannot make exclusive claim as the source and basis of political democracy. For a long time a debate has been waged between Christian and secular leaders on the question whether democracy is the product of the Christian faith or of a secular culture. The debate has been inconclusive because, as a matter of history, both

Christian and secular forces were involved in establishing the political institutions of democracy; and the cultural resources of modern free societies are jointly furnished by both Christianity and modern secularism. Furthermore there are traditional non-democratic Christian cultures to the right of free societies which prove that the Christian faith does not inevitably yield democratic historical fruits. And there are totalitarian regimes to the left of free societies which prove that secular doctrine can, under certain circumstances, furnish grist for the mills of modern tyrannies. The debate is, in short, inconclusive because the evidence for each position is mixed.

Perhaps a fair appraisal of it would lead to the conclusion that free societies are the fortunate products of the confluence of Christian and secular forces. This may be so because democracy requires, on the one hand, a view of man which forbids using him merely as an instrument of a political program or social process. This view the Christian and Jewish faiths have supplied. On the other hand, a free society requires that human ends and ambition, social forces and political powers be judged soberly and critically in order that the false sanctities and idolatries of both traditional societies and modern tyrannies be avoided. This sober and critical view is the fruit both of some types of Christianity and of the secular temper with its interest in efficient causes and in immediate, rather than ultimate, ends.[23]

IV. *Democratic Toleration*

The soberness of a secular pursuit of immediate ends and a tolerant appreciation of the fargmentariness of all human viewpoints is necessary for the "limited warfare" of parliamentary democracy. This spirit of tolerance and the contrasting spirit of fanaticism may each be the fruits of either religious piety or rational enlightenment, contrary to the assumption of each side that fanaticism is exclusively the product of the other while toleration is the characteristic of its own world view. It is as rare an achievement for the pious man to be charitable as for the rational man to be "reasonable." Both achievements depend upon the recognition of the limited character of each one's vision of the truth.[24]

The rationalist-humanist wing of the Renaissance made its contributions to toleration by challenging particular prejudices with the supposed universalities of reason, and by dissolving the false universalities of dogmatic religion by the force of empirical observations. And on certain levels secular Renaissance thought surely meets one of the tests of the problem of toleration: the willingness to entertain views which oppose our own without rancor and without the effort to suppress them.

But on deeper levels the modern position either achieves toleration by taking an irresponsible attitude toward ultimate issues; or it insinuates new and false ultimates into views of life which are ostensibly merely provisional and pragmatic. Here are the twin perils of skepticism and a new fanaticism.[25] In its more naive form, secularism is a covert religion which believes that it has ultimate answers to life's ultimate problems. Its profoundest belief is that the historical process is itself redemptive and guarantees both the meaning of life and its fulfillment. It believes either in the mild fanaticism of the religion of progress or in more vicious forms of political religion. In its more sophisticated form secularism represents a form of skepticism which is conscious of the relativity of all human perspectives. In this form it stands on the abyss of moral nihilism and threatens the whole of life with a sense of meaninglessness. Thus it creates a spiritual vacuum into which demonic religions easily rush. Continental varieties of secularism have on the whole taken this more sophisticated form, while American secularism has been more naive and therefore, on the whole, less dangerous.

But there is a religious solution of the problem of toleration which makes religious and cultural diversity possible within the presuppositions of a free society, without destroying the religious depth of a culture. The solution requires a very high form of religious commitment. It demands that each religion, or each version of a single faith, seek to proclaim its highest insights while yet preserving an humble and contrite recognition of the fact that all actual expressions of religious faith are subject to historical contingency and relativity. Such a recognition creates a spirit of tolerance and makes any religious or cultural movement hesitant to claim official validity for its form of religion or to demand an official monopoly for its cult.

Religious humility is in perfect accord with the presuppositions of a democratic society. Profound religion must recognize the difference between divine majesty and human creatureliness; between the unconditioned character of the divine and the conditioned character of all human enterprise. According to the Christian faith the pride which seeks to hide the conditioned and finite character of all human endeavor is the very quintessence of sin. Religious faith ought therefore to be a constant fount of humility; for it ought to encourage men to moderate their natural pride and to achieve some decent consciousness of the relativity of their own statement of even the most ultimate truth. It ought to teach them that their religion is most certainly true if it recognizes the element of error and sin, of finiteness and contingency which creeps into the statement of even the sublimest truth.

Historically the highest form of democratic toleration is based upon these very religious insights. The real foundation of Anglo-Saxon toleration lies in the religious experience of seventeenth-century England. In the religious conflicts of the Cromwellian period there were religious fanatics who were anxious to secure religious monopoly for their particular version of the Christian faith. There were also some secularists who hoped for toleration through the decay of religion. But the victory for toleration was really won by various groups of Christians, among which were the Independents and the Levellers, certain types of moderate Anglicans touched with Renaissance-humanistic perspectives, and some individuals in other sectarian groups. Their viewpoint was expressed in John Milton's *Areopagitica* and in John Saltmarsh's *Smoke in the Temple.* The latter perfectly expresses the religious humility which must form the basis of religious democracy: "Let us," he declares, "not assume any power of infallibility toward each other . . . for another's evidence is as dark to me as mine to him . . . till the Lord enlighten us both for discerning alike."

Religious idealists usually insist that the primary contribution of religion to democratic life is the cultivation of a moral idealism which inculcates concern for the other rather than the self. But this is only part of the contribution which a profound religion can make. Consistent egoists would, of course, wreck any democratic process; for it requires some decent consideration of the needs of others. But some of the greatest perils to democracy arise from the fanaticism of moral idealists who are not conscious of the corruption of self-interest in their professed ideals. Democracy therefore requires something more than a religious devotion to moral ideals. It requires religious humility. Every absolute devotion to relative political ends (and all political ends are relative) is a threat to communal peace. But religious humility is no simple moral or political achievement. It springs only from the depth of a religion which confronts the individual with a more ultimate majesty and purity than all human majesties and values, and persuades him to confess: "Why callest thou me good? there is none good but one, that is, God." [26] The toleration which democracy requires is difficult to maintain without Christian humility; and the challenges to pretensions of every kind which are furnished in the give and take of democratic life are, on the other hand, strong external supports for the Christian grace of humility which recognizes the partial and particular character of everyone's interest and the fragmentary character of every human virtue.[27]

A genuinely Biblical faith can render a greater service to "democracy" than secularism. For secularism makes democracy or freedom or even some lesser value the final end, and destroys democracy by self-worship.[28]

V. *Democracy as a False Religion*

If one may judge by the various official pronouncements and commencement speeches, Americans have only one religion: devotion to democracy. They extol its virtues, are apprehensive about the perils to which it is exposed, pour maledictions upon its foes, rededicate themselves periodically to its purposes and claim unconditioned validity for its ideals.

It happens that democracy is probably that form of society in which both freedom and order are brought most successfully in support of each other. It is not the only form of society in which justice prevails. The modern prejudice and illusion that there is no middle ground between democracy and totalitarianism is a very parochial viewpoint. Nevertheless democracy is worth preserving. It is a worthy object of qualified loyalty. But is it a proper object of unqualified loyalty? Is it an adequate religion? Does not the very extravagance of our devotion prove that we live in a religiously vapid age, in which even Christians fail to penetrate to the more ultimate issues of life?

Democracy cannot be the final end of life for various reasons. It is a form of human society, and man is only partly fulfilled in his social relations. Ultimately each individual faces not society but God as his judge and redeemer. Democrats talk very much about democratic individualism. But what does it profit a society to refrain from making ultimate claims upon the individual in principle, yet in fact make ultimate claims because it is the kind of society in which the individual is supposedly accorded higher rights than in other societies? And what does it profit an individual to be free of social compulsion if he lacks every ultimate point of reference for the freedom of his soul which exceeds the limits of his social institutions? Democracy is certainly a better form of society than totalitarianism. But many proponents of it share one mistake of communists at least: they know no other dimension of existence except the social one.

Another peril of democracy as a religion is that, without a more inclusive religious faith, we identify our particular brand of democracy with the ultimate values of life. This is a sin to which Americans are particularly prone. American conceptions of democracy are characterized by an excessive individualistic and libertarian note. A large number of parochial Americans are arriving at the absurd conclusion that we are the only surviving democracy in the world. They arrive at this conclusion because they think the emphasis upon community and upon "planning" which is prevalent in Europe is incompatible with democracy. This kind of devotion to a partial and parochial view of democracy might actually become democracy's undoing. There are no historic

institutions, whether political, economic or religious, which can survive a too uncritical devotion. Such devotion accentuates their vices and makes them incapable of adjusting themselves to new situations.

But even if our democracy were more perfect than it is, and if our current notions of it were not so obviously drawn from the peculiar conditions of the world's wealthiest nation, devotion to democracy would still be false as a religion. It tempts us to identify the final meaning of life with a virtue which we possess, and thus to give a false and idolatrous religious note to the conflict between democracy and communism, for instance.

We have to make the best defense we can of our most cherished social and historical values against ruthless foes. But from the standpoint of our Christian faith we have to view such struggles in another dimension. We must recognize the ambiguous and tragic character of a struggle in which a contest of power between two great blocs of power in the world obscures the moral issues involved in the struggle and creates a vicious circle of mutual fear, from which there is no easy escape. There must be a dimension of faith in which, whatever our loyalties and however justified our defense of them, we recognize the tragic character of the human drama, including the particular drama of our own day, and call upon the mercy of God to redeem us, not from the contemporary predicament of democracy, but from the perennial human predicament.[29]

CHAPTER XVII

The Christian in Politics

I. *Idealism, Realism and Christian Responsibility*

We can approach a solution of the problem of relating religious commitments to political decisions by excluding two answers which have already been shown to be in error. The one wrong answer is to find no relevance at all between our faith and our political actions. This answer is wrong because it denies the seriousness of our political decisions and obscures our Christian responsibilities for the good order and justice of our civil community.

The other wrong answer stands at the opposite extreme. It is to equate religious and political commitments and to regard every political decision as simply derived from our faith. This is a wrong answer because political issues deal with complex problems of justice, every solution for which contains morally ambiguous elements. All political positions are morally ambiguous because, in the realm of politics and economics, self-interest and power must be harnessed and beguiled rather than eliminated. In other words, forces which are morally dangerous must be used despite their peril. Politics always aims at some kind of a harmony or balance of interest, and such a harmony cannot be regarded as directly related to the final harmony of love of the Kingdom of God. All men are naturally inclined to obscure the morally ambiguous element in their political cause by investing it with religious sanctity. This is why religion is more frequently a source of confusion than of light in the political realm. The tendency to equate our political with our Christian convictions causes politics to generate idolatry.[1]

An action in the field of politics may be prompted by Christian motives and viewpoints, but it never overcomes the ambiguities indicated and can, therefore, never be regarded as clearly right or clearly wrong. It is the action which we believe to be relevant at the moment in order to bear our Christian witness in the cause of justice. There are no absolutely clear witnesses of faith and love in the political sphere, though there may be highly significant testimonies.[2] It would seem, then, that the first duty of Christian faith is to preserve a certain distance between the sanctities of faith and the ambiguities of politics. This is to say that it is the duty of a Christian in politics to have no specific "Christian politics." [3]

Of course, Christians have been tempted by one or the other of the two wrong answers. There have always been orthodox Christians who have tended to accept the necessities of politics as practically normative and to elaborate a political ethic not very different from that of the cynics. (Thus there are similarities between Lutheran and Machiavellian politics.) On the other hand moralistic Christians tend to be irresponsible toward any political problem in which the realities of sin make coercion and resistance a requirement of justice. Either they give themselves to the illusion that they are seeking to make love prevail in the complex collective behavior of mankind, or they wash their hands of the task of achieving justice because they realize that love does not prevail.[4]

If we rule out these two extremes, we still face the primary question of how politics is to be related to faith. We can advance a little farther toward a solution of the problem if we recognize that political issues represent various grades and levels which range all the way from clear moral issues to problems of strategy and means.

It is obvious, for instance, that the Christian churches of America have, with a fair degree of consistency, espoused the idea of America's responsibility to a world community, and have resisted nationalist and isolationist politics in the name of the Christian faith. They have been right in doing so. But this broad moral purpose must be distinguished from problems of strategy. Various strategic devices will be advanced as the best ways of fulfilling our responsibilities. Such devices can never be invested with full religious sanctity. It would be impossible to claim, for instance, that the Christian faith requires that America give preference to either the European or the Asiatic field of strategy, or that we should defend the free world primarily by air, rather than by land, power.

In the same fashion the commandment "Thou shalt love thy neighbor as thyself" brings us under religious and moral compulsions to eliminate the violations of brotherhood in the field of race relations. But it can hardly compel us to choose between the efficacy of a state as against a federal Fair Employment Practices Act. In such questions of strategy there are reasons for honest differences of opinion.

In actual life, however, no clear distinction between moral principles and strategy can be made. This is why Christian convictions that deal only with ultimate principle and exclude strategic issues tend to become wholly irrelevant. Yet the farther one moves from a principle that is clearly related to the love commandment to detailed applications in particular situations, the more hazardous the decision becomes, and the more impossible it is to compel others to a similar conviction by appeal to a common faith.[5]

But the exclusion of the religious element from pragmatic decisions is only another negative answer to the problem of defining a Christian approach to the economic and political order. How shall we find the positive answer? The basic presupposition of a positive answer must lie in a Christian understanding of the realities of man's social life.[6] We must, then, find a way of dealing with these realities which makes justice something more than the prostitute of power on the one hand, and something more than sentimental day dreams on the other. We must find an understanding of life which is deep enough to save us from vacillating between sentimentality and cynicism or from compounding the two when we are tired of one or the other.[7]

For it is wrong to interpret these realities in purely cynical or in purely sentimental terms. It is important to recognize an admixture of self-seeking in every form of human togetherness and also in every strategy of government required to prevent competitive self-seeking from degenerating into anarchy. We cannot (as does classical liberalism) regard the self-seeking which a bourgeois-liberal economy permits as completely harmless; and we cannot, as does orthodox Protestantism, particularly Lutheranism, be uncritical toward the coercive power of government on the ground that God ordained it to prevent anarchy. For both the economic power which competes in the market place and the political power which sets restraints upon the competition are tainted by motives other than the desire for justice. On the other hand, it would be wrong to be too cynical about this admixture of self-interest in all the vital forces of society. Men do have a residual capacity for justice. Government does express the desire of a community for order and justice; and not merely the will-to-power of the oligarchy which controls the engines of power in government. An attitude which avoids both sentimentality and cynicism must obviously be grounded in a Christian view of human nature which is schooled by the Gospel not to take the pretensions of men at their face value, on the one hand, and, on the other, not to deny the residual capacity for justice among even sinful men.[8]

Thus the real problem of a Christian social ethic is to derive from the Gospel a clear view of the realities with which we must deal in our common or social life, and also to preserve a sense of responsibility for achieving the highest measure of order, freedom and justice despite the hazards of man's collective life.[9] Once again, the necessary idealism and the equally necessary realism can be held together only in terms of a Christian faith which refuses to make sin and self-interest normative, but which also understands that human history offers no simple way out to the kingdom of pure love and complete disinterestedness.[10] Nothing is quite so difficult, yet so genuinely Christian, as to remember that in all political struggles there are no saints but only sinners fighting each other, and to remember at the same time that history from man's, rather than God's, perspective is constituted of significant distinctions between types and degrees of sin. It is well to know that God judges all men and that in His sight no man living is justified. But we are men and not God. We must make historic choices.[11]

Christians ought to be able to analyze a given situation more realistically than moralists and idealists because they are not under the necessity of having illusions about human nature in order to avert despair and preserve their faith in the meaning of life. But it is equally true that they are unable to regard any of the pragmatic policies of politics by which relative justice is achieved in history as ultimately normative. This means that Christians always live in a deeper dimension than the realm in which the political struggle takes place. But they cannot simply flee the world of political contention into a realm of mystic eternity or moralistic illusion.

If the tension between Christian realism and faith in love as the law of life is not to be broken the Christian must become immersed in the claims and counterclaims, the tension, conflict and the risk of overt hostilities which characterize all attempts at justice, while refusing to regard any relative justice so achieved as exhausting his obligations.[12] He must, as a Christian, participate responsibly in the struggle for justice, constantly making significant moral and political decisions amidst and upon perplexing issues and hazardous ventures. He must even make them "with might" and not half-heartedly. But the Christian faith gives him no warrant to lift himself above the world's perplexities and to seek or to claim absolute validity for the stand he takes. It does, instead, encourage him to the charity which is born of humility and contrition. If he claims to possess overtly what remains hidden, he turns the mercy of Christ into an inhuman fanaticism.[13]

In summary, an adequate political morality must do justice to the insights of both idealists and political realists. It must include a political policy which will reduce coercive power to the minimum and bring the most effective social check upon conflicting egoistic impulses in society; it must generate a moral idealism which will make for a moral and rational adjustment of life to life, and exploit every available resource of altruistic impulse and reason to extend life from selfish to social ends; and it must encompass a religious world-view which will do justice to the ideals of the spirit which reach beyond the possibilities of historic achievement.[14]

International peace, political and economic justice, and every form of social achievement represent precarious constructs in which the egoism of man is checked and yet taken for granted; and in which human sympathy and love must be exploited to the full and yet discounted.[15] The field of politics is not helpfully tilled by pure moralists nor by moral cynics. Community must be built by men and nations sufficiently mature and robust to understand that political justice is achieved, not merely by destroying, but also by deflecting, beguiling and harnessing residual self-interest and by finding the greatest possible concurrence between self-interest and the general welfare. They must also be humble enough to understand that the forces of self-interest to be deflected are not always those of the opponent or competitor. They are frequently those of the self, individual or collective, including the interests of the idealist who erroneously imagines himself above the battle.

Since all political and moral striving results in frustration as well as fulfillment, the task of building community requires a faith which is not too easily destroyed by frustration. Such a faith must understand the moral ambiguities of history and know them not merely as accidents or as the consequence of the malevolence of this man or that nation; it must understand them as permanent characteristics of man's historic existence.[16]

II. *Liberalism, Conservatism and Christian Pragmatism*

In our day the labels given to the two most common postures in the arena of practical politics are "liberalism" and "conservatism." It is obviously necessary to make the most careful distinctions between the conservatism and liberalism which are merely moods or ideologies according to which one defends a status quo or seeks to leave it behind, and the conservatism and liberalism which are cogent political philosophies. We can dismiss very simply the sort of conservatism and liberalism which are dispositions toward some status quo by giving an *a priori* preference for liberalism over conservatism on the ground that it is not reasonable to defend any status quo uncritically, and that it is certainly not reasonable to do so in the rapidly changing conditions of a technical society in which "new conditions teach new duties and time makes ancient truth uncouth." If being for or against change were the only issue involved, any critical person would be bound to be a "liberal." [17]

But the debate may mean more than that. It may involve the significance of the two principles of liberty and equality as principles of justice. Traditional conservatism and liberalism have contrasting attitudes toward those principles, conservatism being usually indifferent to them, while liberalism appreciates them as regulative principles and sometimes erroneously regards them as simple historical possibilities.[18] That is, traditional liberalism has a passion for justice but also a blindness to the factors of interest and power in any social situation, as well as a belief that equality and liberty are simple possibilities of communal organization. The average liberal is not an anarchist, but he inclines to be libertarian and equalitarian in an uncritical way.

On the other hand, traditional conservatism possesses the virtue of understanding the inevitability of social hierarchies, the necessity of coercion in establishing social order, and the necessity of dealing with the factors of interest and power.[19] It is also wise enough to trust the organic processes of social cohesion rather than the abstract schemes which liberals are inclined to advance. In the words of Ireton, spoken in the Putney debates of Cromwell's army, it trusts in the "rights of Englishmen" rather than in the "rights of man," preferring to enlarge the rights of persons which had already been mutually acknowledged in the actual course of history rather than to grasp after rights which the liberals regarded as "inalienable," but which must remain abstract until they are actually embodied in a living social organism. This instinct for the possible, only a little advanced beyond the actual, instead of the ideal which hovers so precariously between the possible and the impossible, may be the consequence of experience and responsibility, to be distinguished from the visions of the irresponsible observer. It may also be the fruit of Christian wisdom, which has learned the fragmentariness of all human striving and the measure of egoistic corruption in all human virtue.

But traditional conservatism has been deficient in its sense of justice. Indeed, it has proved itself wedded to aristocratic interests in domestic policy and it has not risen above national or imperial interests in international affairs.[20] * It has further tended to express an uncritical devotion to any existent status quo with its contingent balances of power, its social inequalities, and its forms of relative justice. But any given status quo must be critically surveyed by realistic liberalism; otherwise, differences of privilege may be considered valid *a priori,* thus exceeding those actually justified by function. Likewise, without this critical surveillance, the coercive elements in the community may tend to imperil the liberty of persons—which liberty is necessary above and beyond the demands of the community in order for man to be truly human.[21]

Our problem is how to generate the wisdom of true conservatism without losing the humane virtues which the liberal movement developed. In Western history, liberalism as a spirit connotes a temper of

* Conservatism and liberalism in relation to American foreign policy are treated in Chapter XXIV.

freedom; but it also connotes a specific creed, associated with the rise of both bourgeois life and modern learning. Both the spirit and the creed of liberalism emphasized the value and the dignity of the individual in contrast to traditional forms of culture which did not recognize the individual apart from his social function or position. But in addition the creed of liberalism included some illusions about human nature and human history which have become the source of confusion to our generation. Therefore we must be concerned to preserve the spirit of liberalism, while life refutes the liberal creed.*

But while we cannot condone the spirit of conservatism, at least insofar as it is an ideological defense of some status quo, it is necessary to regain that part of the conservative creed as elaborated in Western, and particularly in British, history. This creed emphasized historical rather than abstract modes of social engineering, and recognized the perennial sources of recalcitrance to moral norms in human life. It was therefore intent upon developing politics as the art of the possible, being cautious not to fall into worse forms of injustice in the effort to eliminate old ones. Perhaps the creed of such a conservatism is most adequately expounded in Edmund Burke's *Reflections on the Revolution in France*.[22]

This blend of the realism of the conservative creed and the idealism of the liberal spirit is put forward as the best contemporary expression of the pragmatic approach to politics required by Christian insight into the human situation. For to know both the law of love as the final standard and the law of self-love as a persistent force is to enable Christians to have a foundation for a pragmatic ethic in which power and self-interest are used, beguiled, harnessed and deflected for the ultimate end of establishing the highest and most inclusive possible community of justice and order.[23]

No political decision should be reached solely in terms of broad principles, whether of "liberalism" or "conservatism," of "freedom" or "justice" or "planning." The evils which have developed from communist pretensions are a reminder and proof of the fact that the worst evils of history are derived not from pure selfishness but from self-interest clothed in the pretensions of ideals. The damage to society is being done by general, abstract programs, serving as weapons of warring groups and classes.[24]

Moreover, inflexible propositions of justice, particularly in the rapidly shifting circumstances of modern technical development, may hinder rather than help the achievement of true justice. One contribution which Christianity certainly ought to make to the problem of political justice is to set all propositions of justice under the law of love,

* For Niebuhr's detailed treatment of the several varieties of liberalism, and particularly the "liberal creed," see Chapter II.

resolving the fruitless debate between relativists and legalists and creating the freedom and maneuverability necessary to achieve a tolerable accord among men and nations in ever more complex human relations. We need a pragmatic attitude toward every institution of property and of government, recognizing that none of them is as sacrosanct as some supposedly Christian or secular system of law has made them, that all of them are subject to corruption and that their abolition is also subject to corruption.[25]

Actually, nothing is intrinsically immoral except ill-will and nothing intrinsically good except goodwill. Since it is very difficult to judge human motives, it is natural that, from an external perspective, the social consequences of an action or policy should be regarded as more adequate tests of its morality than the hidden motives. The good motive is judged by its social goal. Does it have the general welfare as its objective? When viewing a historic situation all moralists become pragmatists and utilitarians. Some general good, some *summum bonum,* "the greatest good of the greatest number" or "the most inclusive harmony of all vital capacities" is set up as the criterion of the morality of specific actions and each action is judged with reference to its relation to the ultimate goal.

The choice of instruments and immediate objectives which fall between motive and ultimate objective raises issues which are pragmatic to such a degree that they may be said to be more political than they are ethical. The realm of politics is a twilight zone where ethical and technical issues meet. A political policy cannot be intrinsically evil if it can be proved to be an efficacious instrument for the achievement of a morally approved end. Neither can it be said to be wholly good merely because it seems to make for ultimately good consequences. Immediate consequences must be weighed against the ultimate consequences. The destruction of a life or the suppression of freedom result in the immediate destruction of moral values. Whether the ultimate good, which is hoped to be accomplished by this immediate destruction, justifies the sacrifice, is a question which depends upon many considerations for its answer. How great is the immediate and less inclusive value which is sacrificed for a more ultimate and more inclusive one? How certain is the attainment of the ultimate value? Is there any certainty that violence can establish equality or that an equality so established can be maintained? These are some of the pragmatic questions which suggest themselves. The questions are important but none of them can be dealt with adequately if it is assumed that any social policy, as violence for instance, is intrinsically immoral.[26]

It is important, in other words, to consider all factors in a social situation, and to have a flexibility in tactics which does justice to momentary contingencies while maintaining an inflexibility in strategy which does justice to the basic principles of human society. But loyalty to principle does not mean loyalty to one principle, when human society is governed by more than one principle. For example, no democratic society can survive if it acts upon the assumption that liberty is the only principle of democracy and does not recognize that community has as much value as liberty. The absolutists like to regard the relativists as opportunists who are devoid of principle. But decent relativists merely recognize, as absolutists do not, that life is governed by more than one principle, and that not even the relation of these various principles is fixed. They know that history is full of novel situations and surprises and that a wise statesmanship must know how to do justice both to immediate exigencies and to perennial human needs.[27]

Nothing is clearer than that ideologically consistent political positions on the whole have been refuted by history, while healthy nations have preserved freedom and extended justice by various pragmatic policies which borrowed from various strategies.[28] Britain has been, until recently, the home of pragmatic politics, where "liberty broadened down from precedent to precedent"; where the complex relation of freedom to order was so well understood that social policy moved from case to case and point to point, informed by experience rather than consistent dogma, thereby avoiding a too great sacrifice of freedom to order or of order to freedom. Britain has not lost her genius for the empirical approach; but we in America may have exceeded her achievements in some respects, partly because we had margins of security which prevented the rise of consistent dogmas. Our success in establishing justice and insuring domestic tranquillity has exceeded the characteristic insights of a bourgeois culture. Frequently our success is due to social and political policies which violate and defy the social creed which characterizes a commercial society. America has developed a pragmatic approach to political and economic questions which would do credit to Edmund Burke, the great exponent of the wisdom of historical experience as opposed to the abstract rationalism of the French Revolution.[29]

Of course, the defects of general political and social and economic programs do not justify the conclusion that no moral choice between general programs is possible and that only narrowly pragmatic approaches to detailed problems of justice are legitimate. General decisions must be made at particular points in history. It was, for instance, morally right as well as historically inevitable that the rising middle classes should have challenged the organic cohesions and the traditional authorities of monarchial absolutism in the early part of the modern period. The bourgeois movement destroyed the monopoly of political power by espousing democracy against monarchism. And it released vast new energies by supporting a system of "natural liberty" against mercantilism and other forms of political restraint upon economic life. It is just as right and inevitable that the sensitive conscience should now support programs for bringing economic power under state control and for insisting upon certain minimal welfare standards in housing, social security, education. The fact that it has been necessary to shift from the emphasis upon liberty to the emphasis upon mutual responsibility and political restraint of economic power simply proves the historical relativity of all socio-moral choices.[30]

The fundamental task of "social Christianity" must be, however, not so much to advocate a particular nostrum for the solution of various economic and social evils, but to bring a full testimony of a Gospel of judgment and grace to bear upon all of human life.[31] The problem of how to maintain freedom under the intense and complex forms of social cohesion in modern technical society and how to achieve justice when freedom is maintained cannot be solved by any neat principles. It must be approached pragmatically from case to case and point to point. We know that it is possible to buy security at too great a price of freedom; and to maintain freedom at too great a price of insecurity for the masses involved in the modern industrial society. The Christian faith as such has no solution for this problem. It ought, however, to be possible for a vital Christian faith to help people to see that both freedom and order are facets of the love commandment which we must approximate; and also that such approximations under conditions of sin and law are bound to be imperfect in all human history. The conflict between order and freedom is perfectly resolved only in the Kingdom of perfect love which cannot be completely realized in history.[32]

III. *The Churches and the State*

Like the individual Christian, the Church as a community and institution must face the challenge of making its social teachings and actions relevant and responsible, while avoiding moralism and fanaticism. This is a peculiarly difficult task, considering how easily religion lends itself to the pretension of possessing absolute truth and virtue.

Ideally, the Church, which defines what is truth or error, is not itself one of the forces contending in society for an advantage, but is a transcendent community above all contending forces. All of us who are Christians believe that the Church holds the "Oracles of God"—that is, that it is a community of grace, testifying to the final truth about life as given in the Christian revelation. But the fact is that this transcendent community is also an interest group, through the sins and interests of its members.[33] Indeed, since the historic Church is always touched with human finiteness, is subject to sociological forces and pressures, and victim of the prejudices and illusions of particular ages, any tendency to obscure or deny this fact becomes the final and most terrible expression of human sinfulness. Yet of that sin no Church has been free.[34]

When the sanctification of the Church is extended to the sanctification of political programs, movements, or systems, the baneful effects are compounded. One need not be a secularist to believe that politics in the name of God is of the devil. This should be obvious to right-minded religious people, for religious politics invariably gives an ultimate sanction to highly ambiguous political programs. Every political policy, however justified, must be regarded as ambiguous when it is related to the ultimate sanctity. Since the political order inevitably deals with power, a religious politics always means the identification of some position of power with God.[35]

Protestants may believe, and not without a measure of truth, that this sin of profaning the Holiness of God, of using His Name in vain, is a particular danger in Catholicism, for Catholicism has a doctrine of the Church in which what is human and what is divine in the Church are constantly subject to a confused identification of the one with the other.[36] The Catholic Church tends to identify the historic Church with the Kingdom of God, and too often its final criterion is what a political movement promises or does not promise to the historic Church. It is therefore forced at times to give preference to movements which deserve plainly to be condemned on grounds of justice. Other expressions of this error are, of course, the Church's commitment to the deductive and intuitive "rational," inflexible propositions of "natural law," and its sanctioning of religious political parties, which are dangerous because they tend to identify the moral ambiguities of politics with eternal sanctities, the result being that almost any kind of struggle can be interpreted as a contest between Christ and Antichrist.[37]

Catholicism's uncritical attitude toward the Church is sometimes transferred even to a Christian state, that is, a state in which God is explicitly acknowledged as Lord. While there is an undoubted difference between a pagan community which acknowledges no sovereignty beyond its own will and knows no majesty beyond its own pride and a "Christian" state which recognizes an ultimate Majesty and Judge, it is the general tendency of Catholic political thought to over-estimate this explicit acknowledgment and to obscure the fact that all particular communities in history, as indeed all individuals, tend to an idolatrous self-worship, even when they are officially or formally "Christian." Thus the inclination of Catholicism to exempt the Church from involvement in sin tends to political views in which Christian states partly participate in this exemption.[38]

A Protestant critic can easily detect that Catholic conceptions of sin and grace underlie this predeliction for an established church and a "Christian state." The Catholic believes that men seek their own ends because they have lost God and that if they find God again they may be redeemed of their self-worship and of the social anarchy which results when the immediate ends of life are transmuted into ultimate ends. The Protestant takes a more serious view of sin. He does not believe that even Christians, who sincerely worship God, are free of the sin of self-glorification. For this reason he is afraid of an authoritarian society. He is quite certain that any elite group endowed with social power will in the end be corrupted.[39]

Despite these serious misgivings, it must be pointed out that most American non-Catholics have a very inaccurate concept of Roman Catholic political thought and life. In this concept, it is assumed that if Catholics anywhere had their way, they would at once build a political structure as much like Spain's as possible. For Catholicism is often judged solely as it shows itself in old and decaying feudal structures, whether in Spain or South America or even in French Canada. People who argue this way usually ignore the relationship of Catholicism to the political life of modern industrial society.[40] Thus they underestimate the resources of Catholicism for preserving justice and stability in a free society, once established. They do not do justice to the role of Catholicism in the free societies in America, France, Germany and Western Europe. They do not realize, for instance, what a contribution the Catholic conception of the superiority of political authority over the economic process made in avoiding the aberrations of both doctrinaire "free enterprise" economics and contrasting Marxist aberrations. Nor do these criticisms take account of the practical effects of the Church's ability to qualify the class antagonisms in industrial society by holding the loyalty of the industrial classes and allowing their viewpoints to color the political positions of Catholic political parties. It was this achievement, together with a Christian check on extreme nationalism, which gave Catholicism such a stabilizing influence in an otherwise unstable Weimar Republic, and which determines the creative force of the Catholic parties in modern France and Western Germany.[41]

It is hardly necessary to expound the realities of the American scene. Fortunately we do not have religious parties. But it would be well for Protestants who talk about the "reactionary" tendencies of Catholicism to remember that, in religious terms, the main political struggles in America would appear to be between Jews and Catholics who are left of the center and Protestants who are right of it.[42]

Of course, the process which makes for this dangerous alliance between religion and power is not confined to any one type of Christian religion, or even to the Christian religion as such. It is in fact such a perennial factor in human history that it must be ascribed to a basic difficulty of human spirituality. Only a religion which worships a God before whom the princes of the world are as nothing, and which is able to convict of sin the mighty as well as the lowly, is capable of dealing with this difficulty of human spirituality.[43]

Thus our constitutional fathers quite obviously and quite rightly wanted to prevent the establishment of religious monopoly. That is the clear meaning of the First Amendment. It is not at all clear that they sought to prevent the state's support of religion absolutely, provided such support could be given equitably to all religious groups. Whether that should be done is a question of public policy upon which we may have different opinions. It may well be that the religious heterogeneity of America is such that the state support of religion is not advisable.

But we ought not to prejudge that issue in the name of a principle of "separation of church and state" which in exact constitutional terms goes no further than the prohibition of the establishment of one religion and the suppression of others.[44] Though it is important to resist all pressures which would give any religious group a special advantage in our nation, it might be worth noting that there is no one ideal solution of the problem of the relation of church and state. Our American principle of complete separation is a valuable heritage; but no one can deny that the price we pay for it is the official secularization of our culture.[45]

Nevertheless for Protestantism it is not so important that a "Christian" society have a Christian ruler as that it have a Christian prophet, which is to say the society must be Christian in its culture rather than officially Christian in its political relations. If the faith of the society is Christian it is possible for the Christian Church to exist within it, and it is possible for individuals on the authority of that Church to preach the judgment of God upon men and upon nations, including their own nation.[46] The Christian Church must bear witness against every form of pride and vainglory, whether in the secular or in the Christian culture, and be particularly intent upon our own sins lest we make Christ the judge of the other but not of ourselves.

But the experience of repentance does not stand alone. It is a part of a total experience of redemption. Positively our task is to present the Gospel of redemption in Christ to nations as well as individuals. According to our faith we are always involved in sin and in death because we try too desperately to live, to preserve our pride, to maintain our prestige. Yet it is possible to live truly if we die to self, if the vainglory of man is broken by divine judgment that life may be truly reformed by divine grace.[47]

IV. *The Insufficiency of Politics*

According to the Christian faith, life is and always will be fragmentary, frustrating, and incomplete. It has intimations of a perfection and completeness which are not attainable by human power.[48] There are no simple congruities in life or history. The cult of happiness erroneously assumes them. It is possible to soften the incongruities of life endlessly by the scientific conquest of nature's caprices, and the social and political triumph over historic injustice. But all such strategies cannot finally overcome the fragmentary character of human existence. The final wisdom of life requires, not the annulment of incongruity, but the achievement of serenity within and above it.[49]

Specifically, any hope for perfection of political life and order is illusory. Politics is always a contest of power. At its best it arrives at a tentative equilibrium of power. "The peace of the world," said Augustine, "is based on strife." There may be long periods of covert rather than overt struggle. But this is not the love and harmony of the Kingdom of God. Perhaps Jesus regarded the political aspect of messianism as such a terrible temptation because illusions about politics lead to the most baneful consequences. The contradictions of human existence which prevent power from ever being good enough to belong to the Kingdom and which equally prevent pure love from being powerful enough to establish itself in the world, must be finally overcome; but they can only be overcome by divine action.[50]

Any illusion of a world of perfect love without these imperfect harmonies of justice must ultimately turn the dream of love into a nightmare of tyranny and injustice. But the tragic character of our moral choices, the contradiction between various equal values of our devotion, and the incompleteness in all our moral striving, prove that "if in this life only we had hoped in Christ, we are of all men most miserable." [51]

Nothing that is worth doing can be fully achieved in our lifetime; therefore we must be saved by hope. Nothing which is true or beautiful or good makes complete sense in any immediate context of history; therefore we must be saved by faith. Nothing we do, however virtuous, can be accomplished alone; therefore we are saved by love. No virtuous act is quite as virtuous from the standpoint of our friend or foe as it is from our standpoint. Therefore we must be saved by the final form of love which is forgiveness.[52]

We cannot contemplate our political life decently without a proper and grateful understanding of the "grace" of God. For the grace of God is on the one hand the providential working in history by which God makes the wrath of man to praise him, and transmutes good out of evil. The other element in divine grace is the element of forgiveness. If we cannot believe that God has resources to negate and to wipe out the corruption of egoism that all our actions betray, if we do not know that we are "justified" not by our goodness but by the goodness of God, we remain in the awful predicament of either trying to find a vantage point in history from which we can act "purely," or persuading ourselves that we have found such a vantage point and declaring a "holy war" from it.

Of course, there can be no acceptance of grace without repentance. If we do not understand how sinful even good men and nations are, we will have no gratitude toward a merciful providence that makes us do good against our will and gives us a chance to serve mankind, even though we want to serve ourselves. But, also, there can be no repentance without faith; for in that case the realization of the awful realities of man's collective life drives us to despair.[53]

So we are "saved by faith" and not "by works"; which is to say that our final peace is not the moral peace of having become what Christ defines as our true nature, but is the religious peace of knowing that a divine mercy accepts our loyalty to Christ despite our continued betrayal of Him.[54]

One of the great resources of this faith for social achievement is the sense of humility which must result from the recognition of our common sinfulness. Christian brotherhood is the brotherhood of common need rather than of common achievement. Jews and Greeks are alike in this, that they are both in need of the mercy of God. To subject human righteousness to the righteousness of God is to realize the imperfection of all our perfections, the taint of interest in all our virtues, and the natural limitations of all our ideals. Men who are thus prompted to humility may differ in their ideals; but they will know themselves one in the fact that they must differ, that their differences are rooted in natural and historic circumstances and that these differences rise to sinful proportions beyond anything which nature knows.

They will not regard either their unities or differences in moral ideals as unimportant. They will know that men are called upon to make fateful decisions in human history and that these decisions sometimes set a son at variance with his father and a daughter with her mother. To subordinate the righteousness to which they are devoted under the righteousness of God does not mean to be less loyal to any cause to which conscience prompts them. Yet they will know that they are finite and sinful men, contending against others who are equally finite and equally sinful.[55]

The only true peace within and among human communities is the peace of forgiveness which grows out of contrition for sin. It is not a peace of perfect accord of life with life, but a peace which is established beyond the frictions of life. And this is a peace beyond the understanding of the moralists, who never fully recognize how much the judgment of the righteous upon the evil doer is below the ultimate and divine judgment. It is the judgment of an unrighteous self upon his fellows. There are of course legitimate judgments of the relatively righteous upon the unrighteous. But even when the unrighteous are obviously so, there is no vantage point in history from which a simple judgment against them can be pronounced. Reconciliation with even the most evil foe requires forgiveness; and forgiveness is possible only to those who have some recognition of common guilt. The pain of contrition is the root of the peace of forgiveness.[56]

Besides judgment, humility and forgiveness, the other great social resource of the faith is the confidence that God can work a redemptive purpose in and beyond the judgment and that His love operates in and beyond His justice. This can be proven true if it is believed, but it must first be believed. It does not of course offer any assurance of the preservation of this or any civilization. It is a confidence and hope which finally transcends the fate of all civilizations. Rightly interpreted, it can give us the serenity required to do our duty in an age in which alternate hopes and fears, fulfillments and frustrations threaten to rob us of the sanity required for the fulfillment of our duty.[57]

Thus the much despised Christian "otherworldliness" becomes a resource for historic striving. We strive for the Kingdom of God in history, but we do not expect its full realization there. Historical realities ought not to tempt the Christian to despair because he ought to know that the final good does not appear in history. The Christian ought to know that we never have, in either individual or collective achievement, the perfect serenity of achieved ideals. Our peace is never a purely moral peace. Our final peace is the peace of forgiveness, of justification by faith. The Kingdom of God always remains fragmentary and corrupted in history. Even the highest historic achievement points beyond itself to a more final consummation, even as every historic judgment points beyond itself to a more ultimate judgment. To know this is to have a final security beyond the securities of history, and a final hope beyond the achievements of history.

Such "otherworldliness" is not an escape from history. It gives us a fulcrum from which we can operate in history. It gives us a faith by which we can seek to fulfill our historic tasks without illusions and without despair.[58]

Only a combination of repose and anxiety, of serenity and preparedness, can do justice to the whole of our life and the whole of our world. For our life is a brief existence, moving within a great stream of finiteness. Yet the stream moves within its bed; and the flux of existence is held together by the eternal purposes of God. We ourselves stand beyond the flux in memory and hope. But we do not stand beyond it so completely that we can touch the eternal in the present moment by our own strength. We touch it by faith. That faith is the source of our serenity, even as alertness for the promises and perils of tomorrow is a reminder of our continued finiteness and sin.[59]

Martyr, prophet and statesman may each in his own way be servant of the Kingdom. Without the martyr we might live under the illusion that the kingdom of Caesar is the Kingdom of Christ in embryo and forget that there is a fundamental contradiction between the two kingdoms. Without the successful prophet, whose moral indictments effect actual changes in the world, we might forget that each moment of human history faces actual and realizable higher possibilities. Without the statesman, who uses power to correct the injustices of power, we might allow the vision of the Kingdom of Christ to become a luxury of those who can afford to acquiesce in present injustice because they do not suffer from it.[60]

PART THREE

Essays in Contemporary Politics

NATIONAL POLITICS

CHAPTER XVIII *

The Problem of Economic Power

I. *Beyond Laissez-Faire and Socialism*

Western civilization has been involved in a war between two political and moral creeds: classical economic liberalism and Marxist socialism. The former has been upheld chiefly by the bourgeoisie, the latter by the industrial workers. The two creeds are almost equally erroneous, and the internecine strife between factions which have countered half-truth with half-truth has even aggravated the chaos of international relations.[1]

The "liberal" society which gradually emerged out of the disintegration of the medieval culture and the feudal-agrarian economy is generally characterized by democratic political institutions and by an organization of economic life which dispenses, as far as possible, with the political, and even the moral, control of economic activities.

It was the great achievement of classical economic liberalism to gain recognition of the doctrine that the vast system of mutual services which constitute the life of economic society could best be maintained by relying on the "self-interest" of men rather than on their "benevolence" or on moral suasion, and by freeing economic activities from irrelevant and often unduly restrictive political controls. It released the "initiative" of men to exploit every possible opportunity for gain and thus to increase the resources of the whole of society, at first through the exploitation of commercial opportunities and subsequently through the endless development of technical and industrial power.[2]

Thus the cobbler would make shoes and the farmer would raise wheat and the tailor would fashion a coat; and they would exchange their several products. Each would gain in the exchange; for it permitted a

* The chapters comprising Part III are not intended to be comprehensive analytical studies. Rather, they are essays on topical problems, gathered together to illustrate Niebuhr's general method of approach, particularly the application of his theoretical insight to actual situations. These materials derive largely from Niebuhr's journalistic and occasional, as opposed to his more systematic, writings.

specialization of labor which improved the efficiency of each. Each would seek his own gain, or rather that of his family; but each would be prompted to serve the other in the system.

There are elements of truth in this discovery of classical economics which remain a permanent treasure of a free society, since some forms of a "free market" are essential to democracy. The alternative is the regulation of economic process through bureaucratic-political decisions. Such regulation, too consistently applied, involves the final peril of combining political and economic power.[3]

But the doctrine of classical economic liberalism accompanied its emancipation of economic life with a theory calculated to set the mind and conscience of society at rest about the possible moral and political consequences of this new freedom.[4] According to the liberal creed it is not necessary to be concerned too much about the problems of justice and brotherhood in an age of technics. All these new powers of man are believed to be governed by a mysterious natural harmony. In the history of mankind this harmony supposedly operates through the automatic processes of a free market and a generally uncontrolled expression of competitive economic interests—uncontrolled, they are supposed to check one another.[5]

In the course of modern experience it became more and more apparent that many cherished values of civilization are not protected by the operations of a "free market" and that there are conflicts in society which are not composed within the limits of a self-regulating competition. The errors and miscalculations which gave liberal society an undue confidence in the possibilities of an automatic harmony of economic and social interests may be finally reduced to two primary ones.

(1) The first basic error of the liberal theory was its strange blindness to the factor of power in man's social life and more particularly to the possibility that great disproportions of power would result in injustice. This error was the more fateful because it was introduced into Western social thought at the precise moment when a technical society began to develop highly collective expressions of economic and political power. This society would quickly transmute the static inequalities of a feudal society into dynamic ones.[6]

The laissez-faire, free market theory left the important fact out of account, that every economic process begins with a disproportion of economic power. Some men have land and some have not. Some gain a foothold in the commercial and industrial process and others do not. Modern technical civilization accentuates, rather than diminishes, these disproportions of economic power. This fact, which Ricardo first saw and which Marx explored more fully, invalidates the basic presuppositions of liberal ideas of property. The development from competitive to monopoly capitalism is the historic refutation of the idea that property is primarily an ordinate and defensive power to be used against the inclinations of others to take advantage of the self. Property, like every other form of power, is both defensive and offensive; and no sharp line can be drawn between its two functions. It is defensive only so long as the individual possesses so little of it that he will not be tempted to use it for domination over others.[7]

Bourgeois ideas of property aggravate the liberal blindness to the power factor by participating in the generally excessive individualism of middle-class life. Just as the individual does not have as discrete an existence as is assumed in liberal thought, so also is it impossible to draw as sharp distinctions between "mine" and "thine" as liberal property ideas imply. One reason for the acrimony of the conflict on property in the modern world is that this individualism was introduced into history at the beginning of the very epoch which would develop highly collective forms of commercial and industrial wealth. There is thus a serious gulf between the social function of modern property and the emphasis upon its "private" character in legal tradition and social thought.

Sometimes the individualism of liberal property theories is derived from the fact that the intricacies and complexities of a commercial and industrial civilization were simply not anticipated in the early period of our epoch. John Locke significantly draws his justification of property from a consideration of the simplest agricultural economy.

In any case, the most glaring contradiction between bourgeois individualism and the social function of property became apparent as commercial civilization was gradually transmuted into an industrial society in which collective production became the primary source of wealth. The modern factory is a great collective process. Technical advance has made it impossible for the worker to own either his own tools or the place of his work. Both the wealth represented by the machine and the wealth which the machine produces are generated by complex mutual services. The "private" ownership of such a process is anachronistic and incongruous; and the individual control of such centralized power is an invitation to injustice.[8]

According to the classical theory, a worker does not require collective power to set against the collective power of the factory which employs him. He will be saved from exploitation by the possibility of accepting a higher bid for his services from some other industry. Unfortunately, however, the worker is much more bound than the theory assumes. He cannot pick up his family and shop around from city to city. Furthermore, his economic weakness, compared with the strength of the company's financial reserves, makes it difficult for him to bargain at all. For he cannot hold out in the hope of securing a better bid from the bargainer. He can hope only that competing companies may bargain against each other for his services rather than that they may bargain with him.

An example from the agrarian side of the economy will reinforce the point. The dairy farmer cannot deliver his milk to the big city or in most areas start his own milk route. Milk processing and distribution, as nearly everything else in the modern economy, require large-scale units. There may even be some good reasons why milk distribution in a given city ought to be a regulated monopoly. But in any event, the dairy farmer has little possibility of getting out of his particular "milk shed" and bargaining with a processor of another city for higher prices than the processor of the city nearest his farm is willing to pay. How can he possibly secure bargaining power except by acting collectively? He may go further and use his political power to secure political intervention as well. He may, in fact, become politically so powerful that he will achieve certain unjustified advantages over the milk consumers of the city. But this merely proves the original contention, that unequal power is always a threat to justice. It does not refute the necessity of individuals' organizing for the sake of gaining collective power. Justice in a technical society requires that the centralization of power inherent in the industrial process be matched by collective social power.[9]

(2) The second great error of economic liberalism was its assumption of an economic rationalism which tended to equate every form of self-interest with economic interest. It believed men both capable of acting, and inclined to act, upon the basis of economic interest, and so obscured the motives of political and religious passion and interest, of ethnic and other loyalties, which impinge upon the economic sphere and are the very stuff of the sphere of politics.[10]

Actually, economic desires are never merely the expression of the hunger or the survival impulse in human life. The desires for "power and glory" are subtly compounded with the more primeval impulse. The lion's desire for food is satisfied when his maw is crammed. Man's desire for food is more easily limited than other human desires; yet the hunger impulse is subject to the endless refinements and perversions of the gourmand. Shelter and raiment have much more extensible limits than food. Man's coat is never merely a cloak for his nakedness, but the badge of his vocation, or the expression of an artistic impulse, or a method of attracting the other sex, or a proof of social position. Man's house is not merely his shelter but the expression of his personality and the symbol of his power, position and prestige.[11]

In short, the laissez-faire theory did not realize that human freedom expresses itself destructively as well as creatively, and that an increase in human freedom and power through the introduction of technics makes the achievement of justice more, rather than less, difficult than in non-technical civilizations. The liberal culture of our era either believed that the egoism of individuals, classes and nations was limited and harmless, or it hoped that the expression of self-interest was due to ignorance which could be overcome by growing social and political intelligence. This optimism misread the facts of human nature, as they are known from the standpoint of the Christian faith and as they are attested by every page of history. It therefore led to pathetic illusions which have been refuted by contemporary history. Thus the political principles which were to guarantee justice actually contributed to ever greater concentrations of power in modern society, and to resulting injustices.[12]

Once it is fully understood that there are no natural harmonies and equilibria of power in history, as there are in nature, and that advancing civilization tends to accentuate, rather than diminish, such disproportions of power as exist in even primitive communities, it must become apparent that property rights become instruments of injustice. In that sense the Marxist interpretation of the effect of property in history is correct.

Yet the Marxist solution for the problem of property is involved in merely another version of the older liberal illusion. Marxism assumes that the socialization of property will destroy all disproportions of economic power in the community. It looks for that perfect equilibrium of power on the other side of the revolution, which liberal theory imagines as a characteristic of the economic process in present society. Marxism does not understand that even universalized property may become the instrument of particular interest.

The Marxist illusion is partly derived from a romantic conception of human nature. It thinks that the inclination of men to take advantage of each other is a corruption which was introduced into history by the institution of property. It therefore assumes that the socialization of property will eliminate human egoism. Its failure to understand the perennial and persistent character of human egoism in any possible society prompts it to make completely erroneous estimates of human behavior on the other side of a revolution.

A second source of Marxist illusions is its belief that the ownership of property is the sole and only source of economic power. The management and manipulation of industrial process represents social power. Such power remains subordinate to the power of ownership in a capitalistic society, but it naturally grows in any society in which the rights of private ownership have been destroyed. The development of a managerial class in Russia, combining economic with political power, is an historic refutation of the Marxist theory.

So the Marxist theory fails to anticipate the inevitable rise of an oligarchy in a new society, partly because it has utopian ideas of idyllic relations in such a society, which obviate the necessity of the use of any form of coercive power; and partly because it identifies economic power too absolutely with the power of private ownership.[13]

Even democratic socialism was, until recently, weighed down with ideological baggage which prevented it from becoming a truly creative third force. It rightly recognized the reality of a class struggle in contrast to sentimental bourgeois concepts of a pre-established harmony in society. But the class forces in modern society are much more complex than Marxism understood. A democratic political strategy requires an understanding of these complexities. Democratic socialism rightly believed in the right and necessity of socializing property. But this strategy of justice still bore a halo of redemption in socialist thought which made it difficult for socialist parties to deal pragmatically with the institution of property. Democratic socialism rightly believed in the dignity and the freedom of the individual; but its materialistic conception of human nature furnished no spiritual foundation for this belief. It took this belief over, partly from Christianity and partly from a liberal culture, without furnishing an adequate framework for it in its own structure of thought. Finally, democratic socialism never fully revised its theory of human nature. It still held to the Marxist belief that human egoism is caused by a social institution and would therefore be eliminated by getting rid of that institution.[14]

The fact that socialism should have been such a creative force in Western democracy and should nevertheless, in its traditional form, be a spent force in current history, is instructive both about the quality of history and about the ability of a free society, with its competing political forces, to come to terms with historical contingencies. Socialism embodied a passion for social justice, but it committed the error of assuming that ownership was the only source of power in economic life. It added to this error its failure to anticipate all the various strategies and forces in a developing society by which undue power would be checked, neutralized and made responsible by the political dialogue and conflict which is possible in a free society.[15]

Adam Smith contributed mightily to a free society, but he almost wrecked that society with the unfulfilled promise that justice would flow inevitably from freedom. Karl Marx contributed mightily to a just society by his partial understanding of the realities of power in an industrial age, but he laid the foundations for a new despotism by not understanding those realities well enough. Fortunately, we are living in a day in which healthy nations do not concern themselves too much with the dogmas of either Smith or Marx, but profit by the truths they have winnowed from the errors of both.[16]

II. *Christian Thought on Economic Power*

According to the classical Christian theory, property, as well as government, is a necessary evil, required by the Fall of man. The Christian theory presupposes an ideal possibility of a perfect accord between life and life which would make a sharp distinction between "mine" and "thine" unnecessary. The sinful selfishness of men, however, had destroyed this ideal possibility and made exclusive possession the only safeguard against the tendency of men to take advantage of one another. Such a theory has the advantage of viewing the "right" of property with circumspection and of justifying it only relatively and not absolutely. It was justified as an expedient tool of justice. The right of possession was not regarded in early Christian thought as a natural extension of the power of the person but rather as a right of defense against the inordinate claims of others.

1. SOME ERRORS OF CHRISTIAN THOUGHT

Even before orthodox Protestantism accepted property distinctions uncritically, Catholic thought had gradually made less of the ideal possibility of common property and accepted private property as either a requirement of the natural law or as an inevitable supplement of positive law. In the modern day, Pope Leo XIII's encyclical *Rerum Novarum* defines property as a necessity in terms which can hardly be distinguished from those of eighteenth-century liberalism, though it must be observed that in Catholic thought economic power always remains under political discipline and moral authority and is not granted the autonomy which eighteenth-century liberalism demanded.

It remained however for orthodox Protestantism, especially Calvinism, to accept property distinctions without scruple or discrimination. In the case of Calvin this uncritical acceptance of property was due to his excessive determinism. Since property existed, he was certain that it must be by the will of God. Calvinism did not, of course, emancipate the administration of property from all moral restraint, as was done in laissez-faire theory. The Christian idea that we are God's stewards of all we possess remained a force in Calvinistic as in Catholic thought. But the idea of stewardship easily degenerated into the idea of philanthropy as a justification for property distinctions, and laid the foundation for the hypocrisies of bourgeois and plutocratic idealism in which charity became a screen for injustice. In extreme reaction to such tendencies, the sectarian Christianity of the sixteenth and seventeenth centuries combined social revolt with religious rebellion against feudalism, and laid the foundation for a primitive equalitarian and communist property ethic.[17]

The social wisdom of regarding property as a relatively effective institution of social peace and justice cannot be challenged. It is a "remedy for sin" in the sense that it gives the person power to defend himself against the inclination of others to take advantage of him. It endows him with instruments for the proper performance of his function, and grants him a measure of security in an insecure world. But both Catholic and Protestant social theory tended to make the right of property much too nearly absolute. The wisdom of some of the early church Fathers was forgotten. They understood that the power of property could be an instrument of injustice as well as of justice; and that it could be the fruit of sin as well as the remedy for sin.[18]

When we turn to American Protestant political and economic theory, we find that it too has gone through immature phases in which "free enterprise" was too uncritically accepted, and in which subsequently the "social gospel" introduced some utopian illusions into the thought of the church. The remarkable fact about developments in recent decades is that these contradictory errors have been overcome.[19] The social gospel movement was a revulsion of the religious conscience against an alliance between Protestant individualism and pietism and classical economic liberalism. It was always rather too moralistic to understand fully the operations of economic and political life with their inevitable contests of power and interest, and its left wing tended to share the Marxist illusions. But these defects now appear to be minor when its achievement is recognized. It insisted that social justice is a proper and necessary concern of the Christian faith, and delivered American Protestantism from meeting complex ethical problems of a technical civilization with an almost completely irrelevant individualistic pietism. Further, through the relation of American Protestantism to the world movement of Protestant churches, it also helped some of the churches of continental Europe overcome their undue social and political defeatism.[20]

Despite such achievements, we must confess that the Christian faith in its various historic forms has become involved in various errors and corruptions. Sometimes it has championed concepts of justice or freedom which were ideologies of the strong. Sometimes it has exceeded secular culture in moralistic illusions based upon the idea of the dignity and goodness of man but lacking in understanding of man's capacity for evil. Sometimes it has fled from these errors into a quasi-Christian Marxism. A genuine Christian faith must always be ready to recognize the periodic involvement of its own historic forms in the various errors against which its true genius forces it to contend.[21]

2. THE CHRISTIAN CONTRIBUTION TO AN ADEQUATE APPROACH

The positive Christian contribution to standards of justice in economic and political life must not be found primarily in a precise formulation of the standards. It must be found rather in strengthening both the inclination to seek the neighbor's good and the contrite awareness that we are not inclined to do this. The inclination to seek the neighbor's good must be accompanied by an awareness that every norm of justice is but a very relative approximation of this goal. The awareness that even good men are not consistently inclined to do this will lay bare the ideological taint, the corruption of self-interest, in every historic standard.

In the perspective of the Christian understanding of human nature, it becomes apparent not only why self-interest must be harnessed and not merely suppressed, but also why the self-interest has a different dimension than was assumed in the theories of classical economics and in the whole of modern naturalistic thought. Self-interest must be harnessed for two reasons. It is too powerful and persistent to be simply suppressed or transmuted. Even if individual life could rise to pure disinterestedness so that no human mind would give the self in which it is incarnate an undue advantage, still it would not be possible for collective man to rise to such a height. The institution of the family would alone prevent a simple substitution of "motives of service" for "motives of profit." For the self as "breadwinner" will seek to serve his family by seeking gain for his toil.

But self-interest must be allowed a certain free play for the additional reason that there is no one in society good or wise enough finally to determine how the individual's capacities had best be used for the common good, or how his labor is to be rewarded, or how the possibilities of useful toil, to which he may be prompted by his own initiative, might be anticipated.[22] Thus even now, when we know that all economic life must submit to moral discipline and political restraint, we must be careful to preserve whatever self-regulating forces exist in the economic process. If we do not, the task of control becomes too stupendous and the organs of control achieve proportions which endanger our liberty.[23]

In the light of modern experience and a balanced concept of human nature, Protestant thought in the twentieth century has achieved some consensus in social and economic philosophy. Its general position might be defined as governed by a concern for both freedom and justice, and as allowing for a great variety of pragmatic approaches to the vexing problems of modern economic life.

This consensus does not assume either that the free play of all economic forces will make for justice automatically, or that the solution of every problem of justice lies in bringing economic life more and more tightly under political control. Christian thought is equally rigorous with both the ideologues who persuade men to fear economic power but not political power, and those who teach that political power is dangerous but economic power is not. It knows that any form of power can be both the occasion of sin and an instrument for organizing the affairs of the community. If both Catholic and Protestant theory tend to justify a subordination of economic to political power, that is because political power can, at its best, express the will of a total community, while economic power is by its nature private and partial.[24]

The problem in modern technical society is so to distribute economic power and so to bring the undistributed centers of power under democratic control that the highest justice may be achieved. This problem can not be solved if property is dogmatically regarded either as the primary instrument of justice or as the primary instrument of injustice. It cannot be achieved if the power of the state is regarded as inevitably evil or dangerous; but neither can it be achieved if it is assumed that the power of a welfare state is inevitably benevolent or that its benevolence will inevitably be wise. We have to move from case to case and from point to point in achieving justice while preserving freedom in a technical society. The dogmatisms of the American right are a great hazard to the achievement of justice either domestically or internationally. But even the mild dogmatisms of socialism are not harmless. There is therefore the bare possibility that the unplanned improvisations of our early New Deal may gradually grow into a purposeful pragmatism in American and world politics.[25]

The foregoing argument leads, thus, to the conclusion that the proper relation of government to economic life presents problems which cannot be solved once for all. The contrasting perils of anarchy and injustice, arising from too little and too much equilibrium of economic power, or from too much or too little social control of it, must be considered in the light of each new situation and technical development. The property issue must, in other words, be continually solved within the framework of the democratic process.

A continuous debate on the property question is possible, however, only if there is some common denominator between opposing factions. The contradictory dogmas about property can most easily be dissolved if the utopianism which underlies both of them is dispelled. In communities such as America, where the Marxist dogma has never developed the power to challenge the bourgeois dogma, the primary requirement of justice is that the dominant dogma be discredited.

The obvious facts about property which both liberal and Marxist theories have obscured are: that all property is power; that some forms of economic power are intrinsically more ordinate than others and therefore more defensive, but that no sharp line can be drawn between what is ordinate and what is inordinate; that property is not the only form of economic power and that the destruction of private property does not therefore guarantee the equalization of economic power in a community; that inordinate power tempts its holders to abuse it, which means to use it for their own ends; that the economic, as well as the political, process requires the best possible distribution of power for the sake of justice and the best possible management of this equilibrium for the sake of order.

None of these propositions solves any specific issue of property in any given instance. But together they set the property issue within the framework of democratic procedure. For democracy is a method of finding proximate solutions for insoluble problems.[26]

III. *The Case of Organized Labor*

In analyzing questions relating to organized labor, we ought to establish two basic presuppositions in regard to the life of trade unionism in our technical culture. The first is that the organized power of labor has done more to increase the health of both our economic and political life than any other factor. It has provided that equilibrium of power without which justice is unattainable. It set organized power against organized power, which is the prerequisite of justice in a highly organized technical society.

The second basic presupposition is that both big business and big labor have acquired semi-governmental functions. They must, therefore, conform to the moral and political standards of our political system or our whole system is imperiled. We have outgrown the old liberal society in which government supposedly was the only power and it dealt with individuals. It is a New Deal achievement that the two great giants are fairly evenly balanced. That solves the over-all problem of justice; but it does not solve the subordinate problem of assuring justice within these subordinate centers of authority which have, in Hobbes' phrase, acquired "chips of the block of sovereignty."

The problem of the giant corporation with its combination of prestige and power, its right to hire and fire, certainly makes big business a part of government. The problem of the big corporation is too great to be solved merely by the enforcement of the Sherman Anti-Trust Act. But it is not the problem which concerns us here. The problem is "big labor," which has become a sovereignty so great that, with big business, our society has features which are as similar to the old feudalism as they are to the old liberalism.

The exercise of power requires more than the inner restraints of a social tradition or a moral mood, desperately as those are needed in some unions. It requires constitutional restraints. The liberal devotion to labor ought not to obscure the fact that even the best unions are defective in the constitutional safeguards against the misuse of power. They have no independent judiciary for one thing, no court to which a member may appeal which is completely independent of the current union leadership. A more important defect is that there is no separation of powers. In theory, the only legislative power rests in the annual convention. There is no representative legislature. But an even more significant defect is that in many unions the executive committee is composed of members who are dependent for their own positions upon the president of the union. There is, in short, no balance of power in many unions.

One additional problem of union democracy cannot be solved by a constitutional separation of powers. It is the problem of "one-party" government. This problem is created by the fact that the means of communication in a union are all controlled by the official leadership of the union. There is no room for a "loyal opposition" because there is no economic base for an opposition press. Unions are not totalitarian in intent; but they approach the totalitarian status because of the peculiar difficulties in organizing parties which will appeal to the general membership rather than to a section of the oligarchy. This matter is important, because in Western democracy many nations have not benefited from the explicit "separation of powers" of our Constitution. But no democracy has maintained its vitality if only one party could function and if the wielders of power were not under the constant scrutiny of an alternative government.[27]

Clearly, then, the day when "liberals" took the virtue of labor unions for granted is past. Much new legislation will be offered, intended to control and check the power of the unions. Some of the legislation will be very necessary, as for instance laws to supervise the scrutiny of the welfare funds. These funds have grown tremendously and constitute a temptation to crooked labor leaders; there must be governmental supervision.[28] Also, it would not be too difficult to require by law secret elections in all unions. Such a law would greatly improve the quality of our labor unions without weakening them. Union shops do rob the workers of the one weapon against badly run unions, which is their right to leave the union. But leaving a union is not in any case the ideal way of remedying abuses in it, just as leaving a church usually does not help very much in giving a church new vitality. What is really needed is the establishment of genuine democratic rights inside the union.[29]

On the other hand, the necessity of trade-union power in the economy of justice makes the weakening of the unions, as is intended by the "right to work" laws adopted or pending in many state legislatures, dangerous to the health of our country. Significantly, these laws are proposed not in the Congress but in the states, many of the legislatures of which have built-in conservative majorities in which the countryside has constitutional advantages over the great urban centers. In these legislatures, the anachronistic individualism of local business leaders who have not come to terms with the social facts of modern society can find alliance with the individualism of the farmers, to whom the collective pressures and counterpressures of industrial society are mysterious and dangerous mechanisms. But this kind of individualism is too anachronistic and too tendentious to prevail in the nation as a whole. The more mature portions of the nation, of whatever economic class or interest, have accepted the realities of both big business and big labor as ineluctable facts of our economy and our democracy.[30]

Something can undoubtedly be done by law in insisting that these quasi-sovereignties of organized power achieve the democratic safeguards which our political society has achieved and which are the source of both our liberty and our justice. But in the long run we must rely on labor itself, not only to develop higher standards and a more healthful moral climate, but also to overcome the hazards of "one party" government and to establish something like an independent judiciary.

Unbiased observers are willing to grant that most of the unions are honest, certainly more honest than the few which have claimed the interest of the public and the McClellan committee. But none of the unions has provided for sufficient safeguards against self-seeking human nature. Some of the most honest and progressive unions have become undemocratic through the great power of the president of the union. Some legislation is necessary to enforce minimal standards. But the real work must be done by the unions themselves. They must realize that their power is sufferable in a democracy only as an instrument of justice; and that even justice may be bought at too high a price of the liberty of the individual.[31]

IV. *Economic Life in Perspective*

The relation of the Christian faith to economic, as to political, life is not exhausted in its real or potential influence upon the moral and social norms of a community, nor in the insights which disclose the heights and depths of human conduct. All religion is an expression of the meaning of human existence. The Christian religion is unique in expressing the meaning of human existence in terms which partly involve and partly transcend man's historic existence.

The significance of man's life upon earth is affirmed, and all historic duties and tasks are taken seriously. But the Christian faith also insists that the final pinnacle of meaning transcends all possibilities of history. It is recognized that physical survival may be bought at too high a price. Thus Christ declares: "Fear not them which kill the body but are not able to kill the soul; but rather fear him which is able to destroy both soul and body in hell" (Matthew 10:28). The warnings in the Scripture against covetousness are frequent and explicit; and they are justified by the observation that "a man's life consisteth not in the abundance of the things which he possesseth" (Luke 12:15).

The final question about the relation of the Christian faith to the economic life of liberal society is concerned with the legitimacy of these warnings and their relevance to a society in which economic efficiency tends to become the final norm by which all things are judged. The general effect of modern economic rationalism has been to exalt the economic means of gain or of efficient production into final ends of human existence. According to Professor Eduard Heimann the effect of this tendency has been that "society has relinquished its control of economic activity and has in turn been made into an appendix to that which is now constituted as economic life."

The issue is the relation between man's immediate and ultimate ends. The question to be resolved is whether the satisfaction of immediate ends will inevitably contribute to the achievement of the more ultimate ends. Naturally any community will devote economic productivity to other than primary needs as soon as these primary needs of food, shelter and security are tolerably met. Therefore economic efficiency and increased productivity will support all higher cultural activity. Human culture depends in fact upon the ability of an economy to establish margins of welfare beyond the satisfaction of primary needs.

There are, however, two reasons why the relation of economic efficiency to culture is subject to a law of diminishing returns. The first is that human needs and desires are, as previously observed, essentially indeterminate. There is therefore no natural limit for their satisfaction. There is further no "natural" system of preferences which will guarantee that economic means will not become ends in themselves and that tangible and immediate satisfactions will not usurp the devotion of men to the exclusion of more ultimate ones. One possible wrong preference involves the violation of the "dignity of man" as a producer for the sake of achieving a high degree of productivity in favor of man as consumer. Furthermore, highly efficient economies may become involved in vulgarities to which more traditional cultures are immune. For in the more traditional cultures the imagination has not been prompted to seek and to desire the unlimited on every level of human satisfactions.

The second reason for the law of diminishing returns in the relation of efficiency to culture is the fact that technical efficiency is more effective in providing the basis for cultural and spiritual values than in contributing to its heights. The invention of writing, and subsequently of printing, were fateful chapters in the cultural history of mankind. Culture depends upon communication. And these arts of communication were creative instruments for all social, as well as for more purely spiritual, achievements of mankind. But the subsequent inventions which made "mass communication" possible and which culminated in the achievement of radio and television have had the general effect of vulgarizing culture.[32]

This is a particularly serious problem for the United States because we are being criticized by both friends and foes in Asia and Europe for having become obsessed with the tools and gadgets of life. When we speak rather idolatrously of the "American way of life," our friends and critics profess not to be certain whether we are recommending certain standards of political freedom or are extolling our living standards. The latter have reached heights of opulence beyond the dreams of avarice for most of the inhabitants of the world.[33] In short, the productive power of our industry threatens to make our culture subordinate to our economy. Too much leisure may become a disvalue and lead to the disintegration of personality. The other alternative of more goods and services may lead to a tremendous pressure upon the consumer to adopt more and more luxurious living standards for the sake of keeping the economy healthy.[34]

In any case, the diminishing returns in the realm of culture are symbolic of the general relation between quantitative and qualitative aspects of life. The quantitative increase of the comforts and securities of life, and of the technical efficiencies which furnish the foundation for every type of human achievement, does not lead to an indeterminate increase of the highest possibilities of life, measured culturally or spiritually. No degree of economic security can finally obviate the basic insecurity of human existence, finally symbolized in the fact of death. If preoccupation with these securities creates a culture in which human beings are incapable of coming to terms with life's basic insecurity through a serenity of faith, the culture stands under Christ's condemnation of the rich fool.

For this reason the Christian faith has a very special function and challenge in a culture in which a high degree of technical efficiency has been attained. If it becomes too defensive about its alleged "otherworldliness," if it fails to call attention to the limits of the "abundance of things which a man possesseth" in achieving the serenity and charity without which life becomes intolerable, if it does not define the dimensions of life which create the possibility of contradiction between the desire to survive and the desire to live in integrity of spirit; if, in short, it capitulates uncritically to the cult of technical efficiency and the culture of abundance, it must lose its uniqueness as religious faith. Perhaps this is the issue on which the Christian faith must come most directly to grips with the prevailing mood of a technical culture. Such a culture is in mortal danger of "gaining the whole world" but "losing its own soul." [35]

CHAPTER XIX

The Problem of Race Relations

On the international scene the relation of white to colored peoples has undoubtedly become the dominant politico-ethical issue of our day. But one aspect of this larger issue, namely the relation between whites and Negroes in specific nations including our own, has achieved even more vivid and tragic proportions than the general racial problem.

Compared with South Africa we are a virtuous nation and have reason to congratulate ourselves that no human being is left absolutely without hope, if not for himself then for his children. For the racial situation among us is obviously in flux and the road to a better tomorrow is not cut off. But the variations in the contest between good and evil are endless and we now face the fact that the very great step forward which the Supreme Court took in its decision abolishing segregated schools has unloosed passions and fears in the white minority in some localities, which reveal the similarity of human nature in the comparatively hopeful America and the hopeless South Africa.[1]

I. *The Problem in Contemporary America*

In 1896 the Supreme Court tried to ease the hiatus between the democratic ideal and the social realities by its doctrine of "separate but equal" rights before the law. It was a very good doctrine for its day; for we must remember that the recent Supreme Court decision would, at the beginning of the century, merely have prompted revolt. And revolt which is so widespread that police power cannot suppress it represents defeat both of the law and the ideal. History had to prepare the nation for the recent Supreme Court decision. By "history" is meant something more embodied than that abstract concept. It includes the thoughts and aspirations of a people, and the dozens of hesitant or bold actions which were taken by individuals and groups to overcome racial bias, to lift the educational standards of the allegedly inferior group and to breach the bar of segregation in every walk of life and in every communal relationship.

The doctrine of "separate but equal" facilities was used effectively by the Supreme Court in the last two decades to open up new opportunities for Negroes, particularly in transportation but also in the schools of higher learning where the force of the court ruling frequently opened the way for non-segregated education in cases where equal, but separate, institutions were unavailable. These revolutionary steps under the prodding of the law prepared the way for the next step which the Supreme Court took in 1954.

In fact, progress had been so rapid that it would have seemed plausible to "let well enough alone" and continue upon this course. But the Court refused to adopt this policy. Challenged with the idea that separate school facilities could not be "equal" because they left a mark upon both white and colored children by the implication of inferiority for the colored group, the Court met the challenge by admitting this indictment of segregated education and proving the correctness of the indictment by an analysis of the "intangible" as well as the tangible factors of education. Thus the Court wrote a great state paper as well as rendering what appeared to be a wise decision.

The statesmanship of the Supreme Court decision was displayed in its combination of boldness and concern for the political realities. It declared a principle, and applied it to a situation without compromise. But it postponed application of the principle for most of the affected states until they had time to adjust themselves to the conditions created by the decision, attempting thus to avoid any undue shock and to lessen the danger that the decision would provoke resistance by Southern authorities.[2]

So the Supreme Court's action was hailed both in this country and abroad as a milestone in the progress of justice. No one quite anticipated that the decision would unloose suppressed prejudices and fears which would complicate the problem of race relations for perhaps decades. The South, or at least the racist minority in the South, is up in arms. The two races are not living exactly at sword's point; but the tension in some localities has become very dangerous. Furthermore, the effort of the racists to defy and circumvent the Court decision has given some Southern states the quality of quasi-fascist terror and intimidation. An organic and slowly developing progress toward justice appears for the present to have been thwarted by a decision which spelled out the ultimate goal of the process. The explicit challenge of the moral standard seems to have aroused subconscious fears and prejudices which might have been gradually beguiled by a slower approach to the ultimate standard.[3]

More specifically, the pattern of reaction seems to be that the sections of the South which were making the most progress in interracial justice have been prompted to still greater progress by the decision, while the recalcitrant sections have been tempted to become more stiff-necked.[4] Thus states and counties vary in their compliance and defiance of the law. When analyzing this record it becomes significant that counties which comply are usually those in which Negroes are a minority of 25 per cent or less. On the other hand, counties which approach the 50 per cent ratio almost invariably seek some form of evasion. No one need be surprised at this phenomenon which shows the relation of moral ideals to mathematical facts. It is easier for a majority to be tolerant of a small than of a large minority. If the minority is large the tension between the two groups shows a corresponding increase. This is a phenomenon of all group relations and does not apply solely to Negro-white relations. It may lead to pessimistic conclusions in regard to certain counties in the South. But it prompts to optimism when we consider the nation as a whole, where the Negroes are in an obvious minority. The relation of morals to percentage points is a reminder to all of us of the frailty of our conscience and the limits of our tolerance.[5]

II. *Liberal and Christian Orientations*

The Christian must recognize that, without reference to capacities, equality is an imperative of love. The loving mother may not speculate whether her children are equally endowed; but she certainly has an instinct to equalize any inequality which "nature" may have left. Furthermore, to affirm that "all men are created equal" is to state a truth which has been amply proved by every kind of anthropological research. That is, men of all races are potentially equal, their inequalities being due to historical, rather than to natural, causes. We can therefore count it fortunate that the Constitution has incorporated this ideal in our law, which represents both an accurate description of the realities and a statement of the ethical implications of our faith.[6]

But Christianity's resources for approaching the problem of race relations do not stop short with a mere statement of the ideal of equality. Christian insights into the human situation afford, for instance, a much more profound illumination of the sources of racial prejudice than does the analysis of secular liberalism. Generally, American liberals have regarded racial prejudices as vestiges of barbarism, which an enlightened education was in the process of overcoming. They were certain, in any event, that racial amalgamation would take place in our nation and were inclined to draw from this fact the most ambitious universalistic conclusions; they thought modern history might be a process of a global assimilation of the races. Our anthropologists rightly insisted that there were no biological roots of inequality among races; and they wrongly drew the conclusion from this fact that racial prejudice is a form of ignorance which could be progressively dispelled by enlightenment.[7]

Liberal educators were fond of calling attention to the fact that children have no race prejudice, from which they drew the conclusion that nothing but a faulty education is responsible for the prejudice. They failed to recognize that the same children who have no race prejudice are also completely oblivious to race distinctions as such. It would be analogous if we argued that nothing but a faulty education caused sex aberrations and proved the contention by pointing to the absence of either sex passion or sex consciousness among children. The mistake is to identify childish innocency with virtue and to attribute the corruption of that virtue to some social source.[8]

All forms of prejudice do feed on stupidity and a certain amount of emancipation from bigotry can be, and has been, effected by social enlightenment. But this scientific assurance that "there are no races" or that "there are no inferior races" is not sufficient, because it does not measure the tragedy of racial bigotry deeply enough. It is of no avail to prove that there are no pure races when actual bigotry expresses itself in history whenever a cultural, religious, ethnic or other group diverges from the characteristics of the majority which presumes to set the standards by which the others are judged.

Very frequently the accusation of group inferiority is actually a betrayal of insecurity in the face of the competition of the minority group. The Japanese were frequently hated on the West Coast because they are incredibly efficient truck gardeners. White competitors veiled their envy and fear by their various accusations. In the same way the intelligence of Jews is feared in the academic competition of many colleges. The fear prompts accusations that the Jewish students are too clannish, or too pushing, or too indifferent to athletics or whatnot.

Most arguments against equal education for Negroes are curiously inconsistent on this score. It is claimed on the one hand that the Negro could not profit by these educational advantages; and on the other hand it is claimed that if he had equal educational advantages nothing would avail to keep him "in his place." Thus the majority group betrays its fears as well as its arrogance and proves that hatred and contempt of the minority group is compounded of both insecurity and a false security. It is the false security of a particular kind of man (Gentile or white man or such) who imagines himself the ultimate man and judges those who do not conform to his standard of beauty, culture, physiognomy, diligence, laziness, or any other characteristic which he ascribes to himself, for falling short of the ultimate of which he is the exemplar. But there is a certain insecurity here also. This ultimate man has a darkly conscious sense of the fact that he is not as ultimate as he pretends; and that the groups which he pretends to hold in contempt might actually beat him at his own game if he relaxed the restraints which he has placed upon them.

Psychological science might make some contribution to the analysis of these sub-rational fears and hatreds. It has in fact already done so. Yet it is also inhibited from a full analysis of these complexities because it does not know the human spirit in the full stature of its freedom. Psychology is not as simply rationalistic as anthropology in dealing with race prejudice. Yet it is always looking for the specific roots of man's insecurity and sense of inferiority. It does not know to what degree the particular forms of pride and arrogance in man are prompted by a *general* predisposition to pride and arrogance; and it does not understand how this general predisposition is man's abortive effort to hide his general insecurity.

Race bigotry is, in short, one form of original sin. Original sin is something darker and more terrible than mere stupidity and is therefore not eradicated by enlightenment alone, though frequently enlightenment can break some of its power by robbing it of some of its instruments of stupidity. While the general predisposition is not malice, it does issue in specific attitudes which have malice in them. Racial bigotry, like every other form of human pride and sin, is something more than ignorance and something less than malice.[9]

Racial prejudice is something less than malice insofar as it is an inevitable concomitant of the ethnic will to live. Wherever life becomes collectively integrated it generates a collective, as well as an individual, survival impulse. But it is something more than ignorance insofar as human life is never content with mere physical survival. There are spiritual elements in every human survival impulse; and the corruption of these elements is pride and the will-to-power. This corruption is deeper and more universal than is understood in our liberal culture.[10]

Group pride, then, is the sinful corruption of group consciousness. Such sinful corruption must not be condoned; but it need not be condoned simply because it is discovered that group pride is more inevitable and perennial than modern idealists have assumed. A profounder study of the tragedy of collective sin will make man less confident of the various panaceas which are intended to eliminate such sin in its various manifestations.

One salutary effect of religious realism is to brush aside all illusions which have hitherto saved us from cynicism and despair, to allow the facts about human nature to become fully revealed, until all men, including ourselves, stand condemned in the disclosure. Once we have recognized that we ourselves are not free of the sin which we see in our enemy and oppressor, no matter how grievous the oppression, it becomes possible for us to deal with the sin with vigor and with grace.

If we imagine that race pride is only a vestigial remnant of barbarism, which civilization is in the process of sloughing off; if we do not understand it as a perennial corruption of man's collective life on every level of social and moral achievement, we are bound to follow wrong policies in dealing with specific aspects of the problem. An engineer who dammed up an ocean inlet under the illusion that he was dealing with a mountain stream would be no more foolish than our social engineers who are constantly underestimating the force and the character of the social stuff which they are manipulating.[11]

In short, it is the illusion of idealistic children of light to imagine that we can destroy evil merely by avowing ideals and demonstrating truths. The Christian knows that the ideal of racial brotherhood is the "law of God" in which we delight "after the inward man"; but he ought also to understand that racial arrogance is "the law in our members which wars against the law that is in our mind." [12]

A Christian orientation to racial pride and prejudice will illuminate the limits, not only of the educational remedy, but also of law, as in the desegregation crisis. The Supreme Court decision ushered in a period of dramatic conflict between the majesty of the law and the power of local custom. There was immediate rejoicing, because the decision had given our democracy a new prestige in our contest with communism, particularly in the sensitive "colored" continents. But it is always premature to anticipate an easy victory of law over custom, for custom is a very stubborn force. Now the sorry realities of "nullification" are being unfolded.

The question is why the "majesty" of the law is not more potent than it has proved to be. That majesty consists of two elements. One is the prestige of justice itself. The other is the authority of the total community over its various members. But when the local community feels itself more integral and compelling than the total community and does not recognize the justice of the law as real justice, the majesty of the law is dissipated and the power of local custom triumphs.[13]

Earlier Supreme Court decisions, forcing Southern states to grant Negroes equality in interstate transportation and in college education, prove that law may be a potent weapon in enforcing rights. Within limits it is possible for a total national community to insist legally that every portion of the community observe its minimal standards of justice. Thus, too, Court decisions have forced some of the Southern states to admit Negroes to party primaries. It is clear, in other words, that the power of law is considerable in raising the democratic standards of a community.

But the law is not omnipotent. The very fact that the Emancipation Proclamation did not abolish slavery absolutely, and that the federal grant of suffrage to all Negroes has been circumvented in Southern states for two generations, proves that there are limits to the power of law. A study of these limits may lead to the conclusion that a federal act enforcing, for example, fair employment, is futile. It obviously cannot be passed; it probably could not be enforced, if it were passed. Such a conclusion flies in the face of an almost unanimous "liberal" opinion, inside and outside of the churches. But liberal opinion has again and again failed to observe that the potency of law has its limits. The lesson of the prohibition era seems already to have been forgotten. That lesson was that a determined minority, if it is locally a majority, whether in a city or a state, is able to defy, evade, or nullify a law passed by a national majority. It will do so if the law goes too far beyond the moral or social standards of the community. Laws can only be enforced upon recalcitrant minorities. The majority of the community must accept a law without enforcement, if it is to be enforceable. But if individual recalcitrance has the support of a local community, if the "conscience" of the community aids and abets defiance, no amount of enforcement by coercion avails.

It would be quite wrong to draw the conclusion that only educational and religious influences upon moral and social standards are of avail, and that it must be regarded futile to change social structures and systems by legal pressure. Too often religious leaders draw this conclusion and assert that goodness by coercion is abortive. A considerable proportion of our social virtue is derived not from our own resources but from the restraints and influences of the community. But the most effective restraints are not those of pure law, patricularly not if the law is in conflict with the "conscience" of the community.[14]

III. *The Churches and Desegregation*

Despite the creative, responsible attitudes and actions of many Christians, especially some heroic ministers in the South, the role of the church in the desegregation crisis has not been impressive; and occasionally we have witnessed the frightening spectacle of religion becoming the simple sanctifier of racial arrogance. Thus we have the ironic fact that the sports field, the trade unions, theaters, and music halls of the nation have been more creative than the churches in establishing community between the races. The churches have been the most segregated communities in the South and, for that matter, in the nation.

Nothing can hide the fact that this religiously sanctified racial parochialism has been a grievous offense against the very ideals of the Christian faith. But it has also been the negative by-product of one of the genuine achievements of the sectarian church in our nation: the creation of integral communities on the level of local congregations. This actual "chumminess" of the local congregation has invalidated the universal principle at the heart of the Gospel. Particular brotherhood, ethnically based, has invalidated the universal brotherhood implicit in the Christian ethic.[15]

This is true despite the fact that every major denomination of the South has unequivocally endorsed the Supreme Court decision on the school question. The difficulty is that the local congregations, and particularly the local ministers, find it difficult to withstand local pressures, particularly when the citizens' councils have infiltrated into the local congregation. Many good ministers in predominantly Negro counties have lost their pastorates because they were courageous; and many more are sick at heart because they do not feel free to follow the dictates of their conscience.[16]

Catholicism has been much more rigorous and successful than the Protestant churches on the racial issue. Partly this success is due to the hierarchial structure of the Catholic church, and the consequent ability of bishops and priests to set standards even in defiance of lay opinion. Catholic schools have been desegregated even when the bishop found it necessary to threaten recalcitrant parents with excommunication. This exceptional achievement of the Catholic church also brings to issue the inclusive community of a sacramental rather than a chummy fellowship. The fellowship of the Protestant church is always degenerating into a sanctified sense of kind, whether of race or class or neighborhood. The sacramental dimensions of the Catholic communion enlarge the communion of saints and conform it more nearly to the universal dimension intended in the Gospel.

If one analyzes the contributions of Catholicism to racial amity, one must be struck by the similarity between its contribution and that of the Bill of Rights. In both cases, one religious and the other secular, one ecclesiastical and the other political, the norm is imposed from above upon a recalcitrant democracy. Perhaps this is just another proof that we must approach this vexing problem from above and from below, both by the authoritative affirmation of norms and by the gradual achievement of community through common interests and pressures.[17]

IV. *Approaches to the Future*

There is no pat formula for resolving the tension between the South and the rest of the nation. Some critics have suggested that the Court should have allowed more time for desegregation. But it did allow time, and more time might have simply encouraged a complacent nullification by tardiness. The people in the North can help the cause if they refrain from unnecessary vilification. They should remember that perfect race amity has scarcely been attained in any part of the country and that, where there is still a considerable cultural difference between the two races, the sense of superiority is aggravated. If the South does not become too hysterical, the adjustments which have begun in those Southern regions where the Negro population is smaller will gradually spread to the hard core of resistance and recalcitrance.[18]

A democratic society must use every stratagem of education and every resource of religion to generate appreciation of the virtues and good intentions of minority groups which diverge from the characteristics of the majority, and to prompt humility and charity in the life of the majority. It must seek to establish contacts between the groups and prevent the aggravation of prejudice through segregation. It must uncover the peculiar hazards to right judgment which reveal themselves in intergroup relations. A democratic society must, in other words, seek proximate solutions for this problem in indeterminate creative ventures.[19]

For example, in 1957, Congress produced the first civil rights law since Reconstruction days. Civil rights purists were not satisfied with the law. But actually both the law and the debate which finally produced it represented a great triumph of democratic justice. The whole process which produced the law was a great triumph, not only because it advanced the rights of Negro citizens, but because it also made some progress in reconciling a recalcitrant South to a higher standard of justice. Another reason for approving the compromise which the law embodied was that it made a sharp distinction between the denial in the South of the very basic right of the franchise and the much less basic right of school integration. The redoubtable Negro leader Martin Luther King was right when he declared: "Give us the vote and we will do the rest." The very debate in Congress, with the two parties contending for the favor of the Northern Negroes, was a vivid justification of the logic which regards all other rights as derived politically from the franchise right.[20]

The success of the Negro bus boycott in Montgomery, Alabama, was also heartening, as the most obviously effective way of bringing pressure for the sake of justice. Violence in any local situation is not only wrong but self-defeating. In the case of a Negro minority in a white society it would be suicidal. The boycott, like the strike, is a recognized form of pressure in a free society. But one cannot help but question the definition of the boycott as "the way of love." Love is a motive and not a method. Love must always be intent on justice, and the boycott is one of the methods of establishing justice. It is justice, rather than love, which becomes relevant whenever one has to deal with conflicting wills and interests. Those of us who are not pacifists will be quick to admit that whenever pacifism is not preoccupied with moral scruples about guiltlessness and personal perfection, whenever it does not occupy itself with the problem of contracting out of responsibilities of justice in the name of personal perfection, whenever it seeks for justice, it becomes impressive. In this case involving a race suffering long from the pride and arrogance of another race, one can have little question about the justice of the boycott against the segregated buses, nor of the adequacy of the method by which justice is being achieved.[21]

In the school integration crisis, account must be taken of the Southern whites' fear of the Negro's cultural backwardness. If we are right in defining this backwardness as cultural rather than biological, it will of course be cured in time by precisely those equal opportunities of education which the Constitution and the Court seek to impose upon the community. But this fact does not immediately help anxious mothers and fathers in those counties of the South that regard a common education as a threat to the cultural adequacy of their children's education.[22] In relations between a cultured people and a backward people whose backwardness cannot hide for a moment the equal potentiality of a common humanity, it is not easy to establish justice. The immediate differences in capacity cannot be ignored. But the equal potentialities must also not be ignored. Therefore, justice means essentially that the hope of the future not be cut off. When that hope is destroyed, every present injustice becomes insufferable to the victims and destroys the humanity of the perpetrators because they are forced to indulge in every kind of self-deception to justify their cruelty to their own conscience.[23]

Probably the only strategy of defiance which is open to the rebel areas is the closing of the public schools. We may expect that that strategy bears its own nemesis; for it aggravates the educational problem which was the concern of the more moderate of the Southern rebels. Thus, with the inevitability of the supremacy of the ultimate norm established, time may be expected to work in favor of the norm and against the local recalcitrance. Even the most rebellious Southerners know that the "Southern way of life" is doomed. But this inevitable triumph of law and morals over custom will not prevent some very tragic local skirmishes.[24]

The church must make its own contribution out of the unique resources of the Gospel, in terms of judgment, repentance and humility. For the mitigation of racial and cultural pride is finally a religious problem in the sense that each man, and each race and culture, must become religiously aware of the sin of self-worship, which is the final form of human evil and of which racial self-worship is the most vivid example. We are not God. We are only creatures. All creatures are conditioned by climate and geography and by every special circumstance. Religious humility, as well as rational enlightenment, must contribute to the elimination of this terrible evil of racial pride.[25]

However, religious experience of repentance and conversion is more efficacious in emancipating us of individual sins which defy common standards of decency than of collective sins which are imbedded in these common standards. Many young people of the South have adopted new race attitudes through religious conversion. Others have changed their attitudes through rational analysis of the implications of their religious commitment and through social experiences which have slowly eroded the mores of their culture. All forms of grace, common grace and saving grace, are necessary to redeem us of our collective sins. And every form of discernment is needed to preserve our common loyalties from becoming collective evils. Our collective sins are the real test of the redeeming efficacy of our Christian faith.[26]

Historically founded and collective evils are corrected and social changes made, on the whole, by implicit rather than explicit processes, by gradual accommodation of social realities and power relations. If we must rely chiefly on the slow erosion of racial prejudice, every common activity of trade or culture in which community is established and men are prompted to recognize a common worth or an uncommon excellence is an important factor.[27] Real statesmanship will be required to uphold the majesty of the law and at the same time win over a custom-bound community to fuller conformity with the law. Prudence is as necessary as courage in the tasks of statesmanship. The fact that it is not very appealing to the victims of a current injustice does not make it any less the course of wisdom in overcoming historic injustices. And a genuine charity is the father of prudence. For genuine love does not propose abstract schemes of justice which leave the human factor out of account.[28]

Upon the basis of humility and charity we can work indeterminately on many proximate solutions for the problem of our ethnic pluralism. Our knowledge that there is no complete solution for the problem should save us from resting in some proximate solution under the illusion that it is an ultimate one.[29]

INTERNATIONAL POLITICS

CHAPTER XX

The International Situation

It is advisable to begin with an analysis of the dominant trends and forces of contemporary history, which have created the unique perils and opportunities confronting us. We may divide these forces and tendencies, complex as they are, chiefly into five great historical movements.*

The first is the increasingly rapid growth of technics which has transmuted every international problem into a global one. The development of technics and the corresponding enlargement of the international community are of course not recent developments. The whole history of mankind has been influenced by the gradual growth of technical competence both in the mastery of nature and in the arts of communication. But these developments proceeded by geometric progression in the latter half of the nineteenth century and the first half of the twentieth century.

Furthermore, world trade increasingly made the economic life of the nations mutually interdependent. It is unnecessary to say that this greater intimacy and interdependence of the nations did not automatically create a world community for which the optimists of the previous century hoped. It created the possibility of such a community but also the possibility of enlarging every conflict between communities. In short, technical progress accentuated all problems of community and gave them new dimensions.

The second development, the advent of the atomic age, is really a part of the first but it has such a significance that it deserves special mention. Modern history moves at incredible speed in all areas, but—ironically enough—particularly in the development of instruments of mutual annihilation. In less than a decade it became apparent that if another world war should occur it would be fought with weapons of such monstrous destructive power as to leave even the victor, in Mr. Churchill's phrase, an empty victory "in a universe of ruins." Thus to all the dimen-

* The themes to be identified briefly in this chapter will be elaborated in the several chapters which compose this section of the volume.

sions of our contemporary international problems this dimension of possible mutual destruction was presented to a generation which had only recently dreamed of historical progress.

The third significant development of modern history which has accentuated what would in any case have been a very large problem of the integration of a potential world community is the growth of the most dynamic and demonic world politico-religious movement in history. International communism has developed aspects both qualitatively and quantitatively that are among the most unpredicted forces in the contemporary scene. For the communist movement has managed to compound power lusts with utopian dreams in such a way as to give its totalitarian practices a dynamism and a plausibility which no one could have foreseen in this age which prides itself on its enlightenment.

It would be difficult to estimate the proportions of illusion and cynicism in the compound of motives that move the oligarchs of the present communist imperium. They must know that the power realities do not conform to the original dream. But they may, for all we know, cling to shreds of the dream in order to validate their ambitions in their own minds and in those of their victims. They have at any rate enough remaining illusions to make their power very dangerous. For in their eyes (at least until the atomic threat became serious) it was not necessary to concern themselves with the problem of mutual accommodation between foes or competitors or with that of integrating a divided world community. For they were privy to an historical logic which promised their cause victory over all its foes. These illusions even more than the unacknowledged power lusts impart a very dangerous irresponsibility to the foes of the free world and render the enmity which separates the communist and the free world doubly dangerous.

The fourth great historical movement that concerns us in describing our contemporary situation is the phenomenal rise of our own nation to the position of undisputed leadership in the world of free nations. This rise has been so phenomenal and rapid that one of our real problems as a nation is to become conscious of the degree of our power and of the responsibility which is the concomitant of power. Before the First World War we were content with our continental security and rather indifferent to the perils and opportunities of the world scene. We entered that war peripherally and subsequent American policies seemed to make it clear that we were determined never to enter another European war. This determination showed that we were not aware either of the growth of our power or of the destruction of our continental security through the technical developments we have already discussed.

The second threat to the European community from a German tyranny proved to be both morally and politically more dangerous to us than the first one. But it did not immediately alter our fixed neutralist determination. Indeed we could probably not have followed the clear dictates of both our conscience and our national interest if Japan had not catapulted us into the war by her attack on Pearl Harbor.

The exertions of World War Two dissipated our neutralist illusions. When the war was over we emerged not only incomparably the most powerful of the free nations but committed to responsibilities commensurate with our power. We moved from continental security to the position of the strongest nation in an alliance of free nations, forced to confront a world-wide communist threat. History probably records no more rapid transformation of a national ethos than the one that was accomplished among us in the Second World War and the subsequent period. Nations which only yesterday feared or affected to fear our lack of a sense of continuing responsibility now have the contrary fear that we will not be flexible enough in leading the free world in its long exertions through a period of not so peaceful co-existence.

The fifth development of which we must take account is the revolutionary ferment that is agitating the Asian and African continents. Our contest with communism on these continents is complicated by three factors which must prove hazards to any immediate success of our cause and which require a great deal of patience and expiation of past sins on our part.

First, there is the resentment felt by the colored peoples of the white man's long tradition of arrogance toward the peoples of darker pigment. Secondly, resentment is felt by the "colonial" peoples against the initial impact of a technical civilization upon a non-technical one. That first impact resulted in the application of the superior technical power of the Western nations for the purpose of bringing the non-technical cultures into the orbit of the powerful nations either as the source of raw materials or as markets for new industrial enterprise. Thirdly, the present impact of a technical civilization upon these older organic cultures tends to destroy their organic forms and to render the feudal structure of their society morally and politically untenable. On the other hand, they can hardly acquire in a few decades the delicate balances of power in both the economic and political spheres by which democratic justice and liberty are achieved and which the Western nations required about four centuries to learn.

The disintegration of a feudal or even a tribal social order under the impact of modern technics, coupled with the inability to create a democratic order in so short a time, is the greatest of the hazards which the free world faces in its contest with communism.

If we summarize the contemporary situation which our nation faces, we can succinctly express our dilemma in this way: We have been called into leadership of the free nations at the moment in history in which a potential world community is forming but has not yet been actualized. Every problem of the world community is aggravated by the world-wide influence of the communist movement, having its power center in Russia but possessing tremendous influence throughout the world and availing itself of every conspiratorial, as well as military, weapon to enhance its power.

We have this position of leadership in the free world chiefly by reason of our tremendous economic power and our consequent military might. Our leadership of the free world is complicated not only by our contest with communism but by the ferment in the Asian and African continents. Nationalistic ambitions and resentments because of previous subjection and the decay of agrarian social orders under the impact of technics all combine to make for political creativity, but also for confusion. They offer communism precisely the initial toehold which it briefly had in Western civilization and which a greater measure of justice in our political and economic life tended to overcome. It will be recognized that this complex of historical conditions, including the brevity of our apprenticeship in world leadership and the swiftness of our rise to power, presents our nation with the most exacting challenge in our history and one more exacting than faced by any nation in world history.[1]

Yet it is doubtful that we are adequately prepared to meet this challenge. The culture in which we have been nurtured has assumed that the comforts, the securities, the satisfactions and achievements of life could be expanded and multiplied without limit, and that nations and individuals could hope for more and more power and privilege.

Now we have come, as a whole nation, before some hard realities of life which all other nations have faced before us. We have discovered a disturbing limit of moral authority for Western civilization in the whole of Asia. We have been forced into the disciplines of an "armed camp." And not the least part of that discipline is the heavy taxation which will be required to sustain it. Very few Americans are willing to admit that all these experiences are due primarily to a combination of historical circumstances which no statesman could have created or deflected. We happen to live in a tragic age in which one world is dying and another seems powerless to be born. It is our destiny to live in this age. We cannot live in another. In this situation we must try to avoid both the spread of communism and the outbreak of an atomic war. To move, act and make decisions within such narrow limits of destiny is a sobering experience for a nation and a culture which thought that historical destiny was completely under the control of human decisions.

One of the most important lessons for our whole nation is therefore to learn how to live within the limits of our epoch's possibilities, to accept what is fragmentary and frustrating in human history, and to bear with patience the adversities of life. The more we can do this with patience and serenity, the more will we be able to act with resolution.[2]

CHAPTER XXI

The Resources and Limits of the International Community

I. *Realists and Idealists in World Politics*

As in other areas of political analysis, it is possible to discern two general types of approach to the problems of international politics. One might be defined as the historical and realistic school of politics. The other is rationalistic in method and idealistic in temper.* In the present situation the idealists rightly insist that the economic interdependence of the world demands new international political organization. They believe in the necessity of some kind of world government, which will make our economic interdependence sufferable and which will organize the potential world community and make it actual.

The realistic and historical school does not deny these new necessities and possibilities. But it views the task of realizing them in the light of its knowledge of the stubborn inertia of human history. It wants to know how nations are to be beguiled into a limitation of their sovereign rights, considering that national pride and parochial self-sufficiency are something more than the mere fruit of ignorance but recurring forces in all efforts at social cohesion.

The task of world organization must be attempted from the standpoint of historical realism. This conclusion could be justified by the simple fact that no historical process has ever, even remotely, conformed to the pattern which the idealists have mapped out for it. It must be added immediately, however, that the truth does not lie simply on the side of the realists. Without an admixture of the temper and the insights of the other school, there could be no genuine advance in social organization at all.

The realists understand the perennial problems of politics, but they are usually deficient in their sense of the urgency of a new situation. They know that politics is a problem of the manipulation of power. But they

* For previous discussions of idealism and realism, see Chapters VI and XVII.

easily interpret the problem of power in too cynical terms. Sometimes they forget that political power is a compound of which physical force, whether economic or military, is only one ingredient. They do not fully appreciate that a proper regard for moral aspirations is a source of political prestige; and that this prestige is itself an indispensable source of power.[1]

More particularly, the realistic school of international thought believes that world politics cannot rise higher than the balance-of-power principle. The balance-of-power theory of world politics, seeing no possibility of a genuine unity of the nations, seeks to construct the most adequate possible mechanism for equilibrating power on a world scale. Such a policy, which holds all factors in the world situation in the most perfect possible equipoise, can undoubtedly mitigate anarchy. A balance of power is in fact a kind of managed anarchy. But a balance of power without the organizing and equilibrating pressure of government, is potential anarchy which in the end becomes actual anarchy.

No participant in a balance is ever quite satisfied with its own position. Every center of power will seek to improve its position, and every such effort will be regarded by the others as an attempt to disturb the equilibrium. There was sufficient mistrust between the great nations, even while they were still locked in the intimate embrace of a great common effort during World War Two, to make it quite certain that a mere equilibrium between them would not suffice to preserve the peace.

Thus a purely realistic approach to the problem of world community offers as little hope of escape from anarchy as a purely idealistic one. Pure idealists underestimate the perennial power of particular and parochial loyalties, operating as a counter force against the achievement of a wider community. But the realists are usually so impressed by the power of these perennial forces that they fail to recognize the novel and unique elements in a revolutionary world situation. The idealists erroneously imagine that a new situation automatically generates the resources for the solution of its problem. The realists erroneously discount the destructive, as well as the creative, power of a revolutionary situation. A catastrophic period of history may not create all the resources required for the solution of its problems; but it does finally destroy some false solutions and some of the inertial obstacles to advance. A view more sober than that of either idealists or realists must persuade us that,

> "If hopes are dupes,
> Fears may be liars." [2]

Surely, the Christian knows, or ought to know, that an adequate Christian political ethic is not established merely by conceiving the most ideal possible solution for a political problem. He must, in all humility, deal with the realities of human nature, as well as the ideal possibilities. He must know that the intransigent elements in every historic situation are derived not merely from the sin of Russia or some other nation, or from the stupidity of statesmen, but from the difficulty which all of us find in conforming our actions to our highest ideals. It is very difficult to establish peaceful and just human communities, because the collective behavior of mankind is even more egoistic than individual behavior.[3] But the Christian also hears the divine command in every new historical situation. He ought to know that the creation of some form of world community, compatible with the necessities of a technical age, is the most compelling command of our day.[4] Our job is therefore to establish a tolerable community within the limits set by man's recalcitrance.[5]

II. *The Illusion of World Government*

The trustful acceptance of false solutions for our perplexing problems adds a touch of pathos to the tragedy of our age.

The tragic character of our age is revealed in the world-wide insecurity which is the fate of modern man. Technical achievements, which a previous generation had believed capable of solving every ill to which the human flesh is heir, have created, or at least accentuated, our insecurity. For, as we have already noted, the growth of technics has given the perennial problems of our common life a more complex form and a scope that has grown to be world-wide.

Our problem is that technics have established a rudimentary world community but have not integrated it organically, morally or politically. They have created a community of mutual dependence, but not one of mutual trust and respect. Without this higher integration, advancing technics tend to sharpen economic rivalries within a general framework of economic interdependence; they change the ocean barriers of yesterday into the battlegrounds of today; and they increase the deadly efficacy of the instruments of war so that vicious circles of mutual fear may end in atomic conflicts and mutual destruction. To these perplexities an ideological conflict has been added, which divides the world into hostile camps.

It is both necessary and laudable that men of good will should, in this situation, seek to strengthen every moral and political force which might give a rudimentary world community a higher degree of integration. It was probably inevitable that the desperate plight of our age should persuade some well-meaning men that the gap between a technically integrated and politically divided community could be closed by the simple expedient of establishing a world government through the fiat of the human will and creating world community by the fiat of world government. It is this hope which adds a touch of pathos to already tragic experiences. The hope not only beguiles some men from urgent moral and political responsibilities. It tempts others into irresponsible criticisms of the necessarily minimal constitutional structure which we have embodied in the United Nations and which is as bad as its critics aver only if a better one is within the realm of possibilities.

Virtually all arguments for world government rest upon the simple presupposition that the desirability of world order proves the attainability of world government. Our precarious situation is unfortunately no proof, either of the moral ability of mankind to create a world government by an act of the will, or of the political ability of such a government to integrate a world community in advance of a more gradual growth of the "social tissue" which every community requires more than government.

Most advocates of world government also assume that nations need merely follow the alleged example of the individuals of another age who are supposed to have achieved community by codifying their agreements into law and by providing an agency of some kind for law enforcement. This assumption ignores the historic fact that the mutual respect for each other's rights in particular communities is older than any code of law; and that machinery for the enforcement of law can be efficacious only when a community as a whole obeys its laws implicitly, so that coercive enforcement may be limited to a recalcitrant minority.*

The fallacy of world government can be stated in three simple propositions. The first is that governments are not created by fiat (though sometimes they can be imposed by tyranny). The second is that governments have only limited efficacy in integrating a community. The third is that the integrative forces in the world community are still minimal.

1. GOVERNMENT IS NOT CREATED BY FIAT

The advocates of world government propose calling a world constitutional convention which would set up the machinery of a global constitutional order and would then call upon the nations to abrogate or abridge their sovereignty in order that this newly created universal sovereignty could have unchallenged sway. No such explicit abnegation has ever taken place in the history of the world. Explicit governmental authority has developed historically from the implicit authority of patriarchal or matriarchal tribal forms. Governments, so established, have extended their dominion over weaker neighbors. But the abridgement of sov-

* For a general treatment of the thesis that government must presuppose community, see Chapter IX.

ereignty has always been indirect rather than direct; or it has been attained by the superimposition of power.

The notion that world government is a fairly simple possibility is the final and most absurd form of the "social contract" conception of government which has confused modern political thought since Hobbes. It must certainly be obvious by this time that the conception of a state of nature in which all men were at war with all, and of a subsequent social contract through which men established a power over themselves to avoid mutual annihilation, is a pure fiction. A small human community is as primordial as the individual. No group of individuals has ever created either government or community out of whole cloth.

When the question is raised whether the nations of the world would voluntarily first create, and then submit to, a super-national authority, the possible reluctance of nations, other than Russia, to take this step is fortunately or unfortunately obscured by Russian intransigence. The Russians have declared again and again that they would leave the United Nations if the veto power were abolished. This means that Russia, as a prospective minority in a world community, is not ready to submit her fate to the will of a majority, even in such a loose organization as the United Nations. It is therefore obvious that she would be even more unwilling to submit her sovereignty to a more highly integrated constitutional order.

The proponents of world government have two answers to the problem posed by Russian intransigence. One is to assert that the Russians never have had the chance to accept or reject a genuinely constitutional world order, and that there are real possibilities of her acceptance of a constitution which is not weighted against her. This answer contains in a nutshell the rationalist illusion implicit in world government theories. It assumes that constitutions can insure the mutual trust upon which community rests. Actually, even the best constitution must, if it be democratic, set up some kind of majority rule. It is not workable if there is not enough common ground between majority and minority to assure that a majority will not take advantage of a minority, or that the minority will not suspect the majority of injustice, even though without cause. There are republics in South America with quite nice constitutions in which a defeated minority starts conspiracies against the government, usually through military channels, on the day after election.

The other answer to the problem of Russian intransigence is a proposed creation of a "world" government without Russia. Thus in the name of "one world" the world would be divided in two. Proponents of world government are always ready with criticisms of the ambiguities in the Charter of the United Nations, without recognizing that those ambiguities correspond to the actual historical situation. The Security

Council is, for instance, a bridge of a sort between the segments of a divided world. They would destroy that bridge for the sake of creating a more logical constitutional system. This done, they look forward to one of two possibilities.

One is that Russia, faced with a united opposition, and concluding that she would not have to sacrifice her communist government but only her ambition to spread communism, would ultimately capitulate and join the world federation. This abstract approach to political problems is completely oblivious of the dynamism of communism.

The other course chosen by some advocates of world government is to create such a government without Russia and to divide the world more consistently in the name of the principle of "one" world. If this should lead to a world conflict they believe that the agonies of war will be assuaged for us by our knowledge that we are at least fighting for a principle of ultimate validity.

There is, of course, a possibility that a closer political integration of the non-communist nations may save the world from war by the creation of an adequate preponderance of power in the West. But such an objective is not to be reached by loftily disavowing "power politics" in favor of "law." The world federalists who accept the inevitability of war walk bravely up the hill of pure idealism and down again into the realm of pure power politics. In this journey they rid themselves of the logical and moral ambiguities of the much despised quasi-constitutional system of the United Nations. Their brethren who are in a less exalted frame of mind will continue to put up with the Charter for the sake of preserving a bridge, however slight, between Russia and the West, making the best arrangements they can to restrain Russia, while trying at the same time to strengthen the existing world security agencies.

2. COMMUNITY IS NOT CREATED BY GOVERNMENT

So far we have considered only the difficulties of creating a world government by constitutional fiat. But a much more serious defect in world government theories is to be found in their conception of the relation of government to community. Governments cannot create communities simply because the authority of government is not primarily the authority of law nor the authority of force, but the authority of the community itself.[6] If the community does not exist in fact, at least in inchoate form, constitutional instruments cannot create it. The authority of law as such is slight, and the fear of police power is useful only to suppress incidental recalcitrance against the will of the community. The community cannot be coerced into basic order; the basic order must come from its innate cohesion.[7]

It is sometimes pointed out that the ancient empires of Egypt, Babylon and Persia were created through the preponderant force of a particular city-state, and that they finally achieved a unity which did not require the constant application of force. But it must also be noted that this pattern of coalescence of communities gives us no analogy for the creation of a world community in democratic terms, that is, without the imposition of preponderant power. The best analogy for our present world situation is to be found in Greece rather than in Egypt or Babylon. The Greek city-states never achieved the imperial unity of the oriental empires. The threat of Persia did finally prompt the organization of the Delian League; but the rivalry of Sparta and Athens for the hegemony of the League resulted in its disintegration. The unity of Greece was finally achieved under Philip and Alexander of Macedon. But this imperial unity was also a tyrannical nemesis for Greek culture. The analogy in present global terms would be the final unification of the world through the preponderant power of either America or Russia, whichever proved herself victorious in a final global struggle. The analogy teaches us nothing about the possibilities of a constitutional world state. It may teach us that though the perils of international anarchy are very great, they may still be preferable to international tyranny.

The coalescence of communities from city-states to empires in the ancient world, and from feudal entities to nations in the modern period, was frequently accomplished only by the imposition of preponderant power. The fact is particularly significant, since all of these communities could rely upon all sorts of "organic" factors for their force of cohesion which the rudimentary world community lacks. By organic factors is meant such forces as the power of ethnic kinship, the force of a common history—particularly the memory of joint struggles against a common foe—a common language, a common culture and a common religion. We do have examples of ethnically and religiously pluralistic nations and empires, but they possess a basic homogeneity of some kind, underlying the differences. In modern India, where religious differences are thoroughgoing and highly localized, it proved impossible to construct a constitutional system which could allay the mutual fears of Hindus and Moslems. The birth in blood of these two nations, once the unifying force of an imperial power was removed, ought to teach our world planners more about the limited efficacy of constitutions than they have evidently learned. There were certainly more common elements in the situation in India than the world community will possess for a long time to come. Despite these common elements, the unity of India proved to be unattainable.[8] *

* Niebuhr has recorded a contrasting, though equally instructive, example: "The new state of Israel is composed of very religious and very consistently secular Zion-

These are tragic facts, and one could wish that they were not true; but it is hardly mature to deny what is so obvious. The world community lacks, in short, the potent elements of "togetherness" which national communities boast. Neither law nor police power can supply this defect. If one trusted to police power alone, the amount required by a universal state to maintain order in a community which did not cohere naturally and organically would be so great as to amount to tyranny. This was Thomas Hobbes' answer to the problem of community. The similarity between his answer and that of many of our modern constitutional idealists is instructive. Fortunately, national communities had a more organic unity than Hobbes supposed. Unfortunately, the international community corresponds at least partly to his picture.[10]

3. THE INTEGRATIVE FORCES IN THE WORLD COMMUNITY ARE STILL MINIMAL

The international community is not totally lacking in social tissue; but it is very scant, compared with that of particular states. Let us briefly assess the various factors in it. Most important as a force of social cohesion in the world community is the increasing economic interdependence of peoples of the world. But it is important to contrast this economic interdependence immediately with the wide disparity in the economic strength of various nations. At the climactic dinner of the World Republic convention, held in Chicago in October 1948, Professor Urey, the atomic scientist, expressed the conviction that the "inclusion of the illiterate, poverty-stricken, overnumerous masses of the Far East" constituted the major problem of the world state. He believed that the white race would not tolerate being outvoted by Asiatics. He therefore proposed a system of weighted votes in favor of nations with high literacy and abundance of raw materials and industrial production. He felt certain that the more "enlightened" Orientals would not object to this procedure. But an objection, from Thomas Tchou, sitting two places to the left of Professor Urey, was immediately forthcoming. Weighted representation, he declared, was immoral. Thus the real problems have an inconvenient habit of peeking through, even at a dinner of a World Republic convention.

---

ists. There is a rumor that when it was proposed to have a constitution for the new state a wise man warned against the venture on the ground that each party would try to secure a maximum of security in the constitution and thus accentuate the differences between them. It was better, he declared, for the two parties to live together as best they could. This common life would allay some of the fears and would throw up some *ad hoc* forms of accommodation which would serve the future as a constitution. So it proved. Life is a better unifier than law. Law can only define and perfect what life has established."[9]

A second factor in the social tissue of the world community is the fear of mutual annihilation, heightened in recent years by the new dimension which atomic discoveries have given to mankind's instruments of death. We must not underestimate this fear as a social force, even as we recognize that some culturally pluralistic communities of past history have achieved some cohesion through the minimal conviction that order is to be preferred to anarchy. But the fear of destruction in itself is less potent than the fear of specific peril from a particular foe. There is no record in history of peoples establishing a common community because they fear each other, though there are many instances when the fear of a common foe acted as the cement of cohesion.

The final and most important factor in the social tissue of the world community is a moral one. Enlightened men in all nations have some sense of obligation to their fellow men, beyond the limits of their nation-state. There is at least an inchoate sense of obligation to the inchoate community of mankind. The desperate necessity for a more integrated world community has undoubtedly increased this sense of obligation, inculcated in the conscience of mankind since the rise of universal, rather than parochial, philosophies and religions. This common moral sense is of tremendous importance for the moral and religious life of mankind; but it does not have as much immediate political relevance as is sometimes supposed. Political cohesion requires common convictions on particular issues of justice; and these are lacking. If there is a "natural law" which is "self-evident" to all men, it certainly does not contain very much specific content beyond such minimal rules as the prohibition of murder and theft and such general principles of justice as the dictum that each man is to have his due. There is little agreement on the criteria by which the due of each man is to be measured.

There is a special irony in the fact that the primary differences in the conceptions of justice in the world do not, however, spring from religious and cultural differences between East and West. They can therefore not be resolved by elaborate efforts at cultural syncretism between East and West. The primary differences arise from a civil war in the heart of Western civilization, in which a fanatical equalitarian creed has been pitted against a libertarian one. This civil war has become nationally localized. Russia has become the national center of the equalitarian creed, while America is the outstanding proponent of the libertarian one. The common use of the word "democracy," together with the contradictory interpretations of the meaning of that word, is the semantic symbol of the conflict. The idea that this conflict would be resolved by greater semantic accuracy is, however, one of the illusions of a too rationalistic culture which fails to understand the power of the social forces expressed in contradictory symbols.

In short, the forces which are operating to integrate the world community are limited. To call attention to this fact does not mean that all striving for a higher and wider integration of the world community is vain. That task must and will engage the conscience of mankind for ages to come. But the edifice of government which we build will be sound and useful if its height is proportionate to the strength of the materials from which it is constructed.[11]

In a day as tragic as our own it would be pleasant to believe that there is a simpler way than the tortuous process by which the nations are finding the road to community with one another. But the short cuts are illusory. Constitutional questions, before sufficient community is established, are divisive rather than unifying. How for instance would we decide how many votes Denmark, let us say, and the United States should have in a World Federalist senate? And what would the debate over that question contribute to the common defense against an immediate peril? In community building, as in other great human enterprises, the motto must be "precept upon precept," "line upon line." [12]

Meanwhile the proponents of world government continue to weary us with the constant reiteration of the proposition that we will have no civilization at all if we do not achieve a genuine world order. The slogan "one world or none" has a limited justification in that it calls attention to the precarious character of our situation and to the very great perils in which we stand. But it is also a very foolish slogan. It is foolish because any sober analysis of the contemporary scene must convince an honest student of the present impossibility of achieving world government. We do not have one world, or any hope of achieving it in the proximate future. Therefore, the logical conclusion from the slogan is that we are fated to have no world at all. Thus logic drives us to despair.[13]

We are living in a world which is neither one in organization nor yet consistently divided in two. Let us not be more consistent than history is. Our hope lies in protecting ourselves at the points where the world is divided, but also in preserving the tenuous threads which still unite it.[14]

III. *Political Integration in a Divided World: the Role of the UN*

The United Nations is not exactly the "Parliament of Mankind and Federation of the World" which the nineteenth century fondly believed to be the "one far-off divine event, to which the whole creation moves." It is nevertheless a symbol of what was true in the illusions of the previous century. It shows how man's communal problem develops toward global proportions. The ambiguities of the United Nations however refute the error in these hopes. The hopes erroneously implied that historical development would, in a sense, guarantee the solution of problems, the dimensions of which were constantly extended.

The most vivid proof that this was an error is given by two contemporary facts which were not at all anticipated. The one is the attempt of communism to organize the whole world upon the basis of its utopian vision. The other is the development of atomic weapons which, in a breathlessly brief time, has confronted us with the dread possibilities of destruction through the hydrogen bomb. The one development has divided the world into two camps. The other has filled the enmity between the two with the awful possibility of mutual annihilation. Both developments are reminders that every historical advance is fraught with possibilities of good and evil. Human history would seem to remain ambiguous, if not to its end, then at least to the present moment.

Thus we face the problem of integrating the world community under unanticipated hazards. The social conditions of community have shifted so rapidly and the factors to be taken into consideration are so endlessly varied that it would seem that the primary necessity is a development of all the social and political sciences with a particular view of overcoming the "cultural lag." This favorite diagnosis for all our ills seems to have acquired new relevance today. Must we not help people to meet the new situations which they confront by measures appropriate to the situation? Must we not establish educational programs to impress upon the new generation the responsibilities and perils of "one world"? Must we not help Americans, living in a paradise of luxury in comparison with world standards, to recognize the problems of peoples emerging from a primitive economy and from colonial tutelage? Must we not, as our sensitive spirits insist, make technical instruments and skills available to them to overcome their poverty? Having done that, must we not be wise enough to send cultural anthropologists along with our technicians in recognition of the fact that "raising living standards" is not a simple procedure? It involves breaking the mold of organic societies and exposing communities to the peril of social disintegration.

In all these problems a greater knowledge of all the factors involved and a larger perspective upon the total situation is certainly a primary necessity for the kind of statesmanship which will guide the nations toward a political and moral integration.

But perhaps this is another instance in which the presuppositions, from the standpoint of which we gather the facts, are as important as the diligence and honesty with which we try to ascertain the facts.

The most diligent elaboration of social and political skills seems not to have challenged the basic presuppositions of our culture in regard to the problem which we confront. That presupposition is that the forces of history are tractable if we only amass sufficient insight and skill to manage them; that even the most complex problems may be solved if we approach them with sufficient knowledge and resolution. In short, we approach them as potential managers of our own and other people's destiny.* It has seemingly not dawned upon us that we have only limited competence in deflecting historical destinies in the drama of history in which we are creatures as well as creators and in which we meet competitive creators who have contrasting ideas of our common destiny.

The immediate consequence of these exaggerated notions of man's competence as an historical creator is that our idealists, as we have seen, project all kinds of programs for integrating the world community purely by artifact and conscious contrivance. It might be noted that there are others who follow contrasting, but essentially similar, pretentious schemes of community. The one dreams of world government; the other would establish the supremacy of our nation in the world community purely by the affirmation of our technical power.

Both propose to solve the problems of the world community by a display of wisdom or of power, by an extension of the artifacts of community and by disregard of the organic factors. Both tend to disregard the possibility of unpredictable emergences in the drama of history. This disregard of the organic growths of the past and of the unpredictable emergences of the future, this emphasis on artifact and contrivance would seem to be plausible enough at first blush. Every extension of community does indeed imply a greater reliance on artifact and less reliance on organic factors. Certainly, as has already been observed, the nascent world community possesses few organic factors of cohesion, lacking even organic historical factors such as memories of a comradeship in meeting a common danger.

It is however significant that this factor is being supplied in each half of a divided world by the enmity between the two halves. There is of course no prospect of peace in these new historical factors on both sides. For the integration of each power bloc increases the tension between the two. But before dismissing this possibility of integration, we must examine the historical forces at work more carefully. They may offer more hope than the explicit contrivances of world community. There are indications that these historical factors are certainly more potent in forming community in the so-called "free" world than all the constitutional arrangements, except as the latter serve the community whose unity has been forged by the fires of present emergencies. The organization of the free world is an historic product with absolutely unforeseen perils and promises. It exists through the organization of various *ad hoc* defensive arrangements under the aegis of the United Nations. The United Nations

* For Niebuhr's complete explication of the errors of scientism in the social sciences, see Chapter V.

itself cannot of course be a final security against war between the two blocs. It was organized on the basis of the idea of unanimity between the great powers, expressed in the right of the veto of the great powers. This idea betrays, on the one hand, the illusions of the past decade that the free world could establish community with communism. The intransigence of this political movement was not correctly estimated. But the right of veto has another justification besides the one furnished by this illusion. It is based upon shrewd insight which the idealists who would abolish the veto do not understand. This insight is that the world community is not sufficiently integrated to permit a majority to be victorious over a minority in the councils of the nations. For in that case the minority, having the power and the inclination, would merely challenge the majority by the arbitrament of war. The grant of the right of veto is based upon the understanding that the world community has not yet reached a degree of integration in which minorities trust majorities. Yet this trust is a basic requirement of the constitutional instruments of which we are so fond.[15] *

Thus the United Nations, incapable of serving its original purposes, serves the very necessary end of integrating the world as far as present realities permit. On the one hand, it is a minimal bridge across the chasm between Russia and the West. On the other hand, it furnishes the meeting ground for the free nations, the aegis for its various *ad hoc* arrangements for defensive communities, and an assembly of peoples in which world opinion serves to check the policies of the most powerful nations in the alliance. These are quite important and yet unintended services to the process of integration. It is one of the interesting revelations of the charm of historical surprises that all these factors of cohesion would probably not have had a chance to become established if the framers of the original United Nations Charter had not been beguiled from their justified fears by an unjustified hope.

The loyalties and mutual trusts which are forming in these *ad hoc* arrangements both within and outside the UN are certainly more potent

* Niebuhr has taken note of the American attitude toward the veto: "All the great nations insisted upon the veto power, and the United Nations Charter would hardly have passed the United States Senate without this provision. Russia is more insistent upon retaining the veto than we are because it is in greater danger of being voted down in the United Nations General Assembly or Security Council. This fact does not deter our constitutional idealists from bombarding the ear of the Administration and the conscience of the nation with proposals for abolishing the veto. Here the constitutional answer to the problem of world peace obviously threatens the delicate and tentative degree of accord which has been achieved politically. We are professedly interested only in establishing a universal sovereignty, and we refuse to admit that we can afford greater devotion to the principle than Russia because we run less danger of being in the minority. This taint in our idealism is obvious enough to the Russians."[16]

than any possible explicit contractual commitments, though as the loyalties grow, they will presumably avail themselves of more adequate institutional arrangements.

In addition to these nascent forms of "social tissue" in the form of mutual trusts and loyalties, the free world is being integrated by another "organic" factor, which is less obviously moral but no less necessary. That is the integration through differentiation of authority, chiefly by power. A hierarchy of power and authority has been furnished for the world community by historical "accidents," chiefly the wholly unanticipated rise of American power and the sudden transformation of an isolationist nation, content with continental security, to the hegemonous power among the free nations. It goes without saying that the American leadership has not been established by explicit consent, though it must deserve the implicit consent of the community to survive. It is also obvious that the preponderance of American power is as valuable for the unity of the free world as it is dangerous to justice.[17]

It ought to be noted incidentally that one of the primary tasks of the United Nations and its various agencies is to relate American power to a weakened world and American prosperity to an impoverished world. For if preponderant American power is an immediate resource for the strength of the free world it is also a hazard. Power and weakness do not march easily in the same harness. It tempts the holders of power to pride and it tempts the weak to envy and resentment.[18] Our loyalty to the United Nations in a sense ought to be a symbol of our loyalty to the principles of international cooperation and our responsibility to the international community.[19]

About the lack of apprenticeship of our nation for these great responsibilities and about other peculiar rather than perennial hazards in this American possession of preponderant power, we must speak presently.* At this point, it is necessary merely to call attention to the fact that the integration of at least half of the world community has proceeded through forces and factors which were less under the conscious control of man than our philosophies would find tolerable. Yet they have been provisionally more successful than the more obvious artifacts.

All this integration leaves us, of course, with the two embattled power blocs and the peril of atomic destruction through a possible conflict between them. If we are to escape disaster, both sides would have to be sufficiently aware of this peril to be more than ordinarily hesitant to take any step which would lead to general conflict. If we are to escape unification of the world through tyrannical power, the loose organization of the free world would have to outlast the monolithic unity of the tyrannical world, and it would also have to be more successful than communism in

* See below, Chapter XXIII.

bidding for the loyalties of the non-committed nations. In that case the present growths might yet contribute to the ultimate integration of the world community. Such an eventuality would of course be possible only if the tyrannical power, having served the purpose of providing the danger which prompted the free nations to integrate their efforts and communities, would gradually lose its power to challenge the world. It is not probable that it will cease to exist as a potent secular religion. But it could well continue to exist without the power to challenge the world.[20]

IV. *Toward an Eventual World Community: a Commentary on UNESCO*

The United Nations Educational, Scientific and Cultural Organization is in the paradoxical position of performing most useful and necessary functions in the nascent world community but of giving very implausible reasons for the performance of its functions.

The most serious threat of conflict arises from the tension between two great centers of power, each of which seeks the political integration of its part of the world, at the expense of dividing the world into two halves. Many of the objections to UNESCO from responsible statesmen arise from the claims, frequently made in behalf of UNESCO, that its functions and services are capable of resolving the conflict between Russia and the West.[21] At the opening session of the Fourth General Conference of UNESCO the chairman of the executive board, the Indian Ambassador to Moscow, suggested that the unresolved conflict between Russia and the West might be resolved if it were taken out of the hands of politicians and men of culture were asked to resolve it. This proposal assumed that men of culture could be found in Russia who would not represent the political viewpoint of the Russian oligarchy. But the suggestion involves an even more serious mistake which is very dear to the heart of many moderns. It is the belief that the difficulties which statesmen face in guiding their nations are due, not so much to their responsible relation to their several nations, as to their intellectual inferiority in comparison with cultural leaders. This misses the whole point in the encounter of nations with each other. Such an encounter is a power-political one, in which statesmen distinguish themselves from philosophers and scientists, not by their smaller degree of intelligence but by their higher degree of responsibility to their respective communities.[22]

The belief that UNESCO programs are directly relevant to the avoidance of overt conflict rests primarily upon the conviction, expressed in the constitution, that "ignorance of each other's ways has been a common cause throughout the history of mankind of that suspicion and mistrust between the peoples of the world through which their differences have all too often broken into war." This proposition is partly true. Ignorance may aggravate fear. But it is not true that knowledge of each other's ways necessarily allays suspicion and mistrust. Some of the most terrible conflicts in history have occurred between neighbors who knew each other quite well, Germany and France for instance. The whole thesis of the direct political relevance of the UNESCO program to the resolution of immediate and overt conflicts in the world community rests to a large degree upon this dubious proposition that conflicts are primarily caused by ignorance of what the parties to a dispute really desire and intend. Actually the most tragic conflicts are between disputants who know very well what the other party intends, but are forced by either principle or interest to oppose it. It is of course possible for a highly integrated community, possessing a rich culture, to establish impartial tribunals with sufficient authority to compose or arbitrate a dispute; and with a sufficiently wise understanding of the points at issue to deflect the disputants from a too direct joining of the issue. But such procedures presuppose something more than an understanding between the disputants. They presuppose a community; and they avail themselves of the community's moral authority as well as of its police force.

UNESCO must, in short, find its justification in the contributions it makes to the integration of the emergent world community rather than in its supposed but usually illusory contributions to "peace."

The literacy programs and the support of fundamental educational projects, particularly in backward portions of the world, offer an especially vivid illustration of the "long range" rather than "short range" character of UNESCO activities. Obviously illiteracy is a bar to participation in any but the narrowest and most limited communities. Literacy is therefore a basic precondition for participation in a wider world community. But literacy and education are no guarantees of peace. Modern wars are fought by the most, rather than the least, literate of nations. A very high degree of intelligence is required for the social cooperation which modern, or even ancient, wars presuppose. Moreover literacy is no simple guarantor of loyalty to a wider community than the nation. In Russia literacy programs run hand in hand with an increasing subordination of the whole educational process to national interests. But the fact that intelligence may be the servant of particular rather than universal interests does not invalidate literacy programs as a part of a general process of building world community: the ability to read and write is the most fundamental of all the arts of communication by which wider communities are created. The strong nations must come to the assistance of the weaker nations in programs of fundamental education; but they will not be able to sustain these efforts if they labor under illusions about the relation of intelligence to community. For such illusions will give rise to periodic disillusionment. These programs can be justified only in very long range terms.

"Peace," declares the UNESCO constitution, "must be founded, if it is not to fail, upon the intellectual and moral solidarity of mankind." Even if the assertion should be interpreted to mean that world community, rather than peace in the more obvious sense, required the intellectual and moral solidarity of mankind, it is a somewhat questionable proposition. In one sense the intellectual and moral solidarity of mankind is an unattainable goal. The world community will be distinguished from particular national communities for ages to come by the higher degree of heterogeneity in its moral, intellectual, ethnic and linguistic forms of culture. It will be very important to achieve minimal common convictions on standards of justice and to establish degrees of tolerance between disparate cultures which do not now exist. It may perhaps be even more important simply to encourage every possible mode of communication between cultures in order that a common social and cultural tissue may slowly develop. Almost every item in the UNESCO program serves this ultimate end. That end must be its justification. Neither the immediate end of composing overt disputes, nor the slightly more remote end of encouraging obvious understanding between nations is necessarily served by these activities.[23]

In short, the difficulty with UNESCO is that its idealism is informed by a too simple universalism. Its idealists burke the tragic realities of life: the conflicts of interests which cannot be easily composed; the perils of war which cannot be simply overcome; the power of collective egoism which is not easily sublimated.

This ideological weakness will, in fact, be corrected by the very realities of contemporary experience which have already dissipated so much of the simple faith of the eighteenth century in the goodness of rational man. But in that case, what will become of the idealism? Will it survive? The spiritual problem of UNESCO is exactly the spiritual problem of modern man, who must find a way of engaging in impossible tasks and not be discouraged when he fails to complete any of them. For here is an organization which seeks to realize the impossible: a world community. It must not regard this end as a simple possibility; but neither can it dismiss the task as an impossibility. It stands, therefore, constantly at the final limit of the human situation where the possible and the impossible are curiously intermingled and where it is difficult to distinguish between God's and our possibilities.

Spiritually an organization such as UNESCO, as well as the whole modern generation, needs a faith which recognizes the completion of life within and above its fragmentariness, the final solution beyond all our solutions. It needs, in short, an apprehension of the grace which makes it possible for men to say, "We are perplexed but not unto despair."[24]

CHAPTER XXII

The Soviet Threat

I. *The Kingdom of God—Without Repentance*

Communism is a religion which has corrupted the Christian version of a Kingdom of God upon earth.* It separated the part of the Christian faith contained in the prayer, "Thy Kingdom come upon earth," from that part of the Christian faith in which the taint of sin on all historic achievements is recognized. It sought for a kingdom of perfect justice, a classless and universal society. It vulgarized this dream even more than did bourgeois secularism. For it thought that the abolition of the institution of property would assure a harmonious society and ultimately a sinless human nature. Thus is promised a Kingdom of God without repentance.[1]

Communism, in its pure form, is a secularized religious apocalyptic creed. The triumph of communism in Russia transferred the religious emotions associated with this apocalyptic hope to a particular locus. The hope that the Kingdom of God would come on earth was related to the assertion that it *had* come on earth and that Russia was the historical embodiment of it.[2]

It may be questioned whether the Russian oligarchy which now controls the destinies of a nation committed to the achievement of such an ideal never-never land, is animated by these utopian dreams. The possession of power is sweet and the corruptions of power are great. We may assume therefore that those who exercise this power do not concern themselves too much with the dreams which originally endowed their power with moral legitimacy. But it is important to recognize that in the eyes of the faithful the power which this oligarchy exercises is still in a completely different category from the power of Nazi oligarchs. Furthermore, the capacity of the human soul for self-deception is so great that some of these Russian oligarchs may, for all we know, feel themselves completely justified by the original dream.

But speculation about the mixture of motives in the soul of the oligarch

* For previous discussions of communism as a false religion, see Chapters I and III.

is comparatively irrelevant.[3] For the end result remains a meretricious compound of Russian nationalism with communist dreams of world dominion; and the creation of a tyrannical oligarchy devoid of either internal or external checks upon its power. Hell knows no fury like the fanaticism of the prophets of a secular religion who have become the priest-kings of an utopian state.[4]

In fact, the history of mankind does not record another instance of this type of enemy. For no previous center of power in human history ever had the advantage of a political religion, scattered beyond its borders, the tenets of which could persuade gullible men to regard even its most tortuous and cynical power politics as proofs of its virtues and good intentions.[5]

II. *The Dictatorship of the Proletariat*

Let us recall how this tyranny developed. The Marxist dogma provided for a "dictatorship of the proletariat." According to the dogma, this dictatorship was necessary because the messianic class (the workers) was bound to be insecure until its class enemies were "liquidated." The theory was that the workers would exercise a dictatorship to eliminate their class enemies, but that among themselves they would enjoy a perfect brotherhood. They would not need courts and policemen because they would put down any anti-social behavior by spontaneous action.

It is well to note the utopian touch in the vision of a democracy within a dictatorship, because it is the first clue to the question why the Marxist utopia turned into a hell. The visionaries did not consider the ordinary problems of a community, the competition of interests, the arbitration of rights, the adjudication of conflict. The only cause for conflict, namely property, was abolished. But meanwhile, the community on the other side of the revolution needed to be organized. It could not rely on spontaneous action. The embryo of the organization lay in the party. The dogma had assumed that, while the workers were the messianic class, they needed the party to inform them of the logic of history and what good things it intended for them. The workers had an existential righteousness, but evidently no wisdom. Lenin declared that, left to themselves, they could not rise above a "trade union psychology." How right he was. The Marxist dogma would always outrage the common sense of common men. It could be believed only by the ideologues. These were the secular prophets who became the priest-kings of the utopian state.

So we proceed from the dictatorship of the workers to the dictatorship of the party. But the party must also be organized. Everywhere the need for government, which the dogma had defined as merely an instrument of oppression, made itself felt. Without integration, the masses were merely a mob. The party must have a "central committee." But the committee was, and is, too large for executive action. The ruling group within the committee was first a mere class war improvisation. But naturally, its powers grew rather than diminished. The real oligarchs emerged. They had the power. This was the "democratic centralism" of Lenin. It must be observed, however, that Lenin, while more subtle than Stalin, was potentially a dictator. He did not allow "factions." He was the charismatic leader who knew the logic of history better than his colleagues. Had he not prophesied correctly?

But without real freedom, either within the party or in the community, there was nothing to prevent a shrewd manipulator, Stalin, from bringing all the organs of power into his own hands, from liquidating even the oldest prophets who did not agree with him, and from terrorizing a whole generation of newer oligarchs—many of whom owed their positions to his favor and had helped him to eliminate his foes. It is this absolute monopoly of power which proved to be so vicious and which is now defined by Khrushchev's euphemism, "the cult of personality." [6]

One must confess, incidentally, an ironic satisfaction in observing orthodox Marxists, who believe that history moves only in terms of "objective conditions," placing all the blame for a horrible tyranny upon the failures of a single individual. They have practiced "the cult of the individual" in reverse. Meanwhile, the "objective condition" which generated the evil is still with them. It is the monopoly of power which proved even more grievous in a revolutionary movement than all history proved it to be when it was used to defend the status quo.[7]

III. *Communist Imperialism*

Marxism projects an ideal international community in which the rivalry between nations will be abolished because that rivalry is ascribed purely to economic causes. Both internal and international friction are ascribed to greed and greed is attributed purely to property ownership. By this double error all power impulses in individuals and groups are attributed to one source. Therefore, the socialization of property is expected to guarantee not only a classless national community but also a harmonious international community.

Thus Marx merely contributed to the structure of communist imperialism the vision of an ideal universal community from which the only cause of disharmony had been removed. He certainly would have been as surprised by the use which Russian power made of this universalism as Augustine would have been surprised by the use which was made of his conception of the "City of God" by the Cluniac monk, Hildebrand, who ruled as Pope Gregory VII and quoted Augustine to justify the power and prestige of the medieval Papacy. Since authority in nation and empire is always compounded of prestige and force, and since prestige always depends upon an ideological framework, it is inevitable that a dominant community should acquire for its prestige whatever ideological framework is most serviceable for its pretensions.

Even Lenin, who had transmuted the Marxist vision of dictatorship to make it politically relevant and dangerous, could not be accused of being the conscious agent of relating Marxist universalism to communist Russian imperialism. Lenin signed the draconic treaty of Brest-Litovsk because he had the illusion that a revolution would break out in Germany which would correct it. The first evidence of the dominance of Russian power in this ideal universal community developed in the relation of the Russian party to the other communist parties of the world through the "Comintern." This development does not yet indicate the flowering of Soviet imperialism for most of these parties had no power in their respective nations. The capstone was placed upon the imperial structure when the Russians, after the Second World War, could use their captive parties as instruments of government in the nations of Eastern Europe which the war had brought under their control; the Red army was, of course, an added and necessary instrument of force.[8]

All of these developments, both internal and imperial, must prompt the student of the political order to question Ferrero's definition of legitimate and illegitimate government, which placed the traditional governments in the category of legitimate government because they governed by implicit consent rather than by force and fraud.* The question is whether there is not a subjective element in the concept of "fraud" both in traditional and in revolutionary governments. And force must be used to prevent the inspection and the discovery of the fraud. Thus communist tyranny, even more than traditional governments, must use force to cover up the defects of its ideology. The years and experience prove the incompatibility between the utopian vision and the necessities of a community even under a revolutionary government.

Obviously there is a more intricate relation between force and fraud than Ferrero assumed. It is also obvious that "fraud" may begin as an honest utopian dream, as in Marx, then become a political tool, as in Lenin, and end in pure fraud, as in Stalin. As this fraud is discovered, or as history transmutes the dream into a nightmare, more force is necessary to protect the ideological basis of the system.

One of the elements of real promise in the present situation is that a power system based upon utopian illusions is discovered more and more to be fraudulent, the further the revolution recedes into the past, and as greater force is needed to prevent the inspection of the fraud.[9]

* See Guglielmo Ferrero, *Principles of Power,* New York, G. P. Putnam's Sons, 1942.

IV. *The Lesson of Sputnik*

The Russian achievements in rocketry and space exploration have illuminated mistaken assumptions that we might not have made had we not been so fat and complacent. These include the following:

(1) Russia is not a "backward" country, except in living standards and political organization. Even the political tyranny is not backward; it is a novel form of harnessing utopian dreams to despotism. We forgot that it required Japan less than a half century to transmute its economy from an agrarian to an industrial and technical pattern. We were wrong to assume that a technical culture, requiring so many centuries to germinate in the West, could not be transplanted in much shorter time. Russia has been even a little quicker than Japan and probably for a reason which illustrates our second mistake.

(2) We were wrong in assuming that despotism excluded democracy in education, at least the democracy of freedom of opportunity. We should have known that the Russian young people had a passion for education and that the communist scholarship program, which recruits the bright sons and daughters of peasants for the most advanced scientific training, is better than our system of free education. We give everyone the right to acquire an education if the family budget and the resourcefulness of the youth are able to cope with our ever higher educational costs. That is "Jacksonian" democracy in practice. The Russian system is "Jeffersonian" in insisting on an aristocracy of excellence.

We can, of course, console ourselves with the comforting and true reflection that this is the only despotism in history which requires efficiency for its survival; and technical efficiency requires brains which may prove themselves ultimately—but only very ultimately—incompatible with tyranny.

(3) We were led astray by the fantastic Lysenko official biology of the Stalin era and imagined that science could not prosper in a dictatorship. The humanities and the arts in general feel the restraining power of the rulers who demand conformity to their standards of "social realism," for this means painting this false utopia according to the illusions of the oligarchs. But the pure scientists are apolitical, and have always been —whether here, or in Russia, or in Nazi Germany.

The technical advances in Russia are the more inevitable because bright young people, anxious to be co-opted as junior partners of the oligarchy which controls Russia, will go into pure science rather than into the humanities where they are bound to bow their knee to the Baal of dictatorship. In pure science and in technology the ambitions of the scientists and the ambitions of the oligarchs for international prestige coincide.

(4) We were probably most grievously in error in the complacency with which we equated all kinds of freedom: the freedom of science, of conscience, of religion, of enterprise and the freedom to buy a new model automobile every year. In short, our indiscriminate freedom and our tremendous productivity have made our culture soft and vulgar, equating joy with happiness and happiness with comfort.

We have in fact become so self-indulgent that one may raise the question whether our position vis-a-vis the Russians is not the old historic situation: the "barbarians," hardy and disciplined, are ready to defeat a civilization in which the very achievements of its technology have made for soft and indulgent living.[10]

At any rate, in the growing competition between East and West for the loyalty of the uncommitted nations of Asia and Africa, the communist countries have an advantage over us because they do not have to take the living standards of their own people into serious consideration. They offer economic aid wherever it seems advantageous to do so. Thus, whether in China or in Russia, a creed which promised to make the poor rich has an advantage over the free nations because it can keep them poor and promise them wealth the day after tomorrow. Surely neither Marx nor the anti-Marxists anticipated this kind of competition. All these unanticipated developments make it dangerous to think in terms of yesterday's thoughts, to say nothing of the slogans of yesteryear.

Meanwhile our benighted representatives in Congress worry about "give-away" programs. Foreign policy is sometimes declared the "Achilles' heel" of democracy. It would seem to be so when a very wealthy and gadget ridden nation cannot compete with a much poorer nation for prestige in helping the even poorer nations because the wealthy nation must take the prejudices and comforts of its citizens into account. This disadvantage of democracy does not make us yearn for dictatorship, but it does prove that only the most enlightened intelligence and conscience can put a democracy upon terms of equality with a tyranny in this kind of competition.[11]

V. *The Re-Stalinization of the Russian Empire*

If no other problem confronted the post-Stalin oligarchy its triumph in competition with the "free world" might be possible particularly since the launching of the earth satellites has given Russia the prestige of superior achievements in advanced technology. But the great problem of the post-Stalin era, which was assumed to be solved by Khrushchev's reconciliation with Tito, remains. The fact that it remains is attested by the subsequent hardening of the Russian line of authority over the satellites and the exclusion of Tito. Why was not the original revision of the dogma that "there are many roads to socialism" maintained? Why was it revised into a new Stalinism after Stalin had been discredited? Why was Hungary suppressed so brutally and Nagy murdered a year after the Hungarian revolt? Why was Poland's semi-autonomous status called in question? What prevented the devolution of the monolithic structure of the empire of Russia, particularly after the first steps to that end were taken after Stalin's death?

The answers to these questions are not simple because no question of dogma is involved. The idea of the dictatorship of the party was derived from the original dogma of the dictatorship of the class. But the dictatorship of Russia itself is not based on any dogma. It has simply been added by the contingencies of history which have made the first nation to have a revolution also the most powerful nation, and by the added fact that Stalin's enforced industrialization and the subsequent technical successes of a once backward nation have added to the Russian prestige in her empire. But the original necessity of exploiting her "colonies" has disappeared. Russia is exporting both capital and techniques to help the satellite nations to a rapid industrialization at a tempo which the creed demands but which is probably too rapid for the good of the satellites. There is no pressing economic reason for the tightened control. There is of course a strategic reason, for Tito has proved no longer a safe ally and if Titoism were to spread the strategic hazards would be multiplied.

But we must find the real reason for the return to Stalinist control of the empire by Russia in the realm of the ideological system from which the prestige of Russia as a ruling nation has drawn. That ideological system, as we have noted repeatedly, was based on utopianism and fanaticism. Russia was not designed to rule the Kingdom of God on Earth according to the Marxist creed. But it was forced to undertake the hegemony of the cohorts of socialism in achieving the victory of the righteous over the unrighteous imperialists. This fanatic and absolute distinction between the righteous and the unrighteous, between the "imperialist" nations and those who were "anti-imperialists by definition," was in conflict with the empirical facts, which anyone could see who was not bound by the dogma. The necessity of a tighter control arose from the dogmatic presuppositions of the communist system. If Russia were not to have this control what was to prevent Tito's policy from proving that the imperialists would not exploit Yugoslavia as the creed asserted? And what was to prevent both Tito and Gomulka from adopting a more melioristic policy toward the peasants than the dogma permitted? It is, of course, still difficult to see why this empirical policy was not permitted, particularly since the Russian oligarchy after Stalin made all kinds of empirical adjustments to the realities, including, for instance, the abolition of the "tractor stations" as a source of power over the collective farms.

But in an empire based upon a creed it is one thing to make slight adjustments to reality at the source of authority, and another to allow "different roads" to develop to such a degree that the original distinction between the socialists and the capitalist world disappears.

In any event the re-Stalinization of the Russian empire proves that an ideological system so glaringly at variance with the historic realities must not only have a fixed dogma, but also only one source of interpretation of the dogma. The dogma did not provide for Russia to be the authoritative source of interpretation any more than early Christian dogma made Rome the source of authority. In each case history supplied the seat of authority but the dogma supplied the necessity for a single authority.[12]

CHAPTER XXIII

America's Precarious Eminence

In less than half a century our nation has emerged from a condition of continental security to a position where its own security is intimately bound to the security of a whole community of free nations. Only yesterday we lived in a state of childlike innocency in which the contentions and alarms of world politics interrupted our youthful dreams only as distant thunder may echo through the happy conversations of a garden party. Today we have become the senior partners in a vast alliance of nations, trying desperately to achieve sufficient unity and health to ward off the threat of tyrannical unification of the world. We are like some adolescent boy, suddenly called upon to assume a father's responsibility for a numerous family.

These responsibilities have come to us at the precise moment in history when technical developments have made the world potentially one, but only potentially so.[1] It was not exactly a kind fate which gave America so great and so precarious an eminence in the world at this precise historical moment. There is an ironic element in this destiny; for the same technical developments which have created the necessity, without achieving the actuality, of such a world community are also responsible for the power which gives our nation such an unchallenged hegemony in the Western world. Technical efficiency and the unusually generous natural resources of a continent have made us economically the most powerful nation on earth in an era in which economic power is more quickly transmuted into political and military power than in any previous age. The same industrial production, which was so quickly transmuted into military power during World War Two, is also the basis of our political hegemony in the post-war period. An impoverished world must wait upon the decisions of the American economic Colossus, not because it trusts our wisdom but because it depends upon our economic resources.[2]

To add to our perplexities it is also the moment in history when a once utopian creed of world unity through world revolution has become an instrument of power in the hands of a cynical group of tyrannical oligarchs, operating from the base of a powerful nation and seeking to bring the nations of the world under its dominion by their fear of its power and their confidence in its virtuous intentions.

Roman and British imperialism both had the advantage of a longer period of apprenticeship before assuming so wide a scope of responsibilities. And neither faced a foe of such formidable proportions. Our position is not an enviable one.[3]

I. *The Prophetic Idea of Destiny*

The prophet Amos was certain of two things. One was that Israel had been particularly chosen of God; and the other was that this special mission gave the nation not a special security but a special peril. "You only have I chosen," he declared in God's name, "therefore will I visit you with your iniquities." Only those who have no sense of the profundities of history would deny that various nations and classes, various social groups and races are at various times placed in such a position that a special measure of the divine mission in history falls upon them. In that sense God has chosen America in this fateful period of world history.

The world requires a wider degree of community. If this community is to be genuine, it cannot, of course, be superimposed by American or any other power. All peoples and nations must find their rightful place in the fellowship. Nevertheless neither the world community nor any other form of human society ever moves as logically or abstractly as some of the "planners" and blueprinters imagine. Some nation or group always has a higher degree of power and responsibility in the formation of community than others.

But the fact is that no nation or individual is ever good enough to deserve the position of leadership which some nations and individuals achieve. If the history which leads to a special mission is carefully analyzed, it always becomes apparent that factors, other than the virtues of the leader, are partly responsible for the position the individual or collective leader holds. Those who do not believe in God's providence in history will call these factors "accidents" or "fortunes." If they are purely accidental then history itself has no meaning for man is destined to live in a completely capricious world. The religious man perceives them as gifts of grace. The grace which determines the lives of men and nations is manifest in all the special circumstances, favors and fortunes of geography and climate, of history and fate which lead to eminence despite the weakness and sinfulness of the beneficiary of such eminence.

If we know that we have been chosen beyond our deserts, we must also begin to realize that we have not been chosen for our particular task in order that our own life may be aggrandized. We ought not derive either special security or special advantages from our high historical mission.

The real fact is that we are placed in a precarious moral and historical position by our special mission. It can be justified only if it results in good for the whole community of mankind. Woe unto us if we fail. For our failure will bring judgment upon both us and the world. That is the meaning of the prophetic word: "Therefore will I visit you with your iniquities." This word must be translated today into meanings relevant to our own history. If this is not done, we are bound to fail. For the natural pride of great nations is such that any special historical success quickly aggravates it until it becomes the source of moral and political confusion.[4]

In this precarious situation our only chance of survival, with which the survival of Western civilization is inextricably joined, lies in a modest recognition of our weaknesses and inadequacies for our task. If ever a nation required the spirit of genuine contrition and humility it is ours. The future of the world literally depends, not upon the display of our power (though the use of it is necessary and inevitable), but upon the acquisition of virtues which can develop only in humility.[5]

II. *The Innocent Nation*

Yet we are (according to our traditional theory) the most innocent nation on earth. It is particularly remarkable that the two great religious-moral traditions which informed our early life—New England Calvinism and Virginian Deism and Jeffersonianism—arrived at remarkably similar conclusions about the meaning of our national character and destiny. Calvinism may have held too pessimistic views of human nature, and too mechanical views of the providential ordering of human life. But when it assessed the significance of the American experiment both its conceptions of American destiny and its appreciation of American virtue finally arrived at conclusions strikingly similar to those of Deism.

The New England conception of our virtue began as the belief that the church which had been established on our soil was purer than any church of Christendom. In Edward Johnson's *Wonder Working Providence of Zion's Saviour* (1650) the belief is expressed that "Jesus Christ had manifested his kingly office toward his churches more fully than ever yet the sons of men saw." Practically every Puritan tract contained the conviction that the Protestant Reformation reached its final culmination here.

Jefferson's conception of the innocency and virtue of the new nation was not informed by the Biblical symbolism of the New England tracts. His religious faith was a form of Christianity which had passed through the rationalism of the French Enlightenment. His sense of providence was expressed in his belief in the power of "nature's God" over the vicissitudes of history. In any event, nature's God had a very special purpose in founding this new community. The purpose was to make a new beginning in a corrupt world.

Whether our nation interprets its spiritual heritage through Massachusetts or Virginia, we came into existence with the sense of being a "separated" nation, which God was using to make a new beginning for mankind. We had renounced the evils of European feudalism. We had escaped from the evils of European religious bigotry. We had found broad spaces for the satisfaction of human desires in place of crowded Europe. Whether, as in the case of the New England theocrats, our forefathers thought of our "experiment" as primarily the creation of a new and purer church, or, as in the case of Jefferson and his coterie, they thought primarily of a new political community, they believed in either case that we had been called out by God to create a new humanity. We were God's "American Israel." Our pretensions of innocency therefore heightened the whole concept of a virtuous humanity which characterizes the culture of our era, and involves us in the ironic incongruity between our illusions and the realities which we experience. We find it almost as difficult as the communists to believe that anyone could think ill of us, since we are as persuaded as they that our society is so essentially virtuous that only malice could prompt criticism of any of our actions.

Every nation has its own form of spiritual pride. These examples of American self-appreciation could be matched by similar sentiments in other nations. But every nation also has its peculiar version. Our version is that our nation turned its back upon the vices of Europe and made a new beginning.[6]

We lived for a century not only in the illusion but in the reality of innocency in our foreign relations. We lacked the power in the first instance to become involved in the guilt of its use. As we gradually achieved power, through the economic consequences of our richly stored continent, the continental unity of our economy and the technical efficiency of our business and industrial enterprise, we sought for a time to preserve innocency by disavowing the responsibilities of power. The surge of our infant strength over a continent, which claimed Oregon, California, Florida and Texas against any sovereignty which may have stood in our way, was not innocent. It was the expression of a will-to-power of a new community in which the land-hunger of hardy pioneers and settlers furnished the force of imperial expansion. The organs of government, whether political or military, played only a secondary role. From those early days to the present moment we have frequently been honestly deceived because our power availed itself of covert rather than overt instruments. One of the most prolific causes of delusion about power in a commercial society is that economic power is more covert than political or military power.

We believed, until the outbreak of the First World War, that there was a generic difference between us and the other nations of the world. This was proved by the difference between their power rivalries and our alleged contentment with our lot. The same President of the United States who ultimately interpreted the First World War as a crusade to "make the world safe for democracy" reacted to its first alarms with the reassuring judgment that the conflict represented trade rivalries with which we need not be concerned. We were drawn into the war by considerations of national interest, which we hardly dared to confess to ourselves. Our European critics may, however, overshoot the mark if they insist that the slogan of making "the world safe for democracy" was merely an expression of that moral cant which we seemed to have inherited from the British, only to express it with less subtlety than they. For the fact is that every nation is caught in the moral paradox of refusing to go to war unless it can be proved that the national interest is imperiled, and of continuing in the war only by proving that something much more than national interest is at stake.

More significant than our actions and interpretations in the First World War was our mood after its conclusion. Our "realists" feared that our sense of responsibility toward a nascent world community had exceeded the canons of a prudent self-interest. Our idealists, of the thirties, sought to preserve our innocence by neutrality. The main force of isolationism came from the "realists," as the slogan "America First" signifies. But the abortive effort to defy the forces of history which were both creating a potential world community and increasing the power of America beyond that of any other nation, was supported by pacifist idealists, Christian and secular, and by other visionaries who desired to preserve our innocency. They had a dim and dark understanding of the fact that power cannot be wielded without guilt, since it is never transcendent over interest, even when it tries to subject itself to universal standards and places itself under the control of a nascent world-wide community. They did not understand that the disavowal of the responsibilities of power can involve an individual or nation in even more grievous guilt.

There are two ways of denying our responsibilities to our fellowmen. The one is the way of imperialism, expressed in seeking to dominate them by our power. The other is the way of isolationism, expressed in seeking to withdraw from our responsibilities to them. Geographic circumstances and the myths of our youth rendered us more susceptible to the latter than the former temptation. This has given our national life a unique color, which is not without some moral advantages. No powerful nation in history has ever been more reluctant to acknowledge the position it has achieved in the world than we. The moral advantage lies in the fact that we do not have a strong lust of power, though we are quickly acquiring the pride of power which always accompanies its possession. Our lack of the lust of power makes the fulminations of our foes against us singularly inept. On the other hand, we have been so deluded by the concept of our innocency that we are ill prepared to deal with the temptations of power which now assail us.

The Second World War quickly dispelled the illusions of both our realists and idealists. We emerged from that war the most powerful nation on earth. To the surprise of our friends and critics we seemed also to have sloughed off the tendencies toward irresponsibility which had characterized us in the long armistice between the world wars. We were determined to exercise the responsibilities of our power.

The exercise of this power required us to hold back the threat of Europe's inundation by communism through the development of all kinds of instruments of mass destruction, including atomic weapons. Thus an "innocent" nation finally arrives at the ironic climax of its history. It finds itself the custodian of the ultimate weapon which perfectly embodies and symbolizes the moral ambiguity of physical warfare. We could not disavow the possible use of the weapon, partly because no imperiled nation is morally able to dispense with weapons which insure its survival. All nations, unlike some individuals, lack the capacity to prefer a noble death to a morally ambiguous survival. But we also could not renounce the weapon because the freedom or survival of our allies depended upon the threat of its use. Yet if we should use it, we would cover ourselves with a terrible guilt. We might insure our survival in a world in which it might be better not to be alive. Thus the moral predicament in which all human striving is involved has been raised to a final pitch for a culture and for a nation which thought it an easy matter to distinguish between justice and injustice and believed itself to be peculiarly innocent. In this way the perennial moral predicaments of human history have caught up with a culture which knew nothing of sin or guilt, and with a nation which seemed to be the most perfect fruit of that culture.[7]

Nations, as individuals, who are completely innocent in their own esteem, are insufferable in their human contacts. The whole world suffers from the pretensions of the communist oligarchs. Our pretensions are of a different order because they are not as consistently held. In any event, we have preserved a system of freedom in which they may be challenged. Yet our American nation, involved in its vast responsibilities, must slough off many illusions which were derived both from the experiences and the ideologies of its childhood. Otherwise either we will seek escape from responsibilities which involve unavoidable guilt, or we will be plunged into avoidable guilt by too great confidence in our virtues.[8]

III. *The Master of Destiny*

There is a deep layer of messianic consciousness in the mind of America. We were always vague, as the whole liberal culture is fortunately vague, about how power is to be related to the allegedly universal values which we hold in trust for mankind. We were, of course, not immune to the temptation of believing that the universal validity of what we held in trust justified our use of power to establish it. Thus in the debate on the annexation of Oregon, in which the imperial impulse of a youthful nation expressed itself, a Congressman could thunder: "If ours is to be the home of the oppressed, we must extend our territory in latitude and longitude to the demand of the millions which are to follow us; as well for our own posterity as for those who are invited to our peaceful shores to partake in our republican institutions."

Generally, however, the legitimization of power was not the purpose of our messianic consciousness. We felt that by example and by unexplained forces in history our dream would become the regnant reality of history.

We have noted that in both the Calvinist and the Jeffersonian concept of our national destiny the emphasis lay at the beginning upon providence rather than human power. Jefferson had proposed for the seal of the United States a picture of "the children of Israel, led by a cloud by day and a pillar of fire by night." Except in moments of aberration we have not thought of ourselves as the potential masters, but as tutors of mankind in its pilgrimage to perfection.

Such messianic dreams, though fortunately not corrupted by the lust of power, have not, of course, been free of the moral pride which creates a hazard to their realization. "God has not been preparing the English-speaking and Teutonic peoples," declared Senator Beveridge of Indiana, "for a thousand years for nothing but vain and idle self-contemplation and self-admiration. He has made us the master organizers of the world to establish system where chaos reigns. He has made us adept in government that we may administer government among savage and senile peoples. Were it not for such a force this world would relapse into barbarism and night. And of all our race He has marked the American people as His chosen nation to finally lead in the regeneration of the world." The concept of administering "government among savage and senile peoples" did of course have power implications. But once again the legitimization of power has generally been subordinate in the American dream to the concept that the nation is committed by divine mandate "to lead in the regeneration of mankind." American government has been regarded as the final and universally valid form of political organization. It was expected to gain its ends by moral attraction and imitation. Only occasionally has an hysterical statesman suggested that we must increase our power and use it in order to gain the ideal ends, of which providence has made us the trustees.

The American dream is not particularly unique. Almost every nation has had a version of it. But the American experience represents a particularly unique and ironic refutation of the illusion in all such dreams. The illusions about the possibility of managing historical destiny from any particular standpoint in history always involve miscalculations both about the power and the wisdom of the managers and about the weakness and manageability of the historical "stuff" which is to be managed.

The first element of irony lies in the fact that our nation has in fact and without particularly seeking it, acquired a greater degree of power than any other nation in history. The same technics, proficiency in the use of which lies at the foundation of American power, have created a "global" political situation in which the responsible use of this power has become a condition of survival of the free world.

But the second element of irony lies in the fact that a strong America is less completely master of its own destiny than was a comparatively weak America.[9] We have grown from infancy to adolescence and from adolescence to maturity in quick and easy strides; and we were inclined to solve every problem, as young people do, by increasing our strength. Now we have suddenly come upon a mystery of life. It is that an infant in his cradle is in some respects more powerful than a man in his maturity. For the infant's every wish is fulfilled by some benevolent attendant; but the wishes of a mature man are subject to the hazards of many conflicting and competing desires. We were stronger as a nation when we rocked in the cradle of our continental security than we are today when we "bestride this narrow world like a huge colossus." For the patterns of history have grown more rapidly than our strength.[10]

The same strength which has extended our power beyond a continent has also interwoven our destiny with the destiny of many peoples and brought us into a vast web of history in which other wills, running in oblique or contrasting directions to our own, inevitably hinder or contradict what we most fervently desire. We cannot simply have our way, not even when we believe our way to have the "happiness of mankind" as its promise. Even in the greatness of our power we are thwarted by a ruthless foe, who is ironically the more recalcitrant and ruthless because his will is informed by an impossible dream of bringing happiness to all men if only he can eliminate our recalcitrance.

But we are thwarted by friends and allies as well as by foes. Our dream of the universal good is sufficiently valid to bring us in voluntary alliance with many peoples who have similar conceptions of the good life. But neither their conceptions of the good, nor their interests, which are always compounded with ideals, are identical with our own. In this situation it is natural that many of our people should fail to perceive that historical destiny may be beguiled, deflected and transfigured by human policy, but that it cannot be coerced.[11]

Moreover, a nation which believed itself to be the master of destiny must now make fateful decisions in an atmosphere of catastrophe. We share this problem with the entire world; but we face it in the most acute form because our responsibilities are very great. Our leaders inform us that our policies are "calculated risks." We have not been accustomed to calculated risks; for we have thrived for a long time on "safe" investments. Our whole culture has predisposed us to justify every action by its promise of rewards. We want to sow where and when we are certain to reap. Now we must sow with no certain guarantee of a harvest. No one can honestly promise us that a given policy will certainly avert a disastrous war or the triumph of communism. It is quite obvious that the world will not enjoy peace for a long while to come. The whole modern generation, even beyond our own nation, finds this prospect difficult to bear, more particularly since we have been informed by a culture which assumed that historical development assured man a more and more secure existence.[12]

The Christian faith offers no escape from life's vicissitudes. It preaches no craven resignation. We must act and assume responsibility within the limits of our powers. But we must also understand that our powers have limits. We are not God. Some of the hysteria in which our nation has been involved derived from the puncturing of the vain delusion that we were a kind of god, who could command the waves of history to obey us.[13]

IV. *Power and Pride*

Powerful men and nations are in greater peril from their own illusions than from their neighbors' hostile designs. Their power secures them against untoward attempts upon their privileges and possessions, even though it may arouse jealous hostility in their neighbors. But it does not protect them against their own follies, which are indeed aggravated by the privileges of power.

Our own nation has achieved a degree of power in the contemporary world community which dwarfs the dominions of the empires of the past. We are in obvious danger of being beguiled by the pride which tends to corrupt the powerful. One form of this pride is the pretension that our power is the natural fruit of our virtue.[14]

It is in fact difficult for all fortunate people to resist the conclusion that their fortune and their power must be regarded as the reward of their virtues. Usually the virtues ostensibly rewarded are those of thrift and diligence. But we add another social virtue to these traditionally respected ones. We assume that we are so fortunate because we are so "free." We do not usually mean that the basic democratic rights are best preserved among us, though we are not above that pretension. We usually mean that our economy is subject to fewer restraints than that of any nation. This is indeed true, though it may be a question how much the freedom of our economy is the consequence, rather than the cause of our productivity. The more meager the social fund to be divided, the greater is the interest in the just division of the fund. This accounts for the fact that the poorer nations of Europe, though boasting of many democratic achievements which we have not attained, have more restraints upon their economic life than we.[15]

We have forgotten to what degree the wealth of our natural resources and the fortuitous circumstance that we conquered a continent just when the advancement of technics made it possible to organize that continent into a single political and economic unit, lay at the foundation of our prosperity.[16] Such religious awe before, and gratitude for, "unmerited" mercies was dissipated fairly early in American life. It remains the frame of our annual presidential Thanksgiving proclamations, which have however contained for many years a contradictory substance within the frame. They have congratulated God on the virtues and ideals of the American people, which have so well merited the blessings of prosperity we enjoy.[17] In this matter we ought to heed the advice in Deuteronomy: "Understand therefore, that the Lord thy God giveth thee this good land to possess, not because of thy righteousness, for thou art a stiff-necked people." There is no greater temptation for a fortunate nation than to transmute its "uncovenanted mercies" into proofs and rewards of its alleged virtues.

Our self-esteem derives also from the fact that we are embattled with a foe who embodies all the evils of a demonic religion. We are by comparison more righteous than our foe, even as we were more righteous than the Nazi tyranny. We will probably be at sword's point with this foe for generations to come. It is difficult to discern the judgments of God upon a person or nation when that person or nation is engaged in mortal combat with an evil foe. All conflicts make for self-righteousness among the disputants. Disputants to a conflict may, in fact, be regarded as constitutionally self-righteous. But if the foe is obviously evil and when he embodies a creed in its most consistent form, which, in its less consistent form had proved to be an instrument of criticism in our own world, the temptation to discount all criticism is very great. Thus we are in danger of sinking into a mood of self-congratulation which must be, as indeed it is, a trial to all of our friends, no matter how grateful they may be that our strength is dedicated to the cause of freedom.

The distinguished English historian, Herbert Butterfield, in his book: *Christianity, Diplomacy and War* has gone so far as to describe the present situation as a conflict between "two organized systems of self-righteousness." We may be offended that he makes no distinction between the quality of self-righteousness among us and that which is encouraged by an explicitly idolatrous religion. Indeed, he is too prone to equate the evils on both sides. But he has at least given us a glimpse of the effect of our national self-esteem upon our most intimate ally, Britain.[18]

Our pride is a great embarrassment in our relation to the democratic world. The more we indulge in an uncritical reverence for the supposed wisdom of our American way of life, the more odious we make it in the eyes of the world, and the more we destroy our moral authority, without which our economic and military power will become impotent. Thus we are undermining the reality of our power by our uncritical pride in it.[19]

We will incarnate the democratic cause the more truly, the more we can overcome the pretension of embodying it perfectly. We will stand the more surely if we "take heed lest we fall." Our power will be used the more justly, if we recognize that our possession of it is not a proof of our virtue. Our possession of it is either an "accident" or it is a gift of grace. It is a gift of grace if we recognize history as a realm of divine providence and not as a series of accidents. If it is recognized as a gift of grace, it must also become apparent that every gift of grace which is pretentiously appropriated as our due turns into a curse. Whether our nation can sense both the grace and the judgment of God in its history is thus the pivotal problem in our national destiny.[20]

Ideally, it is the function of a religion which possesses any prophetic dimension to mediate an ultimate divine judgment upon men and nations who would otherwise sink into a morass of self-esteem. The Christian church must therefore regard it as one of its most important missions to disturb the mood of national self-congratulation into which our nation is sinking. If the church is to perform this task it must know however that the "prophetic" mission to the nation does not come easily or automatically to the church. Religion *qua* religion is naturally idolatrous, accentuating, rather than diminishing, the self-worship of men and nations, by assuring them of an ultimate sanction for their dearest desires.

Insofar as our congregations are merely religious communities in which an uncritical piety is nourished, they also do no more than to mix patriotic self-congratulation with the worship of God. It requires both courage and astuteness to penetrate the armor of the nation's self-righteousness. But above all it requires knowledge of and devotion to the one true God who declares to even the most righteous of nations: "You only have I chosen; therefore will I visit you with your iniquities." [21]

Thus a contrite recognition of our own sins destroys the illusion of eminence through virtue and lays the foundation for the apprehension of "grace" in our national life. We know that we have the position which we hold in the world today, partly by reason of factors and forces in the complex pattern of history which we did not create and from which we do not deserve to benefit. If we apprehend this religiously, the sense of destiny ceases to be a vehicle of pride and becomes the occasion for a new sense of responsibility.[22]

V. *Power and Responsibility*

There is a fateful significance in the fact that America's coming of age coincides with that period of world history when the paramount problem is the creation of some kind of world community. The world must find a way of avoiding complete anarchy in its international life; and America must find a way of using its great power responsibly. These two needs are organically related; for the world problem cannot be solved if America does not accept its full share of responsibility in solving it.[23] From an ultimate standpoint this need not be regretted. For a nation which cannot save itself without at the same time saving a whole world has the possibility of achieving a concurrence between its own interests and "the general welfare" which must be regarded as the highest form of virtue in man's collective life.[24]

One moral resource not usually envisaged among our ideals and values is particularly necessary for a nation which wields as much power as our own. It is a resource which was known in the classical ages of Christianity but which has largely disappeared in a rationalistic and sentimental age. That is an understanding of the moral ambiguity which power and self-interest introduce into political and economic structures.* No political order, whether national or international, is ever a pure incarnation of brotherhood or the fruit of pure unselfishness. Order and justice cannot be maintained by coercion alone; but they cannot be maintained without it. The power which is required to preserve order

* For a full review of the problems of moral ambiguity in international politics, see Chapter XXVI.

is never so perfectly adjusted to the necessities of justice that one may have an easy conscience about its exercise. Self-interest is another source of moral ambiguity in the world of politics. Individuals and nations are capable of considering the interests of others. Without such a capacity for justice human society would degenerate into an anarchy of conflicting claims. But the political order must also harness, deflect, and beguile the self-interest of individuals, classes, and nations. It can never completely suppress or transfigure particular loyalties and motives of self-interest. Politics must, as David Hume asserted, assume the selfishness of man.

Modern culture, particularly in America, has had the greatest difficulty in dealing with the moral ambiguities of the political and economic order. Our political scientists and our men of affairs seem frequently to be divided into three classes: the sentimentalists imagine that the life of nations can be brought into conformity with the purest standards of generosity; the cynics deny every moral standard in political and economic life because they have discerned the morally ambiguous elements in it; and the hypocrites profess one standard and practice another. Sometimes it would seem as if the world were divided merely between sentimentalists who are afraid to exercise power and responsibility because they fear its corruption and the cynics who exercise it without a twinge of conscience. The temptations to sentimentality and cynicism have always existed, but they have increased since the decay of religion. It was one of the merits of the Christian interpretation of the human situation that it understood, as Pascal put it, both the dignity and the misery of man, both his capacity for goodness and his corruption of that goodness. It insisted that men ought to consider the rights of their fellow men; but it also knew that they never did so perfectly. It knew that human sin made coercion in government necessary; but it also knew that the lust for power of the ruler made government dangerous. It regarded all human majesties as, at the same time, derived from the divine majesty and in rebellion against it. This wholesome paradoxical attitude toward the problems of political and economic justice usually disintegrates in modern life and the consequence is either cynicism or sentimentality.

Unlike the communists we do not have a philosophy of life which makes us constitutionally fanatical and self-righteous. But we are constantly tempted to weaken the virtue of our cause by too unqualified claims for it, and to suffer from periodic fits of disillusionment, when the moral ambiguity of our position becomes apparent. We must resist this temptation the more resolutely because we not only have great power but are called upon to exercise its responsibilities in a world situation in which there are no possibilities of pure and unequivocal justice. Yet there are tremendously important moral decisions to be made. Above all, it is important that we fulfill our responsibilities with steadiness and resolution, without the distractions of the alternate moods of cynicism and sentimentality.

We must learn to bear the responsibilities of power in America without imagining either that the exercise of our power will be perfectly just or that we would be a better nation if we disavowed our responsibilities for the sake of being pure.[25] *

It is foolish to hope that America could bear its present responsibilities in the world without regard to national self-interest. It is equally foolish to deny that national self-interest may always become so narrow as to corrupt the virtue of what we are doing. The virtue of every political measure can never be assessed in terms of pure black or white.

If we succumb to the temptation of hypocrisy and claim too pure a virtue for our international politics, we shall merely invite the world's derision and contempt. This derision will be forthcoming the more readily because powerful nations are not generally popular. Moreover, we shall also relax our own moral restraints too much by such a procedure. Power ought always to be exercised with a certain uneasiness of conscience. When the conscience becomes easy, self-righteousness aggravates the moral weakness of the wielder of power. Furthermore, such hypocrisy and self-righteousness always tend to alienate a certain sensitive minority in every nation. This minority is usually quite sentimental about the realities of the political order. But it is, or ought to be, the bearer of the conscience of the nation.

All political justice and order are achieved by men and nations who have a margin of goodness or virtue beyond their self-interest. But they must not deny the interested motives which partly prompt their action. Otherwise their marginal virtue will turn to vice.[27]

A European statesman stated the issue very well recently in the words: "We are grateful to America for saving us from communism. But our

* Late in 1953, Niebuhr cited the following interesting example:

"Several months ago Secretary Dulles experienced the predicament of American power within one short week. At the beginning of the week he vigorously resisted Senator McCarthy's absurd effort to force the Administration to compel our allies to give up East-West trade.

"But before the week was up Secretary Dulles found himself in France and he threatened the French by implication with a possible withdrawal of American power from the Continent if they failed to ratify the European army agreement.

"His predicament proves that the perils and problems of our hegemonous power are indeed very great. We must not reduce our allies to 'satellites.' But we cannot renounce the responsibilities of our power. Among them is the responsibility for the unification of European defense. Mr. Dulles may have been too obvious in his methods, but his seeming contradictions really revealed a permanent predicament of American power."[26]

gratitude does not prevent us from fearing that we might become an American colony. That danger lies in the situation of America's power and Europe's weakness." The statesman, when reminded of the strain of genuine idealism in American life, replied: "The idealism does indeed prevent America from a gross abuse of its power. But it might well accentuate the danger Europeans confront. For American power in the service of American idealism could create a situation in which we would be too impotent to correct you when you are wrong and you would be too idealistic to correct yourself."

Such a measured judgment upon the virtues and perils of America's position in the world community accurately describes the hazards we confront. Our moral perils are not those of conscious malice or the explicit lust for power. They are the perils which can be understood only if we realize the ironic tendency of virtues to turn into vices when too complacently relied upon; and of power to become vexatious if the wisdom which directs it is trusted too confidently. The ironic elements in American history can be overcome, in short, only if American idealism comes to terms with the limits of all human striving, the fragmentariness of all human wisdom, the precariousness of all historic configurations of power, and the mixture of good and evil in all human virtue. America's moral and spiritual success in relating itself creatively to a world community requires, not so much a guard against the gross vices, about which the idealists warn us, as a reorientation of the whole structure of our idealism. That idealism is too oblivious of the ironic perils to which human virtue, wisdom and power are subject. It is too certain that there is a straight path toward the goal of human happiness; too confident of the wisdom and idealism which prompt men and nations toward that goal; and too blind to the curious compounds of good and evil in which the actions of the best men and nations abound.[28]

CHAPTER XXIV

Conservatives, Liberals and American Foreign Policy *

American conservatism has been particularly inept in dealing with the foreign policy issues which confront our nation. These issues would have been difficult for the nation even if American conservatism had not made confusion worse confounded, for we have had world leadership thrust upon us very suddenly, with little opportunity to accustom ourselves to its vexing problems. We are, moreover, a paradise of plenty suspended in a hell of global insecurity, and our good fortune makes it difficult either to understand the needy world in which we have gained so precarious an eminence or to achieve the hardness of discipline required for the exercise of our leadership. But all these difficulties have been accentuated by the fact that American conservatism is bereft of wisdom and imagination in foreign policy.[1]

This failure of American conservatism in the field of foreign policy is the more remarkable because it is the virtue of traditional European conservatism to understand the hazards and responsibilities of foreign policy rather better than traditional liberalism.[2] Traditional conservatism understood that the international community is unorganized or only partly organized; and the contests of power, which are an element of the social life of the human community on every level, are therefore more violent and naked on the international level.[3] It knew in short the relations of the nations to be governed by power factors, to which the liberal mind was usually oblivious.[4]

Traditional liberalism, on the other hand, was informed by a high sense of justice but had little understanding of the power which was required to attain just ends. The liberal creed was avowed either by idealists who had no experience with power or by the new economic overlords of society who wielded a form of power so covert that it betrayed them into sentimental illusions. Thus, in an earlier period, Disraeli was shrewder

* Previous discussions of liberalism and conservatism will be found in Chapters II and XVII.

than Gladstone in the field of foreign relations, and Theodore Roosevelt's understanding of foreign affairs was certainly superior to that of William Jennings Bryan.[5]

I. *American Conservatism and Foreign Policy*

When one turns to examine the role of conservatism in American foreign policy, the distinctive trait appears to be a curious ambivalence between isolationism and imperialism, between a disavowal of the responsibilities of our power and an exercise of that power without a sense of its limits.

In the days of the "interventionist" debate before World War Two, isolationism and neutralism were drawn primarily from the conservative sector of the population. Sometimes isolationism was prompted by fear of the cost of war, thus refuting the Marxist theory that our "capitalists" drive us into war in order to gain profits. Sometimes it was informed by serious miscalculations of the breadth and the depth of the danger which we faced. In other cases it was informed by a simple parochialism arising in a vast economy so nearly self-sufficing that it had learned little of the outside world.

Today it is violently anti-communist, but the violence of its anti-communism has been little help to us. The conservative community thinks that it has uttered the final condemnation of communism when it equates communism with Nazism, obscuring the fact that communism is more dangerous than Nazism.* And the violence of the conservatives' anti-communism imparts to our reactions to world events a kind of apoplectic quality which militates against a shrewd calculation of possibilities. The hysteria of American conservatism is making it almost impossible to analyze the attractive power of communism and equally difficult to state the political and economic program which will eliminate the social conditions and resentments that are exploited by communism.

But whatever its motivation, conservatism very nearly pursued isolation to the extreme of self-destruction. The Republican opposition to Roosevelt came within one vote of destroying our inchoate army before World War Two. It fought the Lend-Lease Plan, which was probably Roosevelt's most imaginative contribution to Allied victory, since it saved our Allies from collapse before we entered the conflict. During the war it frequently endangered a well-conceived global strategy by seeking to subordinate the European to the Asiatic struggle before the time was ripe. Following the conclusion of the war it was hesitant to support the Economic Recovery Program in Europe, by which the communist tide

* Niebuhr's explication of the similarities and differences between communism and Nazism is found in Chapter III.

was stemmed. Most recently, it thought that a complete prohibition of East-West trade in Europe was a smart idea, though it is easy to prove that the health of Western Europe requires as much of such trade as is compatible with strategic necessities.

Isolationism was, however, but one aspect of the conservative reaction to world events. Many conservatives, once we entered World War Two, insisted that the real strategic center of the conflict was Asia, rather than Europe. This special concern for Asia in conservative circles is something of a mystery. It must be noted that since the war the pattern has repeated itself. Whatever lies behind it, it reveals an obvious lack of imagination in weighing the strategic factors on a world scale. One reason for this error is surely a tendency to measure our power too purely in terms of our military strength. This military strength is drawn from our economic power so directly that it can be measured with logistic exactitude. But, of course, the power of a nation or of an alliance of nations consists of other factors than its military strength. The insistence, in the past decade, that Asia was the strategic center of the struggle failed to measure the technical military superiority of Germany over Japan. But it also failed to gauge the moral and political considerations which made Europe the center of the struggle.

Thus American conservatism, insofar as it has been isolationist, has shrunk from the overt application of power, and, insofar as it has conceived of intervention in purely military terms, has conceived of power in terms that are misleadingly simple. The one historic ability of traditional conservatism—its realistic understanding of the nature and application of power—has been conspicuously absent in both of the leading manifestations of American conservatism.

II. *American Conservatism and the Liberal Creed*

Perhaps the answer to this question of the cause of the political incompetence of American conservatism can be most simply supplied by one sweeping generalization: American conservatism is not the traditional conservatism of Western political history. That conservatism was rooted in the aristocratic tradition; American conservatism is a decayed form of nineteenth-century "liberalism." It is the creed of the business community. This community was "liberal" in its historic contest with feudalism. It enlarged many liberties and opposed many traditional injustices. But in America the business community developed in a middle-class paradise without the background of an aristocratic past and therefore without the qualifications which the aristocratic tradition introduced into British politics, for instance. American conservatism is related to the liberalism of the nineteenth century as Herbert Hoover's book entitled

The Challenge to Liberty is related to John Stuart Mill's book *On Liberty*. It has a common emphasis upon "liberty." But liberty for nineteenth-century liberals was a genuine passion. In our day "liberty" tends to become the ideological façade behind which men of great economic power seek to preserve their freedom against a more broadly-based political power and seek to arrest the one process by which modern democracies have achieved a measure of health and refuted the Marxist predictions of their doom.

American conservatism is thus an ossified form of liberalism. It lacks the virtues in domestic politics which the original liberalism had. But it preserves the vices of traditional liberalism in foreign policy.

Traditional liberalism was identified with the business community and ever since has been colored by the business community's views. Such a community predicates its operation upon the containment of the various egoistic drives, individual and collective, within the nicely circumscribed balances of a competitive market. In this realm, life is neither noble, tragic, nor demonic, and the purposes of life are never incalculable. Realists in this world readily assume the force of human selfishness, but they also believe that it is confined to the desire for gain. Hence they are oblivious to the dynamic of the idolatrous political religions of our day, whether Nazi or communist. The idealists of the same world find its chief moral glory in the fact that it repudiates the overt use of force—of which bourgeois culture has a horror—but they do not comprehend the endless complexities of power and the covert forms of force in a human community. Economic power—as distinguished from political and military power—is, in fact, so lacking in the symbols of force that it is easy to describe its operation in purely moral terms, and to hide, either sentimentally or hypocritically, the power elements in economic competition.

Actually the powers which are in cooperation and conflict in the human community are compounded of ethnic loyalties, common traditions, ancient sanctities, common fears, common hopes, and endless other combinations of human motives. The Western "Tory" tradition understands them, simply because it has manipulated them for generations. The business community has never fully understood them. In the Anglo-Saxon tradition the thought of Edmund Burke best summarizes this understanding, and his *Reflections on the French Revolution* represents a perfect refutation of the illusions to which a pure bourgeois rationalism is subject.

But American conservatism is not informed by this tradition. Instead, it is rooted in the business community and shares that community's lack of understanding of the complexities of international power. Therefore it displays a curious ambivalence between isolationism and imperialism, between sentimentality and cynicism. In one moment it is ready to discount all the perils in which we stand and to counsel the nation to "cut its losses" lest further involvement in world responsibilities increase our tax rate. In the next moment it is ready to use our economic power to force European nations into "free enterprise" patterns after our image, however irrelevant these patterns may be to the necessities of the recipient nations, and to employ our economically-based military power in Asia in such a way as to make our struggle with communism appear a purely military venture, thus alienating such vast uncommitted Asiatic nations as India. The enormous social convulsions of a continent in travail are such a mystery to this type of mind that even the most catastrophic upheavals are attributed to mistakes made in our State Department.[6]

In short the business community does not understand the curious compound of forces which go into the making of political power and cohesion; or the dangerous inordinancy of ambition which is exhibited in the realm of politics, particularly in an era of political religions, resulting in demonic political movements. It is characteristic of the business mind that Chamberlain thought that Hitler had a price which reasonable men could meet, and that the typically bourgeois Dutch sought to make themselves safe against Hitler's will-to-power by a meticulous neutrality. When Britain was confronted with great peril, it called Churchill, rooted in an older aristocratic tradition, to the helm.

The American counterparts of Chamberlain were all, or almost all, in the Republican Party. The Republican Party consistently underestimated the Nazi peril and consistently challenged the measures of the Administration, designed to express our responsibility to the imperiled nations of Europe, when they faced, first the Nazi and then the communist peril. If Britain turned to an authentic conservative in the hour of peril, our own nation turned to a "liberal" for leadership, when it was apparent that only a small fraction of Republicanism assessed our position, our perils, and our responsibilities correctly.[7] *

III. *American Liberalism and Foreign Policy*

What was the basis of the left-of-center "liberalism" as espoused by Roosevelt, and why was it superior to the classical "liberalism" of Re-

* Niebuhr has qualified this view as follows: "A balanced view must recognize that not all conservatives fall within the pattern suggested here. The intelligent wing of conservatism, as symbolized, for instance, by Henry L. Stimson and Senator Vandenberg, made important contributions. Some of the irresponsibility of conservative action is, moreover, the irresponsibility of a party in opposition for twenty years rather than the irresponsibility of conservatism as such."[8]

publican conservatism in foreign policy? Roosevelt's "liberalism" was the inheritor of those portions of the liberal tradition which emphasized not so much the freedom of economic forces from control as the development of political institutions to accomplish the liberal objectives of universal suffrage, equal rights under the law, minimal standards of welfare and international comity.[9] If the liberalism left-of-center came under the criticism of its foes on the ground that it tolerated or condoned a collectivism which violated the individualism of traditional liberalism, the liberalism right-of-center could, on the other hand, be accused of frustrating the desire for social change and a broader justice which was also a part of traditional liberalism.

The question is why this left-of-center liberalism was more astute and effective in foreign policy than the liberalism expounded by Republicanism. After all, its moralistic illusions were almost as certain a source of confusion in foreign affairs as the prudential cautions of the conservative liberals. The pacifism and illusionism of Bryan, Wilson's first Secretary of State, are well known. The people in Roosevelt's camp were almost as anxious to preserve the neutrality of the nation for moralistic reasons, as the conservative liberals were for prudential reasons. Labor was almost as isolationist as business, and the pacifism and isolationism of agrarian radicalism, symbolized by Senators Norris and LaFollette, are well known. Perhaps the primary reason for the superiority in foreign policy of the Democratic exponents of liberalism over the Republican exponents must be attributed to the fortuitous circumstance that Democratic presidents were in power when the nation confronted the perils of the First and the Second World Wars. The responsibilities of office are a wonderful school for the party in power.

However, there is another potent cause for the superior wisdom of the Rooseveltian type of liberals despite their weakness in foreign policy. These liberals were genuinely "internationalists" in outlook, as opposed to the prudential isolationist nationalism of the Republicans. In the case of Wilson, the internationalist outlook was devoid of appreciation of the power-political elements in international relations, which characterizes true conservatism. Roosevelt's realism corrected this fault; but both Roosevelt and Wilson were inclined to defy one of the canons of a wise conservatism which restricts policy to limited and foreseeable ends. They had the penchant of the modern liberal for wide and sweeping objectives. Thus Wilson, who at first saw the First World War as only a trade dispute in which we had no interest, ended by interpreting it as a crusade to "make the world safe for democracy." Among his "principles" of democracy, which was to have the consequence of disorganizing some fairly viable social cohesions, was his idea of "the self-determination of nations." The same penchant for wide, abstract, and sweeping objectives is to be noted in the present popularity among American liberals for abstract projects such as world government. The similarity under the difference between Roosevelt's realism and Wilson's idealism is illustrated by Roosevelt's efforts to guard against the charge which the Germans made after the First World War against Wilson. They accused him of violating the promises implied in his "Fourteen Points" in the Versailles Peace Treaty. Roosevelt sought to prevent a similar charge by the simple expedient of insisting on "unconditional surrender." This sweeping correction of Wilson's idealism may have prevented an effective revolution against Hitler's tyranny by destroying the hope of an effective alternative to the fate to which Hitler's Germany was doomed. It was in any case too sweeping a formula to conform to the standards of a pragmatic conservatism in foreign policy.

Whatever may have been the causes of the superior wisdom of Roosevelt's type of liberalism in the realm of foreign policy, and whatever may have been its residual weaknesses, he undoubtedly led the nation with great skill in assuming, in a growing world community, responsibilities to which it was not accustomed by experience and tradition, and which it was inclined to resent. Just as men thought that the achievement was a personal one and that it must be attributed to the political genius of a single man, Roosevelt died, and a successor, who was by general consent no political genius, made the hard decisions required by the peril in which the nation stood when the ally of yesterday turned out to be as dangerous and as tyrannical a foe as the enemy of yesterday. He was opposed on all of these decisions by American conservatism, which exhibited a continued confusion in the realm of foreign policy by alternating between isolationist irresponsibility, which refused to assert the full strength of America, and adventurous irresponsibility which failed to measure the limits of power which even a powerful nation must observe.[10]

IV. *The Vague Universalism of Liberalism*

Our nation, as we have repeatedly observed, is confronted by all the responsibilities of a great power. Indeed, it is now one of the "superpowers." For the performance of these responsibilities it is equipped by only a few decades of experience and a tradition: the liberal-democratic tradition.[11] We have noted the liberal penchant for abstract, sweeping objectives. We must now define more precisely liberalism's approach to the organization of international society.

The liberal democratic theory of international relations seems to have two emphases: (1) an emphasis on the integrity and autonomy of the nation, and (2) a vague universalism or consideration of the "community of mankind" which leaves little room for the configurations of power and authority which develop in history between the nation and the universal community. The liberal theory gives constitutional embodiment to its universalism only at one point: it insists on "collective security" whether through the League of Nations or the United Nations.[12] *

Throughout the millennia of civilization, until the dawn of the modern era, two rather constant structures of community were known: the one the integral community, whether city-state or nation; and the other the larger structure of community and dominion, the empire.

Modern civilization, with its rapidly advancing techniques, particularly in the nineteenth and twentieth centuries, has given the nation a new status as the integral community; and has usually encouraged the development of autonomous nations. On the other hand the same technical developments have made for the disintegration of the imperial structures. Technical advances, particularly printing and the invention of gunpowder, seem to have given the nation an advantage over the imperial structure. The art of communications solidified the integral community rather than the imperial one. And gunpowder hastened the end of the feudal structure of society, which was the political cloth out of which the empires were fashioned.

These rapid developments have persuaded liberal democrats of the West to regard the autonomous nation as an ultimate norm of community, and then to provide for the integration of the nascent global community through the principle of "collective security." The question must be raised whether the politically autonomous nation is really an absolute norm of community; and whether all integral or parochial communities are capable of sustaining the burdens of full autonomy. The further question must be asked whether the empire may not have been prematurely consigned to the limbo of history.[13]

One of the causes of the vagueness of liberal policies beyond the nation is that the democratic form of government has relevance only for the integral community where "consent" can be established and measured in free elections. Proposals for world government are efforts to extend these democratic instruments to the universal community. But most of the proposals ignore the fact that a full-blown system of communication,

* By "collective security" Niebuhr means, not collective defense through traditional alliances, but the principle that all members of the international community are committed to defend any state which has been made the object of aggression. See his chapter titled "Empires, Nations, and Collective Security in a Global Situation," in *The Structure of Nations and Empires*, pp. 256–66.

which overcomes parochial loyalties and permits judgments in the total community transcending these loyalties, is a prerequisite of the "democratic" method.

Democratic liberalism is vague in its universalism, not only because the international structure of dominion and community, as they exist, do not correspond exactly to the norms of the democratic nation, but also because the liberal democrats have had the conviction that democracy has, or will, radically alter the nature and the motives of states. This idea, born in the French Enlightenment, exerted a considerable influence in both Britain and America, but particularly in America. Naturally illusions in regard to the behavior of nations generated corresponding illusions in regard to the structure of the community above the level of the nation.

For centuries the anarchy of European nationalism was slightly mitigated, particularly between the Napoleonic Wars and the First World War, by strategies which generally come under the category of the "balance of power." There was a realist tradition in American thought, exemplified particularly by Madison, Hamilton, and Adams, capable of appreciating the strategy of balanced power. But, since the problems of the international community were beyond the interests of the new nation, isolated on a virgin continent, we must turn to the moderate British liberals for a realistic account of the structures of dominion and community above the level of the nation. The two structures which concern us particularly are the balance of power and the empire.

David Hume's realism prompted him to view the structures of community and power in the international field in a different light than the naive liberals. This applied particularly to the balance of power principle of which Hume gave a classical description. "But whether we ascribe the shifting of sides . . . to jealous emulations or cautious politics, the effects were alike and every prevailing power was sure to meet with a confederacy against it, and that often composed of its friends and allies." [14] This description has the merit of realizing the necessity of some kind of principle of intermediate order within the chaos of international relations, which cannot be overcome by any system of "collective security."

Edmund Burke speaks of the duty of nations to enforce common standards of justice (against Napoleonic imperialism, for instance) and declares, "If England shows herself indifferent or unconcerned when these powers are combined against the enterprises of France she is to look with certainty to the same indifference of these powers when she may be at war with that nation." [15]

Burke's principles of international federation and cooperation not only accurately describe the motives which prompted the alliance against Napoleon, but the alliance which now is loosely formed against Russia.

Both Hume and Burke envisaged the realities which seem to recur in the field of international relations, particularly the reality of defense alliances, far more clearly than did the purer liberal theorists.

The moral ambiguity inherent in the structures of power and community is obviously raised to a high level in the structure of empire. Imperial ventures have given the West an uneasy conscience. Our own nation, with only a brief excursion in imperial dominion after the Spanish American War, has been particularly self-righteous about the alleged sins of its allies. Yet whatever the moral judgment upon empire may be, we must recognize the fact of empire as one of the recurring patterns of large-scale community which will persist as long as strength impinges on weakness, either exploiting that weakness or supplementing it.[16]

V. *American Liberalism and Imperial Power*

The modern world is divided by two opposing alliances of nations. Each is under the hegemony of a nation which has the economic and military strength to determine independent policy. Both the imperial nations, possessing power which dwarfs the power of ancient empires, are informed by creeds that are contradictory in many respects but are identical in one respect: they both believe that imperialism is an outmoded form of political organization. The one believes this by virtue of a liberal democratic creed, which persists in America in its pristine purity. The history of the birth of the nation in a revolutionary war against an imperial power gave us the anti-imperial animus; and the continental expanse of the nation had made imperial ventures, at least of the overt variety, unnecessary. The ironic circumstance of our wielding imperial power, though informed by an anti-imperial ideology, places considerable strain on the "democratic" alliance of nations which includes for instance Great Britain, who, despite her democratic heritage, has been involved in the imperial ventures which characterized the impingement of Western nations upon Asia and Africa throughout the eighteenth and nineteenth centuries. Western imperialism, indeed, had its inception in the sixteenth century so that Western civilization must bear the odium of imperialism of four centuries, an odium which the communist adversary carefully exploits. The ironic fact is that Marxist and liberal democratic theories of power relations are very similar in obscuring the perennial factors, though Marxism attributes imperialism to the very form of liberal political organization (capitalism) which liberalism believes to be a force of emancipation from imperialism.

As we have seen, the ideological system of democratic liberalism has no room for the expression of any power or the formation of any community above the level of the nation and below the level of the universal community. But democratic liberalism is in conflict with a Marxist imperialism which is anti-imperialistic for very different reasons. It is in fact a modern version of the classical imperialisms, much older than the national imperialism of the sixteenth to the nineteenth centuries; of the imperialisms which existed from the dawn of history to the end of the Middle Ages. All these imperial structures combined force with prestige drawn from the claim of having achieved, or being about to achieve, universal community and ideal justice. Marxism is the only version of the universal empire which could achieve relevance in a secular age. For the traditional empires made their ultimate and universal claims in religious terms. Marxism presents an old religious apocalypse in terms of a materialism which pretends to have found the "laws of motion" in history, laws which, if properly understood and manipulated, can lead humanity from the "realm of necessity to the realm of freedom."

There is a vivid contrast between a policy of a hegemonous nation speaking for a whole empire in the name of anti-imperialism, and our own policy of frantically avoiding recognition of the imperialism which we in fact exercise, or ought to exercise if imperialism means the exercise of the responsibilities of power. We regard the United Nations as the true organ of the universal community to which all nations must be subject. This point of view is illustrated in President Eisenhower's policy in the Suez crisis and his subsequent suppression of the Israeli defiance of the United Nations' edict to leave the territory which had been captured from Egypt. The President, it will be remembered, paid tribute to Britain and France for heeding the resolution of the United Nations to quit Egypt "forthwith." They made, he said, "an immense contribution to world order." But he failed to record that they left Egypt because we, with our superior power, sided with Russia in ordering them out; and that their desperate venture was understandable only because we failed to understand their predicament under the pressure of a hitherto "colonial" nation, Egypt, which had taken hold of the life-line of European economy in the name of its emancipation from "colonialism." We declared ourselves sufficiently "anti-colonial" to understand the motives of Egypt. The essential pacifism of the President's policy was expressed in the words, "If the United Nations once admits that international disputes can be settled by force then we will have destroyed the very foundation of the organization and our best hope of establishing a real world order. That would be a disaster for us all."

These eloquent words in favor of the United Nations and world peace manage to obscure the real character of that necessary organization which is not so much a super-government as a forum for international diplomacy. If regarded as the former, the hegemonic responsibility of our own nation is obscured. It will be remembered that all these events took place while Russia was suppressing the Hungarian nation. The President took cognizance of this fact in the words: "I do not believe that Israel's default should be ignored because the United Nations has been unable effectively to carry out its resolutions, condemning the Soviet Union for its armed suppression of the people of Hungary. Perhaps this is the case where the proverb applies that two wrongs do not make a right."

The proverb also obscures the fact that Russia was powerful enough to defy the United Nations and that Israel was not. His analysis of the Suez crisis, in short, places the whole emphasis on the moral and political prestige of the United Nations, and obscures the power factors which are bound to be operative in any situation but particularly in one in which the international organization has no power except that with which it is endowed by the concurrence of the powerful nations. The theory of the United Nations presupposed such concurrence. Since it has been lacking from the beginning it obviously does not promise the kind of world order which the President assumes to be its function.[17]

While the misunderstandings between Britain and America are serious, as recent events in the Suez crisis proved, it is not our present purpose to clarify these misunderstandings but to point to them as symptoms of the failure of modern men, but particularly Americans, to distinguish between the perennial and the contingent and ephemeral in the political communities of mankind. We are now in a situation in which a new imperialism, namely that of the Russian communists, has effectively reconstructed in utopian terms the oldest imperialism of human history. The characteristic of this form of imperialism was to use an ideological universalism as the chief source of its prestige. The utopian form of the imperialism is the more effective because it pretends that its power structures are merely provisional, because its purpose is to eliminate force from human life.

A note of irony is added to present confusions because, superficially considered, the nationalistic form of imperialism, in which the Western nations engaged from the sixteenth to the nineteenth centuries, seems morally inferior to this new imperialism, in which the dominant nations claim to be merely servants of the universal community. These earlier nationalistic imperialisms represented the domination over a weaker people by a stronger one. We are living in a period in which the decay of these nineteenth century empires—occasioned by the war and by the extension of technical competence from the West to the agrarian East—has freed many nations and prompted many still dominated nations to long for their freedom. This means that residual and present resentments against imperialism are bound to color the political thought of the colonial and ex-colonial nations. The Western nations seem therefore to be at a great moral disadvantage. The disadvantage is so great that, as we have seen, the hegemonic nation of the democratic alliance is tempted again and again to share the indictment of its allies which the communist foes make against the West. This is the more pathetic because the communist dogma does not exclude us from the indictment; for the dogma insists that capitalism is the final cause of imperialism even though the facts are at variance with this dogma.

The primary mistake in the liberal and Marxist indictment of imperialism is the failure to recognize the creative as well as baneful effects of the impingement of strong nations upon weak ones, particularly if the strong nations have some cultural, political, or technical resource which the weaker nation can use for its communal integration, for lifting the standards of its economy, or for enriching its cultural life.

India for example lacked means of national cohesion in terms of a common language, a common legal tradition, and means of communication. Despite the resentments against British rule and despite the necessity of winning independence against the reluctant British master, it is obvious that India could have become a nation only by the force of a common resentment against the imperial master on the one hand, and by the instruments of community which the master furnished on the other. The fact that many emancipated nations have not been able to establish either stability or order, and that free Liberia, in which descendants of American Negro slaves have become an uncreative aristocracy in an African nation with lower standards of justice than other nations graduated from the tutelage of colonialism, is proof of the moral ambiguity, rather than the moral evil, of the imperial enterprise in which the Western nations have been engaged. The fact is that imperialism participates in the moral ambiguity of all community as it is related to dominion.[18]

The imperial structure of dominion, as it was known in the traditional ages or even in the nineteenth century, is obviously outmoded. But this fact cannot obscure the necessity and inevitability of various forms of supranational community. These modern forms are much more varied than those in former ages; but the variety of forms corresponds to those necessities of history which modern creeds too easily obscure. They include such remnants of the old European empires which may still be viable as, for instance, the French Community in black Africa and the British Commonwealth of Nations. They also include all the regional alliances such as NATO as well as the more amorphous global anti-communist entente with its Anglo-Saxon hegemony and its secondary hegemony of the Western, chiefly European, nations. Finally, technical developments and the need for economic cooperation have created such new forms of economic supranational sovereignty as the European

Coal and Steel Community and the European Common Market.[19]

In summary, the democratic liberals are right in assuming that the integral nation is, and will increasingly become, the community of significant loyalty for modern men, even though the disparities in the culture and the economy of the various peoples raise the question whether some of the less developed cultures provide the nascent nation with sufficient forces of cohesion to make autonomy feasible. They are right also in assuming that community without the instruments of democratic checks cannot achieve a consistent justice; but they are wrong in affirming that such supranational formations, which lack the democratic instruments, should not be formed. They will inevitably be formed, though the justice they achieve will be more deficient than that in the nation.[20]

Finally, the liberal democrat must understand that, with respect to our own nation, there is no way of applying the liberal democratic standards to the expression of our power in world affairs. Our power is too great to conform to absolute or even to relative standards of justice, though the checks provided by the autonomy of our associates and by our involvement in the United Nations are sufficient to prevent arbitrariness.[21] As the strongest of the democratic nations, the United States must acknowledge the imperial dimensions of its power and accept the responsibilities which are the concomitants of power.[22]

We may claim that we use our power in the interest of the total community with as much justice as is possible for nations, when all nations are instinctively prompted to consider their own interest, and the interests of others only as these are compatible with their own. But our moral claims ought not to go beyond this limit. We are not a sanctified nation and we must not assume that all our actions are dictated by considerations of disinterested justice. If we fall into this error the natural resentments against our power on the part of the weaker nations will be compounded with resentments against our pretensions of a superior virtue. These resentments are indeed a part of the animus of anti-Americanism throughout the world. They may be said to be the fruits of our efforts to govern an empire in terms of the ethos of liberal democratic idealism. We Americans must analyze the permanent and unvarying factors and forces in the anatomy of communities, nations, and empires for many reasons, but chiefly to correct mistakes which the liberal democratic creed was bound to make from the limited perspective of advanced national communities, when it tried to come to terms with the problem of the community on the imperial level.[23]

CHAPTER XXV

Foreign Policy and World Responsibility

I. *Containing Communism*

Both our idealists and our realists conceive patterns which are too logical for the tortuous course of human history. They both persist in confronting us with two horns of a dilemma and beg us to choose between them. All idealistic schemes of world peace insist that we must either achieve world government or resign ourselves to an inevitable war; we must find some way of reaching an understanding with the Russians or face the consequences of a world war. Our realists are convinced that neither world government nor a pragmatic understanding with the Russians is an attainable goal. They are therefore tempted to grasp the second horn of the dilemma. They accept the fact of an inevitable war. From the idea of an inevitable war it is only a short logical step to the concept of a preventive war. For if we must inevitably fight the Russians, why should we not have the right to choose the most opportune time for joining the issue? *

Now it may be that dilemmas, like horned cattle, have only two horns. But there is no reason to assume that history is always impaled on these two horns. Perhaps the real mark of statesmanship is to avoid the horns of a dilemma; or to find a third path at the traditional "fork in the road" where our anxious guides bid us make a choice between the two obvious forks.

A statesmanlike wisdom must certainly reject the "horn" or the "fork" which moves from the idea of an inevitable war to preparations for a preventive one. Even when the historic situation is as tragic as our contemporary one, and when a careful estimate of historic probabilities is bound to lead to more pessimistic than optimistic conclusions, we have no right to speak of "inevitabilities" in history. Men are always agents,

* Naturally the advocates of preventive war have found their position rapidly becoming less tenable as the military capabilities of the Soviet Union have expanded. The reader's attention is called to the fact that the article from which these materials derive was published in 1950.

and not merely the stuff, in the historical process. If modern culture has been inclined, at times, to overestimate the power of the human will over historical destiny, there is yet no reason why we should abdicate the responsibility of that will in this tragic hour. It is foolish to substitute the pretensions of omniscience for the pretensions of omnipotence. We neither fully know nor fully control all the forces operative in a given historical situation; nor can we gauge all the possible consequences of a course of action which we might initiate. We must therefore be slow to bow before any so-called "inevitability" or reluctant to ride any "wave of the future."

We must admit however that most of the apostles of an inevitable war have been driven to hold to their "horn" because they found the other horn implausible. They do not believe that it is possible to "come to terms" with the Russians. There is in fact little plausibility in the various schemes for coming to terms with the Russians. Thus we are told that the Russians might accept world government if only the scheme were sufficiently just to beguile them from their apprehensions. Yet a just government would have to be a democratic one; and the Russians, even if they were not communists, would be loathe to become a prospective minority in such a democratic arrangement. Since no way has yet been invented to run a democracy without requiring a minority to submit to the will of the majority, we cannot expect to solve our problems with the Russians that way. This is particularly obvious when we deal with a minority which believes that it has revolutionary possibilities of becoming a majority in the world community, if only the revolutionary logic of history is allowed to run its course.

Some idealists think we could come to terms with the Russians if only we convinced them that we had no martial designs against them. There is a modicum of virtue in this theory, since it is true that in all international tensions a vicious circle of mutual fear develops. Justified military precautions against all eventualities always seem like prospective aggression from the viewpoint of the other. This is why we should not place undue emphasis upon military strategy alone. But it is idle to hope that the Russian oligarchy could be moved to trust us by any approximation of defenselessness on our part. It is the prisoner of its own conception of the "logic" of history. Its faith in this logic is so great that it could interpret any undue gesture of trust on our part as proof of the decadence which in its opinion is the consequence of our "inner contradictions."

Other idealists think we could beguile the Russian fears and hatreds by more adequate proof of the sincerity of our desire for both greater liberty and greater equality in the so-called free world. There is every reason to work incessantly for the moral and political health of the free world, not only because it is a self-justifying end but also because there are millions in both Europe and Asia, not yet under the Russian yoke, who must be convinced that they can achieve justice and security in a free society so that, in their desperation, they will not be tempted to risk slavery for the sake of security. But there is no reason to believe that the Russian oligarchy could be impressed by these achievements. (We are not speaking of the Russian people, for they cannot be reached.) The oligarchy hates socialism more than capitalism. In pre-fascist Germany it supported Hitler surreptitiously. It prefers reaction to the democratic middle ground because that contributes to the social convulsions out of which it hopes to achieve power. All proponents of social justice are "social fascists" in its estimation because they allegedly confuse the "masses" by dishonest pretensions of achieving justice by other means than their own revolution. The communist dogma is absolutely clear upon all these points. Is there any reason to believe that any virtue on our part could penetrate through this dogma?

Here in fact lies the whole difficulty of all these idealistic approaches. They cannot bring themselves to believe in the reality of the evil which we face in a fanatic creed of this kind. It is tragic that the yearnings of a whole world for peace should be thwarted by such intransigence. But there it is. We serve no useful purpose by obscuring this cruel fact in sentimentalities and illusions.

Yet, though these facts are very discouraging, they must not persuade us that a conflict with Russia is inevitable. While it is not possible to change the minds of these fanatic priest-kings of a secular religion it is possible to provide historical facts which will refute their logic. We need not convince them. We need only convince that part of the world in Europe and Asia which is "halting between two opinions." If we succeed in that enterprise we will preserve a sufficient preponderance of power to prevent Russian aggression. The Russian dogmatism will not necessarily be consciously changed by such a moral defeat. But it will gradually be robbed of its virulence.

Let us consider an historical analogy which supports this hope. The invasion of Europe by Mohammedanism offers the best historical parallel to our present situation. Its fierce equalitarianism and its readiness to use any means to achieve its ends sharpen the analogy. It may be worth observing that it would not have had the chance to conquer Spain in the early Middle Ages or to capture Constantinople in a later period, if political rivalries in Spain had not opened the doors to it and if the jealousies between Western and Eastern Rome had not left Constantinople isolated. These are warnings from the past which we must still heed. But at any rate Islam did conquer large parts of Europe, including some of the Balkan countries now under the communist heel. The seventeenth and eighteenth centuries saw the gradual recession of the Moslem tide from Europe and the First World War finally achieved Islam's expulsion from Europe. Meanwhile Mohammedanism has not changed. It still believes in a holy war, that is, in the right and in the duty to propagate its faith by the sword. The Koran still declares: "Kill those who join the worship of other gods with God wherever you find them; besiege them and lay wait for them in every kind of ambush. But if they shall convert and observe prayer and pay obligatory alms then let them go their way for God is gracious and merciful." Yet Mohammedanism is no longer a peril to the world's peace. It does not believe in itself sufficiently to challenge the whole world.

In the heyday of the Ottoman Empire the Sultan of Turkey combined in his person the political power of a secular ruler and the religious pretensions of the high priest of the Mohammedan faith. He was both Sultan and Caliph. Today there is neither Sultan nor Caliph in Turkey. There is in fact no unified authority in the Moslem world, though there is still a strong sense of religious community beyond national boundaries.

Is it not plausible to suppose that the rigor with which Kremlin orthodoxy deals with satellite leaders who are one hundred per cent communist but also ten per cent patriots reveals both the moral and religious embarrassment of the Kremlin and the inevitable internal opposition to its pretensions? The Sultan could not finally hide the fact that his Turkish interests corrupted his counsels as the high priest of Allah. Nor will the Soviet leaders be able to hide the mixture of a Russian will-to-power in the pretended universalism of orthodox Marxism. Thus all political religions, seeking universal dominion, are finally confined to their own particular locus by the "logic" of history. The processes by which this logic is worked out are not as neat as the maps which the logicians of history conceive for them. But this logic can be more successfully verified empirically than the neat logic by which either communist or Western realists would plunge us into war.

There is however an element in this analogy which will not seem to be reassuring. The Mohammedan tide in Europe did not ebb until after many military defeats in sanguinary conflicts. Charles Martel prevented the early expansion of Moslem power in Europe by his victory at Tours. The defeat which checked the second wave of expansion was administered by the fortuitous intervention of a Polish king in the battle of Vienna. The whole story is one of victories and subsequent defeats in war. Must we draw the conclusion from the analogy that the communist tide will not turn until we have joined the issue in military terms?

Let us, however, be wary in the use of historical analogies. Nothing in history is ever exactly analogous. We must be careful to note both the similarities and the differences in historical recurrences. Mohammedanism was a religious-political creed which rejoiced in martial conflict for the glory of Allah. Communism has no natural desire for martial adventure. It will use any means to achieve its end. But it is also convinced that it has a completely different weapon of world dominion and world redemption than military war. It will certainly use military weapons to maintain its positions. But its primary instruments are always political revolution and conspiracy. Its successes, particularly its triumph in China, are such that it can afford to abide by these weapons for some time to come. No one could guarantee that it might not make a military venture if it became sufficiently strong; or that it might not stumble into one in the desperation of its weakness. It withdraws no armies from satellite nations until it is certain of its political instruments of dominion. But all this cannot change the basic fact that its primary instrument of expansion is political penetration. For this reason the primary instruments of defense against its expansion must be moral, economic, and political. One is almost tempted to prophesy that we will not have to meet communism in overt military conflict unless we have first succumbed politically to such a degree that our cause is hopeless or unless it has succumbed to such a degree that it may be tempted by desperation to join the issue.

Communism must be contained; but the strategy of containment cannot be primarily military. That is why it is important to resist the counsels of desperation on our side which would tempt us to confront communism in Asia primarily in military terms and thus play into the hands of the communist political propaganda by which it would expand still further into Asia.

So much wisdom, imagination, and will to do justice is required to contain communism that we may well feel uncertain about our capacity to accomplish that end. But we ought at least to put our resources where they will be effective and not be beguiled by either sentimental or cynical policies. The idealists must learn that nothing but a preponderance of power in the non-communist world can preserve the peace. And the realists must learn that the power, of which we require preponderance, consists of the unity and the moral and economic health of our world. We must not relax our military defenses. But they must remain subordinate to our main purpose.

Such a course cannot be guaranteed to preserve the peace of the world. No guarantee for any policy can be given in our present predicament. But a policy is possible which saves us from both illusion and despair.[1]

II. *The Anglo-American Alliance*

The Anglo-American partnership remains first in order of importance.[2] It is a *sine qua non* for the preservation of Western civilization.[3] Put in another way, the world is being held together by American power, frequently deflected, though not always guided, by the wider experience and greater political maturity of British statecraft.

The American partner achieved world hegemony very quickly and has had no apprenticeship in the art of carrying great responsibilities. Our authority is derived from our wealth and not from experience in world affairs. Only recently we were tempted to isolationism. We have overcome that temptation; but the world suspects us of succumbing to the opposite temptation of heedlessness in wielding our power. We are certainly more inflexible in policy than the new Russian leadership is. In Asia we are in the toils of a fiction that the communists triumphed in China because we gave inadequate support to the Nationalists. This fiction binds us to the Chinese Nationalists and makes us adamant in the refusal to admit Communist China to the United Nations. We are consequently the symbol of "imperialism" in the Orient though it was the British, and not we, who had imperialistic connections in Asia.

Perhaps it was Britain's success in preserving her health and morale while liquidating an empire which was the chief symbol of British political maturity. It certainly stands in stark contrast to the French embarrassments about her empire, which she has not been able either to hold or to liquidate. The British success has certainly not been uniform. But by and large it is significant that the British ex-imperialists are more respected on the colored continents than we are, who had only a single imperialistic venture in the Philippines.[4] America would be well advised to make use of the prestige of Britain even when its impotence is apparent. The attitude of India toward Britain and toward us is instructive on this point. Anthony Nutting, the former Minister of State for Foreign Affairs, is certainly right in insisting that nothing is as important as the most intimate Anglo-American cooperation in Asia and Africa, for only by this cooperation can the free world benefit from both British prestige and American power.[5] This is the significance of the "Anglo-Saxon" alliance at the heart of the free world. It is one of those providential factors in history which no one could have contrived but for which we can only be grateful.[6]

This partnership is assumed to be comparatively easy of achievement because of the common language, cultural traditions, and democratic ideals which bind the two nations together. But it must be observed that relatives sometimes find a tolerable accord more difficult than strangers. Minor differences against the background of fundamental similarities sometimes offend the imagination more than wider differences which invite no odious comparisons.

For example America's power is preponderantly economic, whereas Britain's is chiefly political. Ours is derived from our continental resources and our unrivaled power of industrial production, while Britain's until recently rested on its vast imperial system. The friction between these two forms of power has produced difficulties on every hand.[7] The more our economic power grows the more we are inclined to assume that political power, being more overt, is less ethical than the more covert economic power. This illusion is generally shared by American liberalism and is one of the most fruitful sources of friction between the two nations, which have been enacting on an international scale the old tension between the landed aristocrats and the rising bourgeoisie. The British own more castles than we; we, increasingly, own the mortgages to these castles. We do not quite know whether we ought to resent the fact that we do not live in the castle or rejoice that we have the mortgage. In this moral predicament we have tended to resolve our difficulty by calling attention to the fact that the owner of the castle has not completely liquidated serfdom on his estate, but we do not mention that the owner is in danger of becoming our serf.[8]

American liberalism has tended to regard British "imperialism" as merely a system of exploitation—a judgment which not only disregards the very great democratic achievement embodied in the "Commonwealth" side of the British Empire, but also obscures some very real accomplishments in British colonial administration. Despite American criticism of British imperialism, we ourselves are having to learn that power, once possessed, must be exercised; that its occasional misuse is no more grievous than an isolationist effort to disavow its responsibilities; that even the most responsible exercise of power is not free of imperial corruption; and that the danger of the exploitation of the weak by the strong can be overcome only by the gradual elaboration of the most careful political and moral restraints.[9]

The rift in the Anglo-Saxon alliance consequent upon the Suez crisis in 1956 made explicit many of these residual differences and tensions between the partners, upon whose continued friendship the solidarity of the alliance of free nations depends. At that time, Secretary Dulles insisted that we would give hope to the nations under the heel of communist despotism by remaining true to our original ideas and convictions.* Those convictions were that our democracy would give an example to the peoples of the world and inspire them to rebel against "alien despots." He was trying to reconstitute the original American innocency, according to which we were the only pure democracy. The Secretary expressed the conviction that our example would have the same wholesome effect upon the world now which our fathers expected it to have in the eighteenth century.

* Address by John Foster Dulles, entitled "Dynamic Peace," before the Associated Press Annual Luncheon, New York, N.Y., April 22, 1957.

The British objected to the tenor of this policy utterance, partly because it was too vague for the nation on whose power and decisions the whole free world depends, and partly because it was too ambiguous. As one British paper asserted, it expressed the desire of our nation to be at once "the pillar of society and the vanguard of the revolution." This protest against our ambiguity expresses the frequent British apprehensions about our "anti-colonialism," our effort to exploit our early history for the sake of currying sympathy with the ex-colonial nations, or, as one British journalist put it, "applying for membership in the Bandung conference." The British object to this particular American gambit because it obscures the creative achievements of British "imperialism" and sanctifies every residual colonial resentment as justified, and also because it obscures the reality of power in the present situation. The reality is that we are the most powerful nation in the alliance of free nations and that Britain is quite content to play second fiddle to us, provided that we understand that the Anglo-Saxon alliance is the core of authority in the free world and that the two nations working together have more authority than one nation, however powerful, working alone. Perhaps the finest fruit of the Anglo-Saxon alliance would be not the combination of the power of the Anglo-Saxon nations, but the mixture of British "realism" and American "idealism." [10]

III. *The Atlantic Community*

We are linked in a bond of common destiny with Europe.[11] For the peace of the world will have to be maintained for years to come primarily by the preponderance of power in the Western world. But let no one imagine that this "power" is, or can be, primarily military. Overt force is like the fist of a hand. But "power," in the moral and political sense of the word, is like the total strength of a body plus the psychic vitality of the soul which is in the body. The preponderance of power in the Western world is constituted primarily of the moral unity and economic health of that world.[12]

The most obvious bond between us is our devotion to what the World Council of Churches defined as a "free and responsible society." Inevitably there are different nuances and accents in the definitions of such a society which the various democratic nations will give.

It is important that we should learn from one another in seeking to define such a society most adequately. Europe suspects us, generally speaking, of defining democracy in too strictly libertarian terms. It thinks we have too great confidence in the possibility of achieving justice as a by-product of freedom. On the other hand, we suspect Europe of sacrificing liberty too easily for the sake of achieving a wider security or a more equal justice.* A part of the difference in emphasis is undoubtedly derived from the difference in economic and political conditions on the two continents, for fewer restraints have to be placed upon various social and economic factors in a situation of abundance than in a situation of scarcity. We are not only in danger of trying to force libertarian conceptions of democracy upon Europe, which are irrelevant to the European situation. We are also in danger of pressing a dogmatic formula upon our own national situation which might be applicable if our national economy were isolated but which is not applicable when our responsibilities to the world, as embodied in economic aid and the military defense program, are considered.

European democrats may on the other hand be too prone to lose the values of an open society in their effort to solve the immediate necessities of justice. They may forget that while equality is the general principle of justice, no society can exist in terms of absolute equality. Every social organism must have room in it for differentiated functions and must provide the best possible incentives for the performance of those functions. Liberty and equality are just as much in contradiction as they are complementary to each other. A society can destroy liberty in its search for equality; it can annul the spirit of equal justice by a too consistent devotion to liberty. A healthy democracy will never regard the problem of liberty and equality as solved, because new historical factors constantly enter a given situation to aggravate old disbalances or to disturb hitherto satisfactory balances between the two.

If the civilization which we are defending is to be something more than a hodgepodge of ancient and modern creeds, of partly discredited traditional dogmas and wholly discredited modern illusions, we must work together on the problem of creating a free and responsible society with as few dogmatic preconceptions as possible. This will require an especially critical attitude toward the dogmas most favored in our portion of the world. All men and nations are much too prone to vaunt themselves for their "ideals."

Our Western civilization could do with fewer "ideals," particularly those which contradict each other and set nations and classes at variance with each other. It would also profit from a higher sense of responsibility: each man for his neighbor. For it is that sense of responsibility which makes freedom both sufferable and possible. When freedom is ex-

* These differences were much more acute when Niebuhr wrote these lines in 1949 than they are today, for political conservatism has followed in the wake of Europe's economic recovery. However, Niebuhr's analysis is still instructive, because basic differences between European and American economic and political philosophy, though covert, still remain.

ercised irresponsibly it creates conditions which lead to its annulment.

On the other hand, a free and responsible society cannot achieve the unity which we confront in the tyranny which opposes us. That unity is established not merely by the coercive instruments of a tyrannical government but by the totalitarian claims of a secular political religion. It is nevertheless important that we achieve a measure of unity and common purpose, not only within the national units of our civilization but within the civilization itself. Unity in a free society must be achieved on the lowest level by an accommodation of rights and interests. On the highest level it must be achieved by a constant interpenetration of ideas and ideals so that mutually supplementary moral values will not degenerate into mutually contradictory creeds. That is why a sense of humility and mutual forbearance in advancing our various notions of democracy is a prerequisite for the spiritual and moral integration of our civilization.[13]

Superficially, much progress has been made in integrating the so-called Atlantic community. But the progress is in the sphere of military and economic organization. In the realm of political, moral, and cultural opinion a deep animus against America, and a consequent "neutralism" have at times made our accord with Europe very difficult.[14]

The anti-American animus of Europe has not all derived from differences of economic and social policy. Some of it has been due simply to the tremendous shift of power which has taken place in international relations in the past two decades. Europe is our spiritual father. We were, until recently, the adventurous son who had gone into a far country whence came back rumors that he had found a way of combining riotous living with a success and prosperity quite unlike "the husks that the swine do eat" in the Biblical story of the Prodigal.

This adventurous rather than wayward son now suddenly returns to dominate the destiny of Europe. Momentary gratitude that his power holds back the tide of communism, and momentary anxiety that he may not have the stability to persevere in this Herculean task, constantly give way to envy of this power and prosperity and resentment at Europe's impotence. Our own experience with isolationism in the days when the lines of power were in Britain's hands should give us some understanding of such neutralism. It is significant that these resentments are actually greater in France than in Britain, though they would be more natural in the nation which held the position of hegemony in Europe until we took it over.

An American may be pardoned for suspecting that French resentments are sometimes an unconscious cover for France's uneasy conscience about its role in recent history. French resentments epitomize and exaggerate the resentments of a "cultured" parent civilization against its uncouth son. All over Europe "Americanization" has become synonymous with the threat of "technics" against the organic and traditional elements of culture. Is not America, asks the French journal *Le Monde,* rather repetitiously, a "technocracy" scarcely distinguishable from the Russian variety? The attack at this point is not upon our capitalistic social organization but upon our culture, upon its real and imagined vulgarities. One is tempted to reply resentfully that the French culture is indeed ripe to the point of overripeness, that the French intellectuals oscillate between an absurd devotion to communist illusions and a sophistication which is bereft of every illusion and ends in the conviction that human existence itself is absurd.

But perhaps these resentful counter-charges have no place if one seeks an understanding between America and the continent. Perhaps we ought to admit that a civilization as preoccupied with technics as our own unavoidably exhibits vulgarities which mellow cultures find difficult to bear. The genuine merits of our culture will prove themselves in time. The "moss" of an organic culture does not easily settle on the shining metal of modern machines. There are evidences in American life that the sense of justice and community can come to terms with technical civilization, though the imponderables of culture require time.

In any event our power would be resented in Europe while at the same time it is courted, even if it had proceeded from an ancient rather than a modern culture. We shall have to learn to bear these resentments with patience. We must not assume that they are all unjustified; for power never impinges upon weakness without some injustice.[15]

Actually, our most creative achievements of statesmanship (the Marshall Plan, for instance) are not acts of generosity. Generosity is probably beyond the moral capacity of collective man. It is therefore foolish for powerful nations to pretend to it. The pretension will merely elicit cynical reactions. But it is not impossible for nations to find the point of concurrence between self-interest and a wider interest than their own. This we have done in the most creative acts of American statesmanship in recent years. We shall have to be content with the knowledge that this is so, neither claiming more moral credit than we deserve nor becoming too disturbed by the fact that our power and our prosperity will arouse both justified and unjustified resentments—even among friends and allies who are inexorably locked with us in a community of common destiny.[16]

IV. *The Colored Continents*

It required years of experience for our nation to come to the rightful conclusion that it is important to "hold the line" against expanding communism in Europe. But meanwhile communism has penetrated into Asia and has conquered China. Should we not, argue the realists, hold whatever military line can be held against further expansion?

This appeal to consistency in foreign policy has a certain degree of plausibility; but formal consistency may be the greatest source of confusion. The real question is: Are the conditions to which we are asked to apply equal measures, really equal? It is because the contingent factors in Europe and Asia are not equal that the realists' appeal to consistency is vain.

In Europe we have helped by both economic and military aid to preserve a viable civilization which is capable of defeating communism in a competition for the allegiance of common men. There were moral weaknesses in that civilization. But it had sufficient health to offer men both freedom and justice, rather than the communist annulment of freedom for the hope of justice. In China, on the other hand, communism conquered the nation precisely because the Nationalist Government lacked the moral and political virtue necessary to claim the allegiance of the vast mass of Chinese people. They accepted communism. To defend such a government from the island of Formosa would mean that we subordinate moral and political to military strategy. Thus formal consistency would involve us in the inconsistency of subordinating military to moral strategy in Europe and making military strategy dominant in Asia.[17]

The plausibility of the communist creed to the two colored continents is given by the fact that the Marxist interpretation of the class struggle and its analysis of the class structure, though always too simple to fit the facts, are much more relevant to the social facts in a decaying feudal structure than in an advanced capitalistic one. It is not surprising that Marxism succeeded only in the agrarian and feudal economies of semi-Asiatic Russia and in China; nor surprising that it still appears to be relevant to the recently emancipated nations of Africa and Asia, who have suffered or still suffer from foreign domination, and whose suffering has not ended with their throwing off the foreign yoke.

American idealists are inclined to neglect all the political complexities of Asia and Africa and to imagine that "free elections" represent a meaningful goal to the people who live there. They think democracy is a matter of accepting a democratic constitution and they are oblivious to the tortuous history by which justice was established in a free society through an equilibrium of political and economic forces. If they are more realistic, our idealists propose a technical assistance program for the non-technical nations, but only few recognize that technical advance breaks the molds of organic communities. Political chaos may go hand in hand with a rise in living standards. A free society is not as simple an alternative to the old feudal society as is the collectivism of communism which promises technical competence; promises, but does not grant, economic justice; and does *not* promise the individual freedom which the peoples of Asia and Africa have never enjoyed and which seems in any case to be beyond their reach.

But whatever mistakes our idealists make in presenting an open society as a simple alternative to past injustices, they are trumped by the mistakes of our realists who insist on regarding our contest with communism in the colored continents as primarily a problem of military strategy.

The right-wing "realists" of the Republican Party still insist, for example, that China might have been saved from communism if the nationalists had been given adequate military support. They close their eyes to obvious political and moral weaknesses of the nationalist cause, and to our loss of prestige in the whole of Asia through our persistent military championship of that cause long after it had proved its inability to win and hold the loyalty of the Chinese masses.

Secretary Dulles managed to combine the mistakes of the idealists *and* the realists. He had a purely "idealistic" approach to the problems of Asia and Africa when he defined the issues between ourselves and the communists as a contest between those who believe in the "moral law" and those who do not. He was a military "realist" when he contrived military defense pacts which enraged our neutralist "allies" by driving a wedge between India and Pakistan, and another in the Middle East between the various members of the Arab League. These defense pacts were modeled after the European NATO model; but Mr. Dulles did not seem to appreciate that the analogy he used to justify them is faulty. For the European community is solid, or nearly solid, in its devotion to the standards of democratic civilization and can be conquered only by military force. In non-European nations on the other hand, subversion and political conspiracy are the communists' chief weapons.

The essential problem which democracy faces in Asia and Africa can be briefly stated: Democracy is at once a more tainted and a more impossible ideal than we have realized. It has been tainted for the Asian and African nations because the democratic nations are also the technically most powerful nations, whose initial impact on the continents was imperialistic. Democracy seems an impossible ideal because it appears to lack the essential conditions for attaining justice and stability, within the framework of a free society. Asians and Africans also usually lack the religio-cultural foundation for individual freedom; their religions either lose the individual in the social whole, the family or the tribe (as in Confucianism and in the more primitive religions of Africa), or are mystical religions which seek for the annulment of individuality.

But even if these peoples should manage to gain an appreciation of the value of the individual, more like our own, they must still prove that individual liberty, so much prized by the West, can be made compatible with *both* justice and stability. Freedom is not an absolute value. We think so because we take the values of justice and stability for granted. But these values have been made compatible with freedom by very slow processes of history in the West. If freedom could not be made compatible with justice, the communist case against a free society would be proved. If free societies could not achieve stability, the communists would finally profit from the resulting chaos. Justice requires an equilibrium of political and economic power. The equilibrium of political power was broadly achieved by universal suffrage. But a tolerable justice was not achieved in Western civilization until the industrial workers achieved both political *and* economic power through political and trade union organizations.

Further, the stability of a free society requires not only justice but a measure of moral and political wisdom which sets limits to party conflicts and the competition of conflicting interests within the community. The wisdom expressed in the "limited warfare" of parliamentary government is not the simple fruit of literacy or even of intelligence. It is also an historical product, usually the fruit of generations of living together in freedom. The justice and stability which we take for granted have not been achieved in most Latin American nations, though they may have ideal Constitutions.

Such an analysis would seem to make our democratic alternative to communism impossible for nations of Asia and Africa. But while the difficulties must be appreciated, the alternative is not impossible. The possibility rests upon the ability of men to transfer political skills and wisdom from one culture in which they matured into another culture in which they are not indigenous. This requires rare cooperation between the tutor nation and the apprentice; and resentments against the imperial tutor frequently make this cooperation extremely difficult. But the experience of Britain in India and our experience in the Philippines, and, less impressively, the Dutch experience in Indonesia, prove that it *is* possible to transfer historically acquired skills. The British have proved in the Gold Coast of Africa (Ghana) that it can be done, even if the apprentice is a budding nation with a primitive culture.

Yet the difficulties of the task make it evident that we have a long-range program before us, requiring not only ingenuity but patience.[18] It is perfectly possible for the nations of Asia and Africa to slip from the tyranny of the older social forms to the new tyranny of communism under the illusion that the new system is better, and not worse. We must therefore expect many a defeat in Asia and Africa before the tragic facts, gradually disclosed to the Western world in the past decades of experience, are revealed to these new nations.[19] In short, the long ardors of competitive co-existence cannot be understood at all or borne with patience, if we do not realize that the contest between a free society and a tyranny is one in which the tyranny has all the immediate advantages in the colored continents, while we have all the ultimate ones. That is why time is on our side, however much the battle may run against us for decades.[20]

A century and a half ago Napoleonic France had the same relation to the bourgeois revolution as Soviet Russia has to the communist revolution. It would have been silly for any military strategist to regard a victory over any of Napoleon's satellites as definitive so long as Napoleon's power remained unbroken. It would have been equally silly for any political strategist to hail Napoleon's defeat as the final triumph over the bourgeois revolution. What was valid in that revolution (and even elements in it which were not valid) affected the life of Europe for a century and more.

Asia will require at least as much time to assimilate and to reject the communist revolution. We in the Western world cannot affect these historical processes very much by military intervention.[21] Naturally it is necessary to resist communism whenever it presents itself in terms of military aggression, as in Korea, and to prevent the communist movement from gaining supremacy in the weapons with which modern warfare is bound to be conducted. Military force is always the *ultima ratio* in the contest between nations.[22] Furthermore we have the right and the duty to protect lands (the island littoral for instance) which are strategically necessary and the defense of which is morally acceptable. Fortunately our relations to both Japan and the Philippines do make their defense morally acceptable to them. But we cannot go much further.[23]

Just as we must not underestimate our moral and spiritual affinities with Europe we must not overestimate our moral resources in the colored continents. Our lack of moral authority in Asia means that when we use military power there we diminish, rather than augment, our moral and political authority. Military power without a moral base is always intolerable. Nor can we cover our moral nakedness by alliance with such regimes as that of Chiang Kai-shek.[24] If we do not understand that the colored people of the world have grievances and resentments against the Western world which communism exploits and if we do not seek to mitigate these resentments by justice and forebearance, we will lose the battle in Asia. If we do not understand that, however orthodox the communist leadership in China, its rank and file consists of Chinese patriots and peasants yearning for security, we will be too clumsy ever to encourage a tension between the masses and the communist leadership or between the Chinese communist leadership and the Russian oligarchy.[25]

The immaturity of American political thought makes it difficult for us to acknowledge the limits of our political and moral authority in various parts of the world, or to distinguish between the military and moral dimensions of our conflict with communism. If we fail to make such distinctions, the possibility of avoiding an atomic war becomes very minimal. For a policy of countering the expansion of communism everywhere in the world by military force must make the final conflict inevitable.[26]

V. *The Cold War, the Nuclear Dilemma, and Co-existence*

The long history of conflict between communities, whether national or imperial, has reached a climax in the cold war and the nuclear dilemma of the present day. The "cold war" means a perpetual tension between the two blocs of nations, communist and anti-communist, of such unique intensity that one may question the adjective used to describe it. Yet it is regarded as "cold" rather than "hot" because there are no overt hostilities on a large scale. These hostilities are prevented by an historical phenomenon as unique as the cold war itself. Both sides have nuclear weapons which have raised military destructiveness to such a degree of suicidal and lethal efficacy that neither side is tempted to initiate the conflict.

Meanwhile, in the arsenals of both sides, bombs are piled on bombs and guided missiles will be piled on guided missiles in an armory of such frightfulness that man's technical progress throughout the ages has taken on a new dimension. The dimension is novel because, for the first time, the balance between the creative and destructive possibilities of the mastery over natural forces would seem to have been destroyed. The destructive possibilities are certainly more apparent and more imminent.

Furthermore, modern technical advances have set man's progress in techniques in a new light. Progress in this field is accomplished, as previously, through human agency, but it outruns human desires so that historical developments become more and more analogous to natural forces "which go on their fateful way unswerving and know not what they are."

In this situation of the cold war and the nuclear stalemate two questions inevitably loom large in scanning the dark future. The most immediate question is whether there is any way of abolishing the dread weapons; and the second is whether there is any way of mitigating the animosities of the conflict. The first question, which is the more unanswerable, looms largest; but the second question is of equal importance.

If we seek to draw lessons from history to instruct us in our present perplexities it is important to note the radical difference between two problems which communities in past history have faced. In the first case, communities were confronted with a crisis in which they were forced to make a choice between their survival or liberty—and some larger good, or the good of a larger community. In this situation nations chose their own existence, security, or interest rather than the more universal value, such as the peace of Europe or any other region.

The second situation is radically different. It is when communities were pressed by historical circumstances to adjust their interests, usually by gradual and even by unconscious steps, to new conditions. In the past, communities have successfully negotiated these adjustments, even when the new conditions presented some radical novelties. The great difference between the two situations is due to the necessity of either a risk or sacrifice of vital interests in the first case, while only an adjustment of interests and a reinterpretation of the peril and promise, given by the new situation, is necessary in the second case.

Thus in the Wars of Religion which followed the Reformation, neither Catholic nor Protestant nations thought of sacrificing their securities for the sake of the peace of Europe. But when it became apparent that neither side could eliminate the power of the other side Catholics and Protestants began those adjustments of a competitive co-existence which gradually transformed the culture of Europe into a religiously pluralistic one.

If the radical distinction between the two situations be validated by this example, and also by many other similar historical instances, it might follow that it is easier to cool off the animosities of the cold war than to agree on nuclear disarmament or the total abolition of nuclear weapons. For nuclear disarmament, even if undertaken mutually, involves some risk to the securities of both sides. There is small prospect that either side would be willing to take the risks. This remains true even if their failure to do so would involve the world in the continued peril of nuclear warfare. One may take for granted that neither side actually intends to begin the dread conflict. But it may come upon them nevertheless by miscalculation or misadventure.[27]

While the prospect of abolishing the nuclear threat completely is slight,* we are also confronted with the less difficult task of sharing the world with a despotic system which we abhor and which decades of polemics have made the more abhorrent. Yet unless we annihilate each other in a nuclear war we must come to terms with the possibilities of co-existence with this regime. This task is easier than the abolition of

* For Niebuhr's detailed analysis of the many problems surrounding a viable system for reducing and controlling armaments, see *The Structure of Nations and Empires*, pp. 269–76.

nuclear weapons but it is not as interesting and does not excite the same devotion among the idealists. It is easier because it does not demand that the impulse for survival of each collective system be challenged directly. It is only required that each side allow historical developments to modify the animosities and to change the power realities within each system.

The first precondition of survival in such competitive co-existence is that both sides come to a full recognition of their involvement in a common fate. Included in this common fate are fear of mutual annihilation and also the common inclination to attribute malice to the other side, particularly the evil design of initiating the ultimate conflict. It would be sobering to the West to make an honest analysis of the situation of a common fate. Such an analysis might well prompt the conclusion that the temptation to begin the ultimate conflict probably is greater on the Western side than on the Russian, because, as we have seen, the Russians have all the immediate political advantages in the Middle East and in Asia and Africa; and their prospective victories there are much more likely to lead to desperation in the democratic alliance.

The task of managing to share the world without bringing disaster on a common civilization must include, on our part, a less rigid and self-righteous attitude toward the power realities of the world and a more hopeful attitude toward the possibilities of internal developments in the Russian despotism. Our rigid and self-righteous attitude is manifest particularly in our insistence that Chinese communism is "ephemeral" and will disappear if we oppose it rigorously enough. Communist despotism in China is undoubtedly more absolute than in Russia. But the system which, according to our official dogma, is fated to extinction has meanwhile gained enough power to influence the Russian strategy, chiefly by exchanging loyalty to Russian hegemony for the tangible benefits of technical equipment and guidance. Our China policy appears to the uncommitted world as dogmatic as anything in the rigid dogmatism of the communist world.

The other side of the problem of co-existence is to hope for, and abet, those aspects of the communist system which offer some promise of gradual change in the despotic rigidity of the communist totalitarianism. It would be foolish to expect an inflexible system either quickly or even gradually to develop into an open society. But it is not wrong to reflect on historical analogies between the monarchical absolutism which gripped Europe only a few centuries ago and the present Russian system. Monarchical absolutism succumbed in France to the Revolution, but in Britain it evolved into an open society because a group of Whig aristocrats, who controlled Parliament, disputed the authority of the monarch; and the tension between King and Parliament gradually benefited the common people of Britain. It may not be too sanguine to draw the analogy and to point to the fact that the remnant and the beginning of democracy in the communist system may be the Central Committee of the Party. Its power seemed to be qualified by the more closely knit oligarchy, originally devised in purely *ad hoc* terms, of the "Politbureau" and now the "Presidium" of the Party. Stalin managed to dominate both this little oligarchy and the Party through terror. Much has been said about the ease with which this despotism established itself in the name of "democratic centralism"; but with the death of Stalin new forces expressed themselves in Soviet society, and the execution of Beria and the abolition of the police terror showed that the surviving oligarchs could express a will to resist absolute tyranny. The system still allows shrewd and ruthless leaders to emerge with almost absolute power; but it is wise to remember that Khrushchev has achieved his present eminence partly by appealing to the Central Committee against the Presidium where he was outvoted. Evidently there is something like a Whig aristocracy in the Russian system of the Central Committee.

The second aspect of the communist system in Russia which offers the prospect for dynamic internal developments, which we must not discount, is the educational system. In Russia children of peasants can receive a university education if their intelligence merits it. The political system may be despotic but the rudiments of democracy are in the educational system. Only a short time ago we regarded Russia condescendingly as a backward community; but now we wonder whether we can match the Russians in training technicians for a technical society. This despotism differs from the traditional despotic communities because it is a dynamic society which requires a great deal of competence for its health on all levels of the community. Technical competence is not synonymous with a humanistic training, aware of all the nuances of culture. Russia probably will be "vulgar" for decades to come; and we might reflect that the vulgarity of our own mass culture may be destroying the humanities as rapidly as the Russians may be becoming conscious of the limits of their technical achievements.

There is, of course, no immediate prospect of achieving political emancipation by raising the level of intellectual competence. Dictatorships have co-opted a technical oligarchy for their purposes; and have kept them quiet and docile by finding the point of concurrence between the prestige and security of the technicians and the ambitions of the oligarchy. We cannot think in short-term goals when we think of leavening the lump of despotism by intellect alone. But the long-term result must be that a technically competent culture cannot avoid a rational ferment which yet may prove politically subversive. We cannot build any immediate hopes on these probabilities. But we must realize that we are not fated to share the world with the present despotism forever. It is under the ferment of a culture which is bound to produce political effects in the long run.

Two characteristics of the communist system discourage even those rather desperate hopes which we have enumerated. One is that it is the first system of government which identifies without reservation the ideal and the real, claiming for its system of power if not the immediate then the ultimate realization of an ideal justice.

The other characteristic of the communist system which tempts even the most hopeful to lose their hope is that none of the oligarchies—rivalry between which must be one of the conditions of increasing freedom—have independent sources of power, not related to the state bureaucracy. The managerial oligarchy, for instance, is distinguished from the rising business class of Western history in early modernity by the fact that they have no property of their own but are only the managers of state property.

The twin forces of freedom in Western history were property and conscience. They are also the sources of freedom in some of the newer countries like Tunisia. There seems no room in the communist system for either of these forces.

Yet political systems and communities are subject to various developments by the shift of historic circumstance. Systems built on revolutionary ardor are particularly subject to development as the revolutionary enthusiasm abates and the oligarchy acquires a sense of responsibility for the preservation of order and the adjustment of interest within the growing system. It must be understood, of course, that these hoped-for developments do not change the common characteristics of communities with reference to their collective self-regard. They can only mitigate the uncommon characteristics of communism, including the fury of its fanaticism and the rigor of its despotism. It would be foolish to expect the development of a democratic system within the foreseeable future, or to hope for any other than a collective self-regard within the communist system, even if a full-blown democracy should develop. All that can be expected is that historical developments finally will reduce the communist system to more or less the same dimensions which are universally manifest in the traditional communities of history. Such a development might make accommodation between the democratic and the communist alliance easier, but it would not eliminate the peril of war. That peril may be avoided in the future, as in the present, by the fear of mutual annihilation and the processes of diplomacy. The peril will be lessened, also, by mutualities of trade and culture which will increase as the revolutionary animus abates in Russia in the second and third generations of post-revolutionary leaders.[28]

VI. *American Power and World Community*

We must now return to a problem which concerned us earlier, that of creating a world community,* and analyze more specifically the responsibilities of the American nation in this undertaking. To begin with, it would be well to concede that our inordinate power offers some real advantages for the world community. It is quite possible that if power had been more evenly distributed in the non-communist world the degree of cohesion actually attained would have been difficult. Many national communities gained their first triumph over chaos by the organizing energy of one particular power, sufficiently dominant to suppress the confusion of competing forces. Thus, dominant city-states in Egypt and in Mesopotamia were responsible for the order and cohesion of these first great empires of human history. The preponderant power of America may have a similar role to play in the present international scene. There is, furthermore, a youthful belief in historic possibilities in our American culture, a confidence that problems can be solved, which frequently stands in creative contrast with the spiritual tiredness of many European nations as also with the defeatism of Oriental cultures. Our hegemonic position in the world community rests upon a buoyant vigor as well as upon our preponderant economic power.

Nevertheless, great disproportions of power are as certainly moral hazards to justice and community as they are foundations of minimal order. They are hazards to community both because they arouse resentments and fears among those who have less power; and because they tempt the strong to wield their power without too much consideration of the interests and views of those upon whom it impinges. Modern democratic nations have sought to bring power into the service of justice in three ways. (a) They have tried to distribute economic and political power and prevent its undue concentration. (b) They have tried to bring it under social and moral review. (c) They have sought to establish inner religious and moral checks upon it.

Of these three methods the first is not relevant to the international community, as at present inchoately organized. The relative power of particular nations must be accepted as fateful historic facts about which little can be done. The preponderance of American power is thus an inexorable fact for decades to come, whether within or without a fuller world constitution than now prevails. If it does disappear it will be eliminated by the emergence of new forces or the new coalition of older forces, rather than by constitutional contrivance.

The strategy of bringing power under social and political review is a possibility for the international community, even in its present nascent

* See above, Chapter XXI.

form. It is a wholesome development for America and the world that the United Nations is becoming firmly established, not so much as an institution capable of bridging the chasm between the communist and the non-communist world, but as an organ in which even the most powerful of the democratic nations must bring their policies under the scrutiny of world public opinion. Thus inevitable aberrations, arising from the pride of power, are corrected. It will be even more hopeful for the peace and justice of the world community if a fragmented Europe should gain the unity to speak with more unanimity in the councils of the nations than is now possible. It is impossible for any nation or individual fully to understand the peculiar circumstances and the unique history of any other nation or individual, which create their special view of reality. It is important, therefore, that the fragmentary wisdom of any nation should be prevented from achieving the bogus omniscience which occurs when the weak are too weak to dare challenge the opinion of the powerful.

If there should be, as many Europeans believe, too great a preoccupation in America with the task of winning a war which Europe wants to avoid; and if there should be in Europe, as some Americans believe, so desperate a desire to avoid war that the danger is run of bringing on the conflict by lack of resolution, it is to be hoped that a creative synthesis of complementary viewpoints will take place.

The third strategy of disciplining the exercise of power, that of an inner religious and moral check, is usually interpreted to mean the cultivation of a sense of justice. The inclination "to give each man his due" is indeed one of the ends of such a discipline. But a too confident sense of justice always leads to injustice. Insofar as men and nations are "judges in their own case" they are bound to betray the human weakness of having a livelier sense of their own interest than of the competing interest. That is why "just" men and nations may easily become involved in ironic refutations of their moral pretensions.

The sense of justice must be supplemented by a sense of religious humility which recognizes that nations are even more incapable than individuals of fully understanding the rights and claims of others. Such humility ought also to reveal that the pretensions and the vanities of the other group, though perhaps different in intensity, are not different in kind from those of our own group. Finally, a genuine religious humility will prompt us to acknowledge the mystery and integrity of "the other," and will reveal to us that this other life represents a boundary which our expansive impulses must not transgress.

Such resources of community are of greater importance in our nation today than abstract constitutional schemes, of which our idealists are so fond. Most of these schemes will be proved, upon close examination, to be indifferent toward the urgencies and anxieties which nations, less favored than we, experience.[29]

Let us, therefore, be less concerned with abstract schemes of world order and more intent to deal realistically with every concrete issue which faces our nation. In some of these issues a powerful nation will be inclined to disregard the wishes of weaker allies. In some of them a proud nation will be inclined to resent criticism of envious or resentful friends. In some of them a frustrated nation will be inclined to become impatient with the slow processes of history. In some of them a nation fearful of the future will be inclined to "fly to evils that it knows not of" in its desire to avoid the "slings and arrows of outrageous fortune."

Our nation is basically committed to the principles of a cooperative world community. The real problem is whether we can give this basic commitment the body of, the flesh and blood of, our daily acts of loyalty and forbearance in the nascent community of mankind. We must learn to bear the burdens of our day, including the burdens of a heavy taxation and the anxieties of a cold war, without any certain knowledge how our acts of fidelity to a nascent community of nations may be rewarded or justified.

While the communists give an interpretation of the difference between our wealth and the world's poverty which is as false as it is plausible, we must be intent to give a right answer to the problems raised by the contrast. We must help the impoverished world to gain greater technical efficiency, and we must strengthen every political instrument of common living which allays suspicions and resentments. We cannot overcome all the hazards to mutual understanding between ourselves and an impoverished world; but we can learn in actual encounters to deal loyally with our allies in the free world. From such loyalty will spring policies which we must refrain from calling generous because they will be in our own long-term interest; but they will be wise in the sense that they will help to cement the unity of the free world.

Our actions and attitudes on detailed questions of daily policy, on questions of tariffs and immigration quotas, on technical assistance programs and investment in undeveloped areas will contribute more to the international community, which all far-seeing Americans see in the making, than any abstract commitments to ideal and impossible world constitutions which some idealistic Americans regard as important. Undoubtedly the constitutional instruments of world order must be perfected in time. But the more perfect instruments must grow out of the more perfect mutualities of daily living together.[30]

CHAPTER XXVI

Foreign Policy and Moral Problems

The question of right and wrong is undoubtedly raised in the realm of international relations. Both individuals and nations either desire to do, or claim to have done, what is right in the relations of nations with each other. Only a few cynics try to dismiss the moral question. A much more frequent attitude than cynicism is that of hypocrisy which makes larger claims for the moral quality of an action than the facts warrant.

Indeed the moral issue is so persistently raised, both in the theory and in the practical conduct of international affairs, not only because men honestly seek to do the right, but also because they cannot follow their interest without claiming to do so in obedience to some general scheme of values. Since men are more inclined to follow their own interests in collective than in individual behavior, moral pretension plays a very large part in politics. This is why the alleged father of modern political cynicism, Machiavelli, made the pretension of moral aims a part of the science of politics even though he specifically disavowed the reality of genuine moral motives in the life of the nation. Certainly the peril of hypocrisy is greater than that of pure cynicism in international, as in all political questions.

The moral issue in international relations is in fact a more vivid explication of the moral question in the whole realm of the political order. Every question of right and wrong is made more complex on the international level because the parochial interests to be dealt with are more precisely exemplified in national communities than in any international groups or interests, and the issues of power, authority, and interests are more explicit variations of the problems faced in the political realm in general. Thus the moral ambiguities of international politics, which we must now examine in some detail, are notorious.[1]

I. *Case Studies of Moral Problems in International Politics* *

1. THE CONFLICT OF MORAL PRINCIPLES: SUEZ

The crisis in Egypt in the fall of 1956—and the evident desire of good people to find a right or "moral" solution for the issues—raised the problem of the precarious relations between moral ideals and international politics, and all politics, for that matter. The reason right and wrong cannot be defined so easily is because two or three moral values and loyalties come into conflict in a political decision, so that our decision in a particular instance usually depends upon historical contingencies which are not anticipated in any statement of Christian or moral principles.

Walter Lippmann, who did not agree with the Administration policy in the Suez crisis, declared that the Egyptian problem could not be solved until we detected the "moral issue" in the crisis. This issue, said Mr. Lippmann, was that the Egyptian dictator was a covert aggressor before the overt aggression of Britain and France. Many of us would agree with Lippmann and regret that both the Administration and the American public did not recognize this important fact. But we must not deny that those who did not agree with us followed other moral principles and values, particularly their sense of loyalty to the United Nations Charter.

Senator Humphrey of Minnesota also did not agree with the Administration; but when asked whether the bitterness toward us in Britain and France would abate, he declared that it would abate, once our allies recognized that we were acting in obedience to "moral principles." He saw these principles in terms of loyalty to the United Nations.

But the British and French criticized us precisely because they thought we were at once loyal to the United Nations and at the same time we destroyed its real authority by putting it under the dominance of the Russian-Arab-Asian bloc. They felt our action to be disloyal to the Western alliance, which had been holding the fort against communism; and we felt their actions to be disloyal to us, who were trying to establish contact with the uncommitted world of Asia and Africa.

These appeals to moral principles in international affairs could be duplicated in all the complex issues of domestic politics. The fact that honest men see the hierarchy of moral values and principles in a different order according to their different perspectives must not discourage

* The "case studies" which follow have been collected from Niebuhr's occasional writings and are included in this compendium as illustrations of his approach to the problem of relating morality to politics in specific situations. The "cases" and moral perplexities reviewed are, of course, suggestive, not exhaustive.

us from honestly seeking to do what is right. But it ought to dissuade us from all self-righteous assumptions that we alone are truly moral.

The late Justice Oliver Wendell Holmes used to say: "People are always extolling the man of principles; but I think the superior man is the one who knows that he must find his way in the maze of principles." [2]

2. THE DANGERS OF MORAL SIMPLIFICATION: SECRETARY DULLES

"The communists," Secretary Dulles told a convention of the National Council of Churches of Christ, held in Cleveland in the fall of 1958, "deny that there is such a thing as justice, in our meaning of the term." Perhaps the phrase "in our meaning of the term" conveys the embarrassment which simple moralism confronts in any political problem. Who is meant by the pronoun "our"? Do Americans, or Western democracies, or all non-communist nations define the meaning of justice? Justice, declared Aristotle, means giving each man his due. But no one has ever accurately defined how, and by whom, the due to men and to nations is to be measured. An ideal justice requires an impartial judgment, which is supplied only in an independent judicial system. Even in the domestic life of advanced democracies, justice is achieved, not through impartial tribunals, but by a tolerable equilibrium of social forces. In international life, the standards of justice are even more inexact.

Naturally the communists do not have a conception of justice "in our meaning of the term." They are informed by a dogmatic Marxist creed, which regards our justice as bogus and which exalts "socialist legality," whatever that may mean. Mr. Dulles believed that communist immorality was responsible for Chinese strategy on the issue of offshore islands. Yet, if China were not communist, it would still have a different perspective from ours on that strategic problem, and might still object to our insistence that the Formosan Government is the real government of China.

Mr. Dulles was as moral in dealing with our allies as he was with our foes. He reminded them that our inflexible policy was a matter of "principle." "Our collective security arrangements would surely collapse," he declared, "if our free world associates felt that they were tied to policies that shifted under the dictates of passing considerations, as to what was expedient from the standpoint of the United States. They do not like it when we adhere to principle, but they would like it even less, if we had no principles."

Mr. Dulles forgot that what our allies like least of all is our tendency to equate our inflexibility with "principle," and their more flexible policy with "expediency."

Mr. Dulles' implied disavowal of the use of force, and his indictment of the communists for using it, was even more simple than his conception of justice. "The communists," he warned at Cleveland, "do not share the [UN] Charter's concept, either with respect to the non-use of force, or the justice of international law." Mr. Dulles went on to say that since "the Soviet Union and the Chinese communists have both repeatedly invoked force to achieve their ends," *we* must use it in self-defense against the communists. "Since we cannot . . . depend on the United Nations alone to safeguard the peace, we must and do take collective action in self-defense, as authorized by the Charter." This leaves us with the impression that only communist recalcitrance prevents the world organization from abolishing force altogether. But if this should be the case, why did we send troops to guard the integrity of Lebanon? But what a foolish question. "International communism" was responsible for the Lebanese crisis, was it not?

Mr. Dulles' moral universe made everything quite clear, too clear, with the result that it complicated our relations with our allies, who found our self-righteousness very vexatious. For self-righteousness is the inevitable fruit of simple moral judgments, placed in the service of moral complacency.[3]

3. MORALITY AND INTEREST: KASHMIR

The defiance of the United Nations by India on the Kashmir issue has gone comparatively unobserved. It will be remembered that Kashmir, a disputed territory claimed by both Moslem Pakistan and Hindu India, has a predominantly Moslem population but a Hindu ruler. To determine the future political orientation of the area, the United Nations ordered a plebiscite. Meanwhile both India and Pakistan refused to move their troops from the zones which each had previously occupied. Finally, Nehru took the law into his own hands and annexed the larger part of Kashmir, which he had already shrewdly integrated into the Indian economy. The Security Council, with only Russia abstaining, unanimously called upon him to obey the United Nations directive, but the Indian government refused. Clearly, Nehru does not want a plebiscite now, for it would surely go against India, though he vaguely promises a plebiscite for the future.

Morally, the incident puts Nehru in a rather bad light. But his embarrassment, if any, merely proves, as Goethe observed, that "conscience is the virtue of observers and not of agents of action." When India's vital interests were at stake, Nehru forgot lofty sentiments, sacrificed admirers in the *New Statesman and Nation,* and subjected himself to the charge of inconsistency.

His policy is either Machiavellian or statesmanlike, according to your point of view. Our conscience may gag at it but on the other hand those eminently moral men, Prime Minister Gladstone of another day and Secretary Dulles of our day, could offer many parallels of policy for Mr. Nehru, though one may doubt whether either statesman could offer a coherent analysis of the mixture of motives which entered into the policy. That is an achievement beyond the competence of very moral men.[4]

4. THE LIMITS OF MORAL IDEALISM: CO-EXISTENCE

The alternatives which face us in the international scene are total war or co-existence. The choice means, or seemed to mean, that our nation had opted for the alternative of co-existence; that is, it had recognized that an atomic war of global proportions is so unthinkable as a conscious choice that we must adjust ourselves to the prospect of making co-existence with a world-wide tyranny as sufferable as possible.

The world is by no means convinced that we are content with co-existence. Most of the European nations, not to speak of the Asian ones, rather suspect us of heedlessness.

It is strange that a nation which, only two decades ago, was suspected of lacking a sense of continuing responsibility in the world community, which was accused of entering the community only at times of crisis and then withdrawing—that this nation should now be suspected of being so frantically engaged in its responsibilities of assuring victory over communism that it has forgotten the other horn of the dilemma, avoiding atomic war.

One key to this contradiction is the knowledge that isolationism and imperialism are but two versions of the same pride and self-centeredness. Isolationism is the selfishness of the weak, and imperialism is the selfishness of the strong. We were some decades in discovering that we were not weak but very strong. Having discovered that, we entered the world community in full force. But we announce that we will stay in it only if our will is obeyed.

The other key to the seeming contradiction is the understanding of what moral idealism contributed to both forms of national heedlessness. When we were tempted to isolationism, the Christian and secular idealism which sanctified this attitude was intent on proving our nation more moral than other nations because it did not become involved in their "quarrels." Now that we are tempted to imperialistic domination of the weak nations by our strength, another form of heedless idealism tries to sanctify our position. We equate a rigorous opposition to communism at all costs with "morality" and accuse our allies of "expediency."

Both types of idealists, who captured the imagination of our nation successively, are blind to the endless complexities in the moral issues in politics, whether on the national or the international level. They do not understand that it is not possible to be both pure and responsible. If we define purity as being untainted with conflict, we deliver our fellow men into the hands of tyrants for lack of resistance to their power. If we define purity as being untainted with comradeship with tyranny, we reject every form of co-existence, and are in peril of falling into the abyss of total war.

This latter is our present "idealistic" mood which the world fears so much. People who are more interested in their purity than in responsibility for the weal of their fellows are rather poor statesmen in any situation. The first type of purist fortunately never had a chance to influence the policies of government; therefore we resisted tyranny successfully. The second type is unfortunately free to influence the policies of government because he is able to pose as a hard-headed "realist."

A realism which sees only one danger to the community when there are in fact always at least two—conflict and tyranny—is rather inadequate. An idealism which sees only one taint to righteousness when there are at least two—complacency with evil and resistance to it without counting the costs to our fellow men—is equally inadequate. Thus the political maturity of our nation must wait not only upon the experience which reveals these complexities of politics, but upon a religious depth which will interpret them. Perhaps we will be given grace to acquire both forms of maturity before it is too late.[5]

5. THE ABSENCE OF ABSOLUTE MORAL SOLUTIONS FOR ULTIMATE MORAL PROBLEMS: NUCLEAR WEAPONS

The dimensions of the moral dilemma of our age continue to expand. The dilemma may be briefly defined. We have come into the tragic position of developing a form of destruction which, if used by our enemies against us, would mean our physical annihilation; and, if used by us against our enemies, would mean our moral annihilation. In short the good that we would do is undoubtedly to create peace in global dimensions. Yet we are caught in the dilemma of doing the "evil that we do not want," namely, running the risk of annihilation in a nuclear global war.

There are Christians who believe that the only solution for such moral dilemmas is the disavowal by our nation of any reliance on atomic weapons. But that is a position which responsible Christians cannot take, though idealistic individuals may advocate it. There is no simple moral answer to this dilemma. It does not avail to suggest that converted men would rather die than purchase their lives at the price of atomic frightfulness. For these good men may feel themselves responsible for the survival of their common civilization; and they have reason to believe that the disavowal of nuclear weapons would merely give modern despotism a simple victory over us.

We face, in short, a moral dilemma for which there is no clear moral solution. It is certainly ironic that our culture, which only a half-century ago was so confident of man's ability to master historical destiny, should find itself in the grip of a destiny which it has no chance of mastering.

If we are wise enough to "discern the signs of the times," we can realize that the depths of wisdom in the Gospel of divine mercy are to be preferred to the secular and pious alternatives to the Gospel, which teach us that we would be redeemed from all our present discontents if only we tried a little harder to be either more "pious" or more "scientific" in mastering the perplexities of our common life and destiny.

The Christian faith has always understood the moral ambiguity of the human situation and has known that there are no moral solutions for the ultimate moral problems of our existence. We may find all sorts of proximate solutions if we have the humility to recognize that the ultimate solution is beyond the competence of mortal men.[6]

II. *Interest, Pretension and Moral Ambiguity*

Moral questions assume moral criteria, by which we measure good and evil. Despite the perennial debate concerning the source and content of moral standards, we need not be detained too long on this question, because only the strictest Aristotelians will define the good as conformity to a pre-established ontological pattern of being. In social ethics at least, the freedom of man and the consequent wide variety of historic and dramatic patterns and configurations which he is able to elaborate, make it necessary to have a more flexible definition of the good. It is usually defined tentatively in the phrase of Santayana as "the harmony of the whole which does not destroy the vitality of the parts." This definition excludes all tyrannically enforced harmonies and makes freedom to assert the unique vitality of each part, the criterion of moral value. We thus arrive at a definition of the good for man's togetherness which makes justice, informed by the transcendent principles of liberty and equality, the criterion of morality. It must be added that equality and liberty are only regulative principles of justice. Community is not possible without a certain degree of subordination of one member to another, and without a modicum of coercion. Therefore liberty and equality are not simple possibilities but only regulative principles. Naturally the debate on how much or how little of either subordination or coercion is necessary or desirable is endless.*

Political morality contains an inevitable ambiguity because the factors of interest and power, which are regarded as an irrelevance in pure morality, must at least tentatively be admitted to the realm of social morality. Self-interest may be a source of discord ultimately; but it is tentatively necessary to prevent the harmony of the whole from destroying the vitality of the parts. In similar fashion, granted the persistence of individual and collective interest, power, despite its dangers, must be admitted tentatively both to assure a proper counterweight against power in the interest of justice; and to provide for the coercion which is necessary for the order of the community. This moral ambiguity is raised to a special height in the morality of international relations because the national community is so large and imposing, from the viewpoint of the individual, that it constantly makes claims upon his conscience, according to which its good is the end of the moral question. In the words of Hegel, the nation represents "concrete universality" for the individual. It is however more obvious in this day of international interdependence than ever before that this is not so, for both the individual and the nation must face the more ultimate question, how the good of the nation may fit into a more general and universal scheme of value.

The force of "alter-egoism" is, however, so strong on the national level that it is almost universally recognized that a nation cannot simply espouse a more universal value at the expense of its interests. The highest morality possible for nations seems to be, not a sacrifice of its interests, but a prudent self-interest, which knows how to find the point of concurrence between its interests and the more universal interest.

This proposition is generally recognized by all sophisticated observers of national behavior. The moral problem in international relations would thus seem to be above debate. But a closer analysis of the facts reveals two very grave moral questions even if these facts be accepted.

First, is not a consistent emphasis upon the national interest as self-defeating in national, as in individual, life? Does not a nation concerned too much with its own interests define those interests so narrowly and so immediately (as for instance in terms of military security) that the interests and securities which depend upon common devotion to principles of justice and upon established mutualities in a community of nations, are sacrificed? To obviate this peril we may have to make more rigorous distinctions between what is possible for governments and what is possible for nations. Perhaps the situation is that a government cannot morally transcend what the nation regards as its interests. But it would be fatal

* A full treatment of the principles of justice is found in Chapter XV.

for the security of the nation if some loyalties beyond its interests were not operative in its moral life to prevent the national interest from being conceived in too narrow and self-defeating terms. We shall return to this problem shortly.

The second question arises from the fact of moral pretension which plays an even larger part in the life of nations than in the life of individuals. The same nation which insists on the one hand that it cannot act beyond its interests, claims, as soon as it acts, that it has acted, not out of self-interest but in obedience to some higher claim of "civilization" or "justice." How shall we deal with these claims? We had an amusing illustration of the problem at the beginning of the war. A British minister, seeking to honor us, declared upon our entry into the war that we had never been neutral since our loyalty to the principles of a democratic civilization had thrown the weight of our sympathies on the anti-Nazi side. This compliment was embarrassing since the Administration was under criticism by our isolationists and nationalists for having dragged us into the war against our interests. Secretary Hull therefore demanded and received an apology from the bewildered British minister.

The problem came to us in another form in the operations of the Marshall Plan, as indeed in the whole exercise of our hegemony in an impoverished world. Despite the strong emphasis upon national interest we have been inclined to claim more benevolence for our policies than they deserve. We have thus aroused the resentments of people already inclined to criticism by their envy of our power and wealth. Particularly in France, we have been accused of compounding the sin of imperialism with the sin of hypocrisy. Though the exercise of our hegemony is a splendid example of the application of a wise self-interest when informed by loyalty to principles transcending national interests, it is important not to claim too much for the moral quality of our policies. This is the more true since some of our "benevolence" is prompted, not so much by concern for the health of the free world but by reluctance to open American markets to a genuinely reciprocal trade.

This issue proves that the problem of moral pretension is a very basic one in international relations. We will be accused of hypocrisy by the world as the British were before us. We will resent this charge. But it will be at least partly true. We must learn how to moderate our moral pretensions. But those who criticize us must learn that hypocrisy is an inevitable by-product in the life of any nation which has some loyalty to moral principles, but whose actions do not fully conform to those principles. The price of eliminating these hypocrisies entirely is to sink into a consistent cynicism in which moral principles are not operative at all. On this point the contrast between the British and the Germans is instructive.

The British could crown their hypocrisies with Lionel Curtis' book *Civitas Dei,* in which the British Empire is absurdly equated with the Kingdom of God. The Germans were naturally scornful of these pretensions but they ended by trying to build an empire which was clearly of the devil. One could make similar comparisons between the inevitable pretensions involved in our failure to realize the "American dream" in our race relations, so poignantly described in Myrdal's *American Dilemma,* and the consistent realism and unhypocritical cruelty of the South-African approach to this problem.

It is significant that the moral issue in international relations should reveal itself in these two dimensions: a) should the nation be bound by moral principles? and b) how can the nation be prevented from claiming too much moral virtue for its actions? These two questions prove the ambiguity in which the actions of nations are enveloped. It must be observed that a full consideration of the problem which is exhibited in the moral pretensions of nations leads us beyond the moral issues, and raises wider questions about the relation of political theory to the practice of statesmen. For moral pretension is but one aspect of the general inclination of modern men, who are undoubtedly agents in history, to forget that they are also creatures in the very historical process in which they must take responsible action.

Refusal to admit the moral ambiguity and the very tentative character of any nation's virtue is one form of this blindness. The realistic statesman, intent upon the national security, who advises his nation that "there is nothing which America cannot do if we approach our problem with sufficient vigor," exhibits another form of this blindness, particularly dangerous to a nation which faces the paradox that it is less master of its own fate in the day of its supreme power than in the day of its impotence.

But the statesmen are relatively free from this blindness, compared with the prevailing social science of our day, which insists that the historical realm is analogous to the realm of nature; and that the proper "scientific technics" can assure men mastery over their historical fate, as complete as their previous mastery over nature. Fortunately, the political sciences are less infected by this illusion than sociology for instance. But they are sufficiently infected to make many of their studies irrelevant to the practice of statecraft in a day, the watchword of which must be "sufficient unto the day is the evil thereof." In other words the paramount problem for the contemporary study of international relations is to supplant the illusions which we have inherited from the French Enlightenment and which are most characteristically expressed in the influence of Auguste Comte upon our social thought, with the wisdom of an Edmund Burke (and, one might add, of a Winston Churchill). This basic problem of political philosophy must be solved before political theory can become relevant to the issues which the statesmen of our nation face.[7] *

III. *Interest and Pretension in American Foreign Policy*

The American situation is such a vivid symbol of the spiritual perplexities of modern man, because the degree of American power tends to generate illusions to which a technocratic culture is already too prone. This technocratic approach to problems of history, which erroneously equates the mastery of nature with the mastery of historical destiny, in turn accentuates a very old failing in human nature: the inclination of the wise, or the powerful, or the virtuous, to obscure and deny the human limitations in all human achievements and pretensions.

The most rigorous and searching criticism of the weaknesses in our foreign policy, which may be ascribed to the special character of our American idealism, has been made by one of our most eminent specialists in foreign policy, Mr. George Kennan.

He ascribes the weaknesses of our policy to a too simple "legalistic-moralistic" approach and defines this approach as informed by an uncritical reliance upon moral and constitutional schemes, and by too little concern for the effect of our policy upon other nations, and too little anticipation of the possible disruption of policies by incalculable future occurrences. In short, he accuses the nation of pretending too much prescience of an unknown future and of an inclination to regard other peoples "in our own image." These are, of course, precisely the perils to which all human idealism is subject and which our technocratic culture has aggravated.

Mr. Kennan's solution for our problem is to return to the policy of making the "national interest" the touch-stone of our diplomacy. He does not intend to be morally cynical in the advocacy of this course. He believes that a modest awareness that our own interests represent the limit

* Niebuhr's assessment of Churchill is indicated in the following observation: "The greatness of Churchill seems to lie primarily in a combination of moral insight with a genius for political strategy. Unlike many of his Tory colleagues, he both hated and understood the Nazis. He knew and predicted with remarkable prescience that the gangsters in Germany would not be beguiled by the various pathetic devices by which both the great and the small nations of Europe sought either to mitigate or to deflect the Nazi fury. He was convinced from the beginning that Hitler meant war. Unlike the Labor and the Liberal leadership he knew what kind of power would be required to frustrate the design of the dictators. 'We are in this war,' declared a young Labor man on the first day of World War Two, 'because the Tories willed the means but not the end; and Labor willed the end but not the means. Only Churchill among our leaders willed both the end and the means.' That is a fairly neat appraisal of Churchill's place in recent history and of the debt to him of the democratic world."[8]

of our competence should prompt such a policy. His theory is that we may know what is good for us but should be less certain that we know what is good for others. This admonition to modesty is valid as far as it goes. Yet his solution is wrong. For egoism is not the proper cure for an abstract and pretentious idealism.

Since the lives and interests of other men and communities always impinge upon our own, a preoccupation with our own interests must lead to an illegitimate indifference toward the interests of others, even when modesty prompts the preoccupation. The cure for a pretentious idealism, which claims to know more about the future and about other men than is given mortal man to know, is not egoism. It is a concern for both the self and the other in which the self, whether individual or collective, preserves a "decent respect for the opinions of mankind," derived from a modest awareness of the limits of its own knowledge and power.

Mr. Kennan rightly points to the evils which arise from the pursuit of unlimited rather than limited ends, even by highly civilized nations in the modern era. The inhumanities of our day, which modern tyrannies exhibit in the nth degree, are due to an idealism in which reason is turned into unreason because it is not conscious of the contingent character of the presuppositions with which the reasoning process begins, and in which idealism is transmuted into inhumanity because the idealist seeks to comprehend the whole realm of ends from his standpoint.

A nice symbol of this difficulty in the policy of even "just" nations is the ironic embarrassment in which the victorious democracies became involved in their program of "demilitarizing" the vanquished "militaristic" nations. In Japan they encouraged a ridiculous article in the new constitution which committed the nation to a perpetual pacifist defenselessness. In less than half a decade they were forced to ask their "demilitarized" former foes to rearm, and become allies in a common defense against a new foe, who had recently been their victorious ally.

We cannot expect even the wisest of nations to escape every peril of moral and spiritual complacency; for nations have always been constitutionally self-righteous. But it will make a difference whether the culture in which the policies of nations are formed is only as deep and as high as the nation's highest ideals; or whether there is a dimension in the culture from the standpoint of which the element of vanity in all human ambitions and achievements is discerned.[9]

IV. *The National Interest—and Beyond*

It is not easy for a nation to be concerned with any other nation in altruistic terms. The difference between individual and collective morality is immense and is established by the fact that collective self-concern is a compound of individual egoism, collectively expressed, and the spirit of loyalty and self-sacrifice of the individual which the community easily appropriates for its own ends. It was a dictum of George Washington that a nation was not to be trusted beyond its own interests; and on the whole this realistic advice has been the guide of all political science. But a mere consideration of the power of concern for the national interest easily obscures another side of the equation, namely, that self-concern can be as self-defeating in collective as in individual behavior. Nations as well as individuals stand under the law: "Whosoever seeketh to gain his life will lose it." In more concrete terms this means that a nation that is too preoccupied with its own interests is bound to define those interests too narrowly. It will do this because it will fail to consider those of its interests which are *bound up in a web of mutual interests* with other nations.

In short, the national interest when conceived only from the standpoint of the self-interest of the nation is bound to be defined too narrowly and therefore to be self-defeating. In both our secular and religious traditions there have been morally idealistic emphases which have recognized this aspect of man's collective life and have sometimes gone so far as to define patriotism as a form of treason to the larger community. But this form of idealism was usually blind to the persistence of the factor of collective self-regard and to the impossibility of either suppressing it completely or of transmuting it. On the other hand, the "realist" reaction to what was regarded as sentimentality was usually blind to the self-defeating nature of pure self-regard. We must draw on the profounder sources in our religious tradition and in our secular disciplines to solve this problem.

There are two aspects in a tolerable solution. First, we must realize that it is not within the realm of moral possibilities to ask a nation to be "self-sacrificing." There are various reasons for this, including the fact that the government which sacrifices the interests of a nation for the "common good" is in a very different situation from that of the individual who may decide to subordinate or sacrifice his own interests for a higher value. The art of statecraft, as we have already pointed out, is to find the point of concurrence between the parochial and the general interest, between the national and the international common good. It does not occur to any statesman to define a desired policy in any other term but that of such concurrence; and to justify it in terms of "wise self-interest." Moralists sometimes suggest that this establishes a too sharp distinction between individual and collective morality; but it must be observed that a free society, in contrast to a tyrannical one, seeks to harness rather than to suppress particular individual interests in establishing the common good. In our immediate situation this policy means that we must try to persuade the nation that what is good for the alliance of the free nations is good for our own nation *in the long run*. A prudent self-regard must obviously prefer long run to short run ends because there are too many conflicts of interest in the short run between the particular and the general interest.

But this "realist" approach to the problem of national morality is obviously defective, even if prudence insists on the long run rather than the short run in calculating the concurrence of interests. The defect arises from the fact that any kind of prudence which estimates common problems from the perspective of a particular interest will define the interest too narrowly. It is necessary, therefore, to draw upon another moral and spiritual resource to widen the conception of interest. The citizens of a nation must have loyalties and responsibilities to a wider system of values than that of the national interest—to a civilization for instance, to a system of justice, and to a community of free nations. These moral concerns will serve to leaven the mind of a nation and prevent a national community from defining its interest too narrowly. The sense of justice must prevent prudence from becoming too prudential in defining interest.[10]

The proposal several years ago to give India two hundred million dollars worth of wheat to stave off famine provides some interesting insights into this problem. The main support for the project came from people who had a great humanitarian concern for the starving people of India without regard to the political situation. But this humanitarian concern would never have been enough to get the bill passed. It is questionable whether nations as nations ever act without reference to national interest.

Yet there were quite a few people in Congress who wanted to spell out the national interest in such specific terms that the whole purpose of the proposal would have been defeated. One Congressman wanted to make the giving of the food conditioned upon a promise from India to vote with us in the United Nations, a proposition which even a starving nation would reject as a violation of its independence. Another group in Congress thought we ought to make India promise to give us in return certain strategic materials which had been on the list of non-exportable materials. If these proposals had carried, India would either have rejected the bargain or, if she had accepted it, would have regarded it as so hard a bargain as to have resented rather than appreciated our turning over the food. There is, in other words, a form of self-interest which is so narrowly conceived as to destroy its own ends.

The generosity of the people who were concerned merely to feed starving people would not have been enough to move our government, if it had not been in our national interest to give the food. Nations are selfish. But the more generous portion of our population prevented our conception of national self-interest from becoming so narrow as to be self-defeating. Thus love and self-love are curiously compounded in the standards of justice which nations are able to achieve.[11]

Such a combination of idealism and realism is given in the great historic faiths. Without the insights of these faiths, realism may degenerate into cynicism and idealism into sentimentality. They may even degenerate within the context of these faiths. But ideally the presuppositions of Biblical faith insist on both the moral imperative of the love commandment and the fact of the persistence of self-love in actual history. There is in this faith, therefore, a safeguard against both sentimentality and moral cynicism. This must be made available to the nation in the present period of critical decisions in which we cannot afford to disregard either the moral possibilities or the moral realities of our common life.[12]

CHAPTER XXVII

Faith for a Hazardous Future

We are living in an age between the ages in which children are coming to birth but there is not strength to bring forth. We can see clearly what ought to be done to bring order and peace into the lives of the nations; but we do not have the strength to do what we ought. In fact this generation of mankind is destined to live in a tragic era between two ages. It is an era when "one age is dead and the other is powerless to be born." The age of absolute national sovereignty is over; but the age of international order under political instruments, powerful enough to regulate the relations of nations and to compose their competing desires, is not yet born.[1]

The fact that world-wide economic and technical interdependence between the nations makes a world-wide system of justice necessary is so obvious that even the most casual observers have become convinced of it. At the beginning of this century, before two world wars had chastened the mood of our culture, it was assumed that the comprehension of an historic task would guarantee its achievement. Since then we have learned that a potential world community may announce itself in history through world conflicts; and that some of the very instruments which were to guarantee the achievement of world-wide community could be used to sharpen conflict and give it global dimensions.

The lack of strength to bring forth is usually interpreted as the consequence of a natural or cultural "lag." This idea of a cultural lag is plausible enough, and partly true. But it does not represent the whole truth about the defect of our will. It obscures the positive and spiritual element in our resistance to necessary change. The lower and narrower loyalties which stand against the newer and wider loyalties are armed not merely with the force of natural inertia but with the guile of spirit and the stubbornness of all forms of idolatry in human history.

Consider, for instance, the position of the great powers in the present world.[2] The will-to-power of the great nations, which involves them in vicious circles of mutual fears, is a manifestation of an age-old force in human history. It accentuates the insecurity which it is intended to destroy. It is never completely overcome in man's history; but every new communal advance requires that it be overcome upon a new level of man's common enterprise. Mutual fears lead so inevitably into overt conflict that one would suppose that the nations would recognize this danger more clearly, and would take more explicit steps for a complete international partnership. The fact that they do not cannot be attributed merely to ignorance or the cultural lag. There is an element of perversity in this failure to see the obvious; and in the unwillingness to act upon the facts and implications which are seen. The stupidity of sin is in this darkness. "They became vain in their imaginations, and their foolish heart was darkened," is the way St. Paul describes this fact in human life. That description fits the international situation exactly.

The self-righteousness of the great powers is also a "vain imagination." Just as the will-to-power is intended to overcome the natural insecurity of men and nations, but actually increases what it would overcome; so also the moral pride of peoples seeks to obscure their common involvement in the sins of nations but actually accentuates what it intends to hide. Both of these forms of vain imagination contribute to the spiritual impotence which prevents the necessary next step in the development of the human community.[3]

There are unique Christian insights into the problem of building this community. One such insight is the realization of the Christian faith that men and nations do not repent of their sins by some simple rational analysis of their past errors. Self-love, whether individual or collective, cannot be destroyed if the self-centered self is not shaken to its very foundations. That is why history is a more tragic process than secular idealism has been able to understand. The self-sufficiency of modern nations has become incompatible with the necessities of a world community, potentially created by a modern technical civilization. But the self-sufficiency of those nations and the egoism of ruling groups within those nations will seek to defy the logic of history until defiance has been beaten down again and again and until the Lord of history has indubitably asserted His majesty over the false majesty of the nations.

It must be observed however that the "objective" judgments which come out of the process of history itself, are not redemptive if they are not interpreted by faith. The world-wide catastrophe in which we live will appear to those who have no frame of meaning into which they can fit it, as merely universal chaos and meaninglessness. In that case it cannot produce repentance. It can only prompt despair, which St. Paul defines as the "sorrow of the world which worketh death."

There are others who have a frame of meaning in which to fit the present catastrophe; but the frame is inadequate. The whole of modern culture has had one cherished form of faith: that history itself is redemptive. Our present calamities refute this idea of historical progress.[4] The crowning irony of our age consists precisely in the fact that the tragic aspects of human existence, man's sin and death, having been denied by our philosophies, express themselves in more terrible terms than in any previous period of history. We thought we had conquered death by our conquest of nature and now we face death in an undeniably social (moral) dimension. We are in peril of destroying each other.

The moral problems which confront us are nicely symbolized by the fact that the atomic weapons which give us immediate security against the outbreak of total war can easily become, in the case of war, the means of our moral destruction. Confronting these problems, Christian moralism offers another inadequate frame of meaning. It declares that all of these horrible ambiguities would not exist if only we loved each other. As such, it is on exactly the same level as a secular idealism which insists that we could easily escape our predicament if only we organized a world government. A Christian moralism which solemnly assures men that peace can be had by "men of good will" but is unavailable if we lack good will, can drive us to as complete a despair as the despair which secular idealism is widely creating. Suppose we have good will but our opponent's fanatic fury is impervious to it? And suppose no amount of good will in us suffices to establish a transcendent ground above the tragic historical struggle? "If Christians were only sufficiently unselfish," declared a Christian moralist recently, "to be willing to sacrifice their life, we could quickly solve the problem of war."

In such terms Christian unselfishness requires that we capitulate to tyranny because democracy happens to be "ours" and tyranny is "theirs." Thus disloyalty and irresponsibility toward the treasures of an historic civilization become equated with Christian love. On the opposite extreme Christian moralists are ready to suppress every moral scruple because we are fighting for a "Christian" civilization against atheism. Neither type of moralism recognizes the moral ambiguity in all our historic responsibilities. There is no recognition in such versions of the Christian faith of the necessity of humility for the defenders of even a just cause and of the necessity of forgiveness and pardon for the "righteous" as well as the "unrighteous."

Religiously we are at the end of an era in which both Christians and secularists indulged in schemes of salvation, which regarded virtue as a simple possibility and hoped that historical destiny would be brought progressively under the control of an ever broader "good will." Now we know that we cannot do good without also doing evil; that we cannot defend what is dearest to us without running the risk of destroying what is even more precious than our life; that we cannot find moral peace in any of our virtues even as we can have no security in the ramparts of our boasted civilization. The whole human enterprise is morally more precarious than we realized.[5] If our moralists were less concerned to validate their faith as directly relevant to the present situation, that faith might be more relevant.

A less relevant faith would, as did the prophets of Israel, give the nation a sense that its primary engagement is with God and not with its foes.[6] For the Christian faith believes that God is the sovereign of history, and that all the tortuous historical processes are finally, though not simply, meaningful. It understands, as it were, the meaning of chaos. Thus it relates the objective judgments of history to the internal judgments of God. The chaos is meaningful because it represents the judgment of God upon all human pride, individual and collective, and proves the futility of all efforts to organize life with the self as the center of it, whether that self be an individual self, or the German or the Russian, or the British or the American collective self. Thus the God Who visits the soul in the secret recesses of its uneasy conscience is identified by Christian faith as the same God Who presides over the processes of history, before Whom the nations are as a drop in the bucket and the judges of the earth are vanity.[7]

This kind of religious engagement, in which the distinction between the righteous and unrighteous nations is obscured, is the only source of humility for a nation so tempted as our own to regard its fortune as proof of its virtue. We could have less friction with our allies and be a better moral match for our foes if our engagement with a divine judge helped us to recognize the fragmentary character of all human virtues and the ambiguous nature of all human achievements. We might also be helped to see that, what we regard as great generosity toward our poorer allies is prompted not so much by Christian charity as prudent consideration of national interest.

The encounter between nations and the divine justice always wipes out a part of the distinction between good and evil men, and between just and unjust nations. But the Christian faith also helps us to understand the necessity of preserving against tyrannical power whatever standards of justice or virtue we have achieved. It does not persuade us that we are wrong to stand resolutely against tyranny, because we happen ourselves to be unjust in God's sight. It helps us to appreciate the responsibilities which even sinful men and nations have to preserve what is relatively good against explicit evil. Neutrality between justice and injustice, whether derived from a too simple moral idealism or a too sophisticated Barthian theology, is untrue to our Gospel.[8]

This combination of moral resoluteness about the immediate issues with a religious awareness of another dimension of meaning and judgment is brilliantly illustrated in the statesmanship of Abraham Lincoln.

Lincoln was devoted both to the Union and to the cause of the abolition of slavery, though he subordinated the latter to the former. Yet his brooding sense of charity was derived from a religious awareness of another dimension of meaning than that of the immediate political conflict. "Both sides," he declared, "read the same Bible and pray to the same God. The prayers of both could not be answered—that of neither has been answered fully."

Lincoln's awareness of the element of pretense in the idealism of both sides was rooted in his confidence in an over-arching providence whose purposes partly contradicted and yet were not irrelevant to the moral issues of the conflict. "The Almighty has His own purposes," he declared; but he also saw that such purposes could not annul the moral purposes of men who were "firm in the right as God gives us to see the right." Slavery was to be condemned even if it claimed divine sanction, for: "It may seem strange that any men should dare to ask a just God's assistance in wringing their bread from the sweat of other men's faces." Yet even this moral condemnation of slavery is followed by the scriptural reservation: "But let us judge not, that we be not judged."

Surely it was this double attitude which made the spirit of Lincoln's, "with malice toward none; with charity for all" possible. There can be no other basis for true charity; for charity cannot be induced by lessons from copybook texts. It can proceed only from a "broken spirit and a contrite heart."

We face today the difficult but not impossible task of remaining loyal and responsible toward the moral treasures of a free civilization while yet having some religious vantage point over the struggle. Applied to the present situation Lincoln's model would rule out the cheap efforts which are frequently made to find some simple moral resolution of our conflict with communism. Modern communist tyranny is certainly as wrong as the slavery which Lincoln opposed. Lincoln's model also rules out our effort to establish the righteousness of our cause by a monotonous reiteration of the virtues of freedom compared with the evils of tyranny. This comparison may be true enough on one level; but it offers us no insight into the corruptions of freedom on our side and it gives us no understanding of the strange attractive power of communism in a chaotic and impoverished world. Even the most "Christian" civilization and even the most pious church must be reminded that the true God can be known only where there is some awareness of a contradiction between divine and human purposes, even on the highest level of human aspirations.

There is, in short, even in a conflict with a foe with whom we have little in common the possibility and necessity of living in a dimension of meaning in which the urgencies of the struggle are subordinated to a sense of awe before the vastness of the historical drama in which we are jointly involved; to a sense of modesty about the virtue, wisdom and power available to us for the resolution of its perplexities; to a sense of contrition about the common human frailties and foibles which lie at the foundation of both the enemy's demonry and our vanities; and to a sense of gratitude for the divine mercies which are promised to those who humble themselves.

Strangely enough, none of the insights derived from this faith is finally contradictory to our purpose and duty of preserving our civilization. They are, in fact, prerequisites for saving it. For if we should perish, the ruthlessness of the foe would be only the secondary cause of the disaster. The primary cause would be that the strength of a giant nation was directed by eyes too blind to see all the hazards of the struggle; and the blindness would be induced not by some accident of nature or history but by hatred and vainglory.[9]

Perhaps the most important relevance of a Christian faith, which is not too immediately relevant to the political situation, is a sense of serenity and a freedom from hysteria in an insecure world full of moral frustrations. We have to do our duty for a long time in a world in which there will be no guarantees of security and in which no duty can be assured the reward of success. The hysteria of our day is partly derived from the disillusion of a humanistic idealism which thought that every virtue could be historically rewarded, and encouraged men to sow by the promise of a certain harvest. Now we must sow without promising whether we can reap. We must come to terms with the fragmentary character of all human achievements and the uncertain character of historic destinies.

There is nothing new in all this. Our present vicissitudes merely remind us of the words of Scripture: "If in this life only we had hoped in Christ we are of all men most miserable." That is an expression of what a humanistic age calls "Christian otherworldliness." It is the Biblical illumination of a dimension of existence which makes sense out of life, when it ceases to make sense as simply upon the plane of history as it was once believed. We are rightly concerned about the probabilities of disaster to our civilization and about our various immediate duties to avert it. But we will perform our duties with greater steadiness if we have something of the faith expressed by St. Paul in the words: "Whether we live, we live unto the Lord; and whether we die, we die unto the Lord: whether we live therefore, or die, we are the Lord's." In this final nonchalance about life and death, which includes some sense of serenity about the life and death of civilizations, there is a resource for doing what we ought to do, though we know not what the day or the hour may bring forth.[10]

In summary the Christian faith finds the final clue to the meaning of life and history in the Christ Whose goodness is at once the virtue which man ought, but does not, achieve in history, and the revelation of a divine mercy which understands and resolves the perpetual contradictions in which history is involved, even on the highest reaches of human achievements. From the standpoint of such a faith it is possible to deal with the ultimate social problem of human history: the creation of community in world dimensions. The insistence of the Christian faith that the love of Christ is the final norm of human existence must express itself socially in unwillingness to stop short of the whole human community in expressing our sense of moral responsibility for the life and welfare of others. The understanding of the Christian faith that the highest achievements of human life are infected with sinful corruption will help men to be prepared for new corruptions on the level of world community which drive simpler idealists to despair. The hope of Christian faith that the divine power which bears history can complete what even the highest human striving must leave incomplete, and can purify the corruptions which appear in even the purest human aspirations, is an indispensable prerequisite for diligent fulfillment of our historic tasks. Without it we are driven to alternate moods of sentimentality and despair, trusting human powers too much in one moment and losing all faith in the meaning of life when we discover the limits of human possibilities.

The world community, toward which all historical forces seem to be driving us, is mankind's final possibility and impossibility. The task of achieving it must be interpreted from the standpoint of a faith which understands the fragmentary and broken character of all historic achievements and yet has confidence in their meaning because it knows their completion to be in the hands of a Divine Power, Whose resources are greater than those of men, and Whose suffering love can overcome the corruptions of man's achievements, without negating the significance of his striving.[11]

NOTES

PART I. THE CRISIS

I. The Contemporary Crisis

1. "God's Design and the Present Disorder of Civilization," *The Church and the Disorder of Society,* Vol. III, Amsterdam Assembly Series (New York: Harper and Brothers, 1949), p. 13.

2. "Faith for History's Greatest Crisis," *Fortune,* Vol. 26 (July, 1942), pp. 99–100.

3. "God's Design and the Present Disorder of Civilization," *op. cit.,* p. 13.

4. *Ibid.,* p. 16.

5. "Will Civilization Survive Technics?" *Commentary,* Vol. 1 (December, 1945), pp. 2–3.

6. "God's Design and the Present Disorder of Civilization," *op. cit.,* pp. 16–17.

7. "A Faith for History's Greatest Crisis," *op. cit.,* p. 100.

8. "God's Design and the Present Disorder of Civilization," *op. cit.,* p. 17.

9. "Will Civilization Survive Technics?" *op. cit.,* p. 4.

10. "God's Design and the Present Disorder of Civilization," *op. cit.,* pp. 17–18.

11. "A Faith for History's Greatest Crisis," *op. cit.,* pp. 100, 122.

12. "Will Civilization Survive Technics?" *op. cit.,* pp. 5–7.

13. "A Faith for History's Greatest Crisis," *op. cit.,* p. 122.

14. "God's Design and the Present Disorder of Civilization," *op. cit.,* pp. 18–21.

15. "The Religious Level of the World Crisis," *Christianity and Crisis,* Vol. 5 (January 21, 1946), p. 4.

II. The Soft Utopians: Liberalism

1. *Faith and History,* p. 1.

2. "Two Forms of Utopianism," *Christianity and Society,* Vol. 12 (Autumn, 1947), p. 6.

3. "The Sickness of American Culture," *Nation,* Vol. 166 (March 6, 1948), p. 268.

4. "Two Forms of Utopianism," *op. cit.,* p. 7.

5. "Liberalism: Illusions and Realities," *New Republic,* Vol. 133 (July 4, 1955), pp. 11–12.

6. *Ibid.,* p. 13.

7. "The Blindness of Liberalism," *Radical Religion,* Vol. 1 (Autumn, 1936), pp. 4–5.

8. "Ten Years That Shook My World," *Christian Century,* Vol. 56 (April 26, 1939), p. 543.

9. "The Blindness of Liberalism," *op. cit.,* p. 5.

10. "Liberalism: Illusions and Realities," *op. cit.,* p. 12.

11. "A Faith for History's Greatest Crisis," *Fortune,* Vol. 26 (July, 1942), pp. 122, 125.

12. "The Sickness of American Culture," *op. cit.,* p. 267.

13. "A Faith for History's Greatest Crisis," *op. cit.,* p. 125.

14. *Faith and History,* p. 5.

15. *Beyond Tragedy,* pp. 232–33.

16. *Moral Man and Immoral Society,* pp. 27–29.

17. *Beyond Tragedy,* pp. 236–37.

18. *Ibid.,* pp. 241–42.

19. "Einstein and the World Situation," *Messenger,* Vol. 19 (December 14, 1954), p. 6.

20. "A Faith for History's Greatest Crisis," *op. cit.,* p. 126.

21. The quotation is from Edmund Noble, *Purposive Evolution,* p. 418.

22. *Faith and History,* pp. 3–7.

23. "A Faith for History's Greatest Crisis," *op. cit.,* p. 128.

24. *Faith and History,* p. 8.

25. "Which Question Comes First for the Church?" *Christianity and Crisis,* Vol. 5 (November 12, 1945), p. 1.
26. *Faith and History,* p. 207.
27. "The Reunion of the Church through the Renewal of the Churches," *Christian Century,* Vol. 7 (November 24, 1947), p. 5.
28. *Faith and History,* p. 208.
29. "A Faith for History's Greatest Crisis," *op. cit.,* pp. 100, 122.
30. *Ibid.,* p. 126.
31. *Christianity and Power Politics,* p. 188.

III. The Hard Utopians: Communism

1. "Two Forms of Tyranny," *Christianity and Crisis,* Vol. 8 (February 2, 1948), pp. 3–4.
2. *Faith and History,* pp. 208–12.
3. *Christian Realism and Political Problems,* pp. 34–36.
4. "Russia and Karl Marx," *Nation,* Vol. 146 (May 7, 1938), p. 530.
5. *Christian Realism and Political Problems,* pp. 36–39.
6. *Christianity and Power Politics,* pp. 145–46.
7. *Christian Realism and Politcial Problems,* pp. 39–42.
8. "Two Forms of Tyranny," *op. cit.,* pp. 3–4.
9. "The Soviet Reality," *Nation,* Vol. 171 (September 23, 1950), p. 270.
10. "Two Forms of Tyranny," *op. cit.,* pp. 4–5.
11. *Christianity and Power Politics,* p. 91.
12. "Communism and the Clergy," *Christian Century,* Vol. 70 (August 19, 1953), p. 937.
13. "Two Forms of Tyranny," *op. cit.,* p. 5.
14. "The Soviet Reality," *op. cit.,* p. 270.
15. *Faith and History,* p. 212.

IV. The Perennial Crisis

1. *Christian Realism and Political Problems,* pp. 106–107.
2. "The Sickness of American Culture," *Nation,* Vol. 166 (March 6, 1948), p. 268.
3. *Faith and History,* pp. 84–85.
4. "The Wisdom of the World," *Christianity and Society,* Vol. 14 (Spring, 1949), p. 4.
5. *The Children of Light and the Children of Darkness,* p. 16.
6. "Faith for History's Greatest Crisis," *Fortune,* Vol. 26 (July, 1942), pp. 128, 131.

PART II. POLITICAL PHILOSOPHY

V. The Illusion of Scientific Politics: A Critique

1. "A Faith to Live By—I. The Dilemma of Modern Man," *Nation,* Vol. 164 (February 22, 1947), pp. 206–207.
2. *Christian Realism and Political Problems,* p. 75.
3. *Ibid.,* p. 82.
4. *Ibid.,* pp. 83–84.
5. *The Self and the Dramas of History,* p. 45.
6. *Christian Realism and Political Problems,* pp. 85–86.
7. *Faith and History,* pp. 55–56.
8. *Christian Realism and Political Problems,* p. 91.
9. *The Self and the Dramas of History,* pp. 44–46.
10. *Discerning the Signs of the Times,* pp. 5–8.

11. *Christian Realism and Political Problems,* pp. 92–93.
12. *Discerning the Signs of the Times,* p. 8.
13. *The Self and the Dramas of History,* p. 54.
14. *Christian Realism and Political Problems,* pp. 93–94.
15. The quotation is from *Science and Common Sense,* p. 25.
16. *The Self and the Dramas of History,* pp. 114–15.
17. *Christian Realism and Political Problems,* pp. 3–4.
18. *Ibid.,* pp. 88–91.
19. "A Faith to Live By," *op. cit.,* p. 207.
20. *Faith and History,* pp. 116–19.
21. *The Self and the Dramas of History,* pp. 41–42.
22. *Christian Realism and Political Problems,* pp. 69–70.
23. *The Irony of American History,* pp. 80–81.
24. *Christian Realism and Political Problems,* pp. 70–71.
25. *The Irony of American History,* p. 84.
26. *Ibid.,* pp. 84–85.
27. *Ibid.,* pp. 88.
28. *The Self and the Dramas of History,* pp. 133–40.
29. *The Irony of American History,* pp. 85–87.
30. *Christian Realism and Political Problems,* p. 124.
31. *Faith and History,* pp. 91–92.
32. "A Faith to Live By," *op. cit.,* p. 207.
33. "Christian Faith and Social Action," in John A. Hutchison, editor, *Christian Faith and Social Action* (New York: Scribners, 1953), pp. 233–34.
34. "A Faith to Live By," *op. cit.,* p. 207.
35. *Christian Realism and Political Problems,* p. 4.
36. "A Faith to Live By," *op. cit.,* pp. 207–208.
37. "The Blind Leaders," *Christianity and Society,* Vol. 14 (Spring, 1949), pp. 5–6.
38. "A Faith to Live By," *op. cit.,* p. 208.
39. "The Blind Leaders," *op. cit.,* p. 6.

VI. The Relevance of Christian Realism: An Orientation

1. *Christian Realism and Political Problems,* pp. 119–20.
2. *The Children of Light and the Children of Darkness,* pp. 9–10.
3. *Christian Realism and Political Problems,* p. 120.
4. "Plans for World Reorganization," *Christianity and Crisis,* Vol. 2 (October 19, 1942), p. 3.
5. *Christian Realism and Political Problems,* pp. 120–27.
6. *Ibid.,* pp. 129–30.
7. "The Idolatry of America," *Christianity and Society,* Vol. 15 (Spring, 1950), p. 3.
8. *Christian Realism and Political Problems,* p. 131.
9. *Ibid.,* pp. 136–37.
10. *Ibid.,* pp. 145–46.

VII. Human Nature and the Will-to-Power

1. *Moral Man and Immoral Society,* pp. xxiv–xxv.
2. *Christianity and Power Politics,* pp. 154–55.
3. "The Contribution of Religion to Cultural Unity," Hazen Pamphlet No. 13 (New Haven: 1945), pp. 13–14.
4. "Christianity and Humanism," *Messenger,* Vol. 17 (September 9, 1952), p. 7.
5. *Human Nature,* p. 12.
6. *Ibid.,* p. 167.
7. *Ibid.,* pp. 13–14.

8. *Ibid.*, p. 3.
9. *The Structure of Nations and Empires,* pp. 287–88.
10. *Human Nature,* pp. 15–16.
11. *Christian Realism and Political Problems,* p. 6.
12. *Human Nature,* pp. 179–85.
13. *Ibid.*, pp. 16–17.
14. *Ibid.*, pp. 178–79.
15. *The Children of Light and the Children of Darkness,* pp. 18–22.
16. *Human Nature,* pp. 188–94.
17. *Ibid.*, p. 188.
18. *Ibid.*, pp. 194–203.

VIII. Groups in the Struggle for Power

1. *Moral Man and Immoral Society,* pp. xi–xii.
2. *Ibid.*, pp. 46–49.
3. *Ibid.*, pp. 93–94.
4. *Ibid.*, pp. xxii–xxiii.
5. *Human Nature,* pp. 208–209.
6. *Moral Man and Immoral Society,* pp. 83–85.
7. *Human Nature,* p. 209.
8. *Moral Man and Immoral Society,* pp. 88–89.
9. *Ibid.*, p. 95.
10. *Human Nature,* pp. 210–12.
11. The quotation is from Philip Leon, *The Ethics of Power.*
12. *Moral Man and Immoral Society,* p. 108.
13. *Reflections on the End of an Era,* p. 43.
14. *Human Nature,* pp. 212–13, 217.
15. *The Children of Light and the Children of Darkness,* pp. 47–49.
16. *Moral Man and Immoral Society,* p. xx.
17. *Human Destiny,* p. 265.
18. "Christian Faith and Social Action," in J. Hutchison, *Christian Faith and Social Action,* pp. 240–41.
19. *Human Destiny,* pp. 258–59.
20. *Discerning the Signs of the Times,* p. 186.
21. *Moral Man and Immoral Society,* p. 19.
22. *Discerning the Signs of the Times,* pp. 186–87.
23. *Human Destiny,* p. 259.
24. "Leaves from the Notebook of a War-bound American," *Christian Century,* Vol. 56 (November 15, 1939), p. 1405.
25. *Christianity and Power Politics,* p. 123.
26. *Discerning the Signs of the Times,* p. 187.
27. *Human Destiny,* pp. 260–63.
28. *Reflections on the End of an Era,* p. 151.
29. *Human Destiny,* pp. 263–64.

IX. The Necessity and Basis of Community

1. *The Self and the Dramas of History,* pp. 34–35.
2. *The Children of Light and the Children of Darkness,* pp. 50–51.
3. *The Self and the Dramas of History,* pp. 35–36, 38.
4. *The Children of Light and the Children of Darkness,* pp. 3–5.
5. *Human Destiny,* p. 244.
6. "Coercion, Self-Interest, and Love," in Kenneth E. Boulding, *The Organizational Revolution* (New York: Harper and Brothers, 1953), pp. 240–41.
7. *Human Destiny,* p. 244.
8. *The Self and the Dramas of History,* pp. 163–64.
9. *Does Civilization Need Religion?,* pp. 151–52.
10. *The Children of Light and the Children of Darkness,* pp. 165–66.
11. "Liberalism: Illusions and Realities," *New Republic,* Vol. 133 (July 4, 1955), p. 13.
12. "Coronation Afterthoughts," *Christian Century,* Vol. 70 (July 1, 1953), p. 771.
13. "The Tyrant as Symbol of Community," *New Leader,* Vol. 39 (May 21, 1956), p. 14.

14. *Christian Realism and Political Problems,* pp. 22–24.
15. *The Self and the Dramas of History,* pp. 165–66.
16. *Christian Realism and Political Problems,* pp. 18–19.
17. *Ibid.,* p. 26.

X. *Structures of Power*

1. *Moral Man and Immoral Society,* p. 3.
2. *Ibid.,* p. 6.
3. *Christianity and Power Politics,* pp. 123–24.
4. *Human Destiny,* pp. 257–58.
5. "The United Nations and World Organization," *Christianity and Crisis,* Vol. 2 (January 25, 1943), p. 2.
6. *Human Destiny,* p. 265.
7. "A Dark Light on Human Nature," *Messenger,* Vol. 13 (April 27, 1948), p. 7.
8. "The Long and the Short Range of History," *Christianity and Society,* Vol. 7 (Winter, 1941), p. 8.
9. *Human Destiny,* p. 284.
10. *Christianity and Power Politics,* p. 104.
11. *Human Destiny,* p. 265.
12. *Christianity and Power Politics,* pp. 26–27.
13. *Human Destiny,* p. 266.
14. "Pacifism and Sanctions," *Radical Religion,* Vol. 1 (Winter, 1936), p. 28.
15. *Human Destiny,* p. 266.
16. *The Children of Light and the Children of Darkness,* p. 174.
17. *The Self and the Dramas of History,* p. 166.
18. *Ibid.,* pp. 183–84.
19. *Ibid.,* pp. 190–92.
20. *Human Destiny,* p. 266.
21. "The Moral Question in International Relations," unpublished paper for Rockefeller Foundation, p. 7.
22. *Human Destiny,* p. 266.
23. *Ibid.,* pp. 198, 192.
24. "Coercion, Self-Interest, and Love," in K. Boulding, *The Organizational Revolution,* pp. 239–40.
25. *The Children of Light and the Children of Darkness,* p. 44.
26. "The Idolatry of America," *Christianity and Society,* Vol. 15 (Spring, 1950), p. 4.
27. "The Moral Question in International Relations," *op. cit.,* pp. 7–8.
28. *The Structure of Nations and Empires,* p. 8.
29. "The Moral Question in International Relations," *op. cit.,* p. 8.
30. *The Structure of Nations and Empires,* p. 49.
31. "Power and Ideology in National and International Affairs," in William T. R. Fox, editor, *Theoretical Aspects of International Relations* (University of Notre Dame Press, 1959), pp. 107–108.
32. *The Structure of Nations and Empires,* p. 3.
33. "Power and Ideology in National and International Affairs," *op. cit.,* pp. 108–109.
34. *The Structure of Nations and Empires,* pp. 45–47.
35. *Ibid.,* pp. 35–36, 39–43.
36. *Ibid.,* p. 123.
37. "Power and Ideology in National and International Affairs," *op. cit.,* pp. 109–110.
38. "The Moral Question in International Relations," pp. 9–10.
39. *Moral Man and Immoral Society,* p. 238.
40. *Faith and History,* pp. 220–21.
41. *Moral Man and Immoral Society,* pp. 239–40.
42. *Human Destiny,* p. 267.
43. The quotation is from Hobbes, *Leviathan,* ch. 19.
44. *The Children of Light and the Children of Darkness,* pp. 45–46.
45. "Tyranny and War," *Radical Religion,* Vol. 4 (Fall, 1939), p. 9.
46. *Moral Man and Immoral Society,* pp. 16–18.

47. "Our Relations to Japan," *Christianity and Crisis,* Vol. 5 (September 17, 1945), p. 7.

48. "A Report on Germany," *Christianity and Crisis,* Vol. 6 (October 14, 1946), p. 6.

49. *The Self and the Dramas of History,* p. 184.

50. *Christianity and Power Politics,* p. 120.

51. *Human Nature,* pp. 225–26.

52. *Beyond Tragedy,* pp. 202–203.

53. "Force and Reason in Politics," *Nation,* Vol. 150 (February 10, 1940), p. 216.

XI. Rational, Moral and Religious Norms

1. *The Irony of American History,* p. 139.

2. "Technics, Logic and Salvation," *Christianity and Society,* Vol. 11 (Spring, 1946), p. 5.

3. *The Self and the Dramas of History,* pp. 149–51.

4. *Ibid.,* p. 160.

5. *An Interpretation of Christian Ethics,* pp. 203–204.

6. *Moral Man and Immoral Society,* p. 34.

7. *The Children of Light and the Children of Darkness,* pp. 66–67.

8. *Human Destiny,* p. 151.

9. *Christian Realism and Political Problems,* p. 76.

10. *Christianity and Power Politics,* p. 112.

11. "Reason and Interest in Politics," *Christianity and Society,* Vol. 10 (Winter, 1944), pp. 8–9.

12. "A Faith to Live By—I. The Dilemma of Modern Man," *Nation,* Vol. 164 (February 22, 1947), p. 208.

13. *The Self and the Dramas of History,* p. 125.

14. *The Children of Light and the Children of Darkness,* p. 72.

15. "The Ultimate Validity and the Ideological Distortions of Moral Concepts in International Politics," paper for American Political Science Association, September 6, 1957, pp. 1–2.

16. *The Self and the Dramas of History,* pp. 14–15.

17. *The Children of Light and the Children of Darkness,* pp. 83–84.

18. *Beyond Tragedy,* p. 285.

19. *Moral Man and Immoral Society,* p. 116.

20. *Human Nature,* p. 225.

21. *Christianity and Power Politics,* pp. 108–109.

22. *Human Destiny,* pp. 248, 252, 256, 257.

23. "Religion and Action," in Ruth N. Anshen, editor, *Science and Man* (New York: Harcourt, Brace and Co., 1942), p. 46.

24. *Moral Man and Immoral Society,* pp. 80–81.

25. *Ibid.,* p. 63.

26. *Human Destiny,* p. 267.

27. *Ibid.,* p. 129.

28. *Beyond Tragedy,* p. 73.

29. *Christianity and Power Politics,* pp. 112–13.

30. *The Structure of Nations and Empires,* pp. 218–19.

31. "Moral Rearmament," *Radical Religion,* Vol. 4 (Autumn, 1939), p. 11.

32. *Christianity and Power Politics,* p. 113.

33. "The Ultimate Validity and the Ideological Distortions of Moral Concepts in International Relations," *op. cit.,* p. 7.

34. "The Hitler-Stalin Pact," *Radical Religion,* Vol. 4 (Autumn, 1939), p. 3.

XII. The Problem of the Love Ethic in Politics

1. *An Interpretation of Christian Ethics,* p. 105.

2. *Human Destiny,* p. 35.

3. *Ibid.,* p. 68.

4. *Beyond Tragedy,* pp. 16–17.
5. *Human Nature,* pp. 288–89; 293–94.
6. *Christianity and Power Politics,* p. 8.
7. *An Interpretation of Christian Ethics,* pp. 48–49.
8. *Ibid.,* p. 39.
9. "The Ethic of Jesus and the Social Problem," *Religion in Life,* Vol. 1 (Spring, 1932), p. 199.
10. *An Interpretation of Christian Ethics,* pp. 46–47.
11. "The Ethic of Jesus and the Social Problem," *op. cit.,* p. 200.
12. "Christian Faith and the Common Life," in N. Ehrenstrom and others, *Christian Faith and the Common Life* (New York: Harper & Brothers, 1938), pp. 69–71.
13. *Christianity and Power Politics,* p. 9.
14. *An Interpretation of Christian Ethics,* pp. 56–57.
15. *Human Destiny,* pp. 49, 87.
16. "The Ethic of Jesus and the Social Problem," *op. cit.,* pp. 198–99.
17. *An Interpretation of Christian Ethics,* p. 148.
18. *Human Nature,* pp. 296–97.
19. *Faith and History,* pp. 197–98.
20. *Human Destiny,* pp. 68–69.
21. *Christianity and Power Politics,* pp. 75–76.
22. *Moral Man and Immoral Society,* pp. 266–67, 272.
23. *Faith and History,* p. 184.
24. *Discerning the Signs of the Times,* p. 186.

XIII. The Case Against Pacifism

1. *Christianity and Power Politics,* pp. ix–x.
2. "Christian Politics and Communist Religion," in John Lewis, *et al.,* editors, *Christianity and the Social Revolution* (New York: Scribners, 1936), p. 458.
3. "If America Enters the War," *Christian Century,* Vol. 57 (December 18, 1940), p. 1579.
4. *Christianity and Power Politics,* pp. 9–10.
5. *Moral Man and Immoral Society,* pp. 242–43.
6. "Is Peace or Justice the Goal?" *World Tomorrow,* Vol. 15 (September 21, 1932), pp. 276–77.
7. *An Interpretation of Christian Ethics,* pp. 188–89.
8. *Christianity and Power Politics,* p. 11.
9. *An Interpretation of Christian Ethics,* p. 186.
10. "God Wills Both Justice and Peace," (with Angus Dun), *Christianity and Crisis,* Vol. 15 (June 13, 1955), p. 76.
11. "Speak Truth to Power: Comment," *The Progressive,* Vol. 19 (October, 1955), p. 14.
12. *An Interpretation of Christian Ethics,* p. 189.
13. "Christ and Our Political Decisions," *Christianity and Crisis,* Vol. 1 (August 11, 1941), p. 1.
14. *Christianity and Power Politics,* pp. 15–16.
15. "God Wills Both Justice and Peace," *op. cit.,* p. 75.
16. "Christ and Our Political Decisions," *op. cit.,* pp. 1–2.
17. *Human Nature,* p. 298.
18. "God Wills Both Justice and Peace," *op. cit.,* pp. 76–78.
19. "The Hydrogen Bomb," *Christianity and Society,* Vol. 15 (Spring, 1950), pp. 5–7.
20. "The Hydrogen Bomb and Moral Responsibility," *Messenger,* Vol. 19 (May 4, 1954), p. 5.
21. "Christ and Our Political Decisions," *op. cit.,* p. 1.
22. *Christianity and Power Politics,* p. 14.
23. *Christianity and Power Politics,* pp. 5, 3–4.
24. *Ibid.,* pp. 20–21.
25. "The Christian Faith and the World Crisis," *Christianity and Crisis,* Vol. 1 (February 10, 1941), p. 5.
26. "An Open Letter to Richard Rob-

erts," *Christianity and Society,* Vol. 5 (Summer, 1940), p. 32.

27. *Christianity and Power Politics,* p. 5.

28. "Christian Politics and Communist Religion," *op. cit.,* pp. 455–56.

29. "If America Enters the War," *op. cit.,* p. 1580.

30. "The Will of God and the Van Zeeland Report," *Christian Century,* Vol. 55 (December 14, 1938), p. 1550.

31. *An Interpretation of Christian Ethics,* p. 188.

32. *Pious and Secular America,* p. 115.

33. "Japan and the Christian Conscience," *Christian Century,* Vol. 54 (November 10, 1937), p. 1391.

34. "The Christian Faith and the World Crisis," *op. cit.,* p. 4.

XIV. The Relevance of the Love Ethic to Politics

1. "Christian Politics and Communist Religion," in J. Lewis, *Christianity and the Social Revolution,* p. 442.

2. "Christian Faith and Social Action," in J. Hutchison, *Christian Faith and Social Action,* pp. 236, 237.

3. "Christian Faith and the Common Life," in N. Ehrenstrom, *Christian Faith and the Common Life,* p. 72.

4. *Christianity and Power Politics,* pp. 214–16.

5. *Human Destiny,* p. 207.

6. "Christian Faith and the Common Life," *op. cit.,* pp. 78–79, 81.

7. *Human Destiny,* p. 85.

8. *Moral Man and Immoral Society,* p. 264.

9. *Human Destiny,* p. 96.

10. *Faith and History,* p. 185.

11. *Human Destiny,* p. 96.

12. *Faith and History,* pp. 178–79.

13. "Christian Politics and Communist Religion," *op. cit.,* p. 470.

14. *Christianity and Power Politics,* pp. 22–23, 25.

15. *Human Destiny,* pp. 246–47.

16. *Pious and Secular America,* pp. 118–19.

17. *Christianity and Power Politics,* p. 26.

18. "Christian Faith and Social Action," *op. cit.,* pp. 228, 239.

19. *Christianity and Power Politics,* p. 22.

20. "Ten Years That Shook My World," *Christian Century,* Vol. 56 (April 26, 1939), p. 545.

21. "Christian Faith and Social Action," *op. cit.,* p. 240.

22. *Christianity and Power Politics,* pp. 2–3.

23. *Faith and History,* p. 144.

24. *Christianity and Power Politics,* p. 30.

25. *Faith and History,* p. 97.

26. *The Self and the Dramas of History,* p. 235.

27. *Faith and History,* p. 97.

28. *Ibid.,* pp. 224, 226, 230.

29. "Christian Faith and Social Action," *op. cit.,* pp. 241–42.

30. *Christian Realism and Political Problems,* pp. 167–69.

31. "Christian Faith and the Common Life," *op. cit.,* pp. 91, 95.

XV. Love, Justice and the Question of Natural Law

1. "The Spirit of Justice," *Christianity and Society,* Vol. 15 (Summer, 1950), pp. 5–6.

2. "Christian Politics and Communist Religion," in J. Lewis, *Christianity and the Social Revolution,* p. 446.

3. "The Spirit of Justice," *op. cit.,* p. 6.

4. "Justice and Love," *Christianity and Society,* Vol. 15 (Autumn, 1950), pp. 6–7.

5. *Christianity and Power Politics,* p. 26.

6. "The Truth in Myths," in *The Nature of Religious Experience* (New York: Harper & Brothers, 1937), pp. 134–35.

7. "Justice and Love," *op. cit.,* p. 7.

8. *Human Destiny,* p. 251.

9. *Human Nature,* p. 285.

10. *Human Destiny,* pp. 247–48.
11. *The Children of Light and the Children of Darkness,* pp. 74–75.
12. *An Interpretation of Christian Ethics,* pp. 144–45.
13. *Human Nature,* pp. 274–75, 280.
14. *Christian Realism and Political Problems,* p. 148.
15. *Human Nature,* pp. 280–84.
16. *Ibid.,* p. 297.
17. *Christian Realism and Political Problems,* pp. 132–33, 157.
18. *Human Nature,* pp. 284–85.
19. *The Children of Light and the Children of Darkness,* p. 72.
20. "Christian Faith and Natural Law," *Theology,* Vol. 40 (February, 1940), pp. 88–89.
21. *Christian Realism and Political Problems,* pp. 188–89.
22. *Human Nature,* p. 272.
23. "Christian Faith and Social Action," in J. Hutchison, *Christian Faith and Social Action,* p. 238.
24. *Christian Realism and Political Problems,* p. 172.
25. *The Self and the Dramas of History,* pp. 101–102.
26. *Human Nature,* p. 284.
27. *The Children of Light and the Children of Darkness,* pp. 67–68.
28. *Human Destiny,* pp. 253–54.
29. *Faith and History,* pp. 188–89, 193.
30. "God's Design and the Present Disorder of Civilization," *The Church and the Disorder of Society,* Vol. III, Amsterdam Assembly Series, pp. 14, 15.
31. "The Limits of Liberty," *Nation,* Vol. 154 (January 24, 1942), p. 87.
32. *An Interpretation of Christian Ethics,* p. 140.
33. "The Perils of Our Foreign Policy," *Christianity and Society,* Vol. 8 (Spring, 1943), p. 18.
34. *Human Destiny,* p. 254.
35. *An Interpretation of Christian Ethics,* p. 147.
36. "Christian Faith and the Common Life," in N. Ehrenstrom, *Christian Faith and the Common Life,* p. 85.
37. *The Children of Light and the Children of Darkness,* p. 83.
38. *Faith and History,* pp. 189–90.
39. "Christian Faith and the Common Life," *op. cit.,* p. 94.
40. *An Interpretation of Christian Ethics,* pp. 108–109.
41. *Human Destiny,* p. 255.
42. "The Limits of Liberty," *op. cit.,* p. 86.
43. *Pious and Secular America,* p. 62.
44. *The Children of Light and the Children of Darkness,* p. 78.
45. *Ibid.,* p. 181.
46. "Hazards and Resources," *Virginia Quarterly Review,* Vol. 25 (Spring, 1949), p. 200.
47. "The Moral Question in International Relations," unpublished paper, pp. 10–11.
48. "Hazards and Resources," *op. cit.,* p. 200.
49. "Christian Faith and Natural Law," *op. cit.,* pp. 89–90.
50. *Faith and History,* p. 195.
51. *Human Destiny,* pp. 256–57, 265.
52. *Faith and History,* p. 183.
53. "Christian Faith and Natural Law," *op. cit.,* p. 94.
54. *Faith and History,* p. 194.

XVI. Government and the Strategy of Democracy

1. "The National Preaching Mission," *Radical Religion,* Vol. 2 (Spring, 1937), p. 3.
2. *Faith and History,* pp. 221–22.
3. *Human Destiny,* pp. 269–70, 281–82.
4. "Coercion, Self-Interest and Love," in K. Boulding, *The Organizational Revolution,* pp. 242, 244.
5. *Christianity and Power Politics,* pp. 14–15.
6. *Human Destiny,* p. 268.
7. *The Children of Light and the Children of Darkness,* pp. 1, 3.

8. *Christianity and Power Politics,* pp. 28, 85, 149.

9. *The Children of Light and the Children of Darkness,* pp. 119–20.

10. *Christianity and Power Politics,* p. 86.

11. "The Contribution of Religion to Cultural Unity," Hazen Pamphlet No. 13 (1945), p. 6.

12. *Christian Realism and Political Problems,* pp. 14, 51.

13. "The Commitment of the Self and the Freedom of the Mind," in *Religion and Freedom of Thought,* by Perry Miller, Robert L. Calhoun, Nathan M. Pusey, and Reinhold Niebuhr (New York: Doubleday, 1954), pp. 58–59.

14. *The Self and the Dramas of History,* p. 198.

15. *Christian Realism and Political Problems,* p. 96.

16. "The Electoral Campaign," *Messenger,* Vol. 13 (September 28, 1948), p. 15.

17. *Human Destiny,* p. 263.

18. "What Is At Stake?" *Christianity and Crisis,* Vol. 1 (May 19, 1941), p. 1.

19. "The Contribution of Religion to Cultural Unity," *op. cit.,* p. 4.

20. *The Children of Light and the Children of Darkness,* pp. 70–71.

21. *Ibid.,* pp. x–xii, 1, 6–7.

22. *Christian Realism and Political Problems,* pp. 100–102.

23. *Ibid.,* pp. 95–96.

24. *Pious and Secular America,* p. 6.

25. *Human Destiny,* pp. 232, 236, 238.

26. *The Children of Light and the Children of Darkness,* pp. 131–36, 150–51.

27. *Christian Realism and Political Problems,* p. 103.

28. "Protestants, Catholics and Secularists," *Christianity and Society,* Vol. 13 (Spring, 1948), p. 5.

29. "Democracy as a Religion," *Christianity and Crisis,* Vol. 7 (August 4, 1947), pp. 1–2.

XVII. The Christian in Politics

1. "Christian Faith and Political Controversy," *Christianity and Crisis,* Vol. 12 (July 21, 1952), p. 97.

2. "Christian Action," *Christianity and Society,* Vol. 20 (Autumn, 1955), pp. 5–6.

3. "Christian Faith and Social Action," in J. Hutchison, *Christian Faith and Social Action,* p. 229.

4. "A Christian Peace Policy," *Radical Religion,* Vol. 4 (Spring, 1939), p. 11.

5. "Christian Faith and Political Controversy," *op. cit.,* pp. 97–98.

6. "Christian Faith and Social Action," *op. cit.,* pp. 229–30.

7. "America in the Hour of Decision," *Christianity and Society,* Vol. 6 (Summer, 1941), p. 3.

8. "Christian Faith and Social Action," *op. cit.,* p. 230.

9. *Ibid.,* p. 236.

10. *Christianity and Power Politics,* pp. 61–62.

11. "Leaves from the Notebook of a War-Bound American," *Christian Century,* Vol. 56 (November 15, 1939), pp. 1405–1406.

12. "A Christian Peace Policy," *op. cit.,* p. 11.

13. "Can the Church Give a Moral Lead?" *Christianity and Crisis,* Vol. 8 (August 2, 1948), p. 106.

14. *Moral Man and Immoral Society,* pp. 20, 233–34; *Reflections on the End of an Era,* p. 229.

15. *Christianity and Power Politics,* pp. 38–39.

16. *The Children of Light and the Children of Darkness,* pp. 186–87.

17. "Liberalism: Illusions and Realities," *New Republic,* Vol. 133 (July 4, 1955), p. 11.

18. *Pious and Secular America,* p. 61.

19. "Liberalism and Conservatism," *Christianity and Society,* Vol. 20, No. 1 (Winter, 1954–55), p. 3.

20. *Christian Realism and Political Problems,* pp. 65–66.

21. "Liberalism and Conservatism," *op. cit.,* p. 3.

22. *Christian Realism and Political Problems,* pp. 67, 71–72.

23. "Christian Faith and Social Action," *op. cit.,* p. 241.

24. *Ibid.,* pp. 230–31.

25. *Christian Realism and Political Problems,* pp. 110–11.

26. *Moral Man and Immoral Society,* pp. 170–71.

27. "The Limits of Liberty," *Nation,* Vol. 154 (January 24, 1942), p. 88.

28. "Our Faith and Concrete Political Decisions," *Christianity and Society,* Vol. 17 (Summer, 1952), p. 4.

29. *The Irony of American History,* pp. 89, 91.

30. "Christian Faith and Social Action," *op. cit.,* pp. 232–33.

31. *Ibid.,* p. 242.

32. "God's Design and the Present Disorder of Civilization," *Man's Disorder and God's Design,* Vol. III, Amsterdam Assembly Series, pp. 22–23.

33. "The Commitment of the Self and the Freedom of the Mind," in *Religion and Freedom of Thought,* p. 59.

34. *Christianity and Power Politics,* p. 218.

35. "Clericalism in Europe," *New Leader,* Vol. 39 (January 2, 1956), p. 17.

36. *Christianity and Power Politics,* p. 218.

37. "Catholics and Protestants: Some Misconceptions," *The Reporter,* Vol. 6 (January 22, 1952), p. 10.

38. *Faith and History,* p. 201.

39. Review of T. S. Eliot, *The Idea of a Christian Society,* in *Radical Religion,* Vol. 5 (Winter, 1940), p. 39.

40. "Catholics and Protestants: Some Misconceptions," *op. cit.,* pp. 9–10.

41. "A Protestant Looks at Catholics," *Commonweal,* Vol. 58 (May 8, 1953), pp. 117–18.

42. "Catholics and Protestants: Some Misconceptions," *op. cit.,* p. 11.

43. "Catholicism and Anarchism in Spain," *Radical Religion,* Vol. 2 (Spring, 1937), p. 28.

44. "Our Relations to Catholicism," *Christianity and Crisis,* Vol. 7 (September 15, 1947), p. 6.

45. "Separation of Church and State," *Messenger,* Vol. 12 (August 5, 1947), p. 21.

46. Review of T. S. Eliot, *The Idea of a Christian Society, op. cit.,* p. 39.

47. *Christian Realism and Political Problems,* p. 111.

48. "We Have This Treasure in Earthen Vessels," *Christianity and Society,* Vol. 14 (Autumn, 1949), p. 3.

49. *The Irony of American History,* pp. 62–63.

50. *Beyond Tragedy,* pp. 178, 180.

51. "Justice and Love," *Christianity and Society,* Vol. 15 (Autumn, 1950), p. 8.

52. *The Irony of American History,* p. 63.

53. "History (God) Has Overtaken Us," *Christianity and Society,* Vol. 7 (Winter, 1941), pp. 4–5.

54. "The Christian Faith and the World Crisis," *Christianity and Crisis,* Vol. 1 (February 10, 1941), p. 5.

55. *Beyond Tragedy,* pp. 246–47.

56. *Discerning the Signs of the Times,* p. 187.

57. "Providence and Historical Confusion," *Christianity and Society,* Vol. 11 (Summer, 1946), p. 10.

58. "Christian Otherworldliness," *Christianity and Society,* Vol. 9 (Winter, 1943), p. 12.

59. *Discerning the Signs of the Times,* pp. 109–10.

60. *Beyond Tragedy,* p. 286.

Part III. ESSAYS IN CONTEMPORARY POLITICS

XVIII. The Problem of Economic Power

1. "The Sickness of American Culture," *Nation,* Vol. 166 (March 6, 1948), p. 267.

2. "The Christian Faith and the Economic Life of Liberal Society," in A. Dud-

ley Ward, editor, *Goals of Economic Life* (New York: Harpers, 1953), p. 433.

3. *The Irony of American History,* p. 93.

4. "The Christian Faith and the Economic Life of Liberal Society," *op. cit.,* p. 434.

5. "The Sickness of American Culture," *op. cit.,* p. 267.

6. "The Christian Faith and the Economic Life of Liberal Society," *op. cit.,* p. 435.

7. *"The Children of Light and the Children of Darkness,* p. 109.

8. *Ibid.,* pp. 99–100, 103.

9. "Coercion, Self-Interest, and Love," in K. Boulding, *The Organizational Revolution,* pp. 231–32.

10. "The Christian Faith and the Economic Life of Liberal Society," *op. cit.,* p. 435.

11. *The Children of Light and the Children of Darkness,* pp. 61–62.

12. "God's Design and the Present Disorder of Civilization," in *The Church and the Disorder of Society,* Vol. III of the Amsterdam Assembly Series, p. 19.

13. *The Children of Light and the Children of Darkness,* pp. 110–12.

14. "The Spiritual Weakness of the Third Force," *Christianity and Society,* Vol. 14 (Summer, 1949), p. 6.

15. "The Fate of European Socialism," *New Leader,* Vol. 38 (June 20, 1955), p. 8.

16. "Neither Adam Smith nor Karl Marx," *New Leader,* Vol. 40 (December 23, 1957), p. 9.

17. *The Children of Light and the Children of Darkness,* pp. 90–95.

18. *Faith and History,* p. 191.

19. "Has the Church Any Authority?" *Christianity and Crisis,* Vol. 10 (April 3, 1950), p. 36.

20. "The Protestant Clergy and U.S. Politics," *The Reporter,* Vol. 6 (February 19, 1952), pp. 24–26.

21. "The Christian Faith and the Economic Life of Liberal Society," *op. cit.,* p. 448.

22. *Ibid.,* pp. 441–42, 445–46.

23. *The Children of Light and the Children of Darkness,* p. 76.

24. "Has the Church Any Authority?" *op. cit.,* pp. 35–36.

25. "Plutocracy and World Responsibilities," *Christianity and Society,* Vol. 14 (Autumn, 1949), p. 8.

26. *The Children of Light and the Children of Darkness,* pp. 115, 117–18.

27. "The Teamsters and Labor's Future," *New Leader,* Vol. 40 (August 26, 1957), pp. 3–5.

28. "Hoffa and the Teamsters," *Christianity and Crisis,* Vol. 17 (October 28, 1957), p. 137.

29. "The Republicans and Labor," *Christianity and Society,* Vol. 12 (Summer, 1947), p. 8.

30. "The Teamsters and Labor's Future," *op. cit.,* p. 3.

31. "Hoffa and the Teamsters," *op. cit.,* p. 137.

32. "The Christian Faith and the Economic Life of Liberal Society," *op. cit.,* pp. 451–56.

33. *Ibid.,* p. 453.

34. "The Next Twenty Years," *Fortune,* Vol. 57 (January, 1958), p. 190.

35. "The Christian Faith and the Economic Life of Liberal Society," *op. cit.,* pp. 456–58.

XIX. The Problem of Race Relations

1. "The Race Problem in America," *Christianity and Crisis,* Vol. 15 (December 26, 1955), p. 169.

2. "The Supreme Court on Segregation in the Schools," *Christianity and Crisis,* Vol. 14 (June 14, 1954), pp. 75, 76.

3. "The Desegregation Issue," *Christianity and Society,* Vol. 21 (Spring, 1956), p. 3.

4. "The Effect of the Supreme Court Decision," *Christianity and Crisis,* Vol. 17 (February 4, 1957), p. 3.

5. "Morals and Percentages," *Christianity and Society,* Vol. 20 (Autumn, 1955), pp. 3–4.

6. "Law and Custom," *Messenger,* Vol. 19 (June 29, 1954), p. 7.

7. *The Children of Light and the Children of Darkness,* pp. 138–39.

8. "The Race Problem," *Christianity and Society,* Vol. 7 (Summer, 1942), p. 3.

9. "Christian Faith and the Race Problem," *Christianity and Society,* Vol. 10 (Spring, 1945), pp. 21–23.

10. *The Children of Light and the Children of Darkness,* p. 139.

11. "The Race Problem," *op. cit.,* pp. 3–5.

12. *The Children of Light and the Children of Darkness,* p. 142.

13. "Nullification," *New Leader,* Vol. 39 (March 5, 1956), p. 3.

14. "Fair Employment Practices Act," *Christianity and Society,* Vol. 15 (Summer, 1950), pp. 3–4.

15. *Pious and Secular America,* p. 82.

16. "The Race Problem in America," *op. cit.,* pp. 169–70.

17. *Pious and Secular America,* pp. 83, 84.

18. "Nullification," *op. cit.,* p. 4.

19. *The Children of Light and the Children of Darkness,* pp. 143–44.

20. "The Civil Rights Bill," *New Leader,* Vol. 40 (September 16, 1957), pp. 9–10.

21. "The Way of Non-Violent Resistance," *Christianity and Society,* Vol. 21 (Spring, 1956), p. 3.

22. *Pious and Secular America,* p. 81.

23. "The South African Tragedy," *Christianity and Society,* Vol. 20 (Spring, 1955), p. 5.

24. "The States' Rights Crisis," *New Leader,* Vol. 41 (September 29, 1958), p. 7.

25. "The Sin of Racial Prejudice," *Messenger,* Vol. 13 (February 3, 1948), p. 6.

26. "Race and Christian Conscience," *Christianity and Crisis,* Vol. 16 (July 23, 1956), p. 99.

27. *Pious and Secular America,* pp. 81–82.

28. "Nullification," *op. cit.,* p. 4.

29. *The Children of Light and the Children of Darkness,* pp. 144–45.

XX. The International Situation

1. "Our Moral and Spiritual Resources for International Cooperation," *Social Action,* Vol. 22 (February, 1956), pp. 5–12.

2. "To Be Abased and To Abound," *Messenger,* Vol. 16 (February 13, 1951), p. 7.

XXI. The Resources and Limits of the International Community

1. "Plans for World Reorganization," *Christianity and Crisis,* Vol. 2 (October 19, 1942), pp. 3–4.

2. *The Children of Light and the Children of Darkness,* pp. 173–76.

3. "World Community and World Government," *Christianity and Crisis,* Vol. 6 (March 4, 1946), p. 5.

4. "Plans for World Reorganization," *op. cit.,* p. 6.

5. "World Community and World Government," *op. cit.,* p. 5.

6. *Christian Realism and Political Problems,* pp. 15–22.

7. "The Myth of World Government," *Nation,* Vol. 162 (March 16, 1946), p. 312.

8. *Christian Realism and Political Problems,* pp. 23–24.

9. "Can We Organize the World?" *Christianity and Crisis,* Vol. 13 (February 2, 1953), p. 1.

10. "The Myth of World Government," *op. cit.,* p. 314.

11. *Christian Realism and Political Problems,* pp. 26–29.

12. "Can We Organize the World?" *Christianity and Crisis,* Vol. 13 (February 2, 1953), p. 1.

13. "One World or None," *Christianity and Crisis,* Vol. 8 (February 16, 1948), p. 9.

14. "The Federation of Western Europe," *Christianity and Crisis,* Vol. 8 (March 1, 1948), p. 18.

15. *The Self and the Dramas of History,* pp. 202–206.

16. "The Myth of World Government," *op. cit.,* pp. 312–13.

17. *The Self and the Dramas of History,* pp. 206–207.

18. "The Moral Implications of Loyalty to the United Nations," Hazen Pamphlet No. 29, New Haven, 1952, pp. 9–10.

19. "The Churches and the United Nations," *Christianity and Society,* Vol. 18 (Winter, 1952–53), p. 3.

20. *The Self and The Dramas of History,* pp. 207–208.

21. "The Theory and Practice of UNESCO," *International Organization,* Vol. 4 (February, 1950), pp. 3, 5.

22. "Peace Through Cultural Cooperation," *Christianity and Crisis,* Vol. 9 (October 17, 1949), p. 132.

23. "The Theory and Practice of UNESCO," *op. cit.,* pp. 6, 8–10.

24. "Peace Through Cultural Cooperation," *op. cit.,* pp. 132–33.

XXII. The Soviet Threat

1. "The Relevance of the Reformation Doctrine in Our Day," in Elmer J. F. Arndt, editor, *The Heritage of the Reformation* (New York: Richard R. Smith, 1950), p. 254.

2. "The Communist Party and Russia," *Christianity and Society,* Vol. 9 (Spring, 1944), p. 8.

3. "Two Forms of Tyranny," *Christianity and Crisis,* Vol. 8 (February 2, 1948), p. 4.

4. "Hazards and Resources," *Virginia Quarterly Review,* Vol. 25 (Spring, 1949), p. 204.

5. "The Conditions of Our Survival," *Virginia Quarterly Review,* Vol. 26 (Autumn, 1950), p. 482.

6. "Is This the Collapse of a Tyranny?" *Christianity and Society,* Vol. 21 (Summer, 1956), pp. 4–6.

7. "Nikita Khrushchev's Meditation on Josef Stalin," *Christianity and Crisis,* Vol. 16 (July 9, 1956), pp. 89–90.

8. *The Structure of Nations and Empires,* pp. 240–43.

9. *Ibid.,* pp. 233–34.

10. "After Sputnik and Explorer," *Christianity and Crisis,* Vol. 18 (March 17, 1958), pp. 29–30.

11. "Yesterday's Anticipations and Today's Realities," *Christianity and Crisis,* Vol. 16 (June 25, 1956), pp. 81–82.

12. *The Structure of Nations and Empires,* pp. 246–48.

XXIII. America's Precarious Eminence

1. "The Conditions of Our Survival," *Virginia Quarterly Review,* Vol. 26 (Autumn, 1950), p. 481.

2. "America's Precarious Eminence," *Virginia Quarterly Review,* Vol. 23 (Autumn, 1947), pp. 481–82.

3. "The Conditions of Our Survival," *op. cit.,* pp. 481–82.

4. "Anglo-Saxon Destiny and Responsibility," *Christianity and Crisis,* Vol. 3 (October 4, 1943), pp. 2–3.

5. "America's Eminence," *Christianity and Society,* Vol. 13 (Summer, 1948), p. 4.

6. *The Irony of American History,* pp. 23–28.

7. *Ibid.,* pp. 35–39.

8. *Ibid.,* p. 42.

9. *Ibid.,* pp. 69–74.

10. "The Moral Implications of Loyalty to the United Nations," Hazen Pamphlet No. 29, New Haven, 1952, pp. 11–12.

11. *The Irony of American History,* pp. 74–75.

12. "The Conditions of Our Survival," *op. cit.,* p. 484.

13. "To Be Abased and To Abound,"

Messenger, Vol. 16 (February 13, 1951), p. 7.

14. "American Pride and Power," *American Scholar*, Vol. 17 (Autumn, 1948), p. 393.

15. "The Peril of Complacency in Our Nation," *Christianity and Crisis*, Vol. 14 (February 8, 1954), p. 1.

16. *The Irony of American History*, p. 49.

17. *Ibid.*, pp. 52–53.

18. "The Peril of Complacency in Our Nation," *op. cit.*, p. 1.

19. "American Pride and Power," *op. cit.*, p. 394.

20. "America's Eminence," *op. cit.*, pp. 3–4.

21. "The Peril of Complacency in Our Nation," *op. cit.*, pp. 1–2.

22. "Anglo-Saxon Destiny and Responsibility," *op. cit.*, p. 3.

23. "American Power and World Responsibility," *Christianity and Crisis*, Vol. 3 (April 5, 1943), p. 2.

24. "The Conditions of Our Survival," *op. cit.*, p. 482.

25. "Hazards and Resources," *Virginia Quarterly Review*, Vol. 24 (Spring, 1949), pp. 201–202, 204, 203.

26. "The Predicament of American Power," *Christianity and Society*, Vol. 19 (Winter, 1953–54), p. 3.

27. "Hazards and Resources," *op. cit.*, p. 203.

28. *The Irony of American History*, pp. 132–33.

XXIV. Conservatives, Liberals and American Foreign Policy

1. "American Conservatism and the World Crisis: I. A Study in Vacillation," *Yale Review*, Vol. 40 (March, 1951), p. 385.

2. *Christian Realism and Political Problems*, p. 54.

3. "American Conservatism and the World Crisis," *op. cit.*, pp. 385–86.

4. *Christian Realism and Political Problems*, p. 54.

5. "American Conservatism and the World Crisis," *op. cit.*, p. 386.

6. *Ibid.*, pp. 388–92.

7. *Christian Realism and Political Problems*, pp. 56–58.

8. "American Conservatism and the World Crisis," *op. cit.*, pp. 396–97.

9. *Christian Realism and Political Problems*, p. 59.

10. *Ibid.*, pp. 61–64.

11. *The Structure of Nations and Empires*, p. 182.

12. *Ibid.*, p. 17.

13. *Ibid.*, pp. 256–57.

14. The quotation is from David Hume, "Of the Balance of Power" in *Essays Moral, Political, and Literary*, Vol. I, Pt. II, Essay VII, p. 349.

15. The quotation is from Edmund Burke, "Heads for Consideration of the Present State of Affairs," *Works of the Right Honorable Edmund Burke*, IV, p. 398.

16. *The Structure of Nations and Empires*, pp. 188–95.

17. *Ibid.*, pp. 10–17.

18. *Ibid.*, pp. 21–25.

19. *Ibid.*, p. 257.

20. *Ibid.*, pp. 196–98.

21. *Ibid.*, p. 29.

22. *Ibid.*, p. 259.

23. *Ibid.*, pp. 29–30.

XXV. Foreign Policy and World Responsibility

1. "A Protest Against A Dilemma's Two Horns," *World Politics*, Vol. 2 (April, 1950), pp. 338–44.

2. "Understanding England," *Nation*, Vol. 157 (August 14, 1943), p. 175.

3. "The Spirit and The Mechanism of Partnership," *Christianity and Crisis*, Vol. 9 (October 3, 1949), p. 121.

4. "British Experience and American Power," *Christianity and Crisis*, Vol. 16 (May 14, 1956), p. 57.

5. "The Decline of Britain and France,"

Christianity and Crisis, Vol. 17 (February 18, 1957), p. 11.

6. "British Experience and American Power," *op. cit.,* p. 57.

7. "Understanding England," *Nation,* Vol. 157 (August 14, 1943), pp. 175, 177.

8. "American Liberals and British Labor," *Nation,* Vol. 162 (June 8, 1946), p. 684.

9. "Understanding England," *op. cit.,* p. 177.

10. "The Anglo-Saxon Alliance," *Christianity and Crisis,* Vol. 17 (May 13, 1957), pp. 58–59.

11. "Hazards and Resources," *Virginia Quarterly Review,* Vol. 25 (Spring, 1949), p. 197.

12. "Streaks of Dawn in the Night," *Christianity and Crisis,* Vol. 9 (December 12, 1949), p. 163.

13. "Hazards and Resources," *op. cit.,* pp. 197–201.

14. "Transatlantic Tension," *The Reporter,* Vol. 5 (September 18, 1951), p. 14.

15. *Ibid.,* p. 16.

16. *Ibid.,* p. 16.

17. "Should We Be Consistent?" *Christianity and Crisis,* Vol. 10 (February 6, 1950), p. 1.

18. "A Qualified Faith," *New Republic,* Vol. 134 (February 13, 1956), pp. 14–15.

19. *The Self and the Dramas of History,* p. 210.

20. "A Qualified Faith," *op. cit.,* p. 15.

21. "The Two Dimensions of the Struggle," *Christianity and Crisis,* Vol. 11 (May 28, 1951), p. 65.

22. "A Qualified Faith," *op. cit.,* p. 15.

23. "The Two Dimensions of the Struggle," *op. cit.,* pp. 65–66.

24. "American Conservatism and the World Crisis: I. A Study in Vacillation," *Yale Review,* Vol. 40 (March, 1951), pp. 394–95.

25. "A Protest Against A Dilemma's Two Horns," *op. cit.,* p. 344.

26. "The Two Dimensions of the Struggle," *op. cit.,* p. 66.

27. *The Structure of Nations and Empires,* pp. 267–69.

28. *Ibid.,* pp. 281–86.

29. *The Irony of American History,* pp. 134–40.

30. "The Moral Implications of Loyalty to the United Nations," Hazen Pamphlet No. 29, New Haven, 1952, pp. 13, 12, 10–11, 13.

XXVI. Foreign Policy and Moral Problems

1. "The Moral Question in International Relations," p. 1, and "The Moral Issue in International Relations," p. 1, unpublished papers for the Rockefeller Foundation.

2. "Politics and Morals," *Messenger,* Vol. 22 (January 1, 1957), p. 5.

3. "The Moral World of Foster Dulles," *New Republic,* Vol. 139 (December 1, 1958), p. 8.

4. "Kashmir and Nehru," *Christianity and Crisis,* Vol. 17 (March 4, 1957), p. 18.

5. "Co-Existence or Total War?" *Christian Century,* Vol. 71 (August 18, 1954), pp. 971–73.

6. The above passage is composed of materials deriving from the following: "Dilemma in a Nuclear Age," *Messenger,* Vol. 22 (July 2, 1957), p. 5; "The Hydrogen Bomb," *Christianity and Society,* Vol. 15 (Spring, 1950), p. 6; "Pauline Doctrine," *Messenger,* Vol. 22 (April 9, 1957), p. 5.

7. "The Moral Issue in International Relations," *op. cit.,* pp. 1–8.

8. "Churchill's Hour," *Nation,* Vol. 166 (June 26, 1948), p. 721.

9. *The Irony of American History,* pp. 147–50.

10. "Our Moral and Spiritual Resources for International Cooperation," *Social Action,* Vol. 22 (February, 1956), pp. 18–19.

11. "Food for India—Self-Interest or Generosity?" *Messenger,* Vol. 16 (June 19, 1951), p. 7.

12. "Our Moral and Spiritual Resources for International Cooperation," *op. cit.,* p. 20.

XXVII. Faith for a Hazardous Future

1. *Discerning the Signs of the Times,* pp. 39–40.
2. *Ibid.,* pp. 42–44.
3. *Ibid.,* pp. 48–49.
4. "The Christian Perspective on the World Crisis," *Christianity and Crisis,* Vol. 4 (May 1, 1944), p. 4.
5. "Ten Fateful Years," *Christianity and Crisis,* Vol. 11 (February 5, 1951), pp. 3–4.
6. "Utilitarian Christianity and the World Crisis," *Christianity and Crisis,* Vol. 10 (May 29, 1950), p. 68.
7. "The Christian Perspective on the World Crisis," *op. cit.,* p. 4.
8. "Utilitarian Christianity and The World Crisis," *op. cit.,* p. 68.
9. *The Irony of American History,* pp. 171–74.
10. "Utilitarian Christianity and the World Crisis," *op. cit.,* pp. 68–69.
11. *The Children of Light and the Children of Darkness,* pp. 188–90.

A COMPLETE LIST OF BOOKS BY REINHOLD NIEBUHR

Does Civilization Need Religion? A Study in the Social Resources and Limitations of Religion in Modern Life. New York: THE MACMILLAN COMPANY, 1927.

Leaves from the Notebook of a Tamed Cynic. New York: WILLETT, CLARK AND COLBY, 1929.

The Contribution of Religion to Social Work. New York: COLUMBIA UNIVERSITY PRESS, 1932.

Moral Man and Immoral Society. A Study in Ethics and Politics. New York: CHARLES SCRIBNER'S SONS, 1932.

Reflections on the End of an Era. New York: CHARLES SCRIBNER'S SONS, 1934.

An Interpretation of Christian Ethics. New York: HARPER AND BROTHERS, 1935.

Beyond Tragedy. Essays on the Christian Interpretation of History. New York: CHARLES SCRIBNER'S SONS, 1937.

Christianity and Power Politics. New York: CHARLES SCRIBNER'S SONS, 1940.

The Children of Light and the Children of Darkness. A Vindication of Democracy and a Critique of Its Traditional Defense. New York: CHARLES SCRIBNER'S SONS, 1944.

Discerning the Signs of the Times. Sermons for Today and Tomorrow. New York: CHARLES SCRIBNER'S SONS, 1946.

The Nature and Destiny of Man. A Christian Interpretation. One Volume Edition. New York: CHARLES SCRIBNER'S SONS, 1949. Originally published in two volumes: Part I *Human Nature* and Part II *Human Destiny*. New York: CHARLES SCRIBNER'S SONS, 1941 and 1943.

Faith and History. A Comparison of Christian and Modern Views of History. New York: CHARLES SCRIBNER'S SONS, 1949.

The Irony of American History. New York: CHARLES SCRIBNER'S SONS, 1952.

Christian Realism and Political Problems. New York: CHARLES SCRIBNER'S SONS, 1953.

The Self and the Dramas of History. New York: CHARLES SCRIBNER'S SONS, 1955.

Pious and Secular America. New York: CHARLES SCRIBNER'S SONS, 1958.

The Structure of Nations and Empires. A Study of the Recurring Patterns and Problems of the Political Order in Relation to the Unique Problems of the Nuclear Age. New York: CHARLES SCRIBNER'S SONS, 1959.

INDEX

"Reinhold Niebuhr: A Symposium" in _Union Seminary Quarterly Review_, Vol. 11, No. 4, May 1956, (Greene, T. M; Heimann, E.; Herberg, Will; Thomas, G.F.